KOHLER ON STRIKE

KOHLER ON STRIKE

Thirty Years of Conflict

BY WALTER H_{Henry} UPHOFF

Illustrated with photographs

BEACON PRESS   BOSTON

28206

Copyright © 1966 by Walter H. Uphoff
Library of Congress catalogue card number: 66–15073
Published simultaneously in Canada by Saunders of Toronto, Ltd.
All rights reserved
Beacon Press books are published under the auspices of
the Unitarian Universalist Association
Printed in the United States of America

To Reverend George L. (Shorty) Collins

whose suggestion that the 1934 Kohler strike would
be an interesting subject for a Master's thesis sparked
a continuing interest in labor-management relations.

ACKNOWLEDGMENTS

MANY helped to make this book a reality but space permits mention only of those who were especially helpful in providing specific insights and information, and those who made files, publications and documents available to me.

Union spokesmen interviewed included Emil Mazey, Donald Rand, Harvey Kitzman, Ray Majerus, E. H. Kohlhagen, Leo Breirather, Charles Heymanns, Rudolph Renn, Robert Treuer, Allan Graskamp and Joseph Burns. Company personnel interviewed were Lyman C. Conger, George Gallati and Herbert V. Kohler, Jr. Other union and company personnel who were helpful during my study of the first strike included L. P. Chase, Maud McCreery, Henry J. Ohl, Jr., Joseph Padway and L. L. Smith.

Many public officials and law enforcement men, past and present, provided information and opinions which helped to fill in pieces of the complicated "jigsaw puzzle" of the history of the strikes: Henry Billman, Judge John G. Buchen, Frank Bunzel, Waldemar G. Capelle, Oakley O. Frank, Steen W. Heimke, LeRoy Hotz, Donald E. Koehn, Al Konz, Harold Kroll, Elmer A. Madson, Joseph Moomaw, Theodore W. Mosch, Robert Nitsch, Rudolph J. Ploetz, Judge F. H. Schlichting, Walter H. Wagner, Robert Winkel, Frank P. Zeidler and Clarence Zimmerman.

To religious and educational leaders — Rabbi Nathan Barack, Dr. Wilford Evans, Dr. T. Parry Jones, Father A. J. Knackert and Principal John W. Hahn — I am indebted for their observations concerning the impact of these events upon the community of Sheboygan. Others from the community who filled in specific information included Marvin Boll, Peter Buteyn, Carl Fiedler, Chuck Fisher, Philip Eirich, Ralph Feudner, Carl Gunther, Walter J. Kohler, Jr., Chris Leining, Fred Liebelt, Gene Loebel, Ewald

Meuser, Mr. and Mrs. Melvin Petersen, Ray Quasius, Frank Reinthaler, Henry Sieber, Claude Spielvogel and Edward Strains.

I am also greatly indebted for source material to *The Sheboygan Press*, and the *Press* staff for permitting me unlimited use
of the *Press* library; to *The Milwaukee Journal*; to UAW Local
833 for access to its files; and to Senator Robert F. Kennedy,
whose book *The Enemy Within*, and to William L. Blachman,
whose unpublished Ph.D. thesis, *The Kohler Strike: A Case Study
in Collective Bargaining*, were valuable references. Thanks are due
to *The Chicago Tribune*, *The Commonweal*, *The Washington
Evening Star*, *Barron's Weekly*, *The Wall Street Journal*, *The
Wisconsin State Journal*, Commerce Clearing House, the Religion
and Labor Foundation, and the League for Industrial Democracy
for permission to quote materials. Monsignor James P. Finucan
graciously allowed me to quote from correspondence concerning
the book on the second Kohler strike by Sylvester Petro.

Especially am I grateful to my academic colleagues: Professors
Joseph S. Smolen, formerly of the Univerity of Minnesota and now
with the Univerity of Connecticut; Robert Repas, Michigan State
University; and J. K. Emery, Joseph Lazar, Conrad L. McBride,
Donald L. McClurg, Edward L. Rose, Donald W. Sears and
George W. Zinke of the University of Colorado for their helpful
suggestions on the manuscript.

Officials and staff of the National Labor Relations Board and
the Federal Mediation and Conciliation Service provided relevant
documents. Several NLRB staff members read for accuracy the
chapters dealing with its role in the dispute. Attorneys Harold
Cranefield, Albert Gore and David Rabinovitz also read all or parts
of the manuscript. The Wisconsin Employment Relations Board
and Wisconsin's Attorney General, Bronson La Follette, provided essential information; and the director and assistant superintendent of the State Crime Laboratory were generous with their
time in answering my questions.

There was no dearth of source material for this book. It has
been a matter of selecting the most significant, representative and
interesting information and episodes to tell the story. Some who
are familiar with the events of the two strikes may feel that certain
incidents were treated with too much generosity, while to others the
treatment may seem too harsh. To satisfy everyone on such a con-

troversial matter as the Kohler strikes is obviously an impossible and unrealistic objective. Nevertheless, this book is an effort to portray with fairness and without undue bias, the dramatic events which spanned more than three decades.

Iris Brace, Marian York, Genevieve Jaeger and Judith Norman typed much of the manuscript with careful eye for details, and transcribed hours of taped interviews. My special thanks go to my wife, Mary Jo, who worked with me on all phases of the book, interviewing, searching documents and publications, as well as editing and re-writing parts of the manuscript. My sincere appreciation also to our four sons, who were willing to forego our vacations and "spare time" with them while the book was being written.

Walter H. Uphoff
Professor of Economics
University of Colorado

CONTENTS

PREFACE

NEVER in the history of American industrial life has there been a labor-management conflict which lasted so long, cost so much and engendered so much bitterness as the two strikes at the Kohler Company near Sheboygan, Wisconsin, from 1934 to 1941 and from 1954 to 1960. Most of this book was written while the controversy was still before the National Labor Relations Board and the U.S. Circuit Court of Appeals, Washington, D.C., and no definite resolution of the conflict was in sight. As the publication date approached, this modern thirty years' industrial "war" was settled on December 17, 1965, after about thirty years of conflict between 1933 and 1965 — allowing for several years of relative peace during World War II. The company agreed to pay $4,500,000 in back wages and pension credits as the price for a settlement of all the unfair labor practice charges still pending before the NLRB and the withdrawal of contempt charges against the company.

What precipitated these strikes? Why did they last so long? What issues were at stake? How and why were they finally settled?

The reader must draw his own conclusions as to what he believes is the best way for labor and management to resolve their differences, and at what point he thinks society, through its elected and appointed officials, should take a hand in regulating industrial disputes to minimize social costs. Today, differences over wages, working conditions, union recognition, and so on are usually resolved by American companies and unions without strikes, lockouts, boycotts or strikebreakers. It is when special, additional factors are present in the industrial-relations climate that costly disputes result, which hurt the workers, the company and the community at large.

It has been much easier to determine "what" was done than "why" it was done, even though there may also have been disagreement as to what actually took place. The author has endeavored to write the story of the long and bitter controversy with sympathy and compassion, but without glossing over the most reasonable or likely explanations of what occurred and the motives behind the events which made this the longest strike in history.

Another observation which impressed itself upon the author during the research for this book is the similarity between industrial warfare and warfare between nations. Both sides used whatever methods they thought would increase their chances for "victory"; both misinterpreted or distorted the motives of the opposition; and both inclined to see only "bad" in their opponents and only the "good" on their side.

This book is written in the hope that the number and severity of industrial disputes can be reduced if there is a broader understanding of the causes of industrial conflict and industrial peace.

THE CAST

(* = role during first strike; ** = role during second strike; *** = role during both strikes. Identification gives position held when most actively involved.)

Kohler Company Personnel and Attorneys

V. Allen Adams: ** private detective for Madson Detective Agency hired by company

Edmund Biever: * management staff; ** plant manager until 1961

Joseph M. Born: ** time-study man and photographer

Frank G. Brotz: * plant manager

Lucius P. Chase: *** general counsel for company

Lyman C. Conger: * company attorney; ** legal counsel for company, chairman of management committee and company vice president

Gerard A. Desmond: ** assistant to general counsel Chase

George C. Gallati: ** public relations director since 1955

E. J. Hammer: ** assistant to legal counsel Conger

Martin Hollander: ** assistant to chairman Conger of management committee

William F. Howe: ** special attorney, member of Washington legal firm of Gall, Lane & Howe

Walter J. Ireland: *** personnel manager

Paul Jacobi: ** photographer

Herbert V. Kohler, Sr.: son of company founder; * company vice president; ** head of company 1940–1962

Herbert V. Kohler, Jr.: associated with company since graduating from Yale in 1965

John Michael Kohler, Jr.: founder of Kohler Company, Sheboygan, Wisconsin, 1873

Walter J. Kohler, Sr.: son of company founder; * head of company 1905–1940; governor of Wisconsin 1929–1931

Walter J. Kohler, Jr.: * management staff; severed connections with company in 1947; governor of Wisconsin 1951–1957

James L. (Les) Kuplic: company employee since 1943; ** management staff; ** succeeded Biever as plant manager in 1961; ** president of company since 1962

Elmer A. Madson: head of Madson Detective Agency; ** private detective for company 1954–1957; subsequently Green Bay, Wisconsin, chief of police

L. L. Smith: * publicity director; ** executive vice president

Union Leaders and Attorneys

Arthur Bauer: ** vice president of the United Auto Workers (UAW) Local 833

Leo Breirather: a chief steward before second strike; ** in charge of boycott campaign; later UAW International representative

Robert Burkart: ** UAW International representative assigned to Local 833, 1953–1955

Joseph Burns: UAW Community Services Department; ** administered strike benefits

Charles W. Conrardy: ** Local 833 president, elected in 1965

Jack Conway: administrative assistant to UAW president Walter Reuther; ** participated in negotiations with company

Jesse Ferrazza: ** administrative assistant to UAW secretary-treasurer Emil Mazey

J. F. Friedrick: * veteran Milwaukee, Wisconsin, labor leader

Catherine Gelles: ** Director of UAW Auxiliaries' Department

Arthur Goldberg: ** legal counsel for UAW, Chicago and Washington, D.C.; later U.S. Secretary of Labor; U.S. Supreme Court Justice; Ambassador to United Nations

Allan Graskamp: ** president of Local 833 from 1953–1958

Duane H. Greathouse: ** UAW International vice president

George Haberman: ** president of Wisconsin State Federation of Labor (WSFL)

Charles Heymanns: * president of Federal Labor Union Local 18545

during most of first strike; ** regional director for American Federation of Labor (AFL) (AFL-CIO after 1955 merger)

Harvey Kitzman: ** regional director of UAW, Milwaukee

Edward Klauser: ** first president of Local 833, 1952–1953

E. H. (Eggie) Kohlhagen: leader of Kohler Workers Association (KWA) until 1952; ** recording secretary of Local 833, and editor of *The Kohlerian*

Arthur F. Kuhn: * first president of Local 18545, 1933–1935

Raymond E. Majerus: one of early supporters of UAW at Kohler; ** UAW Region 10 staff representative

Emil Mazey: ** secretary-treasurer of UAW International Union since 1946

Maud McCreery: * editor of weekly labor paper *The New Deal* in Sheboygan in 1930's

George Meany: ** president of AFL (AFL-CIO after 1955 merger)

Henry J. Ohl, Jr.: * president of WSFL during most of first strike

Joseph A. Padway: * legal counsel for Local 18545 and WSFL

David Rabinovitz: *** legal counsel for unions at Kohler during first and second strikes

Donald Rand: ** UAW Skilled Trades Department; later administrative assistant to Mazey

Max Raskin: ** legal counsel for UAW, Milwaukee

Joseph L. Rauh, Jr.: ** general counsel for UAW, Washington, D.C.

Rudolph Renn: * secretary of Local 18545 and member of bargaining and strike committees

Walter P. Reuther: ** president of UAW International Union since 1946

Frank J. Sahorske: ** assistant regional director of UAW, Milwaukee

Charles Schultz: ** president of Wisconsin CIO during second strike

Herman Seide: * successor to Ohl as president of WSFL

John Stieber: ** one of early leaders in KWA and later financial secretary of UAW Local 833

Robert Treuer: former editor of Wisconsin *CIO News:* ** UAW staff representative in charge of publicity for Local 833

Frank Wallick: ** first publicity director for Local 833; then administrative aide to Congressman Henry Reuss, Wisconsin

State and Local Officials

John G. Buchen: ** Sheboygan county district attorney 1949–1955

Anton Brotz: * president of Kohler Village

Waldemar G. Capelle: ** Kohler Village chief of police since 1947

John (Jack) Case: * Kohler Village chief of police

Charles A. Copp: * Sheboygan county district attorney

Hugh A. Dales: ** Sheboygan alderman, strong company supporter

Oakley Frank: ** Sheboygan police department detective, later chief of police

Lawrence E. Gooding: ** Chairman, Wisconsin Employment Relations Board

Col. John C. P. Hanley: * in command of National Guard sent to Kohler

Steen W. Heimke: Sheboygan police captain; ** later chief of police; then assistant manager of engine and electric plant for the Kohler Company

Walter J. Kohler, Jr.: formerly identified with Kohler company; governor of Wisconsin 1951–1957; president of Vollrath Company, Sheboygan

Harold Kroll: ** Sheboygan county sheriff, 1957–1959

Carl S. Mohar: ** Sheboygan alderman, strong union supporter

Theodore J. Mosch: ** Sheboygan county sheriff 1945–1949 and 1953–1957

Arold F. Murphy: ** circuit judge, Marinette, Wisconsin

Rudolph J. Ploetz: ** Sheboygan mayor 1955–1957

F. H. Schlichting: ** circuit judge, Sheboygan

Albert G. Schmedeman: * governor of Wisconsin 1933–1935

Vernon Thompson: ** Wisconsin attorney general, then governor

Walter H. Wagner: *** Sheboygan chief of police, retired in 1955

David Weber: ** Sheboygan county district attorney 1955–1959

Charles E. Wilson: ** superintendent of Wisconsin State Crime Laboratory in Madison

Ernest Zehms: * Sheboygan county sheriff

Frank P. Zeidler: ** mayor of Milwaukee 1948–1960; involved in "clay boat incident"

Federal Officials and Staff

Charles H. Alsip: ** assistant regional director, Federal Mediation and Conciliation Service (FMCS)

Carmine S. Bellino: ** consultant for McClellan Committee

Gerald A. Brown: ** National Labor Relations Board (NLRB) member during Kennedy and Johnson administrations after 1961

Virgil Burtz: ** conciliator, FMCS, Chicago

Hon. Homer Capehart: ** Senator from Indiana; replaced Senator Ives on McClellan Committee in 1959

Carl Carlgren: ** conciliator, FMCS, Minneapolis

Hon. Frank Church: ** Senator from Idaho; replaced Senator McNamara on McClellan Committee in 1959

Joseph Cohen: ** NLRB field examiner; later assistant regional director NLRB, Milwaukee

Hon. Carl T. Curtis: ** Senator from Nebraska; member of McClellan Committee

James A. Despins: ** conciliator, FMCS, Chicago

Justice William O. Douglas: ** U.S. Supreme Court

George A. Downing: ** trial examiner, NLRB

Judge E. M. DuQuaine: ** special master assigned to hear NLRB case

President Dwight D. Eisenhower: ** 1953–1961

Hon. Sam J. Ervin, Jr.: ** Senator from North Carolina; member of McClellan Committee

Joseph F. Finnegan: ** director, FMCS 1955–1961

Glenn C. Fleshman: ** conciliator, FMCS, Chicago

Lloyd K. Garrison: * chairman of National Labor Relations Board under NIRA, 1934

Hon. Barry Goldwater: ** Senator from Arizona; member of McClellan Committee

Albert Gore: ** NLRB counsel 1949–1957; then went into private practice as labor relations attorney in Chicago

Hon. Irving M. Ives: ** Senator from New York; member of McClellan Committee

Howard Jenkins, Jr.: ** NLRB member during Kennedy and Johnson administrations, 1963–

Joseph A. Jenkins: ** NLRB member during years 1957–1961

Vern Johnson: ** investigator for McClellan Committee

Hon. John F. Kennedy: ** Senator from Massachusetts; member of McClellan Committee; later President of the United States 1961–1963

Robert Kennedy: ** chief counsel for McClellan Committee; later U.S. Attorney General; then U.S. Senator from New York

Jerry Kronenberg: ** NLRB attorney, Chicago

Boyd Leedom: ** NLRB member during Eisenhower, Kennedy, and Johnson administrations 1955–1964

Hon. James Murray: ** Senator from Montana

Father J. W. Maguire: * Catholic priest; mediator for Regional Labor Board

Hon. Joseph McCarthy: ** Senator from Wisconsin

Hon. John J. McClellan: ** Senator from Arkansas; chairman of McClellan Committee

Frank W. McCulloch: ** chairman of NLRB, 1961–

Jack McGovern: ** investigator for McClellan Committee; counsel for Republican members of Committee

Hon. Pat McNamara: ** Senator from Michigan; member of McClellan Committee

James P. Mitchell: ** U.S. Secretary of Labor 1953–1960

Robert H. Moore: ** regional director, FMCS; later deputy director, FMCS

Hon. Karl E. Mundt: ** Senator from South Dakota; member of McClellan Committee

Stuart Rothman: ** general counsel, NLRB 1959–1963

George Squillacote: ** NLRB counsel; later regional director, Milwaukee

Judge Robert E. Tehan: ** Federal judge, Milwaukee

Chief Justice Earl Warren: ** U.S. Supreme Court

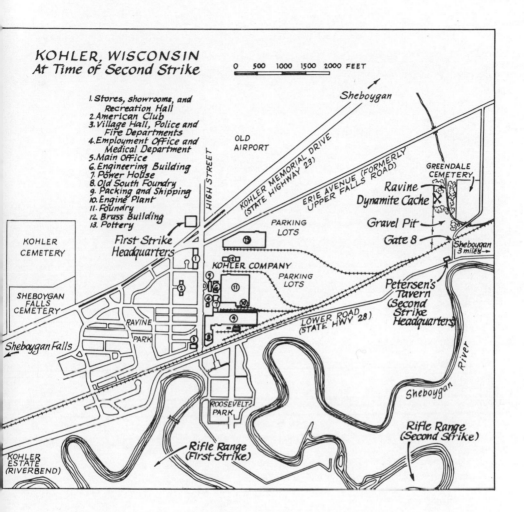

KOHLER, WISCONSIN
At Time of Second Strike

0   500 1000 1500 2000 FEET

1. Stores, showrooms, and
   Recreation Hall
2. American Club
3. Village Hall, Police and
   Fire Departments
4. Employment Office and
   Medical Department
5. Main Office
6. Engineering Building
7. Power House
8. Old South Foundry
9. Packing and Shipping
10. Engine Plant
11. Foundry
12. Brass Building
13. Pottery

Sheboygan

OLD
AIRPORT

KOHLER MEMORIAL DRIVE
(STATE HIGHWAY 23)

ERIE AVENUE (FORMERLY
UPPER FALLS ROAD)

HIGH STREET

GREENDALE
CEMETERY

Ravine
Dynamite Cache

Gravel Pit

Gate 8

Sheboygan
3 miles

First Strike
Headquarters

KOHLER
CEMETERY

SHEBOYGAN
FALLS
CEMETERY

PARKING
LOTS

KOHLER COMPANY

PARKING
LOTS

Petersen's
Tavern
(Second
Strike
Headquarters)

Sheboygan Falls

RAVINE
PARK

LOWER ROAD
(STATE HWY 28)

Sheboygan
River

ROOSEVELT
PARK

Rifle Range
(Second Strike)

Rifle Range
(First Strike)

KOHLER
ESTATE
(RIVERBEND)

I

THE "MODEL VILLAGE" —
DREAMS, REALITIES AND MYTHS

August 26, 1960, marked the beginning of the end of the second long strike at Kohler, Wisconsin. On that day the National Labor Relations Board rocked the community of Sheboygan, Wisconsin, when it announced its decision on the charges of unfair labor practices which had been filed against the company by the union, six years earlier. The Sheboygan Press *carried a banner headline — "NLRB Finds Kohler Company Guilty." It was a day of elation for the strikers. The Kohler Company announced it would appeal.*

Even though the end seemed near at hand, it was to be another five years, three months and twenty-one days before a final settlement between the company and the union was signed, ending thirty years of conflict.

The events which took place during those thirty years seem incongruous to this quiet rural community. It is difficult to comprehend that the ingredients for a full-scale labor-management conflict should be present here to produce events in American industrial history more dramatic than fiction.

KOHLER is a picture-postcard Wisconsin village of flowers, elms, winding streets, vine-clad brick and frame houses; a panorama of parks, ravines and a secluded mansion beside the Sheboygan River — Riverbend, home of the Kohler family.

A sprawling factory, neat behind the formidable fences, bounds the village on the east. Beyond the factory parking lots lies the city of Sheboygan — population about 50,000 — and beyond Sheboygan, Lake Michigan and the blue sky meet.

This peaceful setting, however, is the backdrop against which two bitter strikes have taken place — the longest, bitterest labor-management dispute in United States history. Here, three generations of Kohlers, stemming from a cultural background in Europe where success in business was a matter of extreme personal pride, have operated one of the nation's leading plumbingware firms in a way which has earned both admiration and scorn for its policies.

Founder and head of the Kohler family in the United States was John Michael Kohler, Jr. (1844–1900). At the age of ten, he came to this country from the Austrian Tyrol with his father, John Michael Kohler, Sr. His mother, who had borne eight children, had died in 1853. His father remarried, and from this union ten more children were born.

The family made its way to St. Paul, Minnesota, in 1854, where the elder John M. Kohler purchased a farm on which the children were reared. The *Biographical Record of Sheboygan County* notes that "since eighteen years old he [young John M. Kohler] has battled his own way in the world." He attended Dyrenfurth College in Chicago. His first job was driving a delivery wagon in St. Paul; then he worked as a clerk, and in 1865 became a salesman, first for a wholesale grocery, then for a furniture business. He moved to Sheboygan in 1871.

In 1873, he quit his sales job to start a foundry and machine shop which made agricultural implements. Today the plant comprises a brass foundry, an engine and electric plant, and pottery and enameling departments. In addition to bathroom fixtures, they turn out electric and engine power units for farms, wilderness cabins and boats, as well as for navy installations. The story is that the company got into the bathtub business when a water trough for horses was invented, which could double as a family bathtub.[1] By 1888, the venture, which began with 21 employees,[2] was incorporated as Kohler, Hayssen & Stehn Manufacturing Company, employing 125 men and making enameled bathtubs and kitchenware.[3]

John M. Kohler, Jr., manufacturer and enterprising business-man, reared a family of seven children of whom Walter J., Sr., Robert J., Carl J. and Herbert V. — the only son of a second marriage — were the famous Kohler brothers of Kohler of Kohler. Carl died tragically from carbolic-acid poisoning on August 6, 1904, at the age of twenty-four.[4] Robert, who had become president of the company after his father's death in 1900, died unexpectedly in August, 1905, at the age of thirty-one, just after he returned from a trip abroad.[5] Walter J. Kohler, Sr., succeeded his brother and remained head of the company until his death in 1940 when Herbert V. Kohler, Sr., became its executive head.

The eminence of the Kohler family as the leading industrialists of Sheboygan County and their influence in the political, social and particularly the economic life of that community is not to be underestimated. Every activity of members of the family was grist for the social columns of the Sheboygan newspapers; John M. Kohler, Jr., was a charter member of the Humane Society of Sheboygan and a participant in the political life of the community; the sons belonged to the Masons, the Athletic Association, the Spanish War Veterans; they traveled abroad and participated in important events at home. When John M. Kohler was a candidate for mayor of Sheboygan, *The Sheboygan Telegram*, on February 11, 1897, said:

> Mr. Kohler has always been identified with the material interests and progress of Sheboygan since he came to this city in 1871. He has been one of its mainstays and has always commanded the respect and confidence of the community. To him more than any other citizen, it might be said without fear of successful contradiction, is Sheboygan indebted for its magnificent harbor, which today is the keynote for its prosperity in the future. Other large and successful enterprises have had Mr. Kohler's generous support and influence. He is the founder of the Home for the Friendless, and its president . . . as a large employer of men, he has always possessed their confidence.

It was in his role as "employer of men" that several events occurred worthy of noting here. The strikes of 1934 and 1954 at Kohler are relatively well known, but few are aware that there was an earlier strike at Kohler, Hayssen & Stehn Manufacturing Company. On March 13, 1897, about 25 molders who belonged to the Molders' Union No. 286, left their work, protesting a 50-per-cent cut in wages. The German language newspaper, *Die Sheboygan Zeitung* on March 10, 1897, explained the strike as follows:

> As we came into the factory, we found the work in the various departments in progress, except in the foundry where the work force was reduced. Mr. Kohler explained, in answer to our questions, that a strike had broken out and that 20 to 25 molders laid down their work.
> The workers told [us] approximately the following:
> At the beginning of February, after an interruption, the work was

again resumed and Mr. Kohler explained to us at once that wages must be cut but he didn't say at that time how much. We worked until the 27th of February when Mr. Kohler informed us about the conditions of the wage cut. We considered it too much; Mr. Kohler explained that nevertheless he was not able, because of circumstances, to pay higher wages, and if we didn't want to take the suggested wage cut, we could work until Saturday and then he would close [the plant]. We worked until Saturday; meanwhile we thought over the matter and decided finally not to take the wage cut. We are not on strike, Mr. Kohler just told us that if we would not accept his terms — and that we did not do — we simply do not come to work.

Both parties talked about the matter without regret and both sides appear to bear enough good will so that at this time, it should not be difficult to resolve the differences. [Translation.]

An unnamed member of the company (perhaps John M. Kohler, since his name is mentioned in the article) gave an interview to *The Sheboygan Times* on March 13, 1897, in which he said:

Since we have been manufacturing these 24 years, we have found the contract convict labor system so powerful a competition in some lines of goods that we have been compelled to go into the manufacture of other lines. . . . The work of making bath tubs was a hard one and for the sake of making the work easier we went to great expense in getting machinery, and though the work was easier and more rapid, the bath tub makers were enabled to make 25 percent more and we made no reduction in wages until we found it absolutely necessary. Owing to the hard times, but little building was done last year . . . consequently the sale of bath tubs throughout the United States was greatly reduced. Since last August we have not worked full time, and for six weeks we were obliged to close down the foundry and enameling departments . . . the first time on record since the business was started. . . . We were compelled to so arrange matters that we could compete with the present market and sales or be obliged to keep closed again a part of the foundry. According to our views the first was the best. So we informed the married men of the molders that we could give them work for a short time, but at reduced prices [wages]. . . . According to present prices bath tub molders earn at ten hours work per day, with nine hours Saturday, allowing a ten percent reduction for defections, which is fully covered, a little over $12 a week net, but at the present time bath tub molders are working only half time.

The newspaper also reported the company spokesman as saying that "a committee consisting of three honorable molders informed the company that the officers of the National Molders' Union had notified them not to accept the new scale of prices [wages] offered by the Company, and they left our office without expressing any resentment or hard feelings."

The molders' strike of 1897 dragged on from March into the fall. On the first day of the strike, *The Sheboygan Herald*, in reporting Mr. Kohler's ultimatum (that the men accept a 50-per-cent wage cut or the plant would be closed down) said: "It is understood however, that Mr. Kohler, head of the firm, graciously donated one of the tubs in question to each of those employed in the manufacturing of same as a recompense for the cut to be made."

The men organized marches about the city and picketed the foundry by parading around it every evening and "escorting" home the men who continued to work at the plant. The paper admitted that there had been no "overt" acts by the strikers and one of them, arrested on charges of assault and battery during the summer, was acquitted of the charges. The Molders' Union paid strike benefits of $7 a week to men with families and $5 a week to single men. The attitude of the newspapers, not greatly different from that during the later strikes, was expressed in such comments as the following, in *The Sheboygan Herald*, on July 17, 1897:

> There seems a good deal hold-out-ativeness to both sides. . . . The whole strike business in whatever locality or form is almost always a curse to all parties connected with it and indirectly to every citizen in the nation to a certain extent. Oh! for some St. Patrick to banish the whole strike business into the Atlantic.

On August 21, 1897, the same newspaper commented:

> The whistle of Kohler's strikers is still heard in the land; every morning about 7 o'clock the whistling band march around the Kohler, Hayssen, & Stehn Mfg. Co.'s works and when they can they discourse to the workmen who remain on the subject of "scabs." Sometimes they escort the employees home, one or more on each side, they usually wear red button hole bouquets whether indicative of anarchy or blood, we know not. Sometimes we feel that we would like to live under a monarchy where there is not so much

liberty, where one man or a company cannot have liberty enough to take away the liberty of others. Probably liberty is a good thing, but it seems to be overworked in places.

A sidelight of the 1897 strike was the appearance of Socialist leaders, Eugene V. Debs and Victor L. Berger, in Sheboygan for a speaking engagement on July 10. Heavy rains had fallen earlier that day; the streetcar company shut off service, and many who wanted to hear the speeches could not get to the meeting place on time.

". . . The strikers claim they can stay out for years because the union pays a married man $7.00 per week and a single man they pay $5.00 per week," *The Sheboygan Herald* had written on July 3, 1897, but by fall the strike was given up.

Founding of the "Model Village"

The Kohler Company, in the year following the 1897 strike, bought land southwest of Sheboygan and started what became known as a "model village." Several buildings were erected on the farmland bought in 1898; part of the Kohler production unit was moved to the new location in 1899 and the old plant in Sheboygan was sold. In February, 1901, the new plant at Kohler was partly destroyed by fire, but the factory was rebuilt and the firm prospered.

During the first decade of this century, a number of non-descript buildings were erected by the company at Kohler. Walter J. Kohler had seen many industrial towns in the United States, most of them dismal and unattractive, and he discussed with his architect, W. C. Weeks, his dream for a well-planned village. In 1912, the two men visited Europe to study its garden cities — particularly industrial garden cities — for at that time Europe had many examples of good community planning. Upon their return, the company engaged town planners, landscape men, architects and engineers, and with the help of some other people of the community proceeded to build the model village.[6]

A special organization, the Kohler Improvement Company, was established to acquire title to the land and build neat, attractive homes. These were sold to Kohler employees, although the land ownership in the early years was retained by the company. When houses were to be sold, the company exercised its prerogative to buy them back. In recent years, deeds for property purchased in Kohler Village filed in the Sheboygan County Court House, have often contained a number of restrictive covenants, among them:

> The parties of the second part agree that if the property herein above described is sold by them, their heirs, successors or assignees, the grantor [Kohler Company and its lending agencies] shall have first opportunity to buy said property at the highest bona fide offer made for said property. . . .

Other clauses provide that the "buildings on said property shall not be used for any immoral purposes or for nuisance or for the purpose of a saloon or tavern . . ." or that "it shall never be used as an apartment, tenement, store, public garage, oil or auto service station, public livery stable, etc. nor for any purpose than a single dwelling house." Any "deviation therefrom" requires approval of at least three quarters of the owners within 1,200 feet in any direction as well as of the Kohler Company and any planning board or commission that may be established. These covenants were drawn to "maintain a high-class residential community."

Another organization, the Kohler Building and Loan Association, was chartered under the laws of the State of Wisconsin, subject to the banking laws of the state. During the depression of the early thirties, Walter J. Kohler, Sr., was quoted as saying that the Kohler Company had no official connections with the association except that at times the company loaned money to it. The association had two kinds of stock – paid-up stock for those who wanted to invest money, and "participating stock" for those who bought homes. Five-per-cent interest was paid regularly on the paid-up stocks. According to records in the files of the Sheboygan County Clerk of Court, the Kohler Building and Loan Association had thirteen judgments taken on homes between 1930 and 1935. Two houses were sold at sheriff's sale and other foreclosure actions were started. The association held 268 mortgages in September, 1934.

In 1934, Charles Heymanns, at that time an officer of the newly organized Federal Labor Union No. 18545 in the Kohler plant, said to the author:

The Kohler Company is the controlling factor in both the Kohler Improvement and Association and the Building and Loan Association, according to their own statements on the stand and from actual knowledge of men working in the plant. Men who bought homes were promised and given supervisory positions at the plant, and all payments for stock and loans were deducted from the men's paychecks by the Kohler Company. The great majority of officers of these organizations are also officers of the Kohler Company or dependent upon the good will of the company.

The village itself had grown to a population of about 1,800 by 1934. Most of the construction of new homes occurred between 1922 and 1928 and Kohler was a very attractive place in which to own a home. Lawns were well kept, trees were uniformly trimmed, and flowers added color to the boulevards and bridle paths encircling the community. During the depression of the early nineteen-thirties, when a house in the village needed painting, the company would supply paint if the owner found it impossible to carry through the needed improvement — but only if he agreed to the color and design specified by the company.[7]

Company and Village Policies and Practices

In 1934 there were about 450 houses in the village, most of them built with brick and placed equidistant from the winding streets. More than 90 per cent of the homes were occupied by Kohler employees; over half of these were company officials, superintendents and office workers, with about 200 homes occupied by rank-and-file factory workers. Less than 10 per cent of the factory workers lived in the model village, but many outside Sheboygan County and Wisconsin had the impression that most of the workers lived there. Actually most workers lived in Sheboygan, Sheboygan Falls, Plymouth, or on farms.

The village was governed by a board, similar to that of other Wisconsin villages. Each person had one vote, but in a company town where at least 90 per cent of the adult workers derive their income from one employer, a village board inevitably has a strong majority who identify the village's interests with the company's. This made it easy, for example, for the Kohler village board to vote to annex the Kohler airport which the villagers were then taxed to

The Kohler plant and part of Village of Kohler, with Sheboygan and Lake Michigan in background. Lower Falls Road is the diagonal running from center right to lower left, with High Street intersecting it lower left. This picture was taken before a large addition to the plant beyond the building at center left had been constructed. (Photo Courtesy Thompson Flying Service)

maintain, even though it was the company officials who made most use of the airport.

An American Club with a large dormitory, a dining hall and recreation facilities was built in the village to accommodate single men working in the plant. Many Kohler workers during the twenties were new immigrants from Europe. For a period, the proportion of foreign-born employed in the plant was so large that local people felt "you almost had to be a foreigner" to get a job in the plant. Walter J. Kohler, Sr., spent much time and effort in Americanizing his men. He took them to the county courthouse in Sheboygan on company time to get their first and second citizenship papers. In many cases, groups of newly naturalized citizens were feted at special banquets arranged by the company. They were told that, as United States citizens, they had a better chance for promotion. After World War I labor was scarce and for a time the company sent representatives to New York and to the Canadian border to recruit recent immigrants as workers. Some disenchanted local citizens asserted this was done because immigrants would work for lower wages.

Over the years the Kohler Company initiated a number of practices which were of benefit to employees. A smoking and reading room was provided for the men to use during their lunch hour and a band concert was given on Monday afternoons. They were provided with a recreation club and facilities for baseball, tennis and horseshoes. The company also established a Kohler Benefit Association and a group life-insurance program through the Aetna Life Insurance Company. These fringe benefits were provided years before Kohler production workers thought seriously about forming their own union.

During the early years of the Kohler Company, profits were small. In 1911, taxable income, as reported to the Wisconsin Income Tax Commission was only $14,282.[8] Profits increased to $79,000 in 1912, to $157,000 in 1913, to $380,000 in 1917, and then jumped to $853,000 in 1918, a year after the United States had entered World War I. The company had obtained war contracts to make three-inch projectiles and hand grenades, as well as other munitions.

Workers in the plant during World War I received good wages. The period of postwar prosperity in the twenties led to expanded markets for the company's products and to the need for more men at Kohler; additional factory buildings were constructed during the early twenties. The profits of the Kohler Company dropped from $853,000 in 1918 to $219,000 in 1919; then increased again to a peak, before the first strike, of $3,336,771 taxable income in 1925. The company showed a profit each year until 1930, but in the first four years of the depression, it lost over two million dollars.[9] When the company's markets shrank, it adopted a policy of storing surpluses in available warehouse space in several cities as well as Kohler.

During the middle twenties, when the plant was operating at full capacity, it employed close to 4,000 persons and paid good wages compared with those prevailing in the community. How-

A street of homes (top); the American Club (center), and shops and showrooms (bottom) on High Street in Kohler village. (Kohler of Kohler News *photo, August, 1934*)

ever, some of the first workers to join the union in 1934 claimed that men working in the plant had to work *much harder* than was the case in most factories in Sheboygan, and some of those who left Sheboygan for higher wages at Kohler later returned to their former jobs.

During the twenties, when many thought that prosperity would continue indefinitely, most American workers had steady jobs and were not dissatisfied. This decade saw the advent and expansion of many new programs and innovations in industrial management, such as time-study, piece work and job evaluation. Many companies employed efficiency experts, who timed jobs and put workers on piece-work rates. Piece work at the Kohler Company was urged upon the workers as fair and sensible, as rewarding the diligent worker and eliminating the loafer. When piece rates were first introduced in the plant, the employee who worked hard could usually earn substantially more than he did at his hourly rate. This led many to try to exceed their previous output; men were pitted against one another to see who could do the most work, and before long, efficiency experts, with stopwatch in hand, came along to time the various jobs. If management decided that the established piece rates were too high, a cut was ordered. A Kohler worker remembered that the "efficiency man" would either hide behind the pillars to time the men, or stand alongside them, often stimulating them to surpass their previous records. If a man protested that he could not work at the newly established rate all day, he was told, "Here's a record of the time it took you to do that piece of work." One man said he timed himself, using his own wristwatch, when the efficiency man studied his job, and found that his pay was cut in half even though he worked at the same pace as usual.

Working conditions other than wages and hours are often a source of grievances. The very nature of the Kohler manufacturing processes required some to work under conditions of heat and dust that were far from ideal. L. P. Chase, the Kohler Company attorney, told the author in 1935 that the company had one of the most up-to-date ventilating systems in the country and that dust counts were taken periodically in every department. The men were required to wear respirators in the more hazardous and dusty departments. The company spent a great deal of money to improve its equipment and claimed to have some of the best respirators available. The company also maintained its own medical and dental departments to treat men who were taken sick or injured on the job and it checked periodically on the physical condition of employees. Applicants were given a thorough physical examination, including chest X rays before going to work.

Only men in good physical condition were assigned to the difficult and hazardous jobs. From a health standpoint the most hazardous departments in the factory at that time were the sandblast and grinding rooms. In the sandblast department, sand was blown against the rough plumbingware castings under high pressure as the units passed over a conveyor. The blasting smoothed the surface but shattered the silica (sand) particles, filling the air with dust which had to be kept out of the lungs by means of respirators. This was a very difficult problem to solve because, inevitably, some of the fine silica dust would get through the respirators and lodge in the capillaries of the lungs, causing irritation and congestion. This could lead to fibrosis and multiple-fibrosis, followed by increased calcification, less breathing surface in the lungs, resulting in silicosis and pre-disposition to tuberculosis.

The discovery of silicosis had been fairly recent in medical history. Men working in stone quarries and sandblasts died young from silicosis and never knew why. The Kohler Company, as well as the workers in the sandblast, were confronted with the dilemma of choosing between cheap respirators, which provided little protection, and good ones, which made breathing so difficult that they taxed the lungs. Wages paid in the sandblasting department were necessarily higher because the work was dirty and not everyone would take such assignments. Those who became accustomed to the dust remained on the job for long periods, and eventually the company found itself involved with numerous Workmen's Compensation claims because men developed silicosis or tuberculosis from working in the sandblast. Chest X rays were taken of workers who complained of chest difficulties; hearings were conducted by the Wisconsin Industrial Commission to determine the degree of occupation-induced disability and the company was ordered to settle with the workers where the necessary evidence was presented. Silicosis cases became an item of considerable expense to the Kohler Company, even though it self-insured against claims, and eventually management established the policy that no man could work in the sandblast longer than six months. He would then be transferred to outside work or to another department in the plant. Chest X rays were also taken frequently of men working in dusty places. Rocky Knoll Sanitorium in Sheboygan County near Plymouth, built for tubercular patients, was often referred to by critics of the company as "Kohler Pavilion," the final haven of former Kohler sandblasters.

Men in the grinding room were also required to wear respirators for protection. The mill room, where enamel was made out of fluorspar and other ingredients, was another hazardous place to work. The company doctor kept a medical history on all employees, and there were enough cases of silicosis to make the company very health-conscious. This attitude contributed to the uneasiness among the employees as they became increasingly aware of the health hazards connected with some of the departments in the plant.

Another issue which contributed to the tensions between workers and management at Kohler was the dispute over whether or not the company was within the law in making deductions for defective workmanship. The company asserted that it abided by the law, and workers insisted that they were illegally charged for defective work. If there was no improper charging for defective work, the company evidently did an inadequate job of getting its side of the story to the workers. The author obtained testimony in 1935 from men who claimed that "seconds" and "culls" from the departments were taken to a special department and made over into "firsts," and that the men who did the original work were not paid for their share. One man told about "plugging" imperfect bathtubs and stated that the made-over products were sold close to Kohler so that if the defect were noticed, the company would not have to pay heavy freight charges to return the article.[10] Workers told of instances in which stored goods were taken out of storage to be shipped and, if a crack were found, the man whose number was on the product was charged for it even years later.

The prolonged depression necessitated laying off many men and cutting hours and wages for others. Instead of laying off most of the men and keeping a small number at full time, the company attempted to spread employment and give all the men at least one or two days of work per week. They asserted that this was done because of a long-standing policy of furnishing continuity of employment even though it was not the most economical thing to do. Many workers, however, believed it was done because the company figured it would be cheaper in the long run to keep the men on the payroll, since it is costly to train new employees. Workers also claimed that there were too many different kinds of work to run the plant efficiently with a small crew of full-time employees.

By December, 1933, work had become very scarce and the company's policy of retaining employees who lived in the village, while laying off workers who lived in Sheboygan, caused much dissension. A majority of the villagers still had mortgages on their homes and the Kohler Building and Loan Association got the men to sign agreements, authorizing wage-deductions for mortgage payments, under threat of being included in the next lay-off if they did not sign.

There was not much work to be had; consequently there was much unrest, even among those who lived in the model village. In some cases the men got no money as a result of the deductions; other checks amounted to sums such as $0.85, $2.00 and $5.00 for two-week periods. This unrest culminated in a protest meeting of property holders in May, 1934, to discuss reductions in mortgage payments. They drafted resolutions calling for a reduction in payments, but the men had difficulty finding anyone who would take the resolution to Walter J. Kohler, Sr. Finally, three men were selected. They made an appointment to see Mr. Kohler at 10 A.M. on a Wednesday morning. When they arrived, Walter J. Kohler, Sr., Herbert V. Kohler, L. P. Chase, Walter Ireland and several other officials were there to greet them. This was quite a surprise to the men, since they had made the appointment only with Walter J. Kohler, Sr. The resolution was presented, but not much was said by either side on that occasion.

One of the members of the committee told the author he was laid off within a month after the meeting because he "wasn't working hard enough." He had received a bonus of $7.20 on his last check, which amounted to about 18 cents per hour. He went to the office and asked why they gave him a bonus if he had not worked hard enough; he got no satisfactory answer.[11]

On September 1, 1934, Walter J. Kohler, Sr., stated his ideas on labor-management relations at Kohler thus:

The Kohler Company has had definite labor policies. It has not tried to hire men as cheaply as they could be hired. It was not governed by the surrounding scales of pay, or, rather, the scales of pay in the immediate locality. It kept abreast with the wage payments of its leading competitors, although it is located in a small town where, as a rule, wages are lower than they are in bigger cities. We had a minimum wage at Kohler for many years, long before the N.R.A. brought it up in its code; and we found that some of our competitors . . . have actually had a minimum rate that was only half of what we paid. And during the depression there were some actually paying only one-third of what we were paying. For many years it has been the policy of this company to maintain a happy relationship with the men who worked in the shop. Now, that is based on a very practical experience of my own as a worker. Perhaps part of it was inherited, because my father, I think, was a socially minded man. But I had to work as a boy of fifteen . . . at an age which the young men are not allowed to go to work today. I worked in the enamel shop, on probably the first bath tub made by the dry process in this plant. I worked in the foundry, I have moulded iron, I have worked in the warehouses, assembled goods, shipped them, worked in the office, worked in the scales department, studied finance and naturally played a part in the development of this industry in our particular company in the last thirty years when I became the head of it, and even before that I worked at a very low wage and have worked for a dollar a day. I have lived on it, too, although I confess I did not have a family at that time, but I worked twelve hours a day at the furnaces, which was the schedule throughout the nation, when I was still in my teens. And I changed it to an eight-hour shift because twelve hours was entirely too long. I still thought so, and changed the eight hours later to six. I am a believer in reasonable hours of work, I believe in good wages. I believe in good working conditions, I believe in continuity of employment and regularity of income, which is a substantial factor in the well-being of any worker's life. . . . I have tried to give continuity of employment; we have done so many, many years. That is even before I was born, because that was the policy which I inherited of continuing work. . . . In 1931 there was a shortening of hours until this depression became so prolonged that it was thoroughly impossible to carry it out. We did, however, still attempt to give employment to everybody, recognizing the importance of some regularity of income even if it wasn't as large as would be desired; we kept employed a thousand to fifteen hundred men more than the company should have carried in 1930. If we had laid those men off they probably would have in time gone on public relief, which we did not want, and which they did not want. Laying off men right and left, however, was the policy of most industries. It was the policy, largely, of our competitors . . . they thought it was necessary from a business standpoint, but we attempted to stagger the work and give people some sort of employment, and it was done at a considerable loss and also at considerable inconvenience in manufacture. . . . The company depends for its market on residential building which was active in the middle twenties, particularly in 1922, 1923, and up to 1928. Residential building is one of the indexes of the times. . . . It reached such a low stage of building that in 1932 and 1933, and so far this year it has been running about ten per cent of what it was in the middle twenties. . . . Yesterday I received a report through Dun and Bradstreet's about a manufacturer of boilers and radiators and enamelware. The Richmond Radiator Company — after trying to get funds from the government and unable to do so, closed down and will liquidate the present inventories and its quick assets and will close down indefinitely. This plant was unionized a year ago. I do not say that with any spirit of levity or facetiousness at all. I cite that only as what happened to a unionized A. F. of L. plant in this particular industry. . . . In 1931 the Kohler Company was loaded with goods and there was a reduction in hours. . . . There was a cut in 1931 and two in 1932. In August of last year, however, when the N.R.A. was put into effect and codes came into being, I was active in helping to work out a code, for the industries we are engaged in. . . . We established for that code a forty cent minimum with thirty-five cents in the south because it was insisted upon by the administration. . . . We had increased our rates to forty cents minimum from the first of last August and had raised the other wages thirty percent, irrespective of positions. That was the approximate difference. One manufacturer, a substantial one, admitted to me personally that he was paying a twenty-two cent rate as against the higher minimums we paid. Now, our company lost a good deal of money. That is not generally believed, perhaps, but it is true. . . . It broke down even in 1930. In 1932 it lost nearly $2,000,000 largely because the company kept the men employed, and in 1933 it lost nearly $700,000 — and is losing money this year at the rate of a million dollars a year.[12]

This statement, made by Walter J. Kohler, Sr., six weeks after his model village had become the scene of a bitter strike, reflects his conviction that he was a generous employer who went far beyond what his competitors did to provide jobs during the depression. The Kohler heritage from the "old country" had imparted to him strong paternalism and aristocratic pride, reflected in his sincere efforts to make Kohler a model village. But this pride had not prevented him from working hard at practically every job in the factory. He knew from firsthand experience what could be done and he was not about to permit any "outsiders" to interfere with his business.

Giving a goose or some other gift to Kohler workers on special holidays or anniversaries, and awarding the traditional gold watches for twenty-five years of service, were customs transplanted from Europe; they still exist in some German and Austrian factories and business firms. This paternalism, however, despite its generous aspects, was no substitute for a union. It gave no voice to the workers, and eventually made them turn to unions to gain protection against favoritism and to obtain the right and dignity of having a part in determining wages and working conditions.

The changes in personnel policies at Kohler during the past forty years are the result of union action, together with changes in labor legislation and in company leadership. This period witnessed a major depression, a World War, the McCarthy era, a quadrupling of union membership throughout the United States, and two long strikes at Kohler. It brought increased participation in politics on the part of both management and labor, as well as new developments in economic and political philosophies. The Kohler family had been active in political and community affairs for many years, and during these changing years, two Kohlers became governor of Wisconsin.

2

KOHLER WORKERS BECOME
UNION-CONSCIOUS

Wisconsin Politics — Kohler Elected Governor

POLITICALLY speaking, Wisconsin and progressivism were syn-onomous for most of the first half of this present century. Wisconsin was the first state to introduce workmen's compensation (1911) and the first to adopt unemployment compensation (1932), three years before Congress passed the Social Security Act.

Throughout this period the La Follettes were a profound influence in government and became one of the most famous families in American politics. "Old Bob" — "Fighting Bob" — La Follette began his career when he was elected Dane County district attorney in 1881 and then gained a seat in Congress (1885–91). A biography, *The La Follettes*,[1] by Edward N. Doan, emphasizes the importance of these years: "LaFollette served in the House of Representatives as a regular Republican and began to appreciate the corrupting influence of great wealth and the concentration of economic power."

Early in his career, Robert M. La Follette, Sr., identified with "average" citizens as against the railroads and lumber interests of his day. Although he ran for office as a Republican, except in the 1924 presidential campaign when he ran as a Progressive, his political philosophy came to be far better known as "Progressive" than "Republican." Indeed, the Progressives were viewed more often as a political entity than as a faction within the GOP. In 1900, he was elected governor; from 1905 until his death in 1925, he was Wisconsin's most famous senator. That he was one of six senators who opposed the entry of the United States into World War I, did not diminish the faith of Wisconsin voters in his progressive leadership. When he died, his son Robert, Jr., filled the vacancy in the Senate, serving as one of the nation's ablest senators until his defeat in 1946 by another Wisconsin political figure, Joseph McCarthy.

The younger La Follette son, Philip, was governor of Wisconsin from 1931 to 1933 and again from 1935 to 1939.

Milwaukee, the state's largest city, elected several Socialist mayors: Emil Seidel, elected in 1910, and Daniel Webster Hoan, who served from 1916 to 1940, a period in which Milwaukee achieved a reputation as the best-governed major city in the United States. The leadership of the Wisconsin labor movement, centered in Milwaukee, was also predominately socialist at that time. Another Socialist, Frank P. Zeidler, served three terms as mayor, 1948–1960.

The Republican party dominated state politics throughout most of the nineteen-twenties, but the party was far from united, having within it both the regulars, or stalwarts, and the La Follette Progressives. Wisconsin politics were always lively, often hectic.

It was in this setting that Walter J. Kohler, Sr., entered the political arena. During the last two decades of the nineteenth century, his father, a strong advocate of Republican principles, had served as a member of the Sheboygan County Board of Supervisors and of the Common Council, and also as mayor of Sheboygan.[2] In 1928, Kohler won the Republican endorsement for governor and succeeded in defeating Albert G. Schmedeman, the Democratic incumbent, 547,738 to 394,368. A Socialist candidate, Otto Hauser, received 36,924 votes, a reflection of the sentiment which had repeatedly elected Dan Hoan mayor of Milwaukee.

Kohler conducted a vigorous campaign that took him to all sections of the state, often by private plane and often accompanied by the Kohler band. One resident of Kohler Village, who had been a foreman at the plant for many years, estimated that as many as a hundred men were taken out of the plant and sent throughout the state to put up campaign posters for Kohler and/or make speeches in his behalf. One former employee, with whom the author spoke in 1935, referred to Kohler's campaign crew as "superintendents and henchmen." They received their regular wages or salaries and were free to turn in their own expense accounts.

The large amounts of money spent in the 1928 campaign caused Glenn Roberts, Philip F. La Follette, Alvin C. Reis and William T. Evjue, all progressive Republicans, to bring a law suit against the candidate under the Corrupt Practices Act. The Supreme Court of Wisconsin ruled that a candidate cannot be held responsible for money spent in his behalf where an agency relation-

*Walter J. Kohler, Sr., in a bid for a second term as governor, address-
ing a meeting at Wauwatosa, a Milwaukee suburb, during 1932 campaign.* (Milwaukee Journal *photo*)

ship cannot be established. The defense argued that the spending
was done by voluntary groups of citizens.

The stock-market crash and the Great Depression started in
the fall of 1929 about halfway through Governor Kohler's term of
office. In 1930, Philip F. La Follette won the Republican nomination for governor and defeated Hammersley, his Democratic opponent, by a vote of 392,958 to 170,020.

In the fall of 1932, Kohler Village again became a busy place
when Walter J. Kohler, Sr., attempted to regain the governorship.
Thousands of visitors from all parts of Wisconsin went through the
attractive village and the factory and heard about the "amicable"
relationships which existed between the workers and the management. Four ministers, to whom the author talked in 1934, received
from Kohler shortly before that election free bathtubs for their
parsonages. Kohler won the Republican nomination but lost to
A. G. Schmedeman, the Democratic candidate, by a vote of 470,-
805 to 590,114 when the Democratic landslide elected Franklin D.
Roosevelt as President and started the country on the road of a
New Deal.

By this time there was extensive unemployment and much unrest throughout the state and nation. Metcalfe, the Socialist candidate for governor of Wisconsin, received 63,380 votes, reflection of a growing concern about mass unemployment and poverty in the city and low prices on the farm. Kohler's campaign slogan had been "Cut Costs." He had pledged strenuous efforts to slash cost of government and at the same time provide unemployment relief.

Charles Heymanns, a Kohler worker and a member of the strike committee during the 1934 strike, told the author that during the 1932 primary campaign he had attended a meeting arranged by progressive Republicans in Sheboygan. Incumbent U.S. Senator John J. Blaine of Wisconsin was the speaker. Heymanns was surprised to see many Kohler employees at that rally since another meeting for candidate Kohler had been scheduled on the same day at Vollrath Bowl in Sheboygan. When Blaine's talk was nearly concluded, Heymanns left and went to hear the last of candidate Kohler's address. Three or four days later he was called into the office of Harry Sommers, general plant superintendent, and told, "It is reported that you listened to Blaine while Mr. Kohler was talking." Asked what he had against Mr. Kohler, Heymanns replied, "As an American citizen, I think I have the right to go where I please. I have always been a progressive and I do not agree with Mr. Kohler's political ideas." Heymanns then asked Sommers how it was known to whom he had listened and was told, "The Kohler Company has ways of finding out!" To which Heymanns replied, "I consider this a case of putting out stool pigeons."

Other Kohler workers told the author in 1935 that during the 1932 campaign they had been called into the office and asked to donate the use of their cars to help transport the Kohler band.

Despite the depression, the company had been operating steadily until the fall of 1930 — a fact frequently mentioned in Kohler's unsuccessful campaign for re-election as governor. Economic conditions worsened, however, and this necessitated laying off men, cutting hours and reducing wages in the plant shortly after the election. Many Kohler workers, who did not understand the economics involved in conducting a business enterprise, concluded that they had been kept on the job until after the election for "publicity purposes."

During the entire period from 1873 to 1934, there had been no serious attempt to form a union to bargain collectively for the Kohler workers. Only in 1897 did the molders in the plant, associated with the National Molders' Union, engage in a strike against a 50-per-cent cut in wages. There was no recourse for the individual worker in case he was fired, or received a cut in wages, or was charged too much for defective work. One worker interviewed in 1935 said, "It may be literally true, as Mr. Kohler says, that nobody is scared of him, but a person's fate lies entirely in the hands of the company; and if the individual's demands are considered unreasonable, they are ignored, and if there is a personal grudge or if the worker is considered an agitator, he is fired."

A Rural Heritage Encounters Unions

An agricultural heritage has had a strong influence on the outlook of Sheboygan County citizenry, even though the urban now exceeds the rural population. While the Kohler Company, its model village and the labor disputes associated with that company have given prominence to Sheboygan County, the county also has a reputation for producing delicious bratwurst — Sheboygan celebrates a Bratwurst Day every August. The city is also known as the Chair City because of its furniture factories. The village of Elkhart Lake stages a nationally-known auto race, "Road America," and the city of Plymouth has long been known as the "Cheese Center of the World."

Some of the earliest rural settlers, including the author's great-grandfather, came to Sheboygan County from Langenholzhausen, Lippe, Germany, in 1847 in response to promises made to the immigrants when they landed in Milwaukee. One hundred twelve Germans had left Bremen in the three-mast ship *Agnes* and, after six weeks of rough sailing, came through the Great Lakes on their way to Iowa. A Milwaukee land speculator persuaded the majority to explore the pine forests of Sheboygan County instead of going farther westward. Friedrich Reineking, spokesman for the group, stated in German dialect, "*Nai Kinner, wu wü blüwet, blüwet wü olle.*"[3] (Now children, where we stay we'll *all* stay.)

The author's grandfather, Wilhelm Uphoff, was the first white child born in the township of Herman, Sheboygan County, in 1848.

He reared a family of ten children on a 40-acre farm two miles north of Franklin and the author himself grew up on that homestead. Clearing away timber and breaking the sod occupied much of the time of the early settlers. Farmers hauled their wheat to Sheboygan with oxen over poor roads in those days. A highway from Kiel to Sheboygan, via Millhome, Ada and Howards Grove, was referred to as the "Plank Road" long after the planks had been replaced by gravel. One of the earliest taverns in the county, located in Howards Grove (known as Pitchville), where farmers stopped en route to market, was operated by a man named Schlichting,* jokingly called "Buschkönig" (King of the Woods).

Some Germans came to Sheboygan County to escape the militarism and tyranny that characterized their country during the middle of the nineteenth century, others came in search of economic opportunities. While the county population also includes many whose ancestors hailed from Holland, Belgium and other European countries, the major stock was German and left a strong imprint on the culture of the community. Only a generation ago services in many churches were conducted in German and until very recently some ministers preached both English and German sermons on Sundays. Not many years ago anyone hoping to get a job as a clerk at H. C. Prange's Department Store in Sheboygan had to be able to speak German as well as English.

Some of the early immigrants were free-thinkers, but it was not long before the German Reformed, Evangelical and Lutheran and, later, Catholic churches became important institutions in the community. Opinions as to what was right and wrong were firmly held and new ideas and concepts were slowly adopted. This was evident in the tenacious way their descendants adhered to "pro" or "anti" union sentiments, often depending on the bias of their parents or their "spiritual" leaders.

There was little out-migration from this eastern Wisconsin region except for college students who, in many cases, did not return to their home communities. Mission House Academy, College and Seminary (now known as Lakeland College) east of Elkhart Lake, operated by the German Reformed Church, was the only college in the area. Many of those who remained stayed on the

---

* This is also the name of a circuit judge, F. H. Schlichting, involved in cases during the 1954 strike.

farms or sought work in Sheboygan or at Kohler. As declining profit margins in farming drove people to seek employment in the cities, many were grateful for extra income from regular or part-time jobs in industry. For these people, a regular pay check meant much and seldom did they question whether their wages were equitable.

The depression of the thirties forced many urban workers to rely on government programs such as WPA, CCC and NYA and caused most farmers to turn to agricultural subsidy programs.

When rural Sheboygan County residents entered the industrial world of Kohler, they brought with them into the employer-employee relationship a certain naïveté. Accustomed to working very hard for very little on their farms, they were slow to realize that they were not their own bosses in a factory situation. At the same time, their strong attachment to ownership, as they had experienced it in their homes and farms, gave them a degree of empathy with their employer. The idea of organization and unions was foreign to many of these strongly individualistic people. The newspapers which they read presented little of the viewpoint of the working-man, and what they did read concerning strikes, wage increases, and so on, tended to make them feel that the interests of other workers conflicted with their own.

The advent of the New Deal in 1933 created a changed political climate which brought legislation spelling out the terms under which workers had the right to form and join unions. Skilled craft workers, more than industrial workers, had struggled for years to achieve recognition and legal status after the courts in 1806 declared unions to be "criminal conspiracies." While the criminal-conspiracy doctrine was overruled in 1842, it was ninety years or more before workers saw national policy toward unions expressed in positive terms. Section 7(a)* of the National Industrial Re-

* Section 7(a). Every code of fair competition, agreement and license approved, prescribed or issued under this title shall contain the following conditions: (1) That employees shall have the right to organize and bargain collectively through representatives of their own choosing, and shall be free from the interference, restraint, or coercion of employers of labor, or their agents, in the designation of such representatives or in self-organization or in other concerted activities for the purpose of collective bargaining or other mutual aid or protection; (2) that no employee and no one seeking employment shall be required as a condition of employment to join any company union or to refrain from joining, organizing or assisting a labor organization of his own choosing.

covery Act (NIRA), enacted in 1933 during the early months of the New Deal, stated for the first time that workers had "the right to organize and bargain collectively through representatives of their own choosing" and to be free from interference by employers or their agents.

The Formation of Federal Labor Union No. 18545

Workers at Kohler had grievances — some real and some imaginary. At any rate, not all were satisfied and many felt that a union might help. They were afraid of reprisals if they were to protest against working conditions individually or to ask for higher wages. For a long time there had been sentiment for a collective bargaining agency at Kohler, and when Section 7(a) of the NIRA became law, pressure for a union grew. Some of the Kohler workers felt they now had the law of the land behind them and began to talk about forming a union in the plant. They made contacts with the Wisconsin State Federation of Labor early in the summer of 1933; J. F. Friedrick from Milwaukee was sent to Sheboygan by the federation to address the first public meeting of Kohler workers.[4] He was surprised to find that hundreds had come to hear him and proceeded to give a general union-organizing speech; he explained their rights under the new labor law and urged them to establish a local organizing committee which could set up headquarters and print and distribute membership application cards. Encouraged by early court interpretations of the new labor code, some of the men left application blanks at the work benches of fellow workers and urged them to sign if interested. Small group discussions among the workers followed and by July, 1933, they were well enough organized to become affiliated with the Central Labor Council of Sheboygan. In August, the union applied for and received a charter from the American Federation of Labor designating their organization as Federal Labor Union No. 18545.[5]

In the summer of 1933 workers in the pottery department, employed on a piece-work basis, were getting ten cents for every bowl and six cents for every cover they made. They produced an average of 22 pieces in an eight-hour day. One man working in that department told the author he used to come to work at 6:00 A.M. instead of 6:50 and work "like the dickens," taking a short lunch hour and going back to work with a sandwich still in hand. At that pace he could produce 25 pieces per day and would, on occasion, even finish before quitting time. The foreman insisted that if this man could produce 25, so could the other workers. Then, on or about July 19, 1933, the work schedule was reduced from an eight- to a seven-hour day and the workers were asked to turn out 20 bowls a day; they claimed they could make only 18. The foreman told them to come early, work late, and even work during the noon hour, if necessary, to produce 20 pieces per day. This the workers refused to do and the pottery department was shut down on August 22. This department had been well unionized by this time and men were accused by departmental supervisors of distributing union-application blanks on company time. The company insisted it had a surplus of pottery ware and felt justified in reducing the work force. The workers claimed they were laid off because of their union activity; the company maintained it did not know who belonged to the union.[6]

The labor movement in America was weak during the early thirties (less than 4 million members in the entire United States) and most organized workers, such as carpenters, electricians, machinists, printers, plumbers and locomotive engineers, were members of skilled craft unions with their own national organizations. The only place for industrial workers such as those at Kohler who wanted a union was in a Federal Labor Union chartered directly by the American Federation of Labor.

The Formation of the Kohler Workers Association (KWA)

The impetus which Section 7(a) gave to the formation of new unions also brought a stepped-up drive for counterorganization. Company unions and employee-representation plans were established by many employers during the twenties and early thirties as a means of forestalling organization of unions.

Professor D. D. Lescohier of the University of Wisconsin, in his *History of Labor in the United States*, stated:[7]

> The foundations of what labor now terms "company unions" were laid by the Employers' Mutual Benefit Association of the Milwaukee Electric Railway and Light Company in 1912. . . . Every investigator, whether pro-employer, pro-labor or neutral, seems to

agree that the company unions have interested a majority of the employers because of the potentiality of combating unions. . . . The workers are afraid to appeal grievances and suffer from the discrimination and discharge in spite of the paper promises of the plans. . . . The best that can be said about this scheme is that it is a medium through which the company ascertains "what's in the workers' mind" and that a few minor grievances have been settled in a perfunctory way.

The formation of a company union at Kohler, called the Kohler Workers Association (KWA), took place officially on September 7, 1933, shortly after Local 18545 was chartered. This naturally was looked upon by members of the new Federal Labor Union as a deliberate attempt to break their union. According to testimony given before the National Labor Relations Board * in Washington, D.C., on September 8, 1934, by attorney Joseph A. Padway of Milwaukee, representing Local 18545 and the Wisconsin State Federation of Labor, the Kohler Company was not only willing, but eager, to see the KWA established. Mr. Padway testified that on August 25, 1933, a departmental superintendent at the Kohler Company drew up a petition stating:

> We, the undersigned employees of the Kohler Company, are satisfied with labor policies of the Company during the depression, and we hereby give our unqualified support to the management of the Company at the present time.

He pointed out that about 600 signatures were obtained on this petition, but that most of the men did not realize it would lead to the formation of KWA. On the evening of September 6, 1933, three management personnel men met with Walter J. Kohler, Sr. They told him, according to Mr. Padway, "We have a bright idea. We want to form a company union," and were told by Mr. Kohler, "That is a good idea. Talk to Mr. Thorkelson" (assistant to Mr. Kohler).

At eight o'clock the next morning, the first of three meetings for the three shifts was called, Mr. Padway testified, and Mr. Kohler addressed a select group of 81 persons, telling them ". . . You are free to join or not to join, as you please. . . . Six hundred men

* This was the old NLRB under NIRA — Section 7(a) — before the Wagner Act was passed.

signed a petition and said they wanted to continue working with this company as they have in the past. This was a voluntary petition. A committee of three came to see me last night and asked me if we would consider organization of a shop workers' association."

Application cards and pencils were available at all three of the meetings. Mr. Kohler told those assembled, "Who knows where we will be pretty soon? I wish to continue, and I wish you to co-operate."[8]

Mr. Padway continued: "These men are not fools. That is equivalent to a threat that they will close down entirely unless they join this organization."

According to testimony gathered later by the National Labor Relations Board,[9] John Stieber, a Kohler employee, was called into the office by his superintendent. There he was greeted by Walter J. Kohler, Sr., company president, and Lyman C. Conger, company attorney. Kohler told Stieber that three men had been in to see him the night before to inquire whether he (Mr. Kohler) would recognize an independent union. He had advised them that he would and proceeded to discuss the formation of KWA. A constitution had already been drafted by Attorney Joseph Peters and application cards had been printed. Stieber was made temporary chairman of the group and given copies of the KWA constitution to distribute among the employees. When he returned to his place of work, the works manager sent him to the employment office where, for a time, he was given a full-time assignment to recruit members for the KWA. The Kohler Company supplied KWA with furniture, typewriters and other facilities and permitted frequent meetings to be held on company time.

In November, 1933, Federal Labor Union No. 18545 appealed to the National Labor Relations Board, asking for an election to determine which organization was to represent the workers. Local 18545 had 1,865 active members and its leaders were certain that this union was the choice of the majority of Kohler employees.[10] The appeal was referred to the Labor Board administrators for Wisconsin, who called in Henry J. Ohl, Jr., president of the Wisconsin State Federation of Labor, and Walter J. Kohler, Sr. The union accepted the administrators' proposal to hold an election, but the Kohler Company head rejected it and no settlement was reached.

Attempts at Collective Bargaining

The industrial-relations climate at Kohler was never conducive to genuine and mutually respectful collective bargaining. The
company's encouragement of and assistance in the formation of the
Kohler Workers Association shortly after Local 18545 was organized had caused Local 18545 to turn to newly established government agencies in the belief that the company union (KWA) would
eventually be declared illegal and that collective bargaining procedures between Kohler Company and the union would be established. Three meetings were held between Local 18545 and the
Kohler Campany management during the fall of 1933 with no
meeting of minds. The breach continued to widen. On June 22,
1934, Local 18545 presented the company with a 14-point proposal asking for the adjustment of wage rates and hours of labor.
On June 26, the company shut down indefinitely. It had been a
general practice to close down two to four days around July
Fourth, but since this shutdown came earlier and was termed indefinite, the workers considered it another deliberate attempt to
defeat the union. Several departments continued operation to complete their work and the men were told they would be called back
as needed. The reason given by the company for the shutdown was
"lack of orders."

The hope of Local 18545 leadership for reaching agreement
was shaken by the unsuccessful conferences with the company.
They came to realize how strongly the Kohler Workers Association was supported by the company, yet they felt their union had
the "law of the land" behind it. The union's 14 points were:

1. a request that the principles of collective bargaining be recognized in conformity with Section 7(a);
2. that the Kohler Company agree to confer with a conference
committee of Federal Labor Union No. 18545;
3. that seniority rights be established;
4. that no employee be discharged, demoted or otherwise disciplined except for just and sufficient cause and only after a hearing,
if requested by the employee;
5. a request for a 30-hour work week [Note: Most workers considered themselves lucky if they had four days work per week];
6. employees laid off after August 15, 1933, should be returned to

their positions as soon as possible and before others were afforded employment;

7. employees to be classified into four groups: common labor, semi-skilled, skilled and extra-hazardous;

8. a joint committee to work out job classifications and wage rates;

9. a minimum wage of 65 cents per hour;

10. piece rates to be 30% higher than minimum rates on day work;

11. time-and-one-half for overtime and work on holidays at double-time;

12. no deductions for faulty work unless determined by the worker's representative and the employer that it was due to gross negligence or willfulness;

13. arbitration of grievances not settled at the plant level; and

14. the agreement to remain in effect for six months from date of execution. Unless either party served notice on the other at least 30 days before the expiration date of a desire to modify the agreement, it was to continue automatically in force until changed in accordance with the provisions stated therein.[11]

At a meeting held July 6, 1934, the chief spokesmen for the union were Henry Ohl, Jr., Charles Heymanns and Rudolph Renn. Walter J. Kohler, Sr., did almost all the speaking for the company.[12] During the entire meeting, he was careful to couch his remarks in such a way that they would not conflict with the National Recovery Administration (NRA) codes. Part of the transcript of that meeting is reproduced below:

Mr. Heymanns: About this here: "The Company agrees to confer with a conference committee named by Federal Labor Union No. 18545 on any and all matters affecting the workers of the Kohler plant."

Mr. Kohler: We are discussing with you now, are we not?

Mr. Heymanns: Yes, we are discussing. . . .

Mr. Kohler: No argument on this?

Mr. Heymanns: No further argument on that.

Mr. Kohler: We are meeting with you and we are meeting with individuals. If anyone wants to see me I am willing to see him and to find out what he has to suggest.

Mr. Heymanns: As you know, our local has by far the majority of men at the Kohler Company and those men desire relationship with the Company. We have by far the majority and we are doing this for these men.

Mr. Kohler: You are doing this for the men you represent, whoever they are. Some are now working in the Kohler Company.

Mr. Heymanns: Our constitution states that we cannot take in any men who were not working for the Kohler Company before the lay-off. It is probably thought that we have some who have never worked there. It is in our constitution that unless the men were working for the Kohler Company we cannot accept them for membership. That means the men who were laid off last year, of course. . . . Before we go any further, will the Company agree to that first and second paragraph?

Mr. Kohler: The Company is now working in conformity with Section 7-A of the National Industrial Recovery Act and will continue to do so. It will deal with anybody who represents the workers or deal with individuals.

Mr. Heymanns: The second paragraph, "The Company agrees to confer with a conference committee named by Federal Labor Union No. 18545 on any and all matters affecting the workers of the Kohler plant" — will the Company agree fully with that?

Mr. Kohler: We are now conferring with you. This is an indication that we will confer with you at any time you want to meet.

Mr. Heymanns: Naturally, the Company agrees to that, but will it put that on paper as well as verbally?

Mr. Kohler: The Kohler Company will meet with you. That is a definite statement. We will meet with you at any time you want to meet.

Mr. Ohl: I wonder whether we could get an answer on this question. Whether you will deal with this Committee for conditions in the Kohler plant?

Mr. Kohler: We will for such conditions for the men you represent. Of course, we will deal with other men according to Section 7-A of the National Industrial Recovery Act. We are complying strictly with the conditions of that Act which is incorporated in our Code so far as the labor provisions are concerned, and we can hardly be asked to do anything that is asked.

Mr. Ohl: We recognize the fact that you are receiving this Committee. If you answered the question I did not get it. The point is that if half a dozen different people or groups of men negotiated with the Kohler Company on different bases it may bring about the situation of bargaining for different conditions. We want to bargain in behalf of these men for standards of work to be applicable throughout the plant.

Mr. Kohler: We will, of course, deal with you, but we should also continue to deal with others.

Mr. Ohl: I do know to what extent you are dealing with the others. We were here quite some time ago on two occasions.

At the conclusion of a long discussion, Mr. Ohl said to Mr. Kohler:

> Up to this point there has been no bargaining. I do not think you have sat down with us with that purpose. Maybe the balance of the Committee has a different idea, but my personal opinion is that you have consented to see us, and you will see us later on. We have been here two and a half to three hours. A lot has been said, but nothing has been settled and nothing has been agreed upon. Our only hope now lies in your counter-proposal in which there may be something that will establish this relationship.

The company's reply to the union reiterated its willingness to "confer at any time with any employee, group of employees, or their chosen representatives regardless of their working schedules." The company also called attention to the fact that residential construction, upon which much of the company's business depended, had declined about 90 per cent since 1928 and that, therefore, the company could not commit itself to keeping large numbers of men at work on uneconomical working schedules. In response to the demand for 65 cents per hour minimum-wage scale, the company offered 40 cents (the minimum provided in the NRA code) which it contended was 14 per cent higher than that paid by one of its largest competitors in the South.[13] The company did agree to pay 30 per cent above the 40 cents per hour for "piece rates" and did agree to pay time-and-a-half for overtime and double time for holidays, stating that this was now company practice. On questions of faulty work, the counterproposal merely said that the employee could designate a representative to act for him. Instead of agreeing to arbitration as the last step in the grievance procedure, the Kohler proposal stated, ". . . the Company will consider with them or their chosen representatives, other means that may promise a fair and amicable solution."

Speakers and organizers from the Wisconsin Federation of Labor had been invited to address the local union membership; the men believed they were on the road to genuine collective bargaining, but the three meetings with the company held during the fall of 1933 were disappointing to the union. The case was then turned over to the State Compliance Board where it was held up all winter because the company would not agree to the proposal made by the board. After the fourth meeting held on July 6, 1934, union spokesmen realized they were getting nowhere in resolving the long list of issues they had discussed with the company. On July 13, they decided to call a strike, effective Monday morning, July 16, 1934.

3

THE FIRST STRIKE: 1934–1941

FEDERAL LABOR UNION NO. 18545's decision to strike on July 16 was promptly followed by action on the part of Walter J. Kohler. On July 11, he had sent a statement to the collective bargaining committee of the union, which he withdrew on the morning of the sixteenth with the following public statement:

> In our statement of July 11th to the bargaining committee . . . we said that the Kohler Company would "continue its practice of conferring with individual employees, any group of employees or their chosen representatives who may wish to consider matters of their employment with the Company. . . ." Not only have we received no reply, but since our statement was made, our plant has been surrounded by pickets who have forcibly prevented employees and others from entering and leaving the plant and officers and employees have been intimidated. . . . This strike was inspired by outside labor agitators. Many of those who are picketing the plant and refusing to let law-abiding citizens enter, have never worked for us. They were imported from other cities and have no direct interest in the affairs of the Company or its employees. How can there be any bargaining with law violators who have never worked for us?*

Despite the injured tone of Mr. Kohler's statement, he himself had sought "outside" assistance some days before the strike vote was taken. The La Follette Senate Civil Liberties Committee found this entry [1] in documents subpoenaed from the William J. Burns International Detective Agency, Inc., dated July 7, 1934:

Prospective Business
Kohler Mfg. Co.

Mr. Brotz, Manager of the Wisconsin of the above called at this office. He wanted under-cover men in connection with strike

---

* A student of industrial relations will detect in this statement a firm determination to bargain with any individual rather than accept the collective bargaining procedures delineated by the new labor law. (Section 7(a) of the National Industrial Recovery Act.) Attributing the strike to "outside labor agitators" suggests an unwillingness or inability to recognize that many of his own workers

troubles. Mgr. W. H. C. informed him we could not undertake any labor union work in Wisconsin.

G. W. B.

The Great Depression, beginning in 1929, had made the Kohler Company's economic outlook uncertain. In the period from 1920 through 1929, the company had reported taxable income of over $16 million, but from 1930 to 1933, it had losses of $2,200,000. This strengthened Mr. Kohler's determination to keep a firm hand in company policies and decisions, unencumbered by a union contract. It is true that the company had co-operated with the NRA codes, but only because economic survival in that period demanded it be done.

The Kohler workers felt that, with the enactment of Section 7(a) of NRA, they had a legal right to organize, even though they realized that in a period of widespread unemployment, unionization alone could not solve all their problems. Unsettled grievances arising out of charges for faulty workmanship, indequate seniority and job rights, and the disabilities and injustices resulting from the ominous silicosis hazard — these were the "organizers" that brought the union into the plant.

Mr. Kohler's insistence that "outside agitators" were the instigators of the discontent among his workers accomplished two things:

It made it easier for him to consider the use of force and take measures to turn his plant into a fortress under siege.

It also increased the determination of the strikers to show by sheer numbers how many of them wanted genuine collective bargaining. There is no question that the union, aware of the strike preparations going on in the plant, regarded a large turnout on the picket line as their best protection against the arms and deputies.

In the escalation of the struggle, the tactic of mass picketing was viewed by the Kohlers as a real threat to the plant property. But there was also the matter of adherence to the "principle" that, as owners of the business, they had the legal and moral right to run it as they saw fit and to do whatever they regarded as necessary to continue operating it.

---

were "ungrateful" for the paternalism they had been shown and that they preferred to have their conditions of employment defined by a union contract.

The company's hostile attitude toward unions was well known and widely expressed. Now that the union members had an ally in the government, they were not about to give up their years of seniority and job rights to "scabs" and "strikebreakers" (converse epithets for "agitators" and "Communists" which were used by the company).

The strike which the Kohler Company alleged to be inspired by outsiders was directed by a strike committee of seven members who had worked an aggregate of 82 years with the Kohler Company: Arthur F. Kuhn had been employed 19 years; Otto Reichert, 14; Rudolph Renn, 11; Charles Heymanns, 11; Frank Reinhalter, 10; Christ Gorde, 9; and Fred Zeitler, 8. Members of the strike committee told the author in 1935 that, although the plant had shut down "indefinitely" on June 26, they knew about persons who had been asked by the company to come back at midnight or early in the morning of July 16. They said that for the first time to their knowledge all seven gates to the factory premises were kept open all night. Some men did return to work that night; others joined the picket line which formed at three in the morning. The night before, the company's employment office had been busy calling men back to work, in person and by phone.

Strike Starts July 16, 1934

A picket captain supervised each plant gate and only Kohler workers were supposed to be permitted to picket. By the time the regular office workers came, picketing at the office entrance made it difficult for them to get through the lines. Rudolph Renn, the strike-committee chairman, counted 802 men on the picket line at 7:30 A.M. *The Sheboygan Press* and the union estimated that over a thousand pickets were on duty the first day and the strike committee estimated that at least 95 per cent of them were Kohler workers. L. P. Chase, the company's attorney, estimated that there were perhaps 800 pickets and that not more than 500 or 600 were employees because their foremen could identify only a few over 300 of them by name. A long rope was used by the pickets, who lifted it for Walter J. Kohler, Sr., to go through.

The largest assemblages of pickets were at the entrances on

Pickets lift rope for Walter J. Kohler, Sr., to enter the plant on first day of the strike. In dark coat and overalls behind and left of Kohler, is Charles Heymanns, member of the bargaining and strike committees, now regional director of the AFL-CIO, Milwaukee. (Sheboygan Press photo)

the west side of the office building and plant. Carrying American flags and signs demanding recognition of the union, they circled in endless chains before each gate and sidewalk leading to the industrial plant. At the smaller entrances, less frequently used by employees, small knots of pickets made it difficult for anyone to get through.

The first scuffle occurred when Chris Leining,* a picket, grabbed August Miller, a deputized Kohler employee, when he attempted to go through the line. Leining said that someone, other than Miller, struck him with a club, but the pickets, most of whom could not see what had happened, converged on Miller and pommeled him.[2] Otherwise, everything was relatively peaceful on the picket line. The American flag carried by pickets was snatched

---

* Leining, in an interview, recalled the first day's events in the 1934 strike, and observed that in his opinion, the strike might not have taken place if Walter J. Kohler, Sr., had not been elected governor and left Frank Brotz to run the plant. Leining believed that many of the older workers felt they were able to talk with Kohler about problems in the plant, but that Brotz's authoritarian and driving attitude antagonized the men.

Pickets restrained office manager Al Zibell as he attempted to go through the picket line the first day of the strike. (Milwaukee Journal *photo*)

from them and taken into the office, but Chief of Police Jack Case saw to it that it was returned.

On county trunk highway Y, a quarter-mile north of the village, a lunch stand was set up for the strikers. As far as could be learned, no one inside the office left the building at lunch hour and the strikers figured that the company had obtained a supply of food beforehand.[3]

The strikers permitted doctors, nurses and watchmen to go through the lines; some production workers were prevented from returning to work; others joined the picket line. Mr. Kohler told the press that the strike had been called against a "closed" factory. Rudolph Renn recalled that:

> All men visible on Kohler plant property wore official police badges as did those in the office building and at the gates. The gate guards tried to induce men to slip into the plant from the picket line.

The village of Kohler became the scene of much activity at an early hour on the first day of the strike. Thousands of curious people were on hand from time to time throughout the day to see what was happening. As a result, most of the streets in the village and highways leading to and from Kohler were choked with parked automobiles and cars moving to and fro along the thoroughfares.

Striker Peter Horn had been placed in charge of the pickets at the railroad entrance of the plant. Chief of Police Jack Case and Herbert V. Kohler, vice president of the company, drove up in a squad car that afternoon to drive the pickets off the tracks and get six carloads of coal into the plant. Peter Horn said that Case pointed a pistol and commanded him, "In the name of the law, will you let these cars of coal in?" Horn replied, "No, not until you get a permit from our committee." Case told *The Sheboygan Press* reporter that he had shown the gun merely as a joke and had no intention of using it. He threw some tear-gas bombs at the pickets in an attempt to open the line to get the train through. The men had anticipated some such trouble and were prepared with vinegar-soaked sponges to hold over their noses. They caught the bombs and threw them back at Case and H. V. Kohler, forcing them to flee into the plant. The men then blocked the cars with tin cans and railroad ties and opened the hoppers of four cars, dumping the coal along the tracks.

Because the pickets kept many persons out of the plant, the company publicized a story that 200 men were trapped in the office. Pickets produced a large sign stating that they would furnish an escort and assure safety to those in the plant and office who wanted to go home. The office force would not accept the offer because they felt doing so would admit that the strikers had a right to engage in mass picketing.

Tuesday, July 17

No office or plant workers made an attempt to get through the picket lines on Tuesday morning; all was quiet at Kohler. Workers keeping the delicate kilns in the pottery in operation had been provided with cots and food. Walter J. Kohler, Sr., was hissed and booed when he arrived, but he was permitted to enter, for union leaders had given strict orders that he was not to be molested in any way. Pickets reported seeing flames shooting up through the manhole covers in the street. They interpreted this as indicating that manhole covers were being soldered or welded to permit safe passage through the tunnels under the picket lines over to the main

*Six cars of coal were stopped by pickets the second day of the strike,
four of which were dumped, and cans and railroad ties were used to
block the wheels. Kohler deputies used tear gas in an attempt to drive
away the pickets.* (Milwaukee Journal *photo*)

plant. They looked upon it as another attempt to break the strike
and further evidence that the company did not intend to bargain
with the union. Trucks of the Wisconsin Telephone Company and
the electric company moved into the plant to install telephones and
huge searchlights at strategic points. The drivers of the trucks explained they had come "to make repairs."

The pickets began to come on duty at three o'clock in the
morning. Wives of Kohler employees participated in picketing in
greater numbers than the day before; nearly 2,000 pickets were
walking in the line. The only attempt to get through the line was
made by two telephone operators. Chief of Police Case told Renn
about broken windows on the south side of the plant. The union
alleged that boys and spectators had broken these windows the
night before. Case blamed the pickets. The pickets insisted that the
damage was done in an exchange of stones between persons standing on the railroad tracks and guards on the roof. To prevent fur-

ther incidents, pickets were stationed along the fence to keep spectators away.

No new developments in strike negotiations were reported. L. L. Smith, publicity director for the company, when approached by newspapermen, said the company had not been officially notified of the strike and had received no acknowledgment of the receipt of the company's July eleventh answer to union demands. Mr. Kohler, he said, had "left the doors open for further negotiations," but no effort had been made, so far, by the union. Smith reiterated Mr. Kohler's previous statement that the company was complying with NIRA (NRA) provisions and was ready to bargain individually *or* collectively with the workers.

Apparently, because of the tear-gas episode on Monday, when Chief of Police Case and his deputies arrived on the scene, they were booed by the pickets. Questioned by reporters about a rumor that workers were being deputized in order to get them through the picket lines, Case denied the report.

A mass meeting of the Kohler workers was called at 8:15 A.M. on High Street directly opposite the Kohler office building. Maud McCreery, editor of *The New Deal*, opened the meeting with words of encouragement to the strikers; she introduced Al Benson, Socialist leader and former sheriff of Milwaukee County, who was in the county on a political tour, and C. V. Niland, an organizer from the Washington office of the American Federation of Labor. All speakers expressed hope that Mr. Kohler would "talk things over" with the union representatives and that an amicable and satisfactory settlement would soon be reached.

The Chicago Regional Labor Board sent the Reverend Father J. W. Maguire to Sheboygan County to mediate the strike. Father Maguire,* who had been successful in settling every other labor dispute assigned to him, met with union leaders until after midnight.

Wednesday, July 18

Father Maguire met company officials at 9:30 A.M. in an effort to find a basis for settling the strike. The strike committee said that

* Of Father Maguire, *The Sheboygan Press* said: "Possessing a magnetic personality and an air of confidence, Father Maguire inspired everyone immediately with his competence. Alert, direct and to the point in his statements, he gives the impression of being able to analyze a situation quickly."

all office workers, maintenance men, officials of the company and everybody but actual production men would be provided with credentials to come and go as they wished without interference from the picket line. Office workers, superintendents, foremen and KWA members went to some of the strikers' ıomes, urging them to sign a petition addressed to Anton F. Brotz, president of the village and chief engineer in the plant, which called for opening the plant. They were promised jobs and an increase in pay. (It is interesting to note that on July 6 the company said it could not afford an increase in pay.) Company personnel were also used to recruit more special police for the village.

In contrast with Monday night, when picketing had ceased late in the evening, picket lines continued in force practically all Wednesday night. Some men carried sticks and clubs, but none of them were used.

Thursday, July 19

Most executives, office workers, and all but production workers were able to get through the picket lines in the morning. Walter Kohler, Sr., and H. J. Thorkelson, his assistant, went through the picket lines with no signs of unpleasant demonstration by the strikers.

According to company officials, the water supply of the village of Kohler was threatened unless the strikers allowed coal to be shipped into the Kohler Company yards. Mr. Kohler reported on Wednesday that:

> Six cars of coal were held up, blocked completely and partially damaged outside our plant on Monday by strikers and imported pickets. Under existing conditions, we cannot get more coal into the plant. We told Father Maguire that it is only a question of a few days until the Village of Kohler will be without water, sanitation and fire protection.

Local 18545, through its attorney, David Rabinovitz, replied to Mr. Kohler's letter to the union (sent on Monday the sixteenth and released on Wednesday the eighteenth) as follows:

> Walter J. Kohler had made statements to the newspapers to the effect that the strike is being conducted by outside agitators. He also

refuses to bargain collectively, claiming that he will not bargain with outside agitators. . . . The union absolutely denies that outside agitators have anything to do with the strike. The union was started by Kohler workers on their own initiative, and the strike was ordered by them of their own free will. . . . No people outside the city of Sheboygan, Kohler or Sheboygan Falls have been asked or are picketing at the plant. These men and women are Sheboygan, Kohler and Sheboygan Falls residents and 90 percent of them are Kohler workers. These men are not agitators or law breakers but are honest, law-abiding citizens of our community. This is a strike of the Kohler workers and their purpose is to gain collective bargaining, higher wages and better working conditions. Mr. Kohler has been assured that he will not be bargaining with outsiders but with men who have worked for him twenty years or more.

A press bulletin was released at 3:00 P.M. by Father Maguire after he had conferred with Kohler officials and union leaders:

The question of the introduction of coal into the Kohler plant for the purpose of maintenance, fire protection and water supply for the Village of Kohler has been satisfactorily settled. Mr. Kohler promised me that none of his coal would be used for production purposes, and it would be used only for the purpose of proper maintenance of the plant, for fire protection and water supply. He ordered the chief engineer to keep no reserve on hand and if a reserve began to accumulate he was to order no more coal. Mr. Kohler further stated that in his opinion one carload of coal every two or three days would be sufficient for these purposes. The strike committee has agreed to allow a carload of coal to enter the plant every two or three days to be used for these purposes. This brings to an end any danger for the present of a lack of water supply or fire protection for the Village of Kohler.

The union's agreement also provided that the orders for coal were to be placed with Attorney Rabinovitz.

Rudolph Renn told the author in the fall of 1934 that work on the utilities tunnel from the powerhouse to the American Club had continued during the day and that the company shut off the water for several hours in order to take out a 6-inch pipe to enlarge the tunnel and permit easier passage.[4] One Kohler resident informed the author that the village pipefitter told him a section of 6-inch-diameter pipe had been taken out to enlarge the passage. While the water was shut off, a story was circulated in the community that the village was threatened with a "water famine" because the pickets had refused to let a car of coal enter on the first day. Newspaper cameramen took pictures of women carrying water from neighboring wells, giving some credence to the rumor of a water shortage for which the strikers were blamed. The tunnel was used to take food and supplies into the company premises. The company also used United States mail to get supplies to those who chose to stay inside the plant.

The next incident to attract attention in the community was Father Maguire's speech to the pickets that evening. He explained the coal-car agreement and admonished the pickets not to use violence or violate the law. He addressed between 1,000 and 1,500 pickets, strikers and others from a speaker's stand built especially for that purpose, in the middle of High Street, directly across from the Kohler Company office building. He spoke persuasively and many of his remarks were heartily applauded. "I have been a sincere, true and honest friend of organized labor and I would not counsel you to do anything that would weaken your cause," he declared. He explained that he had been sent to Kohler by the Regional Labor Board and that he had to maintain strict neutrality in the controversy, which he hoped would be settled "within the next few days. Any form of violence," he emphasized, "is morally and legally wrong. The manhandling, jostling or pushing about of persons, or the throwing of missiles is wrong and I strongly urge you to refrain from all things of the sort."

Father Maguire recounted his study of the labor movement in America and his long experience in helping settle labor controversies. "Organized labor, to win, must do nothing wrong and I want to warn you pickets that there is such a thing as peaceful picketing and such a thing as illegal picketing. The juster the cause of labor, the more important it is that labor use the right methods. I have seen many strikes and have never seen a peaceful strike that was lost," he said.

Father Maguire explained the value of united action and emphasized that such action could come only from discipline. He said, "I urge you to give your whole-hearted support to the members of your committee. I have worked with your committee and I know those men to be honest and sincere and it is important that you follow their leadership and I urge you to do so, no matter how un-justly you think you have been treated."

He reported that Battery C, 121st Artillery of the National Guard, would be returning to Kohler on Friday or Saturday after several weeks of training at Camp McCoy, Wisconsin, and asked that the strikers not be alarmed, for they were not coming to "break the strike." The United States Government had for some time rented facilities from the Kohler Company to store this equipment and he asked strikers to permit these men to deposit their equip-ment in the plant and come out again. He asked the pickets and strikers to give him their undivided trust and confidence; he was doing all in his power to get an agreement, he said. Finally, he asked all "to pray to Almighty God" to give strength to his en-deavors to bring about a peaceful agreement between the opposing factions.

Friday, July 20

Battery C of the National Guard arrived in Kohler at 5:30 A.M. and marched through the Kohler Company yards to put their equipment in a warehouse south of the office building. There was no demonstration or trouble of any kind as the members of the Guard returned. The first carload of coal went into the plant be-fore 9:00 A.M. in keeping with the strikers' agreement.

Paul J. Smith, personal representative of William Green, presi-dent of the American Federation of Labor, arrived from Washing-ton to help work out a satisfactory settlement at Kohler. During the day he conferred with the strike committee and with Father Maguire.

The Kohler Company issued this statement concerning strike picketing activities:

Anyone who prevents the free passage of employees and others into and out of our plant is violating the law. We refuse to recognize that these law violators in the picket line have the right to grant passes. To accept their passes is tantamount to admitting that they have authority to take the law into their own hands. Some of our employees who have been in the plant since Monday morning have been given to understand that they will be permitted to leave and re-enter if they show reason why they should be granted passes. They have decided to stay in the plant rather than accept such terms.

We have sufficient food and are prepared to remain in enforced imprisonment indefinitely.

There were rumors that the company tried to buy or borrow trucks to facilitate rapid transportation of the special deputies. Walter J. Kohler, Jr., it was reported, had been in Sheboygan for that purpose. Rumors were also circulating that arms had been shipped to the company from an eastern concern * and that strikebreaking agents had been hired.

Saturday, July 21

The picket lines continued in force throughout the night. A tenseness was noticeable; some of the men carried sticks and clubs, even though the picket captains frequently asked them not to. However, no trouble was reported. Two men, riding in a police car driven by Deputy Oscar Derler, managed to break through the lines and get into the plant. One man jumped out of the car on the north end of High Street and, noting a laxity in the picket lines, made a break for the plant and got through. The car then proceeded south on High Street and while many of the pickets were attracted to the north end of the line, the other man jumped out, made a successful break for the plant on the south end and also managed to get in.

Anton F. Brotz, president of Kohler Village, received a petition signed by 380 women, requesting him to contact legal authorities to see what could be done about the picket-line system which separated men in the plant from their families.

Sunday, July 22

The Central Labor Council, Sheboygan, had voted on Saturday to lend support in mass picketing and many walked, drove or

---

* The La Follette Committee (U.S. Senate) investigation of the Kohler dispute in 1939 reported that: The police of Kohler had received $982.42 worth of ". . . tear and sickening gas and gas equipment" on August 10, 1934, from the Lake Erie Chemical Company, Cleveland, Ohio. Federal Laboratories, Inc., had supplied Frank G. Brotz, Kohler plant manager, with $1,069.60 worth of tear gas and equipment on July 17 and with $773.10 worth on July 23. The Village of Kohler had bought only $76.46 worth before the July 27 riot, but bought $3,984.00 worth between August 1 and 13. Sheboygan County bought $1143.00 worth during the same period. Altogether, Kohler Village bought $6,885.58 worth before and during the first strike.

hitchhiked to Kohler from Sheboygan on Sunday afternoon. The demonstration was planned "for the sole purpose of showing the solidarity of the Sheboygan organized labor movement back of the strike." Approximately 4,000 pickets, strikers, strike sympathizers and spectators milled through the streets during the mass-picketing demonstration. Representatives of the various trade unions, their wives and children marched back and forth carrying their respective banners. More than twenty unions were identified by banners or signs or by well-known members of the various locals. The Amalgamated Clothing Workers came out in large numbers, carrying a huge painted sign advertising their union. A large red silk banner, carried by the brewery workers, reminded old timers in the labor movement of the days when the most precious possession of each trade union was a banner kept in a glass case in the union hall and only brought out on important occasions. Members of the Boot and Shoe Workers' Union No. 197, who had recently won a nine weeks' strike, were in the line with a sign urging the Kohler strikers to "fight until you win." Other signs with similar messages of encouragement were carried by furniture workers, upholsterers, city employees, truck drivers, toy workers and leather workers. Many of these unions also demonstrated their support by giving generous donations from their treasuries.

The Central Labor Auxiliary prepared food for the pickets. Men on the line consumed on an average of 240 loaves of bread, 20 pounds of coffee, 100 gallons of soup and uncounted links of sausage every day. Much of the food was donated by farmers, merchants and others sympathetic to the union.

Arthur F. Kuhn, president of the union, presided at a meeting that afternoon and called upon Maud McCreery, Attorney David Rabinovitz, Paul Smith and Felix Olkives of Kenosha, representing the Wisconsin State Federation of Labor, to speak. Miss McCreery made two talks from the platform, first discussing the demands of the union for recognition and collective bargaining. She said that, if necessary to win, the pickets would keep marching "until next winter." She announced that the tool department at Kohler had signed up with the union 100 per cent and that Theodore Hilgenberg, the president of the "Company union" (KWA) had enrolled as a member of Local 18545. In her final talk, Miss McCreery thanked the unions participating in the demonstration and asked

A makeshift commissary was set up on a nearby farm to feed the pickets. Many strikers lived in Sheboygan and Sheboygan Falls — too far to hike home for lunch. (Milwaukee Journal *photo*)

the pickets to return for duty by 3:00 A.M. Monday. She referred to a "wild rumor" that "five hundred American Legionnaires have been sworn in" to open the picket line on Monday and pointed out that the rumor probably had no basis in fact. She said she believed Walter J. Kohler, Sr., when he said he would not put his plant into production.

While there was much excitement in the streets in front of the Kohler plant because of the union demonstration, everything within the plant, where nonstriking workers had chosen to stay, was peaceful. Two Protestant ministers and a Catholic priest conducted services Sunday morning; a chicken dinner was served at noon.

Monday, July 23

Carl Steffenson, acting secretary of the Chicago Regional Board, arrived in Kohler as the strike moved into its second week. He conferred with Father Maguire and then with the company officials and the union leaders.

Another car of coal arrived at the plant. The men outside

started a slingshot "artillery" because they objected to a beacon light on the roof of the office building which glared into their eyes. They tried to break the light, but found it impossible to hit the "bull's-eye."

Tuesday, July 24

Walter J. Kohler, Sr., issued this statement:

We met last night with Mr. Steffenson, acting secretary of the Regional Labor Board of Chicago. We told him that the Company is determined to stand by its loyal employees. These include the employees who have remained on maintenance in the plant and offices and those who, on the outside, have refrained from unlawful activity. We told him also that the Company cannot deviate from the interpretation of Section 7(a) of the National Recovery Act, and the President's executive order made by General [Hugh] Johnson and Mr. [Donald] Richberg which said: Section 7(a) affirms the right of employees to organize and bargain collectively through representatives of their own choosing; and such concerted activities can be carried on by either majority or minority groups, organizing and selecting such representatives in such manner as they see fit. Also, in affirming this right of collective action, the law lays no limitation upon individual action.

This statement was interpreted by the union officials as a slap in the face and as a determined effort by the company to break the strike. Later in the morning, Father Maguire said publicly, "We had a conference with Mr. Kohler last night in which some slight progress was made." When questioned about Kohler's statement, he explained that he understood the executive order called for the labor board to supervise union elections and "publish the names of those representatives who are selected by a vote of at least a majority of the employees voting for the purposes of collective bargaining, mutual aid and protection."

Events of Wednesday, July 25

Attorney David Rabinovitz, counsel for the strikers, sent the following communication from the union to the Chicago Regional Labor Board:

Gentlemen: We, the undersigned committee of Federal Labor Union No. 18545, petition your honorable body, on behalf of more than thirteen hundred employees of the Kohler Comany, Kohler, Wisconsin, to hold an election among the employees of the Kohler Company to determine the committee that shall represent them for the purpose of collective bargaining under Section 7(a) of the National Industrial Recovery Act.

A strike is now in progress against the Kohler Company, for the purpose of securing recognition of the collective bargaining committee of Federal Labor Union No. 18545. We, therefore, respectfully request an election to determine this main point at issue.

Yours very respectfully,

Collective Bargaining Committee of Federal Labor Union No. 18545.

Charles Heymanns   Fred Zeitler
Arthur Kuhn   Frank Turk
Rudolph Renn

The hot sun beat down on the pickets marching in front of the Kohler Company office building. Water pails and dippers were located all along the line for the relief of picketers. Some of the men and women sought the shade on the lawn nearby. Each time the food car conveying sandwiches and coffee appeared, the pickets crowded around it. At the extreme east end of the plant, they had erected an improvised tent out of railroad ties and gunny sacks. At the picket camp, stood two larger tents — one in which cots had been placed so that pickets could rest, the other providing a spot where women prepared food for the strikers.

Inside the Kohler plant, things went on as usual despite the heat. Some enterprising fellows built a high, backless chair on which haircuts were given for the price of an iron washer. Men in the plant also made their own shoeblack so those with black shoes could get their daily shine.

Thursday, July 26

Specially equipped trucks with heavy gauge metal sides were brought into the village under the cover of darkness and were met by Anton F. Brotz, the village president, at Highway 42 south of Sheboygan Falls.

There was much activity at the company carpenter shop and no picket was allowed to approach it. Reports were circulating that the brass foundry was manufacturing clubs and billies. Rudolph Renn, the strike-committee chairman, recalled that:

> . . . a notice was given to stay out of the village by village officials and villagers were told to stay in their homes after dark.* The tension grew to a "boiling point" due to Company preparations. The Company received a 75-ton car of coal on Wednesday and asked for two more by Saturday which was contrary to the agreement.† No picket or sympathizer was arrested nor was any attempt made to do so on the part of the village police up to this time. Guards, armed with shotguns, appeared at the airport, opposite the picket camp and had their post near the camp. Others doing duty at the barricades were armed.

Picketing continued all night, as usual, and the men were prepared to "dig in for the winter" if necessary to win the strike.

The Inevitable Confrontation

Statements issued by both sides evidenced the tension which was ultimately to erupt in violence. The dumping of coal cars on the second day of the strike had understandably irritated management. The company refused to bargain with the collective bargaining committee of the striking union, claiming that the picket line included imported pickets and that the strike itself was called by "outside agitators." The striking Kohler workers thoroughly resented the allegation, but many in the community believed this charge. Mutual antagonism grew to a point where it was virtually impossible for those involved to act rationally. The throwing of gas bombs on the first day of the strike; the fastening of the manhole covers; the attempts to crash the picket line and the increasing number of deputies on the scene — all helped to fan the rising anger of the strikers. The speeches of encouragement, the large turnout for the mass picketing on the previous Sunday and the liberal support

---

* Rumor had it that the villagers were instructed to darken homes if unusual happenings took place.

† According to the union, the agreement concerning the amount of coal entering the plant stipulated that one car, not to exceed 60 tons, would be permitted to enter every two or three days. The order was to be placed with Attorney David Rabinovitz. The car which entered July 20 contained 58 tons; the one on the twenty-third held 60 tons; the car on July 25 held 75 tons. On July 26 the union attorney was asked by the company to pass one car on the twenty-seventh and another on the twenty-eighth. The men interpreted this increased tonnage and more frequent orders as acts of bad faith on the part of the company.

The Journal *caption reads: "Special deputies are shown, before they were replaced by troops, in one of the Village of Kohler trucks which dashed about during the rioting. The awesome rat-tat-tat of the machine gun mounted on the truck was never heard, but the gun was there to add to the warlike atmosphere." The gun has been identified as a World War I vintage, Browning 30-calibre water-cooled machine gun, by the Denver, Colorado, Police Department Crime Laboratory chief, Joseph Moomaw. A company attorney claimed it was a motion picture camera with telephoto lens. (See page 81.)* (Milwaukee Journal *photo*)

given by the unions, merchants and farmers of the community lent reassurance to the strikers that their case was just and increased their determination to win.

The mass picketing, which in itself was sufficient to irritate the Kohler Company management, plus the carrying of sticks by some pickets and the using of slingshots in attempts to break the beacon light on top of the office, made the company and the village officials more determined than before to open picket lines for resumption of operations with "loyal" employees.

Besides the visible actions, rumors circulated on both sides concerning what was going on behind the scenes. Some people of the community actually believed that many pickets had been shipped in from Milwaukee and that the State Federation of Labor was engineering the strike. Some pickets could not accept Father Maguire's explanation about the return of the National Guard equipment and believed the Kohler Company would use the equipment,* if necessary, to break the strike. Still others believed that strike-breakers had been "imported from Kansas." Accompanying all this activity and speculation there had been considerable shouting and hilarity along with obscene and profane language. As the strike wore on, this increased and some villagers who lived blocks away said they heard the noise all night; others denied this. At any rate, a petition was circulated and presented to the president of Kohler Village:

> We employees of the Kohler Company have an opportunity to work for the company under the terms now in effect and which are satisfactory to us. An organized group, not from Kohler Village, and many not even Kohler employees, are forcibly and riotously interfering with our entering the plant. As American citizens with a right to earn a living, we demand full protection of the legal authorities in entering or leaving the factory and otherwise.

Fifteen hundred workers were reported to have signed the petition. The union men believed it had originated in the Kohler plant.

Mr. Brotz, upon receipt of the petition, issued a public notice:

> I hereby notify all persons that the following acts constitute violations of the law punishable by fine and imprisonment:
>
> Preventing others from engaging in pursuit of lawful work by threat, intimidation or force.
>
> Resisting or assaulting an officer of the law while in the performance of his duty.
>
> Assault and battery.
>
> Assault with intent to do bodily harm.
>
> Carrying concealed weapons.
>
> Trespass upon or damage to property.
>
> Assembly of three or more persons in a violent or tumultuous manner to do an unlawful act.
>
> Vagrancy. (Persons who, having no visible occupation, and unable to give a satisfactory account of themselves, are vagrants.)
>
> Rioting.

---

* There was some basis for this feeling on the part of the strikers. E. R. Schuelke, who was the captain of Battery C of the National Guard at Kohler, was in charge of the Kohler Village special deputies.

Disorderly conduct.

Abusive or obscene language in the presence of others.

Lewd and lascivious behavior.

Drunkenness.

Larceny.

The law gives village officials full power to deal with law violators.

All persons are warned to refrain from abusive or obscene language, assault upon others, and preventing others from engaging in lawful work, or by blocking the entrance to any place of employment with ropes or in any other manner.

All persons except fully authorized officers of the law are warned to refrain from carrying or being in possession and control of any gun, pistol, club, black-jack, hose, stone, knuckles, pointed stock, sling-shot, or any other weapon dangerous to life or limb.

The village of Kohler cannot assume responsibility for the safety of women and children in the picket line in case there is resistance to officers of the law and such persons are warned, for their own safety, to stay away from the vicinity of all unlawful assemblage.

The Village of Kohler has long been known as a law-abiding community and outsiders will not be permitted to continue unlawful and riotous conduct with impunity.[5]

July 27 — A Day of Violence, Riots and Murder

Four special trucks had been obtained by the Village of Kohler on July 26 to facilitate the rapid transportation of large groups of deputies. The newspapers and strikers spoke of these vehicles as "armored." Equipped with heavy-gauge metal sides and wire screening over the radiator and windshield, these trucks sped up and down the streets. The picket lines were generally open for all who wanted to enter the plant after Village President Brotz issued the ultimatum that "from now on law and order will be enforced in the Village of Kohler."

Some misunderstanding had arisen about another carload of coal. The strikers maintained that, according to their agreement, the next car was not due until Saturday. Peter Horn and 11 other pickets stood on the railroad tracks and refused to let the coal pass. According to Horn's testimony, the special deputies approached them with several squad cars and four armored trucks.

Captain Schuelke is supposed to have lined up the deputies, twenty abreast, and ordered, "Forward, march, shoot to kill." Men

Three special deputies with the sticks, clubs and sling-shots taken from the pickets on Friday, July 27. There was no justification for carrying such weapons, but these were no match for guns, in any case. (Milwaukee Journal *photo*)

on the roof of the plant shouted down, "Go back to Russia where you came from!" L. P. Chase, the Kohler Company attorney, said there were 80 deputies in the group; the pickets claimed there were 150. At any rate, the 12 pickets were vastly outnumbered, and the guns and billy clubs were on the other side, so that they gave up without resistance.

A squad of deputies later went to the northeast gate and tore down the tent the strikers had erected there. They threw the debris and sticks lying around into a truck and then drove along the picket line to disarm those pickets who had sticks or slingshots.* This

---

* These were "saved" by the company and twenty-four years later, testifying at the McClellan hearings in 1958, Edmund J. Biever told the committee: "We have some of the clubs we picked up off the picket line that day, [here] in the city of Washington. If you wish to see them we will be happy to bring them in." (p. 9456.) L. C. Conger testified (p. 9196), "They also disarmed the picket line of several barrels full of clubs, sling-shots, stones, rocks, etc. some of which we now have in this very city. . . ."

A special deputy, who in a moment of hysteria, begged for a gun to kill himself, was restrained by deputies, while his daughter pleaded with him to get down from the truck. (Milwaukee Journal *photo*)

collection was piled together and a picture taken by the company's photographer for use in *Kohler of Kohler News* sent to professors, ministers and community leaders.

The union's strike committee responded to the company moves with the following statement:

> Since Mr. Kohler promised no production would be carried on in the plant, there is no necessity of 250 men coming to the scene in armored cars, with clubs and guns, and we feel that such actions are unwarranted at this time. The men in the lines are picketing legally and peacefully and the trouble today was started by the Kohler Company.

Because of the size of the force of special deputies, additional accommodations had to be provided and the American Club was turned over to them. On the afternoon of July 27, the deputies took the trunks and belongings of two striking union members, Steve Graeber and Frank Tradler, and put them out in the street. These men had been living in the club and working for the Kohler Company for many years and the deputies' action angered the pickets. The publicity man for Kohler Company, L. L. Smith, said they had been put out for "getting too much information and using it unwisely." It was later reported that the two men had been informing the union about the supply of ammunition in storage at Kohler.

During the afternoon, a young woman, who was on the picket line with her husband, saw her father on one of the armored trucks and shouted, "Daddy, get down from there!" The deputy, Adolf Meinolf, became hysterical, calling for a gun with which to shoot himself, while the daughter, Mrs. Anton Marver, Jr., wept and begged the deputies to let her father get off the truck. The deputies refused and he was taken to the American Club where he was given treatment and then permitted to quit his job as deputy.[6]

The picket lines continued in motion, carrying their signs as usual. About five in the afternoon, all the deputies and trucks withdrew from the streets. The ultimatum by Village President Brotz proved to be an incentive for excitement-seeking crowds to go to Kohler and between four and five thousand spectators thronged to the scene that evening. Several who had been in the picket line that day told the author that some of the men on the factory roofs threw stones at them. Herbert Schutt, who worked at the cook shanty where the pickets were fed, told the writer that he treated a man who had been hit on the nose by a rock thrown from the south foundry roof that day. It is hard to determine how much stone-throwing took place earlier in the afternoon and evening. Teen-age boys had been throwing stones at the men on the roofs and occasionally had broken windows in the factory. When Rudolph Renn was told about this by Chief of Police Case, he assured the officer that he would station some of his men on the company property to keep the boys away and maintain order.

By 8:00 P.M. the village was filled with spectators and there was much excitement; even under normal conditions it would have been difficult to keep such a crowd under control. The atmosphere was tense and various theories were proposed to explain the absence of the deputies who, for the first time, were not on the scene. The first indications that something was wrong, that something was going to happen, were observed about 8:00 P.M. when the crowd appeared to be concentrating near the south foundry on High

Thousands of window-panes were broken with stones and bricks the night of the riot. Shown here is the pottery of the Kohler plant. Windows were smashed in the south foundry and in the medical and employment offices, the general office and the showrooms along High Street. (Kohler of Kohler News *photo, August, 1934*)

Street. The people were slowly moving along the industrial walk; everything was quiet. Suddenly there was a jangle of crashing glass and the thud of a rock landing within the south foundry. Rocks, chunks of coal and pieces of pavement bricks from the streetcar tracks began flying in all directions. There was much yelling as men and women, young and old, joined in throwing missiles until most of the windows in the factory were broken. The mob moved north on High Street and smashed most of the windows in the office building and twenty-one plate glass windows in the Recreation Club. This attack lasted for ten to fifteen minutes. Shots fired from the American Club and from the office building apparently served as signals for the deputies, for they popped up everywhere. They had evidently been in hiding near the office building. When they came out in the open, they began shooting tear-gas bombs from a distance of about 200 feet, the bombs landing everywhere. Women and children screamed. The crowd started running as they covered their faces with handkerchiefs. Children were separated from their parents, wives from their husbands, and confusion prevailed. Some managed to escape into the drugstore and other nearby buildings. Others in the mob were infuriated. Some of the men shouted, "Let's blow up the place!" "Tear down the office, brick by brick!" and "Let's go back and get those yellow rats!" These threats engendered still more determination on the part of

July 28, 1934 — When the special deputies opened fire, these pickets lost no time in getting out of range. (Milwaukee Journal *photo*)

the deputies to drive the people out of the village and keep them out.

Evidently some of the deputies ran out of tear gas and resorted to their guns shortly before 9:00 P.M. When the shooting stopped, two men had been fatally wounded and forty-seven others were shot, most of them in the back. Most of the shooting occurred at

the north end of High Street near Highway 23. The shooting en-
raged the crowd and the howling, yelling and stone-throwing continued from their gathering place north of Highway 23. The
armored trucks stood cold and specter-like at the end of High
Street and deputies stood ready in the middle of the street, along
the sidewalks, behind the trees and lampposts and on the lawns.
The clang of stones as they struck the iron sides of the trucks rent
the air. Now and then a stone pounded its way past the trucks and
rolled into the gutter.[7]

Every so often the strikers rallied in anger and pushed closer
to the waiting police and trucks, but volleys of tear gas drove them
back across the road. Some spectators had their cars parked on the
south side of the road on Upper 23, but when they attempted to get
to these cars, the deputies repulsed them with gas or lead. The men
who wanted to resume their picketing were also driven out.

The two men who were killed were Lee Wakefield, twenty-
five, and Henry Engelmann, twenty-six, both of Sheboygan. Am-
bulances and available cars were kept busy transporting the injured
to the Sheboygan hospitals and clinic. Cars that happened to be
driving by were commandeered by the crowd to take the injured
to Sheboygan for treatment. The forty-seven injured, including
five women, had been wounded by buckshot and/or bullets.

The company lawyer told the author in 1935 that affidavits
could be produced to prove that there had also been shooting from
the pickets' side, but no evidence was ever released showing that a
single deputy was shot.

Leslie Wakefield, father of one of the men killed, told the
author that he could not walk along with the crowd because he had
rheumatism. Instead, he sat on the running board of a car parked
at the north end of High Street on Highway 23. He described the
shooting incident as follows:

> A man stepped out way ahead of the crowd and shot a revolver
> at the deputies. He stepped back behind a post and reloaded and
> again stepped out and emptied the revolver at the deputies. From
> what I saw, no deputy was hit by his shooting and he acted too
> brazenly to have it appear natural.

Mr. Wakefield was sure that the man had been placed there to
shoot blanks to give the deputies an excuse to justify the slaughter

that took place, since this man was not shot at even though he was in front of the crowd and others were falling left and right.

The Sheboygan Press reported:

It was truly a night of terror — ghastly terror, the like of which the community had never seen and wanted never to see again. The menacing silences, broken by the shrieks of gas shells flying through the air, the cries of the wounded and injured, and the horrible threats stood out vividly in the memories of the witnesses of the frightful happenings of the evening of Friday, July 27, 1934. An order came to the deputies to clear the streets of all villagers and spectators. . . . When groups failed to comply with orders, tear gas shells sent them scurrying. Along High Street in the dark recesses of, and on the balcony above the Recreation Club, police armed with guns and wearing iron helmets hid to wait for any attempt of the pickets to storm the streets again. Word was sent out that any attempt to move across Highway 23 and into the village would be met with machine [gun] fire. The pickets across the road continued to curse and yell and hurtle stones down the street at the trucks and into the village. Slowly, however, their number dwindled and by 2:00 o'clock in the morning, the situation became comparatively quiet.

Little groups of deputies marched up and down the street, gathering on corners, discussed what might happen next. All were tense . . . . The quiet continued as the dawn began to break. When the morning sun came up, more of the damage to the Kohler Company show rooms became evident.[8]

The intense emotional atmosphere which exploded into the tragic riot is vividly illustrated in a recounting of the events as given in the two statements which follow. Rudolph Renn, strike chairman of Federal Union 18545, described what happened on July 27:

Owing to the uncertainty as to what would happen next after the special trucks had appeared, the pickets stayed on duty for twenty-four hours. Some of the men were told to go home for some rest at 7:30 A.M. The sun beat down and there was no wind. The strike committee had gone to the picket camp for a conference. We received the news that the company was determined to get the strikers out of the village so Charles Heymanns, Fred Mattern and myself walked to the south end of the plant on the railroad company property. We were greeted with boos and shouting from the factory guards on the roofs, who seemed drunk with power. Such epithets as "They'll get you out now, hey? Communists, Bolsheviks," etc., as well as stones were hurled at us by the guards. Coming to within 150 feet of the scene of events, a mad rush of some of the power-drunken special deputies in our direction followed. We kept on walking until we met, and swinging their clubs and acting like lunatics, they ordered us off or we would be clubbed off. . . . Walking up the highway we saw four trucks, wired and steel-plated, parked near the south-east railroad entrance. There were some guards with guns on the trucks while many others were standing at the entrance. The number of special police was about 200. . . . Prominent among them were Herbert V. Kohler and other Kohler officials and supervisors, all carrying rifles, guns, pistols or clubs. The pickets had halted a carload of coal, because they felt that it was not due on Friday according to their agreement with the company, and it had been returned to Sheboygan. The carload of coal was ordered out to the plant again and when the train was seen approaching, the four armored trucks manned by about 80–90 blue-shirted special police sped eastward on the Lower Falls road and stopped opposite the railroad entrance to the plant. Simultaneously, an inside force of about 120–150 men in black shirts moved up from the plant yards to the entrance, backed by a huge caterpillar truck with a mounted machine gun. The picket force at that point [location] amounted to 18 men of which 7 were not present at the time, the rest playing sheep-head [a card game] under an improvised shelter. They were driven and clubbed off by the united blue and black forces, which even knocked one picket over the head and shot gas at him, burning his arm by the close discharge, because he would not drop a stick or club that he had grabbed when they were attacked. They were told to get out and stay out of Kohler, but no arrests were made or charges brought against any of those men. . . . We . . . walked back to the picket camp to have a conference to discuss the latest situation. Walking past the picket-posts, we cautioned our men not to resist forcefully but to stay on duty . . . and all picket captains were notified to watch their men to prevent any kind of disorder.

As soon as the coal cars were in and the gates were free, a detachment under the command of E. R. Schuelke combed the east side of the plant, the so-called jungles, in military fashion for any pickets. Every tent and lean-to built by the men was torn down, and all bottles, stones, tent-poles, sticks, bricks, etc., found at the picket posts or elsewhere were collected by a truck and taken inside the plant and photographed as proof of "armed resistance" on the part of the pickets. The only thing they left was a pile of railroad ties, used as a shelter, probably because these were too heavy to load on the truck, or they feared it to be preposterous to claim that they were clubs carried by the pickets. The rounds were made to all picket-posts and Schuelke "read the law" [Village President's proclamation] to them. No arrests were made and no charges were brought against anybody. Having finished the rounds, the victorious "private army" retired to their headquarters for a hearty "victory meal," with refreshments and smokes provided free of charge by the Company. Shortly after noon the trucks paraded up and down High Street, keeping "law and order," displaying their guns and antagonizing the picket line as much as possible. Throughout the afternoon Captain Schuelke could be seen giving orders to his "truck Armada. . . ."

The reports of events spread like wild-fire to Sheboygan, Sheboygan Falls and surrounding territory, and curiosity seekers, union sympathizers and others poured into Kohler, where the air was loaded with tension. Wild rumors and idle talk did the rest to create the feeling that something would happen. One of the rumors was that the company and the village would have the pickets out of the village by Monday, and had ordered men to report for work that day. . . . Picket-line captains were told to allow only regular pickets in the line and to keep orderly despite the jeering and goading of factory guards and special police. As the crowd grew, some stones and bricks were hurled from the crowd against the trucks, and the booing and shouting grew louder. Then, when the police were most needed to maintain order, the whole force retreated, and no one with authority was seen after five o'clock. The crowd continued to grow and at 7:30 had grown to about five thousand. With the withdrawal of the trucks and special police the crowd seemed to calm down and the officers of the union hoped that the crisis was past for that time. . . .

At about eight o'clock in the evening, the crowd became uncontrollable and chaos started. . . . Some factory guards at the south end of the plant treated the crowd like they did the pickets, calling them names, and naturally were acting as if they could "lick" anybody. Some of the crowd took them at their own game, and from throwing names at each other it grew to a point where the missiles became stones instead. Just who started first will probably never be found out, but it is claimed that the guards started the stone bombardment and that the crowd retaliated after several were hit with stones. A furious riot followed. The crowd did not heed the pleading of the pickets to stop; they were an uncontrollable mob, moving north on High Street and leaving in its wake the broken windows. The pickets did not participate in this as was brought out at the [Wakefield-Engelmann] inquest. The mob cooled its anger on broken glass and moved northward as far as the general office, cursing and shouting. . . .[9]

Anton Brotz released his version of what happened. *The Sheboygan Press* headlined it:

Riot at Kohler Planned, Charges Anton Brotz

I have made a personal investigation of the rioting which occurred in Kohler Friday night which confirms my own observations as an eye witness, and the evidence definitely shows that the activities of the mob followed a well-organized program.

After the pickets had broken faith by turning back Friday morning a car of coal consigned to the Kohler Company power plant for maintaining the village water supply and fire protection, the village police consummated the delivery of the coal. Later, the village police cleaned up the area around the plant which had been occupied by pickets and strikers for eleven days, and collected a half a truck load of clubs, iron pipe, sling shots, improvised blackjacks, sharp-pointed sticks, empty whisky bottles, piles of stones and other weapons which the pickets had gathered into piles at strategic points. Later in the day, Maud McCreery and Henry Ohl, leaders of the union, visited the picket lines and talked to the pickets.

The suddenness of the mob's almost simultaneous attack at all points, the effectiveness of its violence and the fact that the wildly yelling and shouting mob was supplied with thousands of rocks and bricks which were not available on the concrete-paved highway all indicate that careful preparations had been made in advance.*

Beginning at two sides of the plant, the mob proceeded as if following an organized plan and carried the attack over a mile long on High Street and the Upper and Lower Falls roads. Practically all the windows in the northwest pottery, south foundry, cleaning and locker buildings, the personnel office and the medical department,

---

* A streetcar track ran between Industrial Road and High Street at that time, a spur of which ran into the plant area. The roadbed was filled with crushed rock; the stops where passengers got on and off were paved with bricks and there were several of these stops near the plant. "There was enough 'ammunition' here to supply an army," E. H. Kohlhagen recalls. "Nothing had to be brought along!"

where a company doctor was working, and in which members of the picket line had been treated without cost during the last two weeks, were shattered by rocks and stones. Meanwhile, strikers had broken through the rear fence in five places.

Still the village police offered no resistance because they wished to avoid injury to anyone. It was not until the mob had wrecked the police car, stoned the car of Miss Nichols, county probation officer, attacked the general office building, broken the glass in the main doors and nearly every plate glass window in the basement and first two floors and was about to rush the entrance of the office, where girl telephone operators were working, that the village police went into action by releasing gas bombs.

By the use of gas bombs, the police drove the maddened mob north to the end of High Street. By this time the effects of the gas had worn off and the mob renewed its attack. Up to this point, not a shot had been fired, and, as far as I have been able to learn, no one was injured. A number of shots were fired by members of the mob, two scores of large plate glass windows in the village recreation hall were broken and the mob thoroughly out of control was moving to attack the village. It was not until the mob was threatening the village that the police resorted to their guns. Only by doing so were they able to drive the rioters from the village and protect the lives of women and children.[10]

It is doubtful whether the entire truth concerning the riot can be ascertained, but some conclusions can be drawn. The ferocious anger displayed by the mob had been fueled by years of growing resentment, not only against some of the Kohler policies as the largest employer in the area, but also against society at a time when people had lost their jobs in the depression and their savings in bank failures. If Kohler had laid off most of his workers when orders dropped off instead of spreading insufficient work among too many workers, it is possible that he might not have become the target of the frustration that pervaded the times. The differences between the way the "boss" lived and his workers had to live were glaring and galling. No doubt he, too, experienced his own frustrations with an economy which had almost come to a halt and no longer provided a market for his bathtubs, but his building up an arsenal to protect his plant and his model village served to increase the resentments in the community. Perhaps Kohler himself did not realize or understand the festering anger of the people who had

"This street [the north end of High Street in front of the company showrooms] was no place to be Friday night," commented the Journal. (Milwaukee Journal *photo*)

chafed for years under indignities, injustices and frustrations of working in his plant. William Bernschein, a Kohler employee, stated in an affidavit, August 6, 1934, that one of Kohler's chauffeurs told him "that Kohler Company must break this strike; that other industrialists depend upon Kohler to break the strike."

There were other factors, too. Families in Sheboygan, hearing rumors that "something is going to happen," were growing more concerned for the safety of their men on the picket line. Ralph Miller, of Sheboygan, stated under oath, that "while working Thursday noon [the day before the riot] the Brother-in-law of Sheriff Zehms, Wm. Schoening, said that 'tomorrow they were going to clean them out' [referring to the Kohler strike]." For eleven days, the pickets watched armed deputies, many of whom they knew well, displaying their authority up and down High Street in Kohler. Brotz's warning not to come to the village was a tip-off that the moment of confrontation had arrived. As most reports verify, it was teen-agers stoning the windows of the south foundry who supplied the "match" which ignited the "powder keg."*

Richard S. Davis, reporting for *The Milwaukee Journal*, met a truckload of men armed with clubs headed for Kohler as he drove toward Sheboygan for dinner that night. Later, on his return to the scene, he saw women who carried stones in their skirts to supplement the "ammunition" of the men. He saw men and women clubbed over the head by deputies; saw a deputy, struck in the head by a brick, "fall like the proverbial steer in the slaughter-house"; and saw Robert Kohler, youngest son of the company president, assist a bleeding fellow deputy to the American Club. He described the rage, the fury, the "blasphemous epithets" of the mob, and told how a change in the wind brought the billowing tear gas around to the club where for a time, deputies also suffered from the stinging, blinding fumes.[11]

When Walter J. Kohler, Sr., gave the press a statement the following day, there was no mention of the killed and wounded — only the expression of regret that women and children had not "heeded the warning of Mr. Brotz" because "their presence hampered the activities of the law-enforcing officers." People wondered afterward how much slaughter there would have been had the women and children not been present. "We deeply abhor this happening," Mr. Kohler said. "It is a tragedy that outsiders dragged this thing into our community."[12] Could he not comprehend — or would he simply not admit — that the acts of the mob were expressions of hate and fear felt by the people, who in an hour of rage and desperation, could defy the Kohler blue- and black-shirted † deputies and their guns, up to the point of death?

* In June, 1935, when the Kohler Company tried to collect $3,988.07 in damages resulting from the riot the previous July, District Attorney Jacob A. Fessler answered the suit instituted by the company by denying all allegations. Earlier, the former District Attorney, Charles A. Copp, had given an opinion to the county board which stated in part: ". . . the claimant was in fact and in law violating the much discussed Section 7(a)" and ". . . that the rebuffs to the federation union created a great tensity of feeling against claimant" and ". . . such damage for which it claims compensation must only be considered as having been inflicted upon itself by persisting in such unlawful act."

† Whatever the reason for choosing black shirts to identify the plant deputies, the color had a most unsavory and provocative connotation in 1934, when Fascist groups who used various black, brown and silver shirts were springing up in parts of Europe and the United States. There were frequent references to these "blackshirts" in statements and news stories; Richard S. Davis, of *The Milwaukee*

The Special Deputies

Most of the deputies used during the strike and the riot were employed by the Village of Kohler as "special deputies" and some were deputized by the Sheboygan County sheriff. The recruiting was done at a rapid pace and by the time the strike was ten days old, it was estimated a thousand men had been deputized. Many of them had little or no previous training, although some Kohler employees were members of Battery C of the National Guard, whose equipment had been stored on company property for years. Captain E. R. Schuelke of Battery C at Kohler was put in charge of the special deputies and had a difficult job to "whip them into shape."

According to Rudolph Renn, men from the payroll department, who had been living in the plant, went out through the picket lines to go to Sheboygan Falls and Sheboygan to induce men to become deputies or to go to work in the plant. The number of deputies had been increased to the point where nearly every available nonstriker in the village, and some men from the surrounding territory, had jobs as deputies at $4.00 a day. They all had badges made in the Kohler plant, according to a deputy, who also told the writer that their billies were made in a chair factory at Sheboygan Falls, and that holes were drilled in them into which lead was poured at the Kohler plant. The deputies were told to bring whatever guns they had at home to supplement the guns and tear-gas sticks available at the headquarters. Renn said:

> The fact that the deputies were taken from the immediate vicinity made it hard for them to command respect because they were known by the pickets. The deputies on the other hand were swollen up with authority because it was the first time they had the law in their own hands and the badge helped them to become indignant about the language hurled at them by the pickets.

Depositions of those who were deputies during the first Kohler strike include such information as:

Dee Endsley, a member of Co. F., 127th Infantry . . . was given

Journal, wrote: "One of the most formidable battalions was made up of Black Shirts from the Company's shops. These men, some 50 or more, were big and husky. In the light of the moon, they looked like nothing but trouble."

A group of deputies with helmets, standing before the showroom entrance, before the National Guard arrived. (Milwaukee Journal *photo*)

a job as a guard at the home of Walter J. Kohler, Sr. He was accused of having been on the picket line and . . . was transferred to the American Club. He told of training at the Club and of firing rifles at the rifle range. They also fired machine guns next to the horse barns (Kohler stables). "Man" type targets were set up. . . . He

Walter J. Kohler, Sr., leaving the main office, amid the broken glass, while a Guardsman stands on duty. (Milwaukee Journal *photo*)

reported often seeing Herbert V. Kohler with a .22 pistol on a 45 frame. Many of the men admired the gun and fired it on the range because it was such a handsome weapon . . . a man from Chicago trained them in the "flying wedge" and "jude." This man hung around the Club with [Edmund] Biever and . . . was reputed to be a Pinkerton Agency man. In Endsley's opinion this expert was "a big phoney."*

* Charles E. Wilson of the Wisconsin Crime Lab told the author that the Kohler Company employed Calvin Goddard of Northwestern Crime Laboratory (Illinois) during the first strike. Wilson's assistant, Joseph Wilomovsky, who administered the polygraph tests during the second strike, told the author he served as a deputy under the Federal Marshal during the first strike and rode the engine when the coal cars were taken into the plant.

George Buss . . . Fred Duxbury [under-sheriff] approached him gawking on west side of High Street, said: "So long as you're hanging around here, you might as well do something. . . ." Sworn in on July 20 at County Jail by Sheriff Zehms, told to be on job next morning. . . . He always wore his badge under coat (was instructed to do so) but on that Sunday was told to wear it out in the open. On morning of July 27th, the deputies received orders to take away the rope carried by pickets in front of the main office . . . Buss and other deputies went over and said, "You boys got to give up the rope. You'll get it back after the strike." . . . there was no resistance. . . . When the armored trucks made their appearance, one fellow deputy said, "If they keep those trucks running around, we're in for a lot of trouble."

Ed Mahnke . . . Ed Biever came to see him (August 10) and recruited him to deputy. . . . He was told to give instructions to Herbert V. Kohler and improve his markmanship. . . . Mahnke also gave pistol instruction to Harry Sommers who . . . couldn't hit the target either. Sommers was a foundry superintendent.

Henry Roehre . . . Case swore them in as deputies in the carpenter shop, . . . were issued dark blue shirts, caps, badges, blue helmets, overalls and baseball bats. Received instruction in the tavern. . . . Training concentrated on clubs first, then use of shot guns and lastly tear gas. . . . The day after the shooting, Walter J. Kohler, Sr. came . . . and addressed the deputies. He thanked them . . . "with tears in his eyes and told us all this wouldn't have happened if outsiders hadn't come in to agitate."

Harold Roepke . . . on July 26th someone . . . told him to come to the carpenter shop . . . was given a star [badge] and drilled in back of the American Club for about ten minutes. . . . That three or four men on each truck had shot guns; that some men brought their guns from home; that some guns were passed around Friday night; that during the shooting, many received guns; . . . that between 1 and 2 [P.M.] I was given a gun; that I was sitting outside the Recreation Hall when 72 guns, forty-fives, were brought up from downstairs; helmets were also brought up; that they gave all of us guns; that I was not a capable user of a gun; that I was not asked if I wanted a gun but was just given a gun; that I was frightened and said I did not want to shoot anyone and I was told that I was yellow.

John Stieber . . . Got to the plant on the first day of the strike. Said he came to work and was given quarters in pottery. Was told by Company officials a professional strikebreaker was in plant, in

charge of security, who trained blackshirts behind Shipping No. 6.
. . . He knew positively who belonged to AFL. Later, when Dewitt * was holding meeting, the KWA sent spies who reported those
in attendance to Ireland [personnel director].

The Arrival of the Militia

Early the next morning after the riot, the 120th Field Artillery
of the Sheboygan National Guard was ordered out to the village.
The 120th had been called out around midnight of the twenty-
seventh, to the armory where Sheriff Zehms wanted to "deputize
the entire outfit," according to Emil Schuette, a member of the
Guard. The men refused and went home. They were called out
the second time upon authorization of Governor Schmedeman,
and arrived by truck at Kohler around five-thirty on the morning
of the twenty-eighth.

Schuette, one of those who "policed the area looking for
shells and guns," said that they "picked up 2 large baskets full [of
shells], not counting what men took as souvenirs. . . . All ammunition boxes and the 45 calibre shell casings were marked for
Smith and Wesson Army Issue." (At the inquest, Captain E. R.
Schuelke had testified that although National Guard equipment
had been issued after he had received permission from the adjutant
general about 1 o'clock on the morning of the twenty-eighth,
none of the ammunition was used and it was checked back in later
with Major Mieding of the National Guard.)[13] Schuette said he
found shells in front of the main office, the employment office,
the recreation club and the village hall; that the Guard was "ordered to disarm the Kohler Blackshirts" who "had rifles and
revolvers, mostly civilian," and that he figured the National Guard
equipment had been ordered back to the recreation building where
it had been stored, before the main body of troops arrived.

Historically, workers and unions have known that when the
National Guard is called out in an industrial dispute, it is to protect
property, but not to protect the workers. The Kohler strike turned
out to be a clear-cut exception. After the rioting and shooting had
ended, County Sheriff Zehms and some of the men in the Kohler
Company office phoned Governor Albert G. Schmedeman. The
union leaders favored calling in the National Guard, so a confer-

* James Dewitt, organizer for UE-CIO.

ence was held at the Foeste Hotel in Sheboygan before daybreak on
July 28. It was attended by District Attorney Charles Copp, Father
J. W. Maguire and Sheriff Zehms. District Attorney Copp suggested that, since special deputies at Kohler were recruited from
the vicinity, it would be advisable to bring in impartial outsiders to
maintain law and order.* The 105th Cavalry squadron of Wisconsin was called and arrived with 15 officers and 210 men by ten-
fifteen that morning. Tents were pitched north of the Kohler
Company office building on the east side of High Street.

Upon agreement with National Guard officers and the Federal Labor Conciliator, peaceful picketing was resumed, with
soldiers encamped between the pickets and the Kohler plant. Union
members took up their picketing activities after hearing talks by
Felix Olkives, representing the State Federation of Labor; Colonel
John C. P. Hanley, who was in charge of the guardsmen; and
Father J. W. Maguire. At first the pickets were hesitant about
returning to picket duty and pointed to the machine guns placed
on the pottery-plant roof, but their fears were dispelled when
Colonel Hanley ordered the weapons taken down.

Three hundred more guardsmen from Camp Williams came to
Kohler on Sunday, the second day the village was under military
control; they pitched their tents west of the pottery plant and north
of the first detachment's encampment. A camp kitchen was established, piles of wood were brought in, and the smoke rising from the
campfires gave an aspect of "military occupation" to the entire scene.
The strikers co-operated with the Guard in every way. The pickets
organized their own "police force" for the purpose of controlling
the picketing.

Contrasting sharply with the tumult and chaos of Friday and
Friday night, Kohler Village, except for the thousands of sight-
seers who came from near and far, was peaceful and serene. The
tenseness and undercurrent of dread, the fear of the unexpected,

---

* Joseph Wilomovsky, assistant superintendent of the Wisconsin Crime
Laboratory, told the author there was "politics" behind the selection of the National Guard units sent to Kohler — that units from the industrial areas were sent
because they would be inclined to be sympathetic to the strikers. Ralph M. Immell,
who was adjutant general of Wisconsin at the time, said this charge was "non-
sense" and recalled that Colonel Hanley told him how Maud McCreery came to
him when the National Guard arrived and asked, "Are you that son-of-a-bitch
from Madison?" to which Hanley replied, "No, I'm that son-of-a-bitch from
Chilton."

The National Guard arrived and received instructions for the enforcement of law and order in Kohler. (Sheboygan Press *photo*)

were gone; the villagers themselves returned to their normal pursuits. The hundreds of special police wearing their metal badges were gone. In their place were the uniformed Guardsmen, well disciplined, courteous and disinterested in either side of the controversy. The National Guard remained on duty at Kohler from July 28 until August 20, when a group of 70 special sheriff's deputies took over. The first payroll for special sheriff's deputies on September 1, according to Sheboygan County Clerk William W. Birkle, amounted to $2,705.60. It covered eleven days' services for the 70 deputies at $4.00 per day, plus meals and lodging, and for two cooks receiving $6.00 per day. Birkle reported that the county would also have to pay $1,600.00 for riot guns, tear-gas bombs and other supplies and $350.00 for 70 cots and bedding. One half of the cost of the cots and bedding was to be refunded when they were returned to the Kohler Company from which they had been purchased.

Four members of the Chicago Regional Labor Board came to Sheboygan County for meetings which began Monday morning,

The Regional Labor Board came immediately to the scene. Meeting in Sheboygan are: Father J. W. Maguire; Carl Steffenson, acting secretary; Professor William Spencer, representing the public interest; and John Compton, industry member of the board. (Sheboygan Press photo)

July 30. They interviewed various persons, including the strike-committee members, concerning the factors that led to the strike and to the riot and the shooting on July 27. Board members were Carl Steffenson, secretary; John Compton, industry member; Professor William Spencer; and Father J. W. Maguire. In the afternoon, the board met with Walter J. Kohler, Sr., and other company officials at the company office building. After a strenuous day of conferences, Father Maguire remained in Sheboygan County while the other three Labor Board members left the city.

The seriousness of the situation in the county necessitated a special session of the County Board of Supervisors to set policies and outline a plan of action to preserve peace. A committee of chairman C. F. Bemis, Supervisors E. E. Truttschel and James Gannon, and Sheriff Zehms went to Madison to talk with Governor Schmedeman and to ask that the National Guard remain until the strike was settled. Father Maguire, invited by this committee to give his version of the conflict, reported to the county board:

This is the first time I know of when the coming of troops was valuable. As a student of labor trouble, I always deemed it unwise to have armed troops in a strike area; but this is a peculiar situation where one community is dominated by one of the contending factions. I am not passing judgment on the present controversy, which is wretched, and I have recommended the continuance of the troops until the controversy is settled. None else than a peace settlement will be satisfactory to me. . . . I would like to urge upon you gentlemen that the greatest service you can perform is to use your influence to have both parties to this strike negotiate for a speedy and a positive settlement. As the situation now stands, it is loaded with dynamite. I have been in many strikes, but I never saw such needless and ruthless killing by supporters of the law. There was a worse strike in Milwaukee, but the authorities found no need to call out troops nor to resort to violence. Not a person was killed or wounded during the strike. When it is understood that most of the people were shot in the back last Friday, the ruthlessness is evident. You don't have to shoot people in the back when they are running away. I examined scores of persons and all except two were shot in the back.

As a member of the Chicago Regional Labor Board, I am not going behind fences to say what I have to say. Human lives and human rights are precious in preserving. They are more sacred than property rights, and I shall do all I can to prevent a repetition of such violence. A deep wrong has been done this county, and you should go to the bother to discover who was responsible by using their influence, and these should be punished as they deserve. . . .

Father Maguire was given a vote of thanks by the board.[14]

On August 4, R. II. Cowdrill of Washington, D.C., replaced Father Maguire as the Regional Labor Board's representative; no explanation was given. Father Maguire's recall was protested by labor; Henry J. Ohl, president of the State Federation of Labor, sent a telegram to the board:

Father Maguire has [been] an influence for peace following the Kohler massacre. His removal at this time is fraught with grave consequences in my opinion. To me and to others representing labor, Father Maguire's removal will be a great accommodation to Kohler. We view it as unwise as we sense an attempt of the Kohlers to subdue the workers even if a repetition of the murderous attack of July 27th must be resorted to.

An overflow crowd stood outside St. Paul's Lutheran Church in She-boygan as funeral services for Henry Engelmann took place. (Milwaukee Journal *photo*)

Sheriff Zehms began, on August 4, to enlarge his department to replace the militia and maintain peace. He secured twenty-five to thirty men on the first day who, he felt, were levelheaded enough to prevent further disorder. Carl Steffenson of the Chicago Labor Board and R. H. Cowdrill met with company and union representatives on August 7 and scheduled a conference for August 10 in Chicago. The board met for two days and submitted a proposal which was acceptable to the union but not to the company.

The Funerals

Funeral services for young Engelmann and Wakefield took place on the thirtieth and thirty-first of July. The mayor of

*Thousands of mourners walked in the Wakefield funeral procession
down 8th Street in Sheboygan, to Moose Park where Henry Ohl
spoke. Note black ribbons worn by the women.* (Sheboygan Press
photo)

Sheboygan proclaimed a public state of mourning and thousands of
shocked and sober citizens walked in the processions and gathered
at St. Paul's Lutheran Church and at Moose Park where the ceremonies were held. Henry J. Ohl, president of the Wisconsin
Federation of Labor, delivered the oration at the Wakefield service
where he urged: ". . . cool heads . . . to determine the next steps
in the struggle of the human race against autocracy and despotism.
. . . There can be no turning back." This is not easy, he added,
when "our brothers have been slain and injured in a massacre, with
human life on the one side and profits on the other."

Maud McCreery, editor of the Sheboygan weekly, *The New
Deal,* recorded that a man standing with her beside the coffin of
Henry Engelmann, said: "God, what a hell of a system that makes
working men do the bidding of the boss and shoot down a man like
that!"

The emotion-laden events brought forth an act of vandalism which was to be repeated frequently in the second strike years later: a milkman informed Leslie Wakefield, early on the morning of his son's funeral, that someone had strewn tacks on the street in the front of the house where the services were to be held.

Through the years, graveside memorial services have been held at the Catholic and the Lutheran cemeteries for Lee Wakefield and Henry Engelmann by members of Local 18545 and United Auto Workers (UAW) Local 833, who organized themselves as the Lee Wakefield-Henry Engelmann Memorial Union.

The Inquest

Coroner C. N. Sonnenberg conducted the inquest into the deaths of the two young men who were killed. The juries for both investigations were combined to "save time and expense," since the testimony was bound to be similar. District Attorney Charles A. Copp did the questioning during the three-day inquest, September 11–13.

Seven doctors, including Doctors Emil and Otto Gunther and the company doctor, M. D. Cottingham, testified that they had attended one or more of the shooting victims the night of July 27. Dr. Otto Gunther had seen Engelmann at Memorial Hospital and reported that ". . . in all, there were about 12 bullets that entered Engelmann's body . . . and all were entered in a posterior position." Dr. Cottingham told how, that night, he had gone to his office in the Kohler medical building about 8 P.M. Although he had noticed that there was much noise, that people were surging through the streets and it was hard to distinguish between pickets and others, he saw no weapons in the picket lines or among the crowd. The missiles hurled through the windows of his office, he said, were large and small stones and pieces of what appeared to be paving bricks.[15]

John Case, the Kohler police chief, testified that he had 120 men under him when the strike started and extra men had been added. He enumerated the weapons the department had on July 27, the day of the riot, including a riot gun, a Thompson submachine gun, eight .38-caliber revolvers, as well as 60 gas grenades, 200 long- and short-range gas cartridges and ammunition for the guns, including some shotgun shells. The men had brought their own guns, he said, but he did not supply them with ammunition. The machine gun, he admitted to Copp, was set up in one of the recreation hall doorways that night, but had not been used. Asked if he had a permit from the sheriff to have a machine gun or gas grenades in his possession July 27, he said he did not.

Edmund Biever, at that time Case's assistant, testified that there were two machine guns, one placed in a truck and the other near the grandstand of the baseball field. He said that Captain E. R. Schuelke, who was his assistant, had issued equipment, including revolvers, Browning machine guns and helmets, from the National Guard armory at 2 A.M. on the 28th.

During a recess on the second day of the inquest, Rabinovitz, the union's attorney, asked Copp if he (Copp) would ask some questions he had prepared. Coroner Sonnenberg stepped in, saying:

> You keep out of this. I'll have you understand that I am conducting this inquest and nobody else. The other side is not allowed to ask questions and neither are you and I want you to understand that. . . . Furthermore, if you persist in trying to butt in . . . I'll have you put out. . . . This inquest is going to be conducted fairly and according to the law.[16]

The Sheboygan Press on September 13, 1934, carried the following account of the first witness's testimony that day:

> Stanley Lastusky, 1419 Jefferson Avenue, was the first witness called to the stand this morning. He told of going out to Kohler and parking his car near the Lower Falls road at about 7:30 P.M. on the fatal night of July 27. He told of walking along the Industrial Road at Kohler, watching the pickets and spectators. During this jaunt, he saw Lee Wakefield with a friend by the name of Clarence, but did not know the last name of Wakefield's friend.
>
> Reaching the Upper Falls road, the witness said he saw some boys throwing stones at factory windows, and that pickets stationed there told the boys not to throw stones. The pickets told him, he said, that they didn't want the boys to destroy property because they were afraid "Kohler had hired the boys to do it to make it look bad for the union."
>
> At that time, Mr. Lastusky said he heard a lot of noise on High Street, heard breaking of glass, and went over there to see what was going on. He said that the Industrial Road was pretty dark then but there was a big crowd and a lot of noise. He said he saw something

"flaming through the air" and heard what sounded like a shot and that the crowd was surging in all directions.

"Then I run," he said, "I got as far as the drug store and I was gassed. I got sick. I went down that little street that goes east and west next to the drug store. I could hardly breathe. I waited behind the Western Union office on that street about fifteen minutes. I parked near the lower road, but I thought it would be better to go to the upper road, go down along Highway 23 to the first road that crossed over and then get my car. When I got up to the drug store, I saw three men with guns walking the same way I was. I run, I run to the Upper Falls Road and there was a crowd on the highway. As I got there I looked back and I saw three men with helmets. As I turned again to go on I was shot in the back. . . ."

Howard Owen of Sheboygan testified that he heard Gene Hansen, Kohler deputy, give orders on the night of July 27; that Hansen had said, "Come on, guys, let 'em have it!" Owen said he saw a man put a gun in Bert Chapman's back and push him along. Someone, he testified, called out, "They're human beings!" to which Hansen replied, "Human beings, hell! They're nothing but rats! Let 'em have it." "This time," Mr. Owen said, "I got a bullet in my left leg which went into the flesh about an inch." He said, ". . . it sounded like forty guns were being shot all at the same time."

August Tasche of Sheboygan, who was wounded by birdshot and buckshot, testified that as he neared Highway 23, some man yelled at him, "We're sheriff's men and it's a riot!" and then the bullets came. The man who shouted at him, Tasche said, was Edmund Biever; he was positive of that. Asked if Biever had a gun, Tasche said he did, but he "did not know if it was a shotgun or a gas gun." Frederick W. Krez, a Plymouth attorney sworn in as a Kohler deputy, was asked where he was when the first tear gas was fired, and testified that he "was standing next to the man who released it."

"Who was that?" Copp asked.

"Ed Biever."[17]

Christ Gorde, who was in charge of the picket line that night, stated that no one was allowed on the line if he wanted to carry a club. The stone-throwing at plant windows, he insisted, was done by the crowd and not by the pickets.

Some witnesses testified they had seen a "young man" in blue overalls walk across the highway, shoot five times, reload behind a lamppost, cross the highway and shoot five more times. None identified the "young man," and there was some speculation on the part of the strikers that this was a "plant."

So much conflicting testimony was given that the facts surrounding the killings could not be established. Officers of the union told the author, when he was conducting a study of the strike for his Master's thesis, that union witnesses were only asked questions arising out of previous testimony and given no chance to tell their own story. They considered the inquest "a whitewash."

The two coroner's juries found that Lee Wakefield and Henry Engelmann "came to their deaths in a general gunfight. . . . The persons who fired the fatal shots . . . remain unknown." The Wakefield jury used the words, "as a result of gunshot wounds by unknown ruthless persons"; the Engelmann verdict omitted the word, "ruthless."

The evidence was overwhelming that the Kohler deputies — not the crowd — had the tear gas and the guns. Not a single deputy was hit by so much as one buckshot, but two "non-deputies" were dead, and forty-seven were wounded, most of them in the back.

KWA and Local 18545 Vie for Support

The National Labor Relations Board got around to holding a hearing (Case 115) September 8, 1934 — twelve months after the KWA organized — and handed down a decision on September 15 calling for an election on September 27. The board found the Kohler Company guilty of violating Section 7(a) of the NIRA by interfering with the self-organization of its employees, but ruled that an election between 18545 and KWA was still in order.

Meanwhile, Federal Labor Union 18545 had gone on strike on July 16; violence, bloodshed and rioting had taken place; some members of 18545 had left the community and others had decided to return to work.

Dean Lloyd K. Garrison of the University of Wisconsin Law School, also chairman of the NLRB at that time, remarked at a labor institute in Madison, Wisconsin, on January 19, 1935, that *"The Regional Labor Boards settled cases by the thousands. Only the*

rotten and tough ones went to Washington." [Emphasis added.]
The Kohler case had to be referred to the national board because
the regional office in Chicago could not settle it. On September 8,
1934, the NLRB heard testimony from the Kohler Company, from
Federal Labor Union No. 18545, and the Kohler Workers Association. Three complaints were brought against the Kohler Company.
On September 15, the NLRB released a summary of its findings and
its decision. Part of that summary follows:

> There are presented for determination, three complaints against
> the company; first, that certain employees were discharged by the
> company for union activity; second, that the company failed and
> refused to bargain collectively with the representatives of the union;
> and third, that the company interfered with the self-organization
> of its employees. There is also before us a petition that an election
> be ordered, and that in connection therewith the Kohler Workers
> Association be dissolved.
> As to the first complaint, the evidence shows that . . . out of
> about 2,500 employees, 485 were laid off (between August 22, 1933,
> and June 26, 1934). . . . There is evidence that these 485 men
> were selected solely by the supervisors who had them directly in
> charge, without knowledge as to their possible union membership.
> . . . There is also proof that these supervisors were guided in their
> selections largely by the efficiency record and versatility of the
> men — those with high loss records and those able to perform only
> a few operations being laid off as of least value in a time of retrench-
> ment. This evidence is given greater weight because of the undis-
> puted facts that a great many men who were retained after these
> layoffs were members of the union, and that union officers, including
> the president, were employed by the company up to the very day of
> the strike. In this state of the record, we are of the opinion that the
> evidence does not justify a finding that the layoffs were made by
> the company because of union activities.

On the question of the company's refusal to bargain, the
NLRB sidestepped the issue, saying:

> . . . since there is a question whether the union or the association
> represents the majority of the employees, the company's obliga-
> tions under Section (a) cannot be definitely established until the
> question of representation has been resolved.

On the third complaint — that of the company's interference with the right of self-organization — the NLRB declared:

> . . . it is clear that the company participated in forming and engaged actively in promoting the new organization, that the workers had no opportunity of expressing an unfettered choice as to whether or not they wished to belong to it, and that the company not only indicated its favorable attitude toward the organization but stood ready to finance its existence. Under such circumstances, the organization could not have the independence which is essential to a true collective bargaining agency, and the sudden and extensive promotion of the plan at a time when an outside union was just being formed can only be considered as a deliberate design to influence the allegiance of the employees and to interfere with their free and unhampered self-organization which Section 7(a) guarantees.

Then the Board's findings continued:

> *The wrong done by the company can, however, be remedied by an election.* [Emphasis added.]

That sentence turned out to be the most important one issued by any agency in influencing the eventual outcome of this dispute. The Kohler Workers Association had not been asked to be a party to the case, and since the hearing was called to determine whether this "company union" had been illegally set up, Joseph Padway, attorney for the American Federation of Labor, objected to KWA being represented on the grounds that the *company* and the *union* were to present their cases to determine whether the "child was illegitimate" and that the union had not been notified that KWA was sending a representative. Chairman Garrison ruled that since a KWA representative had come to Washington, D.C., he could present his case and it would be considered supplementary to whatever evidence was presented.

A campaign then followed in which both Federal Labor Union 18545 and the KWA endeavored to gain support among Kohler employees. Local 18545 felt confident of winning the NLRB election until it saw the volume of propaganda circulated by KWA and the organized way in which its campaign was conducted. Federal Labor Union 18545 stated its position in a circular as follows:

To Our Brother Workers

During the last five years that we were working for the Kohler Company, none of us were satisfied and were all complaining about the wage cutting, the speed kings, the deductions, the wage assignments in the Village of Kohler, the consumption * cases and the unfair treatment by foremen and superintendents; but none of us dared to bring our complaints to the head where they should have been brought, namely to Walter J. Kohler. We had no organization to stand behind us and to support us in case Kohler did not like our complaints and would have discriminated against any one who would have dared to do so. That is the reason why we have organized — so that we, the workers as a whole, can bargain collectively with our employer. That is the reason why we went on the strike — to compel Kohler to treat his workers as human beings and to sit down with them and discuss better wages and working conditions.

Now they treat you with candy, cigars and cigarettes and pat you on the back. Did they come around and ask you before the strike how you were living, or did they show any consideration for your welfare? Ask the Poor Department. Many Kohler employees have been steady customers there for a long time. They tell you that if Labor Union 18545 wins, you will be out of a job or work part-time, while as a matter of fact the union wants to put all Kohler workers to work and increase wages so nobody would depend upon charity for a living. We believe that a man old in the service of the company should be protected through seniority rights, so we can be secure in our jobs. We ask for seniority rights for *all* Kohler employees, and not for a certain group. We do not bear malice toward anybody. We do not intend to take the job from any Kohler worker. This statement by the Kohler Workers Association is a lie and is said by them in hopes that it will prejudice you against our cause. We feel that all of you are our fellow workers, whether you belong to the union or not, and we intend to fight for the betterment of wages and working conditions in the plant for all of you, because you are all human beings and all in the same boat as we are.

When you are in the polling booth to vote for your representation, you will be alone with your conscience and your God. Vote as you think, and not as the Kohler Company wants you to vote. Under pressure you might have forgotten your duty toward your

* Tuberculosis and silicosis.

brother workers, even opposed them openly, but you can right the wrong done by voting for Federal Labor Union No. 18545.

Remember — this is the only election and your only chance to vote for the union of your own choice — Federal Labor Union No. 18545.

The KWA with the aid of the Kohler Company was not to be outdone; its campaign was more extensive and better organized. There had been no membership meetings of KWA during the entire year preceding the election, but several days before the NLRB voting, A. L. Hougen, a Manitowoc, Wisconsin, attorney representing KWA, spoke to a general meeting. The men who had returned to work for the company were given free cigars, cigarettes and candy for "dessert." They were given free meals at the cafeteria from the time of the strike until the election. Carl Sass, vice chairman of KWA, saw to it that KWA members were contacted.*

Committee members were instructed, "Do not tell them specifically to vote for KWA, but to vote right." Mimeographed literature was handed to the men at and within the factory gates as they left work, every few days preceding the election. One of the leaflets stated:

Work or Walk the Streets?

What KWA got for you:

1. 15% increase in radiator floor molding rates.
2. Wages increased in south and north automatic blast from 51¢ to 55¢ an hour.
3. Rates increased on brass department screw machines from 43¢ to 55¢ an hour, day work; from 61¢ to 65¢ per hour piece work.
4. Increased sand treatment standards from 51¢ to 55¢ per hour for helpers and from 55¢ to 60¢ for operators.

What 18545 got for you:

1. Loss of 11 weeks pay through a strike.
2. A RIOT, bloodshed, violence and lawlessness.
3. Loss of dues paid to Union.
4. Permanent loss of jobs for those who took part in violence and lawlessness.
5. NOTHING they promised.

* Hilgenberg, KWA president, had defected to Local 18545.

5. Piece work standards increased to 52¢ per hour minimum throughout the plant.
6. Of 180 complaints presented,
   155 were settled satisfactorily
   and 4 were withdrawn. That
   is a batting average of .880.

Although the Union tried to show that the Kohler Workers Association was illegal, the National Labor Relations Board said:

"We are not willing on the facts before us to order dissolution. If
at the election to be held the Association secures a majority of the
votes, it will be entitled to act as representative of all Kohler employees in bargaining."

Are you working? KWA is trying to keep your job. 18545 is trying to give it to the unemployed. Ride the winner and hang on to
your job. Think for yourself instead of paying big salaries to union
lawyers and officials who only get you into trouble.

Vote for the Kohler Workers Association

Kohler Workers Association
Carl Sass, Vice Chairman
Martin Meves, Sec'y. and Treas.

September 25, 1934

Another KWA leaflet stressed:

But don't be misled by over confidence. We need every vote.
There have been political elections that have been as good as won
but were lost because the side with the most votes got too confident
and did not get the voter to the poll. *The only place the votes will
count is in the ballot box. We want to snow the union under so deep
there won't be any more strikes and riots at Kohler.* So if you are
against strikes and riots, be sure to vote Thursday for the KWA. . . .

So if you want peaceable settlements instead of strikes, riots, agita-
tion and trouble, vote for the KWA Thursday. . . .

The NLRB Election

With the NLRB ruling that *"the wrong done by the company
can, however, be remedied by an election,"* the Kohler Company
and its offspring, the KWA, became more determined than ever
that no "outside" union should represent the workers. The com-

pany's interest in the workers manifested itself in numerous ways. Men who worked in the plant before the NLRB election told the author that some of the workers did not limit themselves to the cigarettes and candy which were distributed on the job, but took several cartons of cigarettes at a time. Sandwiches were wheeled around in carts and distributed freely during working hours. Rumors were circulated about the questionable future of the Kohler Company should Local 18545 win. Some feared they would lose their jobs if the union won. Some workers believed everything they heard about "outside agitators" being responsible for the strike, especially after getting free cigarettes and sandwiches at work and being able to belong to a "company union" without paying any dues. It was some time later that a nominal dues system was established for KWA and it was given the proceeds from the vending machines in the plant.

On election day, September 27, 1934, KWA members and Sheboygan businessmen donated their automobiles to transport men from Kohler to the post office at Sheboygan where the election took place from 7:00 A.M. to 7:00 P.M. To be eligible to vote one had to be an employee of the Kohler Company, actually employed by and on the active payroll of the company on the seventh day of September, 1933, with the following exceptions:

(1) Those who were regularly employed elsewhere.
(2) Those guilty of violence in the existing strike.
(3) Executives and those in supervisory capacities.

Office employees were permitted to vote, and their ballots were sealed — their eligibility to be determined by the National Labor Relations Board. The election was conducted by secret ballot under the supervision of two NLRB representatives.

Both sides had four challengers. They had to check each voter's name on the company payroll before he was allowed to vote. Two thousand two hundred and eighty-eight votes were cast and since the voting had to be conducted during a 12-hour period, this meant that the men had to be identified at the rate of nearly 200 an hour.

At seven in the morning, 18 men were in line to cast their vote. By seven-ten the number had increased to about 40 and ten minutes later over a hundred were standing in line. At eight o'clock the line of voters extended down the corridor and stairway to the front of the building and by nine-thirty the line extended several blocks. Rudolph Renn, secretary of Local 18545, claimed they would have needed at least ten men at a time to challenge and identify adequately all the men "because in so many cases the man's time-clock number and [the] number on the payroll didn't check."

The union sent the following telegram to the NLRB in the afternoon:

> . . . Protest allowance of office force vote in Kohler election. Contrary to previous practice of your board and regional board. No office employee is member of union nor eligible to join union. Unfair to us for their status is well known. Since office force is voting under protest, request that votes be absolutely disregarded in totalling vote after election. Request alleged rioters be counted in total for none proven to date is guilty by any court. Please reply.

By 11:45 P.M., the votes had been counted and certified; the election favored the Kohler Workers Association as shown by the results:

Total votes cast for Local 18545	831	
Challenged by KWA for violence	185	
Challenged by KWA — working regularly elsewhere	3	
Votes counted for Local 18545		643
Total votes cast for KWA	1433	
Challenged by Local 18545, including deputies, supervisors, village employees, office employees, private employment, etc.	370	
Votes counted for KWA		1063
Void	5	
Sealed for further consideration	19	
Total votes cast	2288	

The company sympathizers were jubilant; union supporters were disheartened but determined not to give up. They felt they had been cheated out of the election, and said so the following day.

The Labor Board had set September 7, 1933, as the cutoff date for eligibility to vote in the election. The company had laid off shortly before, on August 22, 250 men who had received their last checks on September 15 — 8 days after the cutoff date. The company had also given Christmas presents to these employees in December and had continued to pay life insurance and sick benefits for them up to the time of the election. The union leaders argued that these men, plus the 185 who were charged with violence, even though not one had been arrested or convicted, would have been enough to win the election for Local 18545. The union also contended that they were allowed too few challengers to check the voters and questioned whether they detected all the supervisors, foremen, chauffeurs, village employees, American Club employees and riding stablemen who came to vote.

The author has read 69 depositions by Kohler workers, in which, over and over, the statements appear: "he was approached by the foreman and told to join the company union"; "he refused to join and was told they did not have any more work for him"; or "he joined the company union because he was afraid of losing his job." The years of employment claimed by these men read: 24 years, 6 years, 9 years, 11 years, 15 years, 11 years, 12 years. . . . Independence of spirit met with threats, actual layoffs or transfers to the most miserable jobs in the plant, regardless of years of seniority. Workers were approached by foremen and urged to sign KWA membership applications with such statements as: "You had better think it over." "If you want to go to work, sign this slip." "We want to know if you are for the union or for the company." "Sign this or you might lose your job."

Two notaries, Fred W. Meifert and John D. Ruppel, were kept busy September 3 to 5, 1934, taking 185 sworn statements from the men as to how good the Kohler Company was and how they voluntarily joined the KWA. Practically all of them stated they had signed an AFL application (some had paid $2.00 AFL dues and attended one or more meetings), but "I joined the K.W.A. of my own free will. I voted at the last K.W.A. election. I want the K.W.A. to represent me in bargaining."

Included in this list were the names of Joseph M. Born, later a time-study man, superintendent of the brass department and company photographer during the second strike; Harold J. Curtiss, an active anti-UAW man in the second strike; Dee Endsley, a Kohler deputy who quit and joined the union; and E. H. Kohlhagen, who later became a leader in the drive to affiliate with the UAW-CIO.

The Kohler strikers could find little aid or comfort in the columns of the nation's press in the summer and fall of 1934. *The Boston Transcript* said:

> This was probably the most heartless demonstration ever attempted in this country, leaving in its wake nothing but disaster for the hitherto contented employees, loss for the employer, and ill repute for the case of organized labor.

Nearer home, *The Milwaukee Sentinel* held the opinion that the strike was "ill-considered, ill-timed and unjustified," adding, "It was directed against a man, who as governor of Wisconsin, did more for labor's cause than any other governor in the state's history," a claim that would be difficult to back up with the facts.

Trade publications were even harsher in their judgments, *Iron Age* terming it "one of the most dastardly moves in the annals of organized labor," a "stench in the nostrils of fair-minded citizens," and a "vicious attack . . . by unscrupulous politicians and self-seeking labor leaders of the coarsest stripe." Small-town papers throughout the country echoed these sentiments with expressions ranging from "most unfortunate episode" to "acts of treason."

The Nation, in an article, "The Kohler Myth Dies," regarded the strike in a different light. Gunnar Mickelson wrote:

> The story behind the strike is the rise and fall of America's most widely advertised venture in industrial paternalism. . . . When it came to a final question of Kohler property or Kohler workers, it was gas, cracked heads, gunshot wounds, and death to the workers for the sake of the property. The crash of windows on that sacred property was reason enough to loose a stream of lead into the well-loved employees.

From letters the company received, it prepared excerpts which were widely published as testimonials of support. A Chicagoan wrote:

> Keep up your good work until Radicalism and Communism are completely routed from the Kohler Organization.

A Mt. Airy, North Carolina, citizen said:

The people I have met have always given your company the highest praise for your efforts to make living conditions good for your employees, better, perhaps than any other place in the country. I believe that had your people been left alone by the paid professional organizers of the American Federation of Labor, you would still be carrying on with confidence and friendship.

Someone from New Jersey warned:

Certain labor leaders, alien to your plant, are conducting one of the most dangerous forms of racketeering with which employers today have to contend.

Another in indignation, wrote from La Porte, Indiana:

Of all the dastardly things undertaken by the American Federation of Labor, that uncalled for strike . . . in the case of your employees is probably the worst. . . .

For the leaders of the strike, particularly, the consequence of defying the company was a hand-to-mouth existence at such work as they could find during the depression years. "There were many, many days," a striker's wife recalled, with surprisingly little bitterness, "when we didn't have a nickel in the house." Families were forced to accept government assistance or help from relatives. Except for other unions, most of the community was silent; those who sympathized supported the strikers with food or money to help feed the pickets, some of whom walked before the plant gates until 1941. For the Kohler strikers of 1934 it was indeed a lonely battle.

Union Resorts to Boycott

The union membership was somewhat broken in spirit, but not defeated, after the representation election in September, 1934. Union leaders felt the NLRB had ruled improperly in permitting KWA on the ballot after declaring that the company had "interfered with the free and unhampered self-organization of employees." The union decided to take its case to the public by asking for a national boycott of Kohler products. A resolution requesting that the Kohler Company be placed on the "We Don't Patronize" list was introduced at the convention of the American Federation of Labor in San Francisco in October, 1934. Henry Ohl, Jr., president of the Wisconsin Federation, wired the local union, telling them to continue the strike and to picket the Kohler plant in protest against what they charged was dishonesty on the part of the company and its shop association, the KWA, in packing the election with several hundred of ineligible voters. Discouraged by the delay of the NLRB in hearing the charges of intimidation brought against the Kohler Company, Federal Labor Union 18545 officially instituted a boycott against Kohler in the latter part of October, 1934, and asked the Wisconsin Federation of Labor to assist in making it state- and nation-wide. Organized labor had less than four million members in the entire country at the time the boycott of Kohler was launched and the boycott did not have enough effect on the company's sales to bring about a settlement of the strike.

The CIO Is Started

In October, 1935, organizations representing about one third of the members within the American Federation of Labor, decided to form a Committee on Industrial Organization. While craft workers were fairly well organized, workers in industrial plants were largely without unions. Under the leadership of John L. Lewis, intensive organization was launched in auto, steel, rubber and textile manufacturing. Taking all the workers in a plant into the same union posed a threat to certain craft unions. They regarded this as an invasion of their jurisdiction and the result was the expulsion of the Committee by the AFL in 1937. Under Lewis' leadership, the delegates from the unions interested in industry-wide organization and from newly formed organizing committees then formed the more permanent Congress of Industrial Organizations (CIO). Union membership in the United States rose to over 9 million by 1940, attributable to the economic conditions of the thirties, the enactment of the Wagner Act (1935) with the provisions of the controversial Section 7(a) of the NIRA embodied therein, and the competition for membership between the rival AFL and CIO federations.

The organizing drives of unions in industrial plants during the middle and late thirties were accompanied, at times, by bitter opposition and violence. In the auto industry, there were several sit-down strikes before General Motors, Ford and Chrysler recognized the union.* It took a number of years before employers generally agreed to accept the Federal law protecting the right of workers to join unions.

The Strike Continues

The strike at Kohler which started in July, 1934, dragged on through the remainder of that decade. Most strikers sought work elsewhere, but a small group of dedicated adherents to Federal Labor Union No. 18545 continued to picket the Kohler plant.

Nonstrikers and new employees, who had gone to work in the Kohler plant, provided sufficient manpower to meet the production needs of the depression period; work was hard to find and those who had been given employment at Kohler were thankful to have a job. Not many questions were asked about wages and working conditions. The Kohler Workers Association, which enjoyed an intimate association with the company, dealt with enough of the routine grievances to remain in the good graces of the workers. The management and most of the employees were glad there was no "outside" union in the plant. When plant operations resumed, John Stieber (one of the first men to go into the plant after the strike started) was elected full-time secretary-treasurer of the KWA. Its offices were maintained within the plant for about a year and a half; then KWA rented two rooms equipped with office furnishings in the Building and Loan Association building for $7.50 a month with the privilege of using the recreation hall for meetings. No dues were charged at first; later, employees paid $1.00 per year, then a nominal $2.50 a year, and $5.00 per year after World War II. KWA officers transacted union business within the plant on company time without limitations. The executive board met daily on company time; the checkoff of dues was facilitated by the company even to the extent of sending employees to KWA officers to be signed up. The KWA was given the income from the vending machines for which they paid a nominal rental of $1.00 per machine per month and received revenues of $800.00 to $1,500.00 a month.

---

* Herbert V. Kohler, twenty years later, referred to these sit-down strikes as justification for not dealing with the United Auto Workers-CIO, even though there had been a change in the leadership of that union (Walter P. Reuther was elected president in 1946) and there had been no sit-down strikes for many years.

The Impact on the Community

The human suffering, the economic cost and the strained relationships between partisans in the community created an industrial-
relations climate that continued much further into the future than
was foreseen by those involved in the dispute. The tragic and costly
events of 1934 were to enter into discussion and debate on many
occasions during the nineteen-fifties when a new union became the
spokesman for Kohler workers, when law-enforcement officials
considered what course of action to follow in mass-picketing situations, and when the McClellan Committee probed events of the
second strike.

There was widespread agreement that such a costly episode
must never reoccur in the community, but there was no consensus
as to who was responsible or what should be done to avoid a repetition of such a strike. Unionism was still a new concept for many
Sheboygan County residents and many did not understand or agree
with the goals of union workers. When every fourth or fifth
worker throughout the country was unemployed and many had to
work on public works projects or live on relief, a strike, even
against a paternalistic employer, was hard to fathom.

The doubts and questions which grew out of the riot were
never completely laid to rest. For months letters to the editor in
The New Deal and *The Sheboygan Press* raised questions about the
responsibility for the killings. Friends and families of the dead and
injured felt that the jury verdict placed the responsibility upon the
strikers because of the coroner's statement that they "came to their
death in a general gunfight." The rumors and accusations circulated
in the community rankled and left their mark, not only on the men
involved, but upon families as well. Sides were taken, even among
the neighborhood children, who bore the labels of "pickets' kids"
and "strikebreakers' kids," and whose elders wanted them to have
nothing to do with each other.

Bitterness against strikers found overt expression in a number
of ways. Charlie Heymanns, who followed Arthur Kuhn as president of Local 18545, had joined the union at its inception. To him,
the union became a way of life and he gave unstintingly of his time.
He hauled a carload of pickets from Sheboygan to Kohler every
morning in his old Model-A Ford and called for them in the eve-

ning. In January, 1935, his car was stolen and driven north of the
city where all the tires were cut, the radiator and windshield
smashed and the spark plugs taken out. Some Village of Kohler
residents believed "he did that himself just for publicity."

Individuals in the community, mainly businessmen, organized
the Sheboygan County Law and Order League, which the leading
department store saluted in an ad, August 24, 1934.

> *We Are With You!* Sheboygan County Law and Order League!
> Sheboygan Dry Goods Co. heartily endorses the newly formed She-
> boygan Law and Order League and the lofty ideals for which it
> stands. Every one of our employees believes in the absolute suppres-
> sion of communism, radicalism and intimidation and we will lend
> every effort to cooperate with the League in the prevention and
> eradication of any acts of rioting, violence or other display of unlaw-
> fulness.
>
> We have never countenanced any acts which were not in accord-
> ance with the principles of good Americanism and good citizenship
> and we take this opportunity of applauding the efforts of the She-
> boygan County Law and Order League to maintain a county-wide
> feeling and knowledge of personal security and mutual good will.

The county board, greatly concerned that the National Guard
might have to be called in again if further violence erupted, was
urged by District Attorney Charles Copp:

> . . . it behooves this board to legislate and establish a uniform and
> solid policy concerning the maintenance of law and order. . . . The
> sheriff must find men of intelligence and with individual good judge-
> ment; men who are not partial to either the Kohler Company or the
> workers. He would have to scour the county and induce men to
> enlist as deputies. Our sheriff did this Tuesday and found that the
> number of such men willing to serve . . . was negligible.

Results of a Questionnaire

The author prepared a questionnaire in the fall of 1934 to
determine the psychological impact and degree of community involvement in the strike, and to help point the way for the study he
had undertaken. While the sample was limited, the responses (120
out of 200) did provide some interesting clues to impressions of the
dispute. Respondents included 7 teachers, 6 businessmen, 7 profes-

sional men, 6 ministers, 9 university students living in the county, 12 farmers, 38 union men and 35 laborers. Ninety-five of the 120 had visited Kohler at some time during the strike; 59 thought the strike had been planned months in advance and 9 believed it was called *because* Kohler was a model village. Thirty-two of 115 who answered this question believed "outside agitators" were responsible for the strike — all 6 ministers, 4 out of 6 college students, 3 out of 6 teachers and 4 out of 5 businessmen who responded were of that opinion.

Ninety-six out of 109 respondents thought the AFL union helped the workers more than a company union, but only 5 out of 8 students and 1 out of 4 ministers felt this way. Eleven out of 116 who answered thought it was necessary for the deputies to shoot to quiet the mob; 11 thought an employer should have the right to drill men in military tactics to protect his property, 3 of the 6 businessmen who responded being of that opinion. Only 4 of 109 were of the opinion that the Law and Order League did anything constructive; 3 of them were ministers. Eight of 109 who answered thought real effort had been made to convict the deputies responsible for the killings and of the 69 who had read a feature story on the Kohler strike in *The Saturday Evening Post* all but 8 claimed it to be a one-sided story. On the question, "Can forced arbitration settle conflict?" 29 out of 103 said yes; many respondents wrote, "No, not with Kohler."

A University of Wisconsin graduate, living in Sheboygan, who had a keen interest in the causes and effects of the strike, added the following comment in response to the questionnaire:

> It is very comforting to the local reactionaries to believe that outsiders called the strike; when one asks who these might be, the redoubtable Maud McCreery is the only one ever mentioned. She herself told me that she was flatly against the strike at the time it was called, thinking that the union was not yet strong enough, but that the men themselves overrode her judgement. The outsiders are purely mythical.
>
> The strike was called by the union; certain members of the Central Labor Council conferred as they did with all the striking bodies. Certainly no group called them all. Personal opinion[s] in matters such as this may be interesting, but have no bearing on the facts.
>
> In all the papers, the NEW DEAL [labor paper] included, the reports

were dishonest in my opinion, in that they never included news that might have tended to show the opposing side in its true light.

The Law and Order League served only to draw a sharper line between pro and anti-labor sentiment.

You may know that there is considerable evidence to support the view that the first stones were thrown by men hired by the company to begin the riot. Of course, the original violence was started by deputies roughing up the picket line that morning. Once started, the violence gathered momentum and ran its course.[18]

Responses obtained on the questionnaire provided clues and insight for making a study of the first strike. They are suggestive of the opinions held and the depth of feeling that pervaded the community. No evidence that the company had hired men to throw the "first stones" was found, but neither was there evidence that "outside agitators" had provoked the strike.

"Settlement" of the First Strike

Rudolph Renn, secretary of Federal Labor Union No. 18545 at the time of the settlement, told the author that a representative of the Kohler Company contacted Herman Seide, who had been elected president of the Wisconsin Federation of Labor after Henry J. Ohl, Jr., died (1940), to discuss ways of settling the strike. Renn's account of the details of that settlement is as follows:

The union had maintained picketing at the Kohler Company from 1934 until 1941. While the union maintained just a skeleton crew after the first few months, the picket line was always a sign that a labor dispute existed. The Company wanted to expand its plant so it could get government war contracts, but it realized that members of the building trades unions weren't going to violate a picket line. So they said, "You've got us over a barrel," and offered to settle the strike and take back union members in good standing who could pass the company's physical examination, and give them two years' seniority rights. "But," the spokesman said, "there are three people we won't take back — Charlie Heymanns [president of the local], Rudolph Renn [secretary] and Otto Janisch [treasurer]."

Mr. Seide reported this conversation to the union officers and asked them if they would ever be interested in working at the Kohler Company again. They said, "No, not after what we have gone through" — so Seide then said, "Will you write a letter to the

Engelmann-Wakefield memorial ceremony at strike headquarters out-side Kohler, in 1936. Standing behind left wreath is Charles Heymanns; to his right is David Rabinovitz, the union's attorney. The tall man in dark suit near wreath on right is Rudolph Renn, and at extreme right is Arthur F. Kuhn.

company and tell them you are not interested in working there?" I told him, "If we did, everyone would know it was a 'sell-out!'" Seide then said, "Well, will you write *me* a letter stating you are not interested in working for the Kohler Company?" I told him, "If it will settle things, I guess we won't mind."

The letters were sent to Seide and then turned over to the Kohler Company. When the agreement ending the strike was concluded, the list of workers eligible to return to work was posted by the Kohler Company, including the names of Heymanns, Renn and Janisch, all in proper alphabetical order. If these names had not been on the list, the rest of the union members would have suspected "a deal." But all three of us knew very well that if we ever went to Kohler to ask for a job, we would have our letters shoved under our noses.

Herbert V. Kohler, head of the company since Walter J. Kohler's death, in 1940 addressed a two-page letter, dated April 29, 1941, to Herman Seide, Peter Schoemann, Arthur Olson, and

Theodore Weisman, the committee representing the American Federation of Labor, which stated (in part):

Gentlemen:

As a result of recent conferences at our office, we are submitting the following proposal:

1. Persons whose names appear on Schedule A attached hereto, selected from a list of those whom you would have the company employ, shall constitute a special hiring list for the period ending May 1, 1942. There have been eliminated from your list the names of those who were not on the company's payroll as of August 15, 1933, those who subsequently left the employ of the company for reasons other than the strike, those who we now know are not citizens, and several who are personally objectionable to the company for reasons not attributable to the strike. . . .

3. The physical fitness of an individual to do the work available will be determined by the company's medical department when he is called for examination. In the event of a determination that the company will have no employment for which the individual will be suited, and such finding is disputed, it shall be submitted to a physician selected by the Director of Workmen's Compensation of the Wisconsin Industrial Commission for confirmation. . . .

7. Persons employed in accordance with this proposal will be entitled to the same amount of group insurance as they had when their insurance was cancelled. In other respects their seniority shall date from December 31, 1938. . . .

9. This proposal by the Company is not to be construed as recognition of any organization for purposes of collective bargaining. The Company can extend such recognition only to persons or organizations duly chosen for such purposes by a majority of all its employees.

As we discussed at our meetings, *neither you or we will publicize these negotiations, and in the event of settlement there is to be no publicity of the terms and conditions beyond a simple statement that the strike has been disposed of on a mutually satisfactory basis.* [Emphasis added.]

This proposal is tendered in full settlement of the controversy between us, and is conditional upon the cessation of all strike activities directed against this company by the American Federation of

The 1934 strike headquarters with placards, wreaths and a flag at half-mast for the memorial service four years after the riot.

Labor and organizations affiliated with it. It will become effective upon receipt of a letter of acceptance from your committee.

Signed:
Herbert V. Kohler, President

Thus ended Kohler Strike Number One.

4

BETWEEN THE FIRST
AND SECOND STRIKE

1941–45: The War Years

AFTER the strike was "settled," the Kohler Company started an expansion program which employed union members from the building trades to construct additional plant facilities in preparation for defense contracts. During World War II, the company devoted most of its production to defense work which generally guaranteed production cost plus a profit. Kohler manufactured torpedo tubes, 105-mm. shells, piston rings and precision controls for the United States Government.

Labor costs were not a primary concern of manufacturers during the war period, since production costs were guaranteed by the government. In fact, there were many reports that employers hired extra help to pad their payrolls since their profit was based on total production costs. Government wage controls and price controls during the wartime period, designed to speed up production, minimize inequities and control inflation, restricted the areas in which collective bargaining could take place. Wage increases were granted, within the framework of wage controls established by the Federal government, and generally workers were glad to have a job instead of serving in the military forces.

1945–52: Attempts at Outside Affiliation

A company union, by its very nature, is more closely identified with the employer and thus less free to speak for the workers than is a union affiliated with locals in other communities and in other parts of the country. The KWA was conceived on company property. It did provide a mechanism for the settlement of minor grievances and disputes which interfered with employee morale, but there was no established procedure for taking difficult cases to arbitration. Many decisions on wage increases, rates, et cetera, were made unilaterally by the company.

Income from candy vending machine sales within the plant, which supported the KWA, amounted to $3,763.50 in 1945. In 1946 and 1947 this income increased to over $5,000 per year. In 1948, income from soft-drink sales was added to the candy income. That year KWA began paying a minimal rental charge of $257.43 for vending machines. By 1951 combined KWA income from candy and soft-drink sales amounted to $15,699.28 and rental fees were $772.00.[1]

On August 31, 1950, the Kohler Company and the Kohler Workers Association signed an agreement patterned after contracts negotiated by other unions. It spelled out the basic terms of agreement on recognition, nondiscrimination, dues assignments, merit increases, working schedules, procedures for transfers and discharge, grievances, and so on. Article VII of the agreement provided in part,

> . . . it may be terminated by either party by sixty days' written notice of such termination to be sent by registered mail to the last known address of the other party. Unless so terminated, this contract shall remain in full force and effect as long as the Kohler Workers Association is legally designated as bargaining agent of the employees in the bargaining unit specified in Article II, Section 1, but not later than December 31, 1951. It shall automatically renew itself thereafter for successive calendar years unless prior to November 1st of any year in which the contract would otherwise expire, written notice is given. . . .

Lyman C. Conger, Kohler Company attorney, has been credited with calling from 1934 to 1954 "twenty years of labor peace." It would have been more accurate to call it a period of "cold war." Shortly after World War II ended, signs of discontent manifested themselves in the plant. Some workers made contacts for affiliation with an outside union.

After contacts were made with the Wisconsin State Federation of Labor (WSFL), the federation assigned Ted James, William Wright and R. J. Oudinot to assist in the first postwar attempt to establish an independent union at Kohler.[2] The WSFL, represented by the legal firm of Padway, Goldberg, and Previant of Milwaukee, petitioned the Wisconsin Employment Relations Board (WERB) (pursuant to Section 111.05 of the Wisconsin Statutes), for an election to determine "representatives for certain employees of the Kohler Company." The WERB held a hearing on March 6, 1946, and conducted an election for Kohler employees on April 11. Two questions were placed on the ballot: (1) to determine the bargaining unit, *i.e.*, whether production and maintenance employees should be treated as a separate group from office employees and (2) whether employees wished to be represented by the AFL or the KWA for purposes of collective bargaining.

Those who favored the KWA felt they had a better chance of winning the election if office employees were included in the bargaining unit; AFL supporters favored a separate unit for production and maintenance workers. On this question the results were as follows:

Total number claimed eligible to vote	2,478
Total ballots cast	2,404
Total ballots challenged	29
Total ballots void	3
Total ballots blank	153
Total valid ballots counted	2,219
Ballots cast in favor of a separate unit	749
Ballots cast against a separate unit	1,470

The results of the vote on the first question plainly forecast what the vote on the second question would be, since office workers seldom favor an industrial union. Philip H. Smith, Lambert C. Sage and James Dewitt of the United Electrical, Radio and Machine Workers of America (UE-CIO)* had made efforts to win support among Kohler workers, but withdrew from the campaign and requested that the UE be omitted from the ballot. The Wisconsin State Federation of Labor had planned to establish a new local (Federal Labor Union No. 18545 having become inoperative after the strike "settlement" in 1941) and to arrange for affiliation with

---

* The UE had acquired the reputation of following the Communist party line at that time and could not get a significant following. Leo Breirather, a Kohler worker who joined the UAW-CIO, was of the opinion that the UE had "invited itself" into the community.

some national union if the majority of Kohler workers favored an independent union at that time. The results on this question were:

Total valid votes counted	2,342
Ballots cast for the AFL	716
Ballots cast for KWA	1,561
Ballots cast for neither	65

About 2 out of 3 still supported the company union at that time.

After the April, 1946, employees' election, those interested in affiliation with an independent union were relatively quiet until 1949–50 when unresolved grievances, disputes over cull deductions, and growing discontent led the more aggressive Kohler workers to shop around for a union free from company domination. Some interpreted this activity as a device for getting a better contract for KWA, rather than a serious move to affiliate with a national union. During this period exploratory contacts were made with a number of outside unions, including the United Auto Workers-CIO, the International Association of Machinists-AFL, the Plumbers' Union, and the Wisconsin State Federation of Labor. *Business Week*, in retrospect, quoted a KWA member's argument: "If we're going to affiliate with an international union, let's get into the biggest one."[3]

Eric Bjurman, a staff representative of the International Association of Machinists-AFL * told the author in 1954 that after some Kohler workers contacted his union in 1950, he was sent to Sheboygan County to explore the feasibility of helping Kohler workers form an independent local which might affiliate with the Machinists' union. After examining the situation, he decided the company's attitude toward unions would make it a long, tough assignment, which might cost two million dollars before genuine collective bargaining could be established. The Machinists concluded that this was too costly a project to undertake. Shortly thereafter, contacts were again made with the United Auto Workers-CIO. Although the UAW staff representatives also agreed that

---

* A "national" union confines its jurisdiction to the United States while an "international" union may include locals in Canada. During the period from 1936 to 1955, when the AFL and CIO were rival labor federations, raiding and competing organizational drives were not uncommon.

it would be a long, hard pull in view of the long history of company unionism at the Kohler plant, Harvey Kitzman, the UAW regional director, estimated that the cost would be substantially less than Bjurman's estimate.*

Kitzman told the author in the fall of 1964: "I have never felt bad, and never will in spite of the fact that we spent over 13 million dollars. . . . I don't think that was spent in vain — this was fighting the 'open shop' movement." Kitzman told an anecdote in connection with the decision by the UAW to organize at the Kohler plant:

> Dan Hoan called me in after it came out that we were in there organizing. He looked at me and said, "Harvey, I have known you far a good many years. I always used to think you were a pretty smart kid, but you're completely nuts, man! You know what this is going to cost you? This is going to cost you at least a million dollars!" Well, you know, Dan was only about 12 million off!

A few Kohler workers got together in August, 1950, to determine what national union to ask to help them with their collective bargaining problems and they decided it should be the UAW-CIO. Attending that meeting were: Edward C. Kalupa, Robert H. Matthias, Wilfred C. Bauer, Arbor L. Brewer, Joseph E. Lorier, George Allman, Bernard Kalupa, John Melger, Maynard Richardson and Robert Daily. Ed Kalupa and Brewer acted as unofficial co-chairmen and spokesmen for the group.[4]

Shortly after this meeting, Kalupa was interrogated by Kohler superintendent, Gordon Gavin, concerning his UAW-CIO activities.† Among other things, Gavin said he hated to see an intelligent young man being misled by some union, and he cautioned Kalupa about signing union cards on company time, even though KWA officials were still permitted to engage in union activity on company time.[5]

---

* Jurisdictional lines have never been strictly observed among American unions. In the early fifties the CIO and the AFL were still rival organizations; thus it became a matter of which the workers preferred and which was willing to provide help in organizing the local. The Kohler Company had an engine plant department, so it was not as far-fetched as it might seem for the UAW to represent plumbingware workers.

† An alleged 8(a)(3) violation under the National Labor Relations Act by the company.

Negotiations between KWA and the company broke down for the first time on December 31, 1949, when the company refused to extend the existing contract. Kohler workers voted 2,570 to 750 for an all-union shop on March 8, 1950, and on June 6 they voted 2,549 to 876 to reject the company's contract proposal offering a union shop clause but no other major changes. In July, 1950, the company submitted a new proposal, including hospitalization insurance, pension plan improvements, and a token wage increase, but withdrew the all-union shop offer. KWA accepted a new contract in August which called for wage increases of from six to ten cents per hour and then negotiated another 5 per cent wage increase retroactive to May 1, 1950.

UAW Regional Director Harvey Kitzman assigned several staff members to assist in an organizing campaign among Kohler workers. They met with small groups during the latter part of 1950 and early 1951 and then arranged to petition the National Labor Relations Board to hold a representation election. They obtained more than the number of signatures required by law and an election was scheduled for March 27, 1951.

Harold Neuwith and Floyd Schuette, two enamelers active in in-plant organizing efforts of the UAW-CIO, were discharged on February 22, 1951, because they refused to sign cull deduction slips which they considered inaccurate. The cull deduction system was an issue that helped pave the way for greater support for an outside union. The Kohler Company's assistance to KWA in the pre-election campaign included radio broadcasts and full-page advertisements in *The Sheboygan Press*.[6]

KWA won the election, but the margin of victory was much smaller than in 1946, indicating that a growing proportion of workers favored affiliation with a national union. The election, in which nearly all eligible voters participated, resulted in the following vote:

KWA	2,064
UAW-CIO	1,575
Neither	76
Challenged	12
Total votes cast	3,727

The UAW-CIO continued its organizational campaign after losing the 1951 election. Raymond Majerus, who had been involved in a dispute over working conditions in the enamel shop, was dismissed, allegedly for union activity. He joined the UAW staff and assisted in the organizing drive which was to prove successful the following year.

During the summer of 1951 Herbert V. Kohler, company president; Walter Ireland, personnel director; and Edmund Biever, plant manager, attended a meeting of supervisors in the main office of the Kohler Company.[7] The NLRB summary of that meeting reads as follows:

> At this meeting, Mr. Kohler and Ireland told lower supervision to watch employees who were promoting, organizing or passing out cards for the UAW-CIO in their respective departments, and to report any infractions of shop rules by these employees to Ireland so that the Respondent [Kohler Company] could endeavor to sustain a discharge. (Transcript pages 2357-58, 2364)

The NLRB transcript contains details on a number of instances involving company efforts to discourage employees from joining the UAW. One such citation reads:

> On October 10, employee Ertel refused foreman Mertz's request to work overtime, stating that the employees would not be requested to work overtime if they had a union (Kohler Co., 108 NLRB 224). Mertz grabbed Ertel by the back of the neck and told him he had to work; that it was because of Ertel that "none of the other inspectors wanted to work overtime" and that "it was this CIO business and all the union talk that was creating trouble there"; that Mertz was going to tell Messner that Ertel "was talking about the union too much" and that 10 other men on the enamel shop were "wise guys" like Ertel who "were talking about the union and trying to get the union in there" and that they would be discharged too. On the following day Ertel was discharged for his activities on behalf of the UAW-CIO.[8]

The Enamel Shop Controversy

"They've been doing it for 36 years," Lyman C. Conger told the McClellan Committee, ". . . I am sure they can do it." He was telling an amazed Robert Kennedy that it *was* possible for the men in the enamel shop to eat lunch in 2 to 5 minute intervals between tending pieces of equipment in the ovens. Work in the enamel department was a continuous operation; the men had to wear heavy clothing and asbestos equipment to protect them from heat as high as 240 degrees. Lunches were eaten on the run, the men taking a bite, then putting a sandwich down somewhere while they tended the machinery. Enamel dust was everywhere. The work was extremely fatiguing * and the shift there was 6 hours instead of 8 hours — an adjustment which enamelers had won under the KWA. The enamel shop, understandably, was the department in which the union had its strongest and most active supporters.

On April 21 and 22, 1952, 12 workers in the enamel shop were fired. Allan Graskamp testified before the McClellan Committee that:

> With the fans off, the people, from the heat, got dizzy and some got sick . . . some of them that went to the medical department got sent home, but the most active UAW guys didn't get cards to go home but were told to go back to their jobs.

When the twelve refused to return to work and were discharged, the company claimed it was for insubordination; the union maintained that it was because they were active in the union.

In May, the company unilaterally increased the enamel-shop day to 8 hours and a new incentive rate was put into effect so that the "take-home pay was less after 40 hours of work than it had been for 30 hours." The workers viewed this as reprisal against their "talking union."

Other Kohler workers who became more interested in an outside union after the 1951 vote included Bernard, Ray and Gordon Majerus, Elmer Gross and Edward Klauser.† Later in 1951, UAW-

---

* Attorney Albert Gore emphasized in an interview with the author (December 29, 1964) that conditions of work in the enamel shop were utterly exhausting, to the point that it was a detriment to the workers' family life. About a year after the strike began, he observed, there was a rash of announcements of new arrivals in enamel-shop-worker's families. Leo Breirather modified this statement by saying that the birth rate among strikers generally went up to a point where it put a drain on the Health and Welfare program.

† Ray Majerus, who still supported the KWA at the time of the 1951 election, became one of the most enthusiastic supporters of the UAW after he and eleven others were fired from the enamel shop, April, 1952. He recalled that it

CIO secretary-treasurer Emil Mazey met with leaders of KWA at the recreation hall in Kohler Village, where Mazey explained the structure of the UAW, the benefits of membership and the ways it could help Kohler workers. At this meeting were the general chairman, all the group chairmen, and nearly all the leadership of KWA – about 75 in all. Mazey invited questions and an extensive give-and-take discussion followed in which his forthright answers to questions impressed KWA officials. Mazey recognized that there was a growing interest in the UAW and invited the KWA 12-man executive board to visit Detroit at the union's expense. There they observed the International union in operation at Solidarity House, the UAW headquarters; toured the Briggs plant, a Kohler competitor where the UAW had a contract; and returned to Kohler with a better idea of what other organized workers were doing.

The Kohler Company was not ready to consummate a new agreement with the increasingly aggressive KWA. On February 4, 1952, KWA filed with the NLRB "failure to bargain charges" against the company. The NLRB did not issue a complaint because the charges were "not properly documented."

Officers of KWA Become Disenchanted

Christ Zittel had been chosen president of KWA in 1950. He showed more aggressiveness and independence than former KWA officers and it was not long thereafter until more difficulties arose about grievance and contract interpretation.[9] About this time the character of *The Kohlerian*, the KWA newspaper, changed from the "folksy-newsy" type of publication to a union organ publishing information about collective bargaining, wages and conditions of employment. On many occasions Conger objected to the new format and policy of *The Kohlerian*. He told the editor, E. H. (Eggie) Kohlhagen, that the relationship between the company and the KWA would be much better if he did not publish what happened at meetings between the company and KWA representatives.[10] At about the same time, the company imposed restrictions on the KWA chairman's movement from department to department

was the way Max Raskin, CIO Attorney, handled the cull deduction cases that sparked his interest in the UAW-CIO.

to deal with workers' grievances, and discontinued the policy of paying KWA spokesmen for the time spent on union affairs.

On October 22, 1951, the Kohler Company complained to the KWA about Kohlhagen's use of company time to write grievances involving *other than his own* department, admitting thereby the right to do so in his own department, yet endeavoring to change a long-standing procedure with respect to other departments.[11] According to other testimony presented during the NLRB hearings:

> In January 1952, employee Lacy . . . was told by Kolb (foreman) that if the employees knew what was good for them they would leave the UAW out and be satisfied with what they had. . . . Kolb told employees Reseburg and Pfister that "if a big union such as the CIO came in the Company would step on us, make us work that much harder, we couldn't go down five minutes before wash up time, stuff like that."
>
> In March of that year (1952) foreman Govek told employee Wilcox that if the UAW got into the plant the men would probably be required to stay on the job until the last five minutes before taking their showers instead of being permitted to leave a few minutes earlier as was customary, and that they probably would lose their Christmas bonus. Govek also told Wilcox to watch his step because he "was under surveillance by roving guards."[12]

The KWA endured much longer than most company unions, yet the time came when the association officers concluded that the employees would be better off with a union which was not subservient to the company. But as KWA became more militant and started acting more like a union, the company began withdrawing privileges and favors, one by one.[13]

In less than a year after the March, 1951, victory, KWA's own officers took the leading role in a campaign to affiliate with the UAW, a campaign which succeeded by a 2 to 1 margin among eligible employees. One of the KWA leaders who favored affiliation with the UAW-CIO, when asked about the vote to affiliate, replied: "The Company said that if they hadn't gotten into the fight, we would have bungled the election and they would be dealing with somebody else. So we told them that the next time they would see who had won the election for the KWA."* This

* KWA officers in a meeting with Kohler management after the March, 1951, election, had called attention to the vote and observed that the company's injecting

OF VITAL CONCERN TO THE COMMUNITY

KOHLER CO. FILES PETITION FOR LABOR BOARD ELECTION

recent months Kohler Co. engaged in negotiations with the K.W.A. for a collective bargaining agreement. Those negotiations were terminated by the K.W.A.

Because the matter now has become one of vital concern the community, Kohler Co. feels that this frank, public statement of the Company's basic position is necessary.

The Company's business — that of many other companies — and for reasons beyond our control — has been declining since the middle of last December.

The Company — even with reduced hours — has been able to sell only a part of the goods produced. Rather than lay men off, the Company has built up large stocks of unsold goods.

To increase wages and expensive fringe benefits at such a time would be to gamble with the future of the Company as an employer.

The Company proposed an "open end" contract under which the matter of wages can be brought up at any time and adjusted if business conditions warrant.

The K.W.A. insisted that the Company make immediate commitments to assure large, additional wage and fringe costs and — when the Company refused to do so — broke off negotiations.

Now pressure tactics are being used — such as the recent work stoppage in the Enamel Shop — thinly disguised as an issue of health.

Regardless of what union represents its employees or what bargaining or coercive tactics are employed — the Company's first concern is to preserve itself as an employer of labor and a principal source of income for the community.

It intends to perform that function.

KOHLER CO.

Kohler Co. is filing a petition with the National Labor Relations Board for an election to determine what union, if any, the employees who are members of the Kohler Co. bargaining unit desire to have represent them.

Kohler Co. does not recognize the poll of KWA members, which KWA held Tuesday and Wednesday, as having an official status.

In granting permission that the poll be taken in the plant, the company informed the KWA in writing that it was consenting in order not to inconvenience the employees and that the company was not participating in the poll and would not be bound by it.

This poll was conducted without any of the necessary and usual safeguards. Many of the people in the bargaining unit were excluded from voting. It was an unofficial straw vote. There was not even a poll list such as the Labor Board always insists upon.

It was conducted in extreme haste. Apparently the reason for this great haste was to rush the vote before employees had an opportunity to consider the matter, and to "railroad" a commitment.

The election for which Kohler Co. is petitioning the National Labor Relations Board would be held by secret ballot with proper safeguards and with all employees of Kohler Co. who are to be represented by the bargaining agent having an opportunity to vote.

This is the only type of election which Kohler Co. will recognize

KOHLER CO.

Typical company advertisements in the Sheboygan Press — *April-May,* 1952.

attitude on the part of the company, perhaps more than anything else, hastened the day when a showdown was to come.

The Kohlerian served as a good barometer of sentiment among the employees. The strong interest in affiliation with the UAW among the officers of the KWA made it easy for UAW staff representatives to build the support which was to lead to a UAW victory.

KWA membership had grown to about 3,500 by 1952. In February of that year, some of the KWA officers actively sought affiliation and invited representatives of the AFL and the CIO to

itself into the campaign had nearly cost KWA the election. Conger felt otherwise: "We are the ones that won that election for you; we got on the air and put ads in the papers and we are certain that is what changed the picture — otherwise we might be meeting with somebody else right now."[14]

speak before the KWA. On April 9, 1952, company supervisors took down copies of *The Kohlerian* posted on vending machines in the plant. This issue contained an analysis of bargaining between KWA and the company and recommendations that the company's proposal be rejected at the forthcoming membership meeting. Kohler Company employees voted 2,888 to 487 against accepting the company's contract offer on April 15.[15] A week later, twelve enamel shop men, referred to earlier, were fired and another week later, a referendum on union affiliation was held.

United Auto Workers Win — IUKWA Is Formed

With the 6 to 1 turn-down of the company's contract proposal, the situation was ripe for a move to affiliate with the UAW. On April 24 KWA leaders posted a notice of a general membership meeting to be held on April 27 at which time the members were to discuss "the advisability of a strike" and "the advisability of affiliating with another union." At that meeting it was moved to defer the strike question until the question of affiliation was settled and a motion was then passed to conduct a general referendum on the question of affiliation with the UAW-CIO. Handbills were distributed and also posted on the KWA bulletin boards announcing the referendum for UAW affiliation for April 29 and 30. The vote was:

Yes	2,248
No	1,129
Blank	39
Void	16

The KWA officers applied for a charter establishing "Kohler Workers' Association Local No. 833, affiliated with International Union United Automobile, Aircraft and Agricultural Implement Workers of America (UAW-CIO)," abbreviated as KWA-UAW-CIO Local No. 833. The local made arrangements to have all accounts and securities transferred to the new organization with the proviso that none of the funds go to the treasury of the international union and that if the employees in the General Office Group (Group 8) formed a separate bargaining unit within 60 days, they were to receive a sum of money proportionate to their membership in KWA at the time of the affiliation.[16]

Twenty-eight members of KWA, who opposed affiliation, formed a new organization called "Independent Union of Kohler Workers' Association" – IUKWA – and contributed $1 each as a membership fee.[17] This group initiated court action against the UAW and named 33 persons as defendants, including all the officers of the company union (KWA), Harvey Kitzman, regional director of the UAW, and key Kohler employees who decided to affiliate with the UAW. The trial commenced December 1, 1952, in Sheboygan County Circuit Court. Circuit Judge Henry A. Detling took testimony for four days, heard legal arguments for nearly a full day, and ruled on December 22, 1952:

> I look upon this case in this way: Both of these unions have the same objective, and the Kohler Workers' Association voted to affiliate with the CIO Local 833.
>
> The funds in the possession of the KWA, the amount of which is now in dispute, was a trust fund, and the money can only be used for the purpose of the trust – there seems to be no argument about that. . . .
>
> When the vote was taken, the vote was taken on the question of affiliation, and a big majority voted to affiliate its organization with the CIO. Now, the majority of the Kohler Workers' Association had a right to determine whether or not they would affiliate, and when the majority so decided and so voted to affiliate, it seems to me that that was the organization of Kohler Workers' Association as the majority voted to do so; and when the majority voted to do so, they took with them the Kohler Workers' Association. . . .

On January 10, 1953, the Circuit Court of Sheboygan County dismissed the plaintiff's complaint and taxed "costs against such plaintiffs in the sum of $469.40."

The IUKWA appealed the case to the Wisconsin Supreme Court. The Supreme Court heard the appeal on June 6, 1953, and on July 3 affirmed the judgement of the Circuit Court of Sheboygan County.

Justice Broadfoot, of the Wisconsin Supreme Court, after hearing both sides of the argument,[18] cited *Callahan v. Order of Railway Conductors*, 169 Wis. 43, 171 N.W. 658, as follows:

> . . . courts will not look into the technical correctness of either the proceedings prescribed or the proceedings followed and . . . reasonable or permissible construction which an order gives to its own

constitution, laws or rules will govern unless clearly subversive of personal or property rights.

The newly formed KWA-UAW local had, in the meantime, received its charter on May 5, 1952, and transferred the bank accounts and securities to Local 833. The 2 to 1 victory for the UAW in the referendum on April 29 and 30 was not enough, however, to settle the dispute. The Kohler Company refused to recognize the UAW-CIO and insisted on an NLRB-conducted election. There followed six weeks of intensive campaigning, with leaflets, radio broadcasts and advertisements in *The Sheboygan Press* by both the UAW and IUKWA.

Rivalry, raiding and jurisdictional disputes were not uncommon among American unions in the days of a divided AFL and CIO, so it was no great surprise that in the election which the NLRB scheduled for June 10 and 11, 1952, the United Auto Workers-AFL, a rival to the UAW-CIO, also sought the right to represent the Kohler workers. In spite of a three-way split, the KWA-UAW-CIO Local 833 won a clear-cut majority and was certified as bargaining agent by the board. The vote was as follows:

KWA-UAW-CIO Local 833	1,831
IUKWA (Independent)	850
UAW-AFL	710
No Union	52
Void	15
Challenged	23
	3,481
Number of eligible voters	3,529

Several theories were advanced to explain why the UAW-AFL had sought to represent the Kohler workers when the UAW-CIO was already on the scene. Some speculated as to whether the Kohler Company had encouraged the AFL union to enter the contest. Others figured that the UAW-AFL, on its own initiative, had decided to make a bid for support; and still others explained that there were some skilled craftsmen in the plant who favored the AFL.* (The support for the AFL union in this election was

* Majerus recalls that George Haberman, president of the WSFL, and Anthony Doria of the UAW-AFL appeared before the KWA leadership before the election and that Doria remarked, "You don't need a 10-ton truck to haul a 2-ton load."

A union meeting in the Sheboygan Armory. (UAW photo)

almost identical with the vote cast for the AFL in the 1946 vote: 710 as compared with 716.)

At a special membership meeting of Local 833, held October 10, 1953, the members voted unanimously to drop KWA from the name of KWA-UAW-CIO, Local No. 833, and adopted the name Kohler Local 833, UAW-CIO. Later it was shortened to Local 833, UAW. The State Supreme Court had upheld the Circuit Court ruling that the members had the right, by a majority vote, to affiliate with the UAW, and the membership decided that the continued use of KWA in its name would be confusing and serve no useful purpose.

A Temporary Truce

There was hope that a new era of labor relations was to begin at Kohler after the UAW won the NLRB-conducted election. Some Kohler officials assumed that new officers would be chosen and that they would not have to continue dealing with former KWA officials whom they had come to dislike intensely because they led the campaign for affiliation with the UAW. Company publicity implied that these KWA officers had dreams of becoming union leaders "rising to prominence in the UAW-CIO" and accused them of "systematically fomenting trouble," and "boring from within" to lead the KWA into the UAW-CIO.

Negotiations continued intermittently from June, 1952, until February, 1953, often with the help of Federal conciliators. Local 833 members voted (92.3 per cent) on February 14, 1953, to empower the bargaining committee to "strike if necessary." In the week that followed, Federal conciliators kept the union bargaining committee closeted all week with Kohler Company negotiators, hoping to break the deadlock. Meetings, which filled the Sheboygan armory with Kohler workers, were held on three successive weekends. Agreement for the first UAW contract at Kohler was reached about 11 A.M., Sunday, February 22, just prior to a strike deadline set for Monday morning. ". . . Thank God for a guy like L. L. Smith [who] came in and saved the situation . . . he made enough concessions so that the contract was . . . taken back to the membership and signed," Kitzman told the McClellan Committee.* Kitzman also told the committee that he and Emil Mazey, in February, 1953, "recommended to the members of Local 833 that they accept a contract which most of them knew offered them far less than they were entitled to." Radio station WHBL carried a spot announcement that an agreement had been reached and there was jubilation and relaxation of tensions.

After eight months of no progress, Emil Mazey, secretary-treasurer of the UAW, had come to Sheboygan to join the negotiating sessions, and stayed in the city three weeks. Mazey's entrance into the sessions started movement toward an agreement. He spelled out the provisions agreed on by the union negotiators and at a "hurry-up" meeting Sunday afternoon, February 23, 1953, asked for membership approval of the contract. Mazey, reporting to the membership for the third time at weekly intervals on progress in negotiations, was genuinely glad that a strike had been averted.

* Kitzman was not aware that the Reverend Wilford Evans of Sheboygan had discussed the community's stake in the threatened strike with L. L. Smith, who was a member of his congregation.

He talked about agreement reached on seniority, arbitration, a checkoff for union dues, time study, pensions, a wage reopening clause, and progress in establishing grievance machinery, including incentives, holidays and vacations, work schedules, health and safety, et cetera. He told the members:

> When you walk into the shop tomorrow morning, if you should accept this agreement, it does not mean that everything is going to be rosy, because it's going to take hard work on the part of your committee to start [dealing with] gripes that you have had for a long time, and the document itself will not automatically wipe them out overnight.

The agreement called for 12 cents an hour wage hike, plus 6 cents in estimated fringe benefits, full arbitration and improved hiring rates and wage progression. Edward Klauser, the first president of Local 833, said:

> I think more important than the wage increases we have gained are the other provisions of the contract. Under the new contract, Kohler workers are no longer going to feel that they are second-class citizens. *They have full arbitration.* Some of the gimmicks have been taken out of social security [Health and Welfare] benefits. We have joint time study, and we have all the things other unions have — and that's extremely important to us. *This arbitration thing alone I think is worth 10 cents per hour.*[19]

Eggie Kohlhagen, recording secretary, remarked, "The 'hopeless' days are over. Now we can go to an impartial umpire if we reach the end of the line in trying to untangle our grievances."

John Stieber, who had helped organize KWA and who later became secretary of Local 833, stated that the 12-cent increase granted instead of the company's old offer of 7 cents, "puts $104 a year in the pockets of Kohler workers — a net increase of $74 per person after paying union dues."

Plans were made to print the contract, with a union label, for distribution to all members of the local. The first of a new series of steward training classes were announced by Arthur Bauer, vice chairman of the local and chairman of the stewards' group, and by Elmer Gross, one of the early UAW supporters, who had been named education chairman. Bill Dodds and Clayton Carpenter of the UAW educational staff were asked to lead off with classes designed to equip stewards to interpret and live with the new contract. Elmer Gross commented, "This time we'll have our own contract as the textbook."

Approval to use sound equipment to announce the settlement was obtained from Kohler Village officials and a very noticeable thaw pervaded the entire county. Part of the credit for working out the settlement was due to the efforts of Virgil Burtz, Chicago; James Despins, Green Bay, Wisconsin; and Carl Carlgren, Minneapolis; the three Federal conciliators who kept negotiations from breaking up at the end. Carlgren's Swedish accent and general good will were definite factors in keeping the sessions in good humor.

The wage reopening provision of the contract was utilized at the end of the first three-month period. The union requested a reopening on May 23 and after almost three months of negotiations, settled for a 3-cent increase on August 20. Kitzman and Ferrazza, Mazey's assistant, were greeted with boos when they urged the union not to call a strike over the company's offer of a 3-cents-an-hour increase "which they knew did practically nothing to close the gap . . . between their wages and the wages of Kohler Company competitors." Mazey had instructed Ferrazza that the UAW would not approve a strike over wages during the life of the contract and had "stipulated that the terms and conditions would lie within the scope of contracts of competitors of the Kohler Company," *i.e.*, the union definitely did not want to impose terms which would put the company at a disadvantage.[20] The contract was to be in effect until March 1, 1954, and thereafter from year to year, unless 60 days' notice was given by either party.

While the contract fell far short of providing everything the union had hoped for, it did provide for union security and arbitration, and wage gains — including fringe benefits — of 18 cents per hour. The union leaders had termed the contract "a good one" and one "we can accept with pride"; they referred to the "important" and "tremendous" gains which had been achieved and to "key concessions" which the company had made.

Life under the first UAW contract was not easy for the union or the company. Both sides played it "close to the chest." The company was not reconciled to dealing with an "outside" union and the union members knew too much about the history of the company to feel comfortable with their new contract.

Attempts at a Second Contract

Negotiations to amend the '53–'54 contract were begun on February 2, 1954, with contract proposals from both parties, as well as the 1953 contract, on the table. The first round was devoted to going through the proposals point by point, noting differences of opinion between the two parties. The second round, begun about the middle of February and continuing until the end of the month, found company and union becoming more vehement in their arguments. Robert Burkart, who had been assigned by the UAW-CIO to the Kohler Local in September, 1953, claimed that any agreements reached during the first month of negotiations were confined to minor points. The company counsel then proposed that they turn to the "meat" of the contract. The union, although objecting that this might lead to the minor issues being lost in the shuffle, yielded. Discussion then turned to the seven major issues: arbitration, union security, seniority, pensions, insurance (life, medical and hospitalization), wages, and a 4-per-cent increase for the workers in the enamel shop. Once attention was directed to the major issues, it seemed apparent to the union negotiators that the company had no intention of yielding on these issues. Burkart stated that the issues were "on the bargaining table to this date" when he testified at NLRB hearings three years later.[21]

The company's panel was headed by its counsel, Lyman C. Conger. Robert Burkart, an international representative of the UAW, usually headed the union's panel, together with three officers of the local, Allan J. Graskamp, president; Arthur E. Bauer, vice president; and Egbert H. Kohlhagen, secretary; although sometimes other local officers and international representatives took part. The latter included Mazey, Kitzman, Ferrazza, and Rand.

The union, around February 23, requested an extension of the contract through the month of March, in order to give time for orderly bargaining on the new contract. The company, in its reply on February 25, rejected the union's request and offered instead to extend the expiring contract for a year, with the provision for a wage reopener once each quarter. The company proposition was, in turn, rejected the next day by the union with the claim that it was "more . . . a propaganda weapon than . . . a reasonable proposal." The company came back on the same date (February

26) with an alternative offer of 3 cents an hour general wage increase, dependent on acceptance of the company's earlier proposal of February 15, with such changes as had been agreed upon.

The union turned down the final proposal, asking that bargaining sessions be continued while the arrival of the Federal conciliator from the Federal Mediation and Conciliation Service (FMCS), who had been requested by the union, was awaited. On the grounds that everything would have to be gone over again when the conciliator arrived, the company refused to go on with the discussions.

During negotiations in March, neither side was inclined to yield any further. The union had announced, on March 8, that it would take a strike vote March 14 to ascertain the support it had at the bargaining table. It also invited the president of the Kohler Company, Herbert V. Kohler, to participate "in our deadlocked negotiations." Kohler declined, saying that positions taken by the company's representatives were taken with his full knowledge and approval. NLRB Examiner Downing's intermediate report, concerning the board's conclusions as to whether the company bargained in good faith, stated:[22]

> Though, as will be seen, the record does not support the conclusion that Respondent bargained before the strike with intent to avoid reaching an agreement, there came a time when that was no longer so.*

The report continues:

> The fact that Respondent had proved much the tougher trade [sic], yielding little while holding fast to much, does not establish a claim of bad faith bargaining, unless it occurred in connection with other circumstances which reflect its adamancy was itself part of a technique to avoid reaching an agreement . . . though good faith bargaining is inconsistent with a *predetermined* resolve not to budge from an initial position, "it is not necessarily incompatible with stubbornness or even with what to an outsider may seem unreasonableness." *N.L.R.B.* v. *Truitt Manufacturing Company*, U.S. 149, 154–155 (concurring and dissenting opinion): cf. *Commercial Printing Co.* 99 NLRB 469, 477. . . .

* See chapter 9 regarding 1964 NLRB decision.

Open and obvious strike preparations were made on both sides. Yet, significantly, the same sort of strategy had led on two earlier occasions (the '53 contract and the August '53 supplements) to the reaching of agreement.[23]

Over 20 meetings, consuming more than 100 hours, had been held prior to April 3, when negotiations were broken off. From March 7, 1954, all meetings had been held before a conciliator or a panel of conciliators of the Federal Mediation and Conciliation Service. Except for a few so-called two-man meetings (Conger and Kitzman), both sides were represented by a panel of 4 to 10 members each.

The company's attitude that it knew what was best for the workers and what it could afford to pay them, and arbitrary decisions concerning work assignments contributed to the growing feeling among the workers that a showdown would have to come.* The company adhered to the proposals made in February; and the last meeting before the strike, called for April 5, took place on April 3. Both sides seemed to assume that a strike was inevitable and made plans accordingly.

Strike Preparations

The first UAW contract with the Kohler Company had expired on February 28. After working for five weeks without a contract, the collective-bargaining climate had deteriorated to a point where everyone expected a strike. The company had again erected the watchtowers on top of the plant which had been built when the first contract was negotiated. It had installed additional searchlights on the plant roofs, and had brought in cots, food, cooking equipment, and so on in preparation for a prolonged "siege" if necessary.

It is difficult, and often impossible, for rival parties in a con-

---

* Gordon Majerus was the chief steward of the union. Some 5 or 6 weeks before the strike, while he was processing a grievance for another employee, his foreman, Willard Kohlhagen, told him he was "a fine fellow" who "could go far" with the company and he should not "stick his neck out" for the kind of fellow whom the grievances concerned. Majerus replied that he believed the employee had a legitimate grievance and that he would continue to process it. Kohlhagen told Majerus it would not do him any good to do so, that it would put him in "a bad light," which Majerus understood to mean "would hurt his record with the company."

flict situation to predict with any accuracy how certain actions will be interpreted and what counteractions will result. In 1953, the taking of a strike vote and the company's acquisition of guns and tear gas *did not* prevent the reaching of an agreement; but in 1954 the company's "military" preparations were interpreted by the union as an effort to resist union demands and to get rid of the union.

It is common practice in the United States for unions to take a "strike authorization" vote early in negotiations. This does not mean that a strike will necessarily follow, but it is a way of determining the degree of membership solidarity which exists and this then becomes one factor to consider at the bargaining table. The size of the company inventory and the demand in the marketplace are factors on the company's side of the ledger over which the workers have no control, but which also exert an influence in negotiations. Only in rare cases, when one or both of the contending parties misjudge the strength or the determination of the other, do negotiations break down and a strike or lockout result.

Contrary to the widely held public opinion, union members do not relish the idea of going on strike because it means a great reduction in income even when the union is able to pay some strike benefits, and a complete loss of income when the union cannot pay benefits. Once a strike is called, there is no way to tell how long it will last — days, months, or years; whether it will be won or lost, or how long it will take to recoup lost earnings through the increased benefits which may be obtained. Consequently strikes are usually called only when there is strong sentiment among the workers for risking what they have for something better. The workers at Kohler Company who voted for a strike by an 11 to 1 margin on February 14 were no exception. As an unaffiliated union, KWA could never have seriously entertained the idea of striking to improve working conditions. After they were affiliated with the UAW, they felt they had both the moral and economic support of the international union, if needed.

The union had made preliminary contracts with Petersen's Tavern near Kohler for a headquarters, if a strike should take place, and plans to provide coffee, doughnuts, etc. for the pickets had been discussed. The International Union put 25 cents of its per capita per month into a strike fund and 5 cents from the local went

Searchlight and shanty placed on plant roof as part of the company's strike preparation. (UAW photo)

for the same purpose. The local knew it could call upon this fund for help if necessary.

An examination of the available records discloses that the Kohler Company made more elaborate, far-reaching "defenses" against a possible strike than is recorded anywhere in modern American industrial history. Not only did the company's interests and policies dominate the policies and actions of the Kohler Village officials, as is to be expected in a company town, but special deputy cards, issued years before to five officials and a chauffeur of the Kohler Company, were automatically renewed each term by the county sheriff's office.[24] A company official used this deputy title when ordering tear gas from Federal Laboratories, Inc., Pittsburgh, Pennsylvania.

Lyman C. Conger, the Kohler Company counsel, had been quoted on a number of occasions as saying that the company had achieved twenty years of labor peace by not yielding during the 1934 strike. Union leaders felt quite sure that Conger had made up his mind early in the 1954 negotiations to "teach them another lesson." Evidence of the company's acquisition of weaponry was admitted in testimony given by Herbert V. Kohler, president of the company, at the NLRB hearing at Sheboygan, February 9, 1955. Herbert V. Kohler is the witness.

The Witness: We had armed guards in the plant from the time we took our first munitions contract for the United States government, and I might say we had very good reason to be apprehensive about the UAW-CIO. It advertises itself as a militant union.

The CIO had made a shambles of the Kalamazoo plant, I think it was in 1936. I saw the UAW-CIO sit around the plants in the yards of Chrysler and of G.M. and Ford, I think that was about 1937.

Q (*by Mr. Squillacote*): So you felt you had good reason to feel so strongly against the CIO, is that it?

A: I felt that we had to take precautions against any disorder.

Q: So that you accumulated various weapons?

A: I told you that our guards were armed.

Trial Examiner: You said that was when you took on the government contracts?

The Witness: Yes sir.

Trial Examiner: When was that?

The Witness: We have had . . .

Trial Examiner: When did you take the contracts?

The Witness: Was that around 1940? . . . I can't recall it, but it was some time around there, it was at the beginning of the war, sir. We had more or less government work right along.

Today we are making valves and fittings and devices for the jet engines, for various airplane factories, and for ultimate government end use. We are making shells, and very good ones.

Q (*by Mr. Squillacote*): Did I understand you to say, though, that you also accumulated weapons because of the CIO and what you knew about the union?

A: Well, it advertises itself as a militant union, as a riotous union. . . .[25]

Extensive preparations had been undertaken by the company before any strike was called. Testimony before the Wisconsin Employment Relations Board and the National Labor Relations Board described how far the company went to "protect its property" and to "preserve its management prerogatives." According to the records furnished by the Kohler Company to Carmine S. Bellino, accountant and consultant for the McClellan Committee in 1957–58, the company had acquired the following ammunition and equipment between May, 1952, and April, 1954, when the strike started. Much of the material listed was purchased during the week preceding the 1953 strike vote, taken on February 14, 1953, which did *not* result in a strike. Bellino's testimony does not always give date of purchase, so only items identified as bought before the strike are listed:

8	12-gauge Remington shotguns 2/10/53
375	gas shells, 2/12/53
	gas guns 1½" .37 mm. gas riot guns 8/12/53
24,000	.38 special cartridges 5/13/52 − 3/3/53
2,000	.22 long-range cartridges 6/16/52
600	rounds .45-caliber cartridges 6/16/52
400	police training targets and other targets
6	binoculars 2/8/53
300	army cots (about) 2/7/53
300	sleeping bags 2/7/53
1	8-burner restaurant-type Magic Chef stove 2/13/53
1	round stove 2/14/53
50	McDonald type-T safety hats 2/5/53
21	revolvers between 5/13/52 and 2/25/53
9,200	shotgun shells were reported as purchased between 1952 and 1955 and that most of the ammunition was bought 1952–53.

Lyman C. Conger, company attorney, testified, "We have had a gun club there, a rifle club, at least 35 years, and we have pistol clubs, and we have trapshooting clubs.[26] Some of the ammunition was used for trapshooting." In referring to 4 pounds of gunpowder purchased, he said that it was "sent to me personally, and that I used it for hand-loading of pistol cartridges which were used for training the guards in the plant."[27]

In questioning Waldemar Capelle, Kohler police chief, before the McClellan Committee, about the company's strike preparations, Senator Barry Goldwater defended Kohler Company's preparations thus:

> I might say again that they had ample justification for expecting a rough strike, because of 13 strikes that the Bureau of Labor Statistics reports on, prior to this engaged in by the CIO, had 37 deaths. This is not an isolated example. This is an example of what this union has been doing in violence ever since its inception. I think the Kohler Company, I think the police chief, and the sheriff, were perfectly right in anticipating trouble.[28]

What Senator Goldwater did not add was that it was mostly strikers who were killed in these CIO strikes.[29]

E. H. Kohlhagen, secretary of Local 833, gave an affidavit recording his impressions of certain events at the meeting of April 3, 1954, the last attempt at negotiation before the strike was called:

> In my capacity as a member and recording secretary of the Local 833 Bargaining Committee, I was present at a negotiation meeting held April 3, 1934. When we advised the Company we had no other alternative but to go on strike, Mr. Lyman C. Conger, Chairman of the Kohler Co. Bargaining Committee said: "We've been preparing for this (meaning the strike) for a long time!"
>
> Mr. William Howe, the Kohler Co.'s attorney from Washington, D.C., added these words: "If we're going to have a strike, we might as well have a show down right now!"

Allan J. Graskamp, president of Local 833, stated under oath:

> . . . that before signing the agreement in February 1953, he personally saw the company construct at least six (6) wooden shanties, approximately 4′ x 4′ x 8′ height and place them on the roof of the plant in various places;
>
> That he personally saw the placing of at least one searchlight at each shanty;
>
> That after the signing of the 1953 agreement, the Company did not take these shanties down, but merely left them in their place and laid them on their side;
>
> That before a strike vote was taken in 1954 and during the time the union was still negotiating with the Company for an agreement, the Company uprighted those shanties, placed more windows in them than they had in 1953, and installed many more searchlights

around the confines of the plant and also installed direct communications in these shanties;

That on April 4, 1954, the Company constructed wooden walls across the two (2) driveways leading into the plant which closed off any views of activities inside the confines of the plant, so that no activities on the part of the Company could be seen from the streets.

Leo J. Breirather, chief steward of Local 833, in connection with the 1953 and 1954 negotiations stated in a sworn affidavit:

That he personally saw other employees of the Kohler Company cart cots and bedding equipment into the North Foundry and store them on the second floor of the core department during the immediate period preceding the agreement on a contract between the Kohler Company and Local 833 in 1953;

That he personally saw the same preparations for a strike during the immediate period prior to the agreement between the Kohler Company and Local 833 on the question of a wage increase in August 1953;

That he personally saw identical preparations for a strike being made during the period immediately preceding April 5, 1954, the beginning of the strike;

That he personally heard much kidding going on between members of the supervision in regard to the assignments of cots in the event a strike would take place.

The Role of the Special Police

Normally the Village of Kohler had 3 to 5 special police. They were increased to about 45 in 1952 around the time that the UAW first won the election. Waldemar Capelle, chief of police of the village, testified that this number was increased to approximately 90 by April 5, 1954, the first day of the strike. Capelle also testified that the special policemen who were employees of the Kohler Company were given a leave of absence by the company. All that was required was a letter from Capelle to Walter J. Ireland, personnel director.

On May 13, Chief Capelle issued 24 "Rules and Regulations for Kohler Special Police." The introduction to the rules reads, in part,

. . . the entire plan of operation of this organization is based on the assumption that its members are anxious to serve and are willing to adhere strictly to the rules even at the cost of some personal sacrifices of comforts and conveniences.

Rule 1 stated:

The term Kohler Special Police shall mean an organization of civilian volunteers selected by the Chief of Police to assist regularly appointed police officers in the discharge of police duties in emergencies arising from fires, floods, earthquakes, or other natural causes, or any destructiveness resulting from enemy attack, sabotage, or other hostile action, under the direction of the Chief of Police.

Other rules required:

unity of purpose; prompt response to all reasonable directions; courtesy and civility; keeping cool; familiarity with all laws (Federal, State and Village Ordinances) pertaining to Civil Defense; remaining free from influence of intoxicating liquor when on active duty; *saying nothing, if the truth will not answer* [Emphasis added.]; no issuing of statements except with approval of Chief of Police; badges to be worn on outside of outermost garment over the left breast, unless otherwise ordered; constantly being alert and responding immediately to signals and warnings; reporting grievances to the Chief of Police — no arguing or altercation; no political or religious discussion, and no speaking slightingly of the nationality of any person; keeping a memorandum book at all times; submitting reports in writing as soon as possible.

Rule No. 12 is of particular interest:

It is always unwise for persons whose duty includes the protection of life and property to place themselves under obligation. Members of the Special Police are therefore expected to refuse all gifts or personal rewards offered them by any person liable to arrest or complaint. No officer can discharge his duties impartially if he places himself under obligation to anyone. No member of the Special Police force should interfere in any manner with the lawful procedures against any person arrested or liable to arrest.

It is a matter of record that insurance benefits, vacation and holidays of the Special Police were covered by the Kohler Company.

Why a Second Strike?
Psychological vs. Economic Considerations

Workers do not go on strike "for the fun of it." Neither do employers, as a rule, lock out workers because of a personal whim or intense feelings against unions. Fortunately, most collective-bargaining situations provide for enough give-and-take accommodation and compromise to resolve differences in order that workers can earn their daily bread and employers can operate their firms at a profit. But at Kohler, there were many factors which seem, in retrospect, to have made a showdown inevitable.

One of the factors which made industrial relations at Kohler different from those of most firms was the difficulty its management had in understanding that some of their own workers actually desired to have a voice in shaping their destiny. Management's paternalism satisfied some of the workers, but by no means all of them. The inability or unwillingness to understand this fact led the Kohler Company to assume, or at least to charge, that "outside agitators" had stirred up trouble.* That practically all of the leadership and two thirds of the membership of KWA had voted to affiliate with the UAW-CIO did not seem to provide any clue to the Kohler management. Instead, it took refuge in the argument that the union had taken a strike vote and this justified the preparations that were made for the "defense" of the plant. The statements by the Kohler management representatives before the WERB, the NLRB and the McClellan Committee indicate that they believed a strike vote was tantamount to a strike and acted accordingly. The union leaders' counterclaim was that the company was determined not to bargain in good faith because it felt it could "break" the union.

The family-owned Kohler Company had been operated for three quarters of a century on a paternalistic, we-know-what-is-best-for-you-and-what-is-best-for-us basis. The managerial staff was comprised of men who shared the attitudes and outlook of the Kohlers under the militant leadership of Lyman C. Conger, attorney for the company and chairman of the negotiating committee.

---

* When journeymen carpenters struck for a ten-hour day in Boston, in 1825 the employer said, "We cannot believe this project to have originated with any of the faithful and industrious sons of New England but are compelled to consider it an evil of foreign growth."

No one, the management was convinced, should or could tell the owner of a company how to run it. They knew how much they could afford to pay and how much work an employee could be expected to do safely. They had successfully staved off an "outside" union in the thirties and had established a close relationship from 1933–49 with their own Kohler Workers Association.

The language in which Conger referred to the KWA leaders who had "defected" to the UAW revealed the underlying psychological interactions which were at least as important as any economic factors in the strike. He accused them of trying to "become militant labor leaders" and trying to further their own ambitions; "they brought Kohler employees more trouble than benefits in the last two years," he said, and "have been aping typical abusive CIO tactics for the past two years."

That the company had feared the union and felt justified in building up their own private arsenal, there was little doubt. They would not tolerate "interference" from their own employees or anyone else. They believed, adamantly, that no one could tell them whom to hire or fire; and once having established a position of *no compromise* in which they viewed themselves as embattled crusaders against "government and big labor" encroachment, any degree of accommodation meant losing face. Paul McMahon, writing for *The Milwaukee Journal*, recorded a description of Herbert V. Kohler by Conger:

> There is nothing stubborn about Herbert Kohler. You can get anything you want from him if you approach him on a friendship basis. Mr. Kohler likes to run his business by giving a good deal to all the workers but the worst way to get a deal from him is to try to scare him. A Kohler doesn't scare easy.[30]

John T. Ward appraised the situation in *The Baltimore Sun* thus:

> The Company is stung by the fact that its troubles have been heralded far beyond its once peaceful town, but it is buoyed up by the belief that it is "carrying the flag" for American business against socializing tendencies.[31]

In the calm, attractive environs of Kohler Village, with its fine schools and handsome auditorium (gift of the Kohlers, where concerts, lectures and plays such as only larger cities could generally boast were presented), the Kohlers undoubtedly felt that they were providing "the good life" not only for themselves but for a large segment of the Sheboygan community. Hard work, good stewardship, risk of private capital, and a good product for the market, they apparently believed, entitled them to assume all the responsibilities and decisions affecting their plant operations; entitled them, also, to the enjoyment of their handsome homes at Riverbend and in Kohler Village; and to the recognition, prestige and influence which accompanied all this. The Kohler family, and many others in the community, stoutly maintained: Take Kohler away from Sheboygan and what would you have?*

Kohler workers in 1954 still lived in the shadow of the 1934 strike and in the memories of its dead and wounded. The people of Kohler and Sheboygan communities, according to present-day standards, knew each other relatively well, and not even the Kohlers were insulated from the gossip, the jealousies, the facts and the misinformation which fed the emotions. These residual fears and the existence of the arsenal and the village special police were ever-present psychological facts of life for Kohler workers. Conger could testify that when he "worked in the enamel shop 36 years ago," he could work 8 hours and eat lunch on the run, but the Kohler employees knew that by modern standards, the working conditions were dirty, hot and physically exhausting.

The company's medical and legal staff fought each claim vigorously. The general awareness of the silicosis hazards in some of the departments and the company's refusal to let workers see their chest X rays, lest they become hypochrondriacs, contributed to the psychological insecurity prevalent among the employees. They knew that theirs was one of only a few plants of its kind where workers did not have an independent union. When grievances were put off, or were not satisfactorily settled, the discontent and resentment grew. Moreover, it was common knowledge that workers who showed independence or talked about an "outside" union, were warned and threatened by the foremen and supervisors. Their sense of dignity and worth was offended, and they blamed the company for penuriousness and a lack of concern for them as people.

* When the UAW checked reported incomes for Kohler Company officials in 1949 (Appleton office of the Wisconsin Tax Department) they found: H. V. Kohler $224,813.44; John M. Kohler $180,960.00; Carl J. Kohler $156,220.47; and Oscar Kroos $127,343.48.

Most of the men who worked at Kohler never really were a part of the model village which was publicized near and far. To them this was the "Sunday face" the company presented to the world — a façade of progressivism covering what the union sarcastically dubbed Kohler's "horse and buggy industrial relations."

When contract negotiations were in session, Conger's constant reference to discussion of issues important to the union as "a waste of time" gradually built up an atmosphere of frustration and futility which made bargaining and negotiation impossible. There were economic issues at stake as well: seniority, wages, rates, pensions, insurance, checkoff of dues, et cetera. These were the tangible issues over which the sparring took place. But to this observer, the psychological issues were the weighty determinants in the struggle which culminated in the union's decision to strike.

Workers who have joined unions in most major industries have achieved a sense of dignity and belonging that is absent when there is no organization and the worker's future and security depends upon the employer's decisions. There are instances where unorganized firms have paid as high, or higher, wages than unionized firms — perhaps to get and hold qualified workers — but the ingredient of the psychological security which a union provides is missing. Dale Yoder, Professor of Industrial Relations at Stanford University, writes:

> The whole practice of collective bargaining has developed about the theory that the individual employee as such is an ineffective participant in most labor markets. He has, according to this viewpoint, neither the knowledge nor the resources to discover and take advantage of the best opportunities for disposing of his services. For him to act as an individual under these circumstances tends to result in a less effective application of his labor and, as a result, a lower level of compensation for these services.[32]

Many a worker in unorganized plants goes through life with a grudge, feeling he'd like to "tell the boss off," but he seldom gets up courage to do it because of the factors discussed by Yoder. Union organizers often remark that "the foreman is the best union organizer we've got in the plant," meaning that when plant conditions are difficult or intolerable, workers are much more inclined to seek the protection afforded by a union and united action. This factor played a prominent role at Kohler, both in the formation of an outside union and the willingness to strike.

Leo Breirather, whose father had been a caretaker at the Walter J. Kohler estate during the thirties and who had first gone to work for the company in the fall of '34 when the first strike was in progress, described some of the conditions, as he viewed them, which contributed to the sentiment within the KWA for an "outside" union, and a strike if necessary. He attributed his taking a job as a strikebreaker to youthful "innocence" as he discussed dissatisfaction in the enamel shop, safety hazards, company surveillance of union activity, inadequate grievance procedures, et cetera.[33] When the union complained to the Wisconsin Industrial Commission about safety hazards in the plant, management refused to let union representatives accompany the state inspector around the plant and instead, said Breirather, "conducted him on a guided tour through the plant and we rarely ever heard of what happened. . . . Certainly this did not satisfy the people in the plant. It was one of the determining factors of why they voted for a stronger union and eventually to strike."[34]

Although wages were not the paramount issue in the dispute, there were conflicting claims as to whether the Kohler Company led the field in the plumbing industry or lagged behind. Conger pointed out:

> . . . Kohler has since, around 1936, reported its wages to the State's Industrial Commission, which passed them on to its bureau of labor statistics. He added that matching the Company's overall wage averages against those of the State, Milwaukee County, Sheboygan and various Wisconsin communities, was, although "not completely satisfactory," the only accurate way of making such a comparison. . . . Conger, singling out the enamel shop, reported that at the time of the strike, the pay there averaged about $2.50 per hour; at present, he said, it is $2.90 to $2.95 per hour.[35]

Statistics supplied the McClellan Committee by Emil Mazey challenged Conger's contentions. Mazey declared:

> At Kohler [1954], an enameler of large ware received $2.64 per hour, at American Standard, $3.25 and at Universal Rundle $3.60; an enameler of small ware at Kohler, $1.78, Rundle $2.60, and Briggs Beautyware, a third competitor located in Detroit, $2.36 . . .[36]

Arguments became more heated as the negotiations continued, although certain areas of agreement had been reached by February 26.

There was agreement on a "no strike or lockout during the life of the contract" clause; however, the union sought a subsection which would limit the ability of the company to subcontract work normally done by its own employees. On this no agreement could be reached. The union sought a checkoff of union dues as a part of a standard union-shop clause, a feature bitterly opposed by the company. The company proposed changes in the arbitration clause of the contract which caused the union to assert that such proposals "eliminate arbitration for all practical purposes." One proposal made by the company read:

> Proceeding with an arbitration proceeding shall not be deemed to be a waiver by either party of its right to challenge any ruling or award of an arbitrator on the ground that this is in excess of his jurisdiction or that the matter is not subject to arbitration.

The issues in dispute are, as a rule, spelled out specifically by labor and management during early steps in the grievance procedure; since the union is usually in the position of "asking" and the company of "giving," it is usually the union that decides whether to go to arbitration, with both sides paying half the costs. Unions generally will not risk the costs of arbitration unless they believe they have a good case.

The company wanted the contract to specify that no International * time-study man could visit the plant to make a time study on a disputed rate. The union agreed that any such request would be subject to the fourth step in the grievance procedure but not to arbitration.[37] No agreement was reached on the rights of temporary employees, but they did agree on "shift transfers." The company and the union agreed to a 10-per-cent deviation from seniority in layoffs, subject to the fourth step in the grievance procedure.† The union also wanted the right to go to arbitration on this issue, but the company refused.

---

* i.e., UAW staff man.
† The last step in the grievance procedure, before arbitration — in which the grievance goes before the top union and the top management representatives.

The 1953 contract had provided for a 90-day recall list on seniority. The union wanted to strengthen this provision but could not reach agreement. No agreement was reached on a clause for "transfers from department to department." The union originally asked for job posting and bidding for advancement, and later asked that promotions be made on the basis of ability to perform the work *and* seniority. The company wanted seniority to be considered only if other factors were substantially equal. They further proposed that, if the union objected to their choice for a job opening, it would be subject to the grievance procedure, but not arbitration. The union proposed an additional clause which would guarantee that no chief steward would be transferred involuntarily out of line of seniority, but the company would not agree.

There was some give and take with regard to a clause on "notification of discharges," but they could not agree on going to arbitration on unresolved differences.[38] The articles on "Leaves of Absence" and "Sick Leave" proposed by the union encountered resistance from the company. The 1953 contract, Article VI, Section 5, stated in part, "Female employees who become pregnant may be required to terminate their employment after five months of pregnancy." The union sought a one-year maternity leave for the new contract, but no agreement was reached on this section. Section 6 on "Military Service" was undisputed and remained the same as in the 1953 contract. General agreement was reached on Article VII, "Premium and Overtime Rates," but not on Article VIII, dealing with "Standards and Rates." Articles XIII, "Emergency work," and XIV, "Recess and Washup" were satisfactory to both parties, but the company would not go along with the union's request for a 4-per-cent wage increase and lunchtime allowance for the enamel shop.

The union suggested a section prohibiting supervisors from performing work of employees covered by the contract, except in case of emergency or for instruction purposes, but the company did not agree.

The union had first asked for a general 20-cents-an-hour wage increase, while the company's first offer included no wage change, although later, a 3-cent increase was offered contingent upon the union's acceptance of the company's contract proposals and continuance of the company's insurance and pension program. The company felt strongly enough about limiting the role of arbitration so that it offered 3 cents in wage increases if the union agreed to a weakening of the 1953 arbitration clause. In making the 3-cent offer, the company insisted that the union must accept the company's interpretation of the old contract on all issues. They also proposed that the old contract be extended for a year with no wage increases.

Both parties used the press and radio to make charges against each other while negotiations were being carried on.

A conciliator from the Federal Mediation and Conciliation Service met with the negotiating teams from March 3 to 8 and then requested that both sides put their positions in writing. The company responded to the union statement of position by saying, "You have our final position," and the union announced that it had also reached its basic position and was going to take a strike vote on March 14.

Further meetings were held on March 17, 18 and 19 with no substantial progress. By April 3 the positions of both parties had become so fixed that a strike was inevitable. Harvey Kitzman suggested that "articles of war" be drawn up (for care of pottery furnaces, etc.) to prevent any damage to the plant. He suggested that the union was prepared to agree on the number of maintenance employees who would be allowed to pass the picket lines, but Lyman Conger rejected the proposal, declaring the intention of the company to continue operations within the plant without the union's help.[39] Kitzman testified before the McClellan Committee:

> I was pleading with them, since there obviously was going to be a strike here, that we ought to sit down as men and agree on some rules. . . . And the Company management asked me, "What are you talking about, rules of War?" and I said, "Yes, that is what this is, rules of war."[40]

The Company's Position

The company's position can perhaps best be presented by excerpts from speeches and publications prepared for the general public. Herbert V. Kohler, president of the company, gave an address to the Freedom Club of the First Congregational Church of

Los Angeles, April 17, 1956 (after the strike was 2 years old), entitled "In Freedom's Cause – the Menace of UAW-CIO Coercion."

. . . I am deeply appreciative of this opportunity to reaffirm my right of free speech, given to me by the Constitution, and reestablished by the Taft-Hartley Act. . . .

The issue at Kohler Co. is not collective bargaining on wages, hours and working conditions.

We acknowledge the employee's right to join a labor union and to be represented by a union if he so chooses.

Our wages exceed those for our industry, for the State of Wisconsin, and for Milwaukee County, and greatly exceed those for the neighboring city of Sheboygan. . . .

The UAW-CIO did not come to Kohler with the high purpose of protecting down-trodden workingmen. They came to a company where physical working conditions are exemplary, where real wages had been maintained and earnings were high, to a field which appeared ripe for a harvest of dues.

In a Labor Board election in 1952 the UAW won by a bare majority displacing a local independent union.

When the UAW first won the bargaining rights, we hoped for a time that we would be able to get along better with the "professionals. . . ."

The principal demand was for some form of "union shop" – *i.e.*, compulsory unionism.

It is our belief that the company has no more right to force an employee to join a union to get or hold a job than it has to prohibit his joining a union. Kohler Co. is opposed to any form of compulsory unionism.

The widespread public support of our position in this respect has caused the union to drop this demand temporarily.

But, and make no mistake about it, this issue is never abandoned. The UAW-CIO is as violently opposed as ever to "right-to-work laws."

The union's demands for increased power included:
— No shop rules to be established except with the union's agreement.
— Work schedules to be fixed by agreement with the union, with no increase or reduction of hours except with the union's approval.

— The union to have control of what work should be done by the company and what work should be sub-contracted.

— Automatic wage progression with elimination of merit increases in "non-incentive" day-work pay.

— Super-seniority for union officials and shop stewards.

— Strict seniority with no regard to competence and reliability in promotion to better jobs — in transfers, in layoffs and recalls.

— Arbitration of practically everything except wages. . . .

In closing may I give you a summary of our basic position as it appears in the preface to the April 1955 issue of the *Kohler News:*

"Unions have been vested with great power by law, which lends aid to their organization and to their bargaining. Union leaders who exercise this power recklessly and improvidently cannot disavow responsibility for the consequences.

"We take exception to union abuses, not to unions per se. The practices of some unions, briefly here stated, we believe threaten industry, the economy, and our country.

"*Discounting the Individual* — The dignity and worth of the American workman is theoretically stressed by unions. The theory is valid — the practice is often exactly the opposite.

"Strict seniority without regard to individual merit — equal pay for unequal work — these and similar bargaining demands of union leaders treat the workmen en masse, not as individuals.

"*Compulsory Unionism* — Neither the union nor the employer can justifiably usurp the individual employee's right to judge for himself the worth of a union's services to him.

"*Inflation* — Demands for 'gains' not justified by increase in production only promote inflation. To increase wages before an increase in production occurs does not benefit the workman whose 'gains' are wiped out by price increases. Industry must not be burned out by the forced draft of inflation.

"*Joint Management* — Union demands for joint management, or at least a veto power over the decision of management, if granted would destroy responsibility and make the economy sterile. The law calls for collective bargaining — not for joint management, something entirely different.

" '*Pattern*' *Settlements* — The strength of American industry is in its diversification. There is no more reason for regimentation in industrial relations than in manufacturing techniques or in any other industrial practice.

"*Coercion and Violence* — Goon squads, mass picket lines, physical assaults, destruction of property, attacks on workmen's homes and intimidation of their families are the acts of gangsters and hoodlums — not of the American workman.

"The Class Struggle — The promotion of class hatred and class warfare aids only those who would supplant our economy with a socialist economy. Union leaders who convince the workman that his employer is his natural enemy — that his interests call for 'militancy' and constant conflict — serve only the Marxian doctrine.

"These are typical UAW-CIO abuses. All unions do not indulge in these practices to an equal degree, if at all. But their prevalence calls for serious consideration by every citizen, union member or not, as to where these practices will lead us. . . ."

In a talk before the Economic Club of Detroit, February 25, 1957 — the text of which was attractively printed and widely distributed to university professors and others — Herbert V. Kohler asserted:

The right to strike is a legal right. I would not wish that right denied. But — does the right to strike override all other legal rights in this country? To what extent are unions to be especially privileged and above the law? And if they have special privileges and immunities, what will be the effect upon our economy?

The union shop was one of the demands we refused the UAW-CIO in bargaining for a second contract. We have strong convictions on that subject. They are continuing to grow stronger as some unions use funds from membership dues to finance political campaigns and propaganda with which a large part of their members do not agree. . . .*

* It should be pointed out that state laws of all the major industrial states permit unions and management to negotiate a "union shop" agreement which makes union membership a condition of employment.

Since U.S. labor law provides that whichever union wins a representation election in a plant must negotiate for all members of the bargaining unit and handle all grievances of the workers, union leaders have argued that all workers who share in the benefits should contribute their share toward the cost of maintaining the organization. The U.S. Bureau of Labor Statistics reports that over four fifths of union members work under union-shop conditions.

The Taft-Hartley Act of 1947 outlaws the use of union dues for political action which might influence the outcome of any Federal election. Unions do collect voluntary COPE (Committee on Political Education) contributions and unions do buy tickets to political dinners, a practice which has not been seriously challenged even though the cost of the ticket is more than that of the food served.

It should also be noted that Kohler in this 1957 talk, still linked the UAW with the CIO, presumably because it was more militant or aggressive, even though it had merged with the AFL in December, 1955, and become the UAW-AFL-CIO.

The April, 1955, issue of *Kohler of Kohler News* made reference to the "UAW-CIO mob," "imported goons," "hoodlums," "lawlessness," "violence on the picket line," coercion, sulphuric-acid damage, paint bombs, beatings, slashed tires, smashed windows, vandalism, "refusing to bargain under duress," et cetera.

The Union's Position

The UAW International Union and its Local 833 presented their position in a pamphlet published September, 1955, entitled *The Kohler Worker's Story*:

Before we get into the story, we would like to get the demands clearly established. Kohler Co. has just one basic demand on the Union — that it cease to exist. Kohler workers believe the root cause of the strike is the Company's fanatical hatred of unions and its willingness to go to almost any length to deprive its workers of their right to join a bona fide trade union.

To that end, Kohler Co. announced that 90 men will "never" be rehired. The discharged men include every officer, every Local 833 Executive Board member, every steward except one (who has been out of town since the strike started), and most of the chairmen of the various strike committees . . . in other words, everybody in leadership. These 90 individuals have worked for Kohler Co. for a combined total of more than 1,000 years.

Late this past July, Kohler Co. told the Federal Mediation and Conciliation Service the only basis for settling the strike would be by leaving the present scab force intact. It said it would call back a "minimum" of 500 strikers.

Kohler Co.'s chief spokesman, Lyman Conger, puts it quite bluntly: "Frankly (we) would not grieve to see Local 833 broken in this struggle."

The 7 basic issues which the pamphlet recapitulates are:

1. *Arbitration* — The Union asks for a standard arbitration-grievance procedure including arbitration of disciplinary action and discharges. . . .

2. *Seniority* — Kohler workers are asking for full seniority protection. . . .

3. *Wage Increase* — Local 833 originally asked for a 20-cent general increase plus an additional 10 cents for skilled trades workers as

a step toward bringing Kohler rates in line with those paid elsewhere in the industry. In the hope of expediting bargaining, it reduced its demand to 10 cents across the board plus an additional nickel for skilled trades. . . .

4. *Pensions* — Kohler workers are asking for non-contributory pensions such as are standard in the automobile, steel, rubber and most of the plumbingware industry. . . .

5. *Lunch Period for Enamel Shop* — Enamelers are entitled to the same company-paid 20-minute lunch period received by workers on other 3-shift operations. . . .

6. *Really 90 More Issues* — Local 833 members demand that the 90 strike leaders discharged by the Company . . . during the strike . . . be returned to the seniority lists . . . and that all be returned to their jobs when the strike is over.

7. *When the Strike Ends,* every striker must have his job back. The more than 2,000 on strike have a combined total of more than 23,000 years of seniority.

Kohler Co. has offered to take back a "minimum" of 500 workers; demands that the strikebreaking force be left intact. . . .

Heading for a Showdown

Only three grievances were taken to arbitration during the one-year life of the 1953 contract; the union won two and lost one. Local 833 leadership believed that winning recognition and bargaining rights could well be the beginning of a new era in labor relations at Kohler. Some fairly good provisions had been included in KWA's last contract, but there was no aggressive enforcement of the contract terms. The company management, on the other hand, resented the KWA officers helping win the election for the UAW, and to management's dismay and irritation, the leadership of the new UAW union showed more aggressiveness in enforcing the somewhat weaker terms which had been negotiated.[41] Concepts such as "union shop" and "arbitration" were red flags to the company, and as later events witnessed, reinforced their determination to get rid of the union. During negotiations, before the strike vote was taken, the company again erected the shanties and spotlights on top of the plant buildings — an act which the union interpreted as preparation for "war."

The UAW made arrangements with Petersen's tavern near Kohler for a strike headquarters where coffee and food could be prepared for the pickets if a strike were called. It had made similar arrangements the previous year before an agreement had been reached with the company. The Kohler Company's "defense budget" provided for the purchase of tear gas and ammunition. Both sides intensified propaganda campaigns with ads in *The Sheboygan Press;* and the distorted image each side had of the other culminated in a climate in which a confrontation and showdown was bound to come.

The final stumbling block in negotiations was the fear on the part of the union that an ineffective clause on discipline and discharge, with no chance to have an arbitrator decide what was proper in this area, could lead to the defeat of the union. After many hours of sitting together with company representatives and Federal conciliators, during which no agreement could be reached, the union called a strike for April 5, 1954.

5

THE FIRST YEAR OF THE SECOND STRIKE

AS SOON as the decision to strike became definite on April 3, phones at union headquarters began ringing; excitement mounted and serious plans were undertaken for conducting a massive but orderly strike. Conger had told Kitzman that the company intended to operate with whatever loyal employees it could get to work and the union, viewing this as a strikebreaking threat, was determined to keep nonstrikers, other than office workers and company executives, out of the plant. The dance hall at Petersen's Tavern, a popular hangout for Kohler workers, about a half-mile east of the plant on the Lower Falls Road, was converted into a "soup kitchen" and strike headquarters.

Mass Picketing

Emotions ran high as over 2,000 pickets assembled at the company gates at five o'clock on the morning of April 5. This turnout on the picket line was an obvious show of union solidarity and determination to "close the plant" until a contract settlement was reached. The company had alleged that the strike was called by a minority led by "outsiders," a technique described in the "Mohawk Valley Formula" (*see* Appendix). It made the union members more determined to show the company that a large majority supported the union. According to Allan J. Graskamp, president of Local 833, practically all pickets were employees of the Kohler Company and only 12 to 15 came from other locals and the UAW International Union to help the local with its strike.[1] Kitzman, Sahorske, Majerus, Ferrazza, Rand, Fiore, Barber, Burkart and Wallick were the only "outsiders" on hand during the first day of the strike. Although there were a total of 8 entrances to the plant, the largest number of pickets gathered on the west side at High Street entrances. Picket captains were assigned to each gate and pickets served 4-hour shifts starting at 5:00 A.M. Picket signs were carried with slogans such as: " '34 Was Before the War, We'll

*Petersen's Tavern on the Lower Falls Road, showing the large hall at
the rear which was used as strike headquarters and soup kitchen in the
1954 strike.*

be Free in '54," "Pensions — Not Tensions," "We are Stronger than
L. C. Conger!" "We Want Seniority," "Injunctions Won't Build
Bathtubs!"

The presence of such large numbers of pickets at the gates made
it virtually impossible for anyone to penetrate the lines and get into
the plant. There was singing and shouting among the pickets as
the special police patrolled the streets. Any attempts on the part of
small groups of workers to enter the plant were met with massive
resistance.

During the first days of the strike, a close walking formation
termed "belly to back" was used, to keep nonstrikers and the
deputies who attempted to escort them from penetrating the lines.
With pickets standing 10 to 12 deep at the main gates, whoever came
up to the picket line was bound to be pushed back; those in the
front line of pickets were unable to avoid bodily contact even if
they had wanted to, because of all the pushing and shoving done
by picketers behind them. Later Robert Burkart was to tell the
McClellan Committee that moving pictures prepared by the company did not give "this committee a fair representation of what
occurred on that picket line at all. . . . I have seen more violence

in the New York subway than I saw in the Kohler picket lines," he maintained.

The mass picketing effectively kept the plant from operating for 54 days, even though several hundred persons, mostly management and supervision staff, slept and lived in the plant, to perform necessary maintenance functions and assist in various activities designed to break the strike. Company personnel with still and movie cameras equipped with telephoto lenses were present, taking pictures of activities on the picket line. Some pickets — irked by the omnipresent company photographers — brought mirrors with which to flash light into the cameras. Attempts were made with microphone and tape recorders to pick up conversations on the picket line, but with limited success. An "incident file" was started into which went all kinds of tidbits of information about the activities of hundreds of strikers both on and away from the picket line. Many Kohler workers and their families received telephone calls — from supervisory personnel, urging them to return to work, and from union members, asking them to stay out of the plant until the strike was settled — at times accompanied by abusive language and threats. Homes of some nonstrikers were picketed in an attempt to get them to join the union's ranks.

The war was on and both sides resorted to activities and tactics which they considered most helpful for their cause. Both sides aired their position via radio station WHBL and the *Sheboygan Press*. The union also published a mimeographed daily *Strike Bulletin*.

When the strike was one week old, Chief of Police Capelle urged Sheriff Theodore Mosch to assist him in opening the picket lines with tear gas. Mosch, remembering what had happened when tear gas was used in 1934, refused to co-operate in this venture.[2]

From the first day of the strike, the company contended that the mass picketing was illegal and strengthened their determination not to deal with "criminals and goons." One section of the Wisconsin law on which the company based its position reads:

343.683 *Preventing pursuit of work.* Any persons who by threats, intimidation, force or coercion of any kind shall hinder or prevent any other person from engaging in or continuing any lawful work of employment, either for himself or as a wage-worker, or who shall attempt to so hinder or prevent shall be punished by fine not

Picket line in the early morning on April 12, 1954, in front of company's main offices. Man in dark coat (center left) walking toward Police Chief Capelle is Harvey Kitzman, regional director of the UAW. (Sheboygan Press *photo*)

exceeding $100 or by imprisonment in the discretion of the court. Nothing herein contained shall be construed to prohibit any person or persons off of the premises of such work or employment from recommending, advising or persuading others by peaceful means to refrain from working at a place where a strike or lockout is in progress.

When this statute was read into the McClellan Committee record, Local 833 president Graskamp replied:

May I say, Mr. Chairman, that as far as I am concerned, this [mass picketing] is no more against the Wisconsin law than the illegal possession of tear gas and riot guns is against the law.[3]

The above statement provides a key to an understanding of

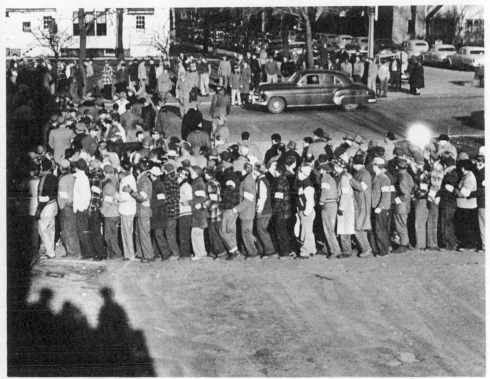

Picket line at employment office gate 6:30 A.M., April 12. Pickets block gate "belly-to-back" as nonstrikers across street prepare to go through line. Note spot of light (right) — a mirror flashing at camera lens of company photographers whose shadows from employment office building appear at lower left. (Paul Jacobi photo, courtesy of W. Capelle)

the second long conflict at Kohler. The company could see only the illegality of the mass picketing by the union, but claimed there was nothing wrong with its acquisition of tear gas and guns to combat the union and its "goons," if necessary; the union viewed the strike preparations of the company — which included moving cots, food and a cook stove into the plant while negotiations were still in session — as an effort to break the union and was convinced that mass picketing was the only way it could protect the jobs of its members — *i.e.*, keeping the minority who wanted to work and any strikebreakers from operating the plant until the strike was settled — even though the state outlawed mass picketing. Although the union eventually lost ground, for a time it appeared as if an irresistible force had met an immovable object.

Company Asks WERB to Intervene — Union Turns to NLRB

When the strike was ten days old (April 15), the Kohler Company filed an appeal with the Wisconsin Employment Relations Board[4] charging the union with mass picketing, and with violation of Section 111.06(2)(a) of the Wisconsin Employment Peace Act "by picketing the domicile of persons desiring to work at the Kohler Company," and of Section 111.06(2)(f) "by hindering and preventing persons desiring to be employed at the Kohler Company by means of massed picketing and by means of obstructing and interference with entrance to and egress from the plant. . . ." There had been gatherings at homes and anonymous phone calls urging nonstrikers not to go to work. The union argued that the company had waited ten days before filing the appeal with the WERB so it could strengthen its case by taking pictures and preparing individual "spy files" on hundreds of pickets, rather than relying on the fact of mass picketing per se.

While the Kohler Company was preparing to take its case to the WERB in Madison, Wisconsin, the UAW turned to the Federal Court to seek NLRB jurisdiction in the dispute. Max Raskin of Milwaukee, attorney for the Wisconsin CIO Council, acting on behalf of the United Auto Workers CIO and its Kohler affiliate, Local 833, appeared before Federal Judge Robert E. Tehan, in Milwaukee, on April 27, and asked that court to bar the WERB from considering the Kohler Company's charges of strike violence and mass picketing. In its petition for a Federal injunction, the union asserted that the WERB lacked jurisdiction in the case because the Kohler Company was engaged in interstate commerce, and that the NLRB, a Federal agency, should assume jurisdiction. Judge Tehan ordered a hearing for May 3. Lyman C. Conger, chairman of the company's negotiating committee, charged that this was "a deliberate stall for time in the hope that the illegal and indefensible picketing may be prolonged, pending the hearings."[5]

The issue came before the WERB on May 4. Chairman Lawrence E. Gooding suggested that a WERB decision would not resolve the Kohler issues and urged the parties to try to settle the strike. Conger replied, "I just want it understood right now that many of the strikers are not going to be hired back because of their acts."[6] He said he was not going to trade negotiations for compliance with 'the law and that the company would not bargain with the union so long as it was conducting a strike illegally.[7] Max Raskin reported that, on the day before (May 3), he had appeared in Federal Court in Milwaukee to request that any action by the WERB be enjoined and that Judge Tehan had asked that briefs be filed by the WERB, the company and the unions. Raskin requested that the WERB hearing be postponed for a week. Conger objected, saying that the Federal Court could have filed an injunction to stop the hearing "had it felt so, but did not do so."

At the hearing on May 3, after considerable discussion, Judge Tehan proposed a truce which provided for a restriction on the number picketing at any one time and the resumption of bargaining by the company and union.

Gooding, at the WERB hearing on May 4, likewise proposed that the company and the union resume bargaining and that the union agree to certain limitations on picketing. The union representatives agreed to recommend acceptance of Gooding's proposal to the membership on condition that the company engage in *bona fide* collective bargaining. On May 5, the union membership voted to accept the conditions of "truce," but authorized the executive board of the union to discontinue the truce if the company "failed to live up to its commitment."[8] Picket lines were drastically reduced in numbers and the gates were unobstructed the weekend of May 7, in hope that bargaining could be resumed and the strike settled. The case was recessed because the WERB and Governor Walter J. Kohler, Jr., nephew of Herbert V. Kohler, were anxious to have the dispute settled.[9]

The first bargaining session, after the strike began, convened May 7. Burkart raised the question of health insurance, suggesting some improvements, whereupon Conger said, "If that is your position, we are right back where we were on February 2 and any agreements made in the interim period are washed out."

"If you are back there," Ferrazza replied, "we are back there too."[10]

After some discussion, Burkart's position — that negotiations continue from the point of breakoff on April 3, with all interim agreements intact — prevailed. When negotiations got down to main issues, spokesmen for the company stated that they had given the union their final offer prior to the strike and that they had nothing further to offer. When the union representatives suggested that negotiations continue that evening (Friday) and over the weekend, company representatives objected strongly, saying they "did not want to submit to any wearing-down process," and that they were "not going into lengthy marathon sessions."[11] Further-more, they said, they also had to prepare briefs which were to be in the hands of Federal Judge Tehan by May 10 or 11.

At a membership meeting called outside Petersen's Tavern on Sunday, May 9, Union President Graskamp reported on the com-pany's refusal to bargain over the weekend; the strikers voted to call off the truce and to resume mass picketing on Monday morn-ing. Union leaders feared that nonstrikers and others looking for work would resume production in the plant and thus weaken the union's chances for an early settlement. Monday morning, the Federal conciliators and the union representatives waited in vain for the company's representatives to appear at a negotiation session which had been set for that day.[12]

On May 14, the arguments on the injunction proceedings in Federal Court were concluded, after which Judge Tehan invited the spokesmen for both parties into his chambers.[13] The judge was provoked by statements in the press to the effect that the company was using the filing of briefs before the U.S. District Court as an excuse for not continuing bargaining after May 7. He told Conger, "You know our rules are quite flexible and if you wanted an ad-journment on the filing of briefs, you could have gotten it for days and months; if this would help settle the strike, that is a more im-portant thing than the filing of briefs."[14]

Judge Tehan endeavored to help settle the strike by proposing:

1. that the Union agree to the reinstatement of the picketing limitations of the "truce" (not more than 200 pickets or more than 25 at one gate)

2. that the Union scale down its wage demands, and

3. that the Company indicate willingness to modify its position on arbitration, seniority, insurance and wages.[15]

Sheriff Mosch (white hat) and deputies endeavored to get nonstrikers (foreground left and right) through picket line at employment office but met good-natured but determined line of pickets. Man in dark jacket (foreground) is Don Rand of the UAW. (Sheboygan Press photo)

Conger stated that he saw nothing new or different in the proposal and that he was there on a legal case and not to make any commitments. Union representatives caucused and then informed Gooding of WERB that the "Tehan formula" was acceptable to them — that they were prepared to reduce the number of pickets and to cut their wage demands from 20 cents to 10 cents per hour providing "that there was some movement" [on the part of the company].[16] Conger resented Tehan's intercession. He labeled it "uncalled for" because it prescribed a willingness to change position.[17]

WERB hearings resumed on May 12 and continued May 13, 17, 18 and 19. On May 21 the board released its decision, found the union guilty of mass picketing and ordered it to cease and desist from:

1. Coercing or intimidating any person desiring to be employed by the Kohler Company in the enjoyment of his legal rights, intimi-

*The Sheboygan County courtroom, as the WERB held hearings on the
company's mass picketing charges against the union. On bench in
foreground (left to right) are Herbert V. Kohler, speaking with Edmund J. Biever, the plant manager. Fourth from left is Arthur Bauer,
then William Rawlings and Allan Graskamp, all officers of Local 833,
UAW. (Sheboygan Press Photo)*

dating his family, picketing his domicile, or injuring the person or
property of such persons or his employe.

2. Hindering or preventing by mass picketing, threats, intimidation, force or coercion of any kind the pursuit of lawful work or
employment by any person desirous of being employed by the
Kohler Company.

3. Obstructing or interfering in any way with entrance to and
egress from the premises of the Kohler Company.

4. Obstructing or interfering with the free and uninterrupted use
of public roads, streets, highways, railways or private drives leading
to the premises of the Kohler Company.

The WERB order further ordered the respondent unions,
their officers, members and agents to "limit the number of pickets

An incident on the picket line before employment office; it was considered one of the "peaks" of "violent" action; a deputy had just been knocked down and assisted to his feet. News photographers are at rear of crowd. Target pinned on man's back in foreground refers to shooting of strikers in the '34 strike. There are at least 10 law enforcement officers and a number of women in the crowd. (C. Pagnucco, courtesy of W. Capelle)

around the Kohler Company premises to a total of not more than 200, with not more than 25 at any one entrance. . . ."

In the memo accompanying the order the three WERB commissioners stated:

> We are thoroughly convinced after spending an entire day in conference with the parties and after listening to some five days of testimony that neither the employer nor the union are free from fault. . . .
>
> The union readily agreed that the company had a legal right to operate its plant as it desired and was able during the time of the strike and that persons desiring to enter or leave the premises should have free access thereto.
>
> By the same token the employer agreed that the union and its

The most widely publicized picture of the strike. Moments after this picture was taken, a nonstriker was arrested for disorderly conduct, in a scuffle with deputies. This picture appeared on the cover of the April, 1954, Kohler of Kohler News, *of which thousands of copies were printed and distributed by the Kohler Company, and at least 50,000 copies were reportedly sold for scrap paper.* (Milwaukee Sentinel photo)

members were entitled to picket and to advise the public of the facts of the strike and demonstrate the solidarity of the employes. While the parties were unable to agree on the mechanics by which these premises could be implemented, the Board laid down certain conditions, largely limitations on the type of picketing theretofore conducted, that if accepted by the union would result in a continuance of the hearing. The conditions laid down by the Board were accepted by the union.

Acceptance of such conditions was contingent on the company agreeing that it would immediately commence bargaining with representatives of the union in a bona fide attempt to reach a mutually satisfactory collective bargaining agreement. . . . At the conclusion of the Friday conference, notwithstanding that the Federal mediators were willing, and the union representatives were desirous, of

Sheriff Mosch (in white hat) talking with Don Rand, UAW staff, as Chief Capelle — who regarded the hour 6 to 7 A.M. as a "strenuous morning workout" — endeavored to assist nonstrikers through the line with the assistance of a deputy (wearing glasses, hat, gloves). Note company photographers at upper right center, on top of low building. (Milwaukee Sentinel photo)

continuing the negotiations both on Saturday and Sunday if necessary, the company representatives arbitrarily refused to bargain on either of those days. This refusal on the part of employer representatives, appearing to the executive board of the union to be arbitrary and without reason, caused the union to again resort to the law of the jungle. Union representatives announced their withdrawal from the truce agreement, again commenced to block driveways, and to forcibly prevent persons desiring to enter the plant from entering. . . .

We are thoroughly satisfied that had the company representatives honestly desired to arrive at a settlement of the dispute, they would have been anxious to continue to bargain and would honestly have tried to arrive at a settlement of the issues responsible for this unfortunate work stoppage. By the same token we do not condone the action of the union in deliberately engaging in activities they knew

After Herbert V. Kohler at the WERB hearings admitted "a strong suspicion" that there was tear gas in his plant, five hundred pickets needled him by wearing war-surplus gas masks on the picketline. Scotty Schrader, member of another Sheboygan union, tried a mask on his dog, Duchess. (Sheboygan Press photo)

to be illegal merely because they were of the belief that the action of company representatives in refusing to bargain on Saturday and Sunday constituted stalling tactics.

If such refusal on the part of the employer is wrongful and constituted a violation of the law, the union had a legal remedy which it was free to pursue and did not have to resort to the illegal tactics which it did resort to.

One very unusual and astounding incident occurred during this proceeding. There was testimony by the president of the company to the effect that the company had equipped and has in its plant a small arsenal. He testified that there were clubs and guns provided for in the plant. His testimony also indicated that either there were tear [gas] bombs provided for in the plant but if not the presence of tear gas bombs would have his approval.

With all the legislation on the books today, both Federal and State, aimed at protecting, not only the rights of employes and employers in labor disputes, but the rights of the public as well, it seems inconceivable that in a forward looking community in a state as progressive as the state of Wisconsin any employer would feel it necessary to resort to self help by the means of arms, ammunition and tear gas bombs. There is no possible justification for an employer today to resort to the use of such means in any strike.

If this dispute is ever to be settled it will be necessary that both sides make some concessions. . . .

It would seem to us that this work stoppage could most quickly be ended if both parties to the dispute would immediately recognize and respect the rights of the opposing party. We are convinced that the union can under no conditions win by engaging in attempting to prevent the operations of the plant by the use of force, violence, and other illegal actions. . . .

We believe that in order to settle this dispute first the union must see to it that the activities of their members comply with the law. Second, the employer must sit down with the union and bargain in good faith. . . .[18]

On May 24, some members of the union picketed the Hildebrand dock at Sheboygan where a clay boat * was being unloaded for the company. The company's next move was to boycott another bargaining session which had been scheduled by the Federal conciliators for the last week in May.[19] On May 28, the question of enforcement of the WERB's May 21 order came before Judge F. H. Schlichting's Court in Sheboygan. The union's attorney, Max Raskin, advised Judge Schlichting that the union would voluntarily comply with the order. After persistent efforts, Judge Schlichting persuaded Conger to agree to meet with union representatives on June 1, but Conger insisted that if, in his judgment, the union was not living up to the WERB order, he would again break off negotiations.[20]

Judge Schlichting announced an agreement reached by the parties, and approved by the Court, which provided a day-to-day adjournment of the enforcement order; a reconvening of the Court on 12 hours' telephone notice "if any violation occurs"; a final hearing on petition for enforcement on 24 hours' notice after June 8; and the resumption of negotiations on June 1.

On the next day, May 29, the company issued a statement published in *The Sheboygan Press*, that no commitment of any kind

* Imported clay is used in making porcelain plumbing fixtures.

had been made to get the union to comply with the WERB order; that the arrangement was not a "truce" in the sense of an agreement between the union and the company; and that the company "will make no concession to get the Union to obey the law."[21] The statement asserted that the obligation to bargain was to meet and confer in good faith. "It does not require either party to agree to a proposal and it does not require either to make a concession." On May 31, *The Milwaukee Journal* published a report of an interview with President H. V. Kohler, which reflected his viewpoint on collective bargaining: "You don't have to give them anything to bargain."

Enforcement of the WERB order which limited pickets to a total of 200 and not more than 25 per gate, with a 20-foot opening, meant that nonstrikers and newly hired strikebreakers could come and go as they wished with no interference except name-calling, as they passed through the opening in the lines. The 54-day shutdown of the plant was at an end and the company resumed as much of its production as it could with nonstriking employees and others recruited from surrounding communities and farms.

The Strike Bulletin

A daily strike bulletin * was distributed to the pickets as a way of disseminating news and keeping up morale. Rather quickly, the bulletin began referring to the plant as "the Fortress," the fence as "the cast-iron curtain," Herbert V. Kohler's presidential offices as "the Ivory Tower." Edmund J. Biever, the plant manager, was variously referred to as "Eager Biever" and "Field Marshal" Biever. Considerable interest was shown in what was taking place within the plant and in what Conger's next moves would be. The nonstrikers were alternately ridiculed for attempts to go through the lines, or cajoled in hope of getting them to join the pickets. Many of the items were rumors or pure speculation, as the union tried to second-guess the next moves of the company.

---

* Burkart put out the first two daily strike bulletins, after which Kohlhagen and Breirather took over. When Breirather became boycott coordinator, Harold Najacht and Peter Bichler co-edited the *Bulletin* for several months. Then Kohlhagen again had major responsibility for it, with Treuer and Breirather sharing editorship. Wallick and Treuer contributed articles occasionally; during the McClellan hearings, Treuer put out the publication. However, the responsibility for the *Bulletin* remained with Local 833.

Primarily intended for the strikers, the bulletin was widely distributed. The community was often irked by the references therein to individuals and groups in the community who were not supporting the strike or were unsympathetic. The daily cartoons which Hank Weber drew had an enormous morale-building effect. Weber, an enamel buffer at Kohler for nineteen years, caricatured the principals in the strike, portraying Kohler as "The Bathtub Baron," rotund, towering, cigar-chewing; Biever and Conger as gnomelike busybodies engaged in antiunion pursuits. Nonstrikers — the "scabs" — were represented by two lean, red-nosed, confused workers, "Ben" and "Arnold." Somewhere in nearly every cartoon was a horse — symbol of what the union labeled as "Kohler's horse and buggy" labor policies. One of the editors' gimmicks was a joking reference to union "spies" inside the plant variously dubbed "U-2," "Q-T," etc. The company later attempted to introduce this at NLRB hearings as evidence that the union was engaged in counterespionage against the company. The bulletin reported that Kohler's chauffeur had been seen buying "long johns" in a Sheboygan store. The editor mused as to whether or not he would dare call it a "union suit." This item, it was alleged, indicated that the union had been "surveilling" company personnel. Trial Examiner Downing rejected this and 32 similar exhibits.

On the Picket Line

The WERB order of May 21 stipulated that a 20-foot clearance be maintained at each plant entrance — an area promptly dubbed "Scab Alley." The union set out large pails of sand, 22 feet apart, to mark the limits for the pickets, and signs reading "Local 833 on Strike" were stuck in the pails or in piles of rocks accumulated to designate the limits. At one point Police Chief Cappelle substituted rubber traffic cones for the stationery objects. Graskamp explained that the pails and piles of stones also served as protection for pickets when nonstrikers drove through the gates at high speeds. The union also set out barrels on the sidewalks to collect rubbish such as paper cups, cigarette packages, sandwich bags, et cetera. (A station wagon made the rounds every two hours to provide the pickets with coffee, soup, sandwiches and doughnuts.) When Chief

Capelle objected to the barrels, he was asked, "What do we do then? Throw the paper on the road?" to which Capelle replied, "Oh my God, no!" and nothing further was said about the barrels.

The pickets, who took their shifts in all kinds of weather, were cheered by visits from union officials. Harvey Kitzman and Emil Mazey walked the line on a number of occasions. The Wisconsin CIO arranged for a long motorcade which visited Sheboygan on Sunday, April 25. A mass meeting of the strikers was addressed by Walter P. Reuther, president of the United Auto Workers-CIO on May 22. Radio station WHBL carried a daily union-sponsored "Strike Bulletin" broadcast, directed first by Frank Wallick and later by Bob Treuer.

As the strike wore on, picketing became a matter of demonstrating to the company and the public that a labor dispute still existed; the number participating gradually declined and activities became routine. The leadership of the union made a concerted effort to avoid assaults and violence. If the specter of the 1934 bloodshed haunted Sheriff Mosch and his deputies, it was also in the minds of the strikers. When Allan Graskamp was asked by Mrs. Beatrice Lampert, assistant attorney general, what he understood by the word "peaceful," he replied that it depended upon the situation. "I don't presume that 'peaceful' has the same meaning in a strike that it does at a Sunday-school picnic. On the other hand, I realize that 'peaceful' does not mean hitting anybody, or pushing anybody, or I don't suppose you have to say 'please.' . . ."

When a number of strikers were charged with disorderly conduct on the picket line in Justice Donald Koehn's court at Sheboygan Falls, William Quick, attorney for the union, said the "only weapon appearing on the line was the club carried by Herbert V. Kohler, president of the Company."[22] On the night of April 25, Kohler had approached the picket line with a billy club in his hand and was accosted by pickets who questioned his right to carry a club. He told them testily, "I am the law!"

The Sheboygan Press, on August 18, 1954, quoted District Attorney John Buchen as saying: "The picket line conduct has been good and I would like to compliment those in charge. It has been much better than in most cities where strikes have taken place."

Sheriff's Deputies

Sheriff Mosch, who had the responsibility for law enforcement throughout Sheboygan County, recruited about 30 additional deputies for his staff when the strike started. Some of them were sent out to Kohler early in the strike, but they were more concerned with preserving the peace than in opening the picket line.

In an unusual category of deputy sheriffs, were Edmund J. Biever, plant manager; Lyman C. Conger; Herbert V. Kohler; Walter J. Ireland, personnel director; Gilbert H. Buffington, assistant personnel director; and Heinz G. Mertes, H. V. Kohler's personal chauffeur; all of whom carried cards issued by the Sheboygan County sheriff's office designating them as deputies. Sheriff Mosch [23] verified that they had these cards for years and the appointments were automatically renewed when he took over the office.*

Forty-six days after the strike started (May 21), Sheriff Mosch wrote to the six company deputies:

Due to the present strike situation at the Kohler Company, I believe it unwise for me to have armed deputies within the plant proper.

I am therefore advising you that I am suspending your Deputy's authorization effective immediately. Please return your Deputy Sheriff's card to me as soon as possible.

I shall be more than happy to again reinstate you as a deputy if you desire whenever the strike is settled and the situation is back to normal. I feel this move is necessary not only for my own protection but also to serve the best interests of the citizens of Sheboygan County.

No release of this action will be made by me either to the press or radio so as not to cause any embarrassment to anyone concerned.

Mosch was taken to task by 5 of the 6 deposed deputies in a letter, dated May 24. (Heinz Mertes, the chauffeur, did not sign the letter):

This will acknowledge your letter of May 21, 1954, advising that you are suspending our deputies' authorization.

* According to Sheboygan County Clerk of Court, Walter J. Ireland, Sr., was deputized in 1933 and Herbert V. Kohler (and Carl J. Kohler) in 1939.

The coincidence of this action with union publicity of the fact that we were deputies makes your motives obvious. This, together with your failure to enforce the law over the past seven weeks, makes it evident that your purpose is something other than to secure better law enforcement.

You speak of this move being necessary "for my own protection."

We would think that "for your own protection" you would be concerned about the open and flagrant lawlessness which has prevailed in this county since the beginning of the strike, with little, if any, interference from your office.

Your own protection and the best interests of the citizens of Sheboygan in particular, have been violated day after day, at times in your personal presence. . . .

We would think that you would be embarrassed by the open praise of your inaction from the very people who have been found by a responsible state agency to be law violators.

At your request, we are herewith returning our deputy sheriff's cards. As you are well aware, these cards were issued for the purpose of assisting us to protect our persons and property, the safety of persons within the plant, the plant property, and the property of the United States Government within the plant, which we have a contractual obligation to protect.

Attempts to dissuade law-abiding citizens from exercising their legal rights or to disable them from providing for themselves the protection for their persons and property which you are unwilling or unable to provide will not make law enforcement any easier.

We and countless other citizens of this community do not intend to surrender our rights so that you may avoid your responsibilities.

As citizens and taxpayers, we demand that you enforce the law.

If you continue to fail to do so, we will take steps to see that the penalties for your failure are enforced.

Although you stated in your letter that no release of your action would be made by you to the press or radio, it has been announced by both; and therefore, we are making the contents of this letter public.[24]

Herbert V. Kohler's testimony before the Wisconsin Employment Relations Board had indicated that ammunition was stored in the plant. District Attorney John G. Buchen, at the request of the union, called for a John Doe investigation. The testimony established that Edmund J. Biever, plant manager, using his position as sheriff's deputy, had purchased ammunition and tear gas for the company. Sheriff Mosch maintained that he had not authorized the Kohler Company or the deputy in question to buy tear gas. He held the possession of tear gas by any deputy to be illegal, in the absence of the sheriff's permission.[25]

District Attorney Buchen held the opinion that company officials had violated "the spirit of the law" even though no crime was committed as long as the company personnel were "deputized."

When the company personnel were suspended as deputy sheriffs, the ammunition, weapons and tear gas stored in the factory were transferred to the custody of the village chief of police (May 22, 1954). A week later, under instructions from Attorney General Vernon Thompson, Sheriff Mosch, accompanied by Buchen, confiscated 11 boxes of tear-gas equipment, 8 of which still had shipping tags from Pittsburgh, Pa., dated April 8, 1954. The Village of Kohler had its own supply of ammunition, which it retained.

Tear Gas and Machine Guns — Available But Not Used

The tear gas that remained in the village hall continued to be a source of controversy for months to come. Early in June, Kitzman voiced the apprehension of the strikers when he said, ". . . as long as tear gas remains within a block of the Kohler main gate . . . Kohler still has the potential of a tear gas and guns labor policy."

In letters to Governor Walter J. Kohler, Jr., and Attorney General Vernon Thompson, Harvey Kitzman and Allan Graskamp questioned the legality of the village possession of tear gas. They wrote: "In view of the close ties between Kohler Village and Kohler Co., we believe the public interest can best be promoted by the transfer of Kohler Village tear gas equipment to a person or persons authorized to possess it."

Chief Capelle issued a reply which read, in part:

> It cannot be news to the Sheriff or the District Attorney of Sheboygan County that the Police Department of the Village of Kohler possesses tear gas. Both the sheriff and the district attorney were advised last week that the police department possesses tear gas.
>
> I consider tear gas as part of the standard equipment of any well-run Police Department.
>
> The Sheriff has been aware of this for several years. At one time,

On orders from the Wisconsin Attorney General's office, Sheriff Mosch confiscated 11 boxes of tear gas and equipment purchased by the company, but which had been turned over to the village when the company's right to have such materials was challenged. Chief Waldemar Capelle and District Attorney John Buchen look on. (Sheboygan Press *photo*)

at the Sheriff's request, I instructed him and his deputies in the proper use of tear gas.

The tear gas now in my possession was purchased long ago, on my recommendation. It is not a part of the tear gas placed in my custody by a deputy sheriff after his appointment was revoked. . . .[26]

While Police Chief Capelle contended that he had been advised by the village attorney that it was legal for village police officials to possess tear gas, District Attorney Buchen interpreted the law as restricting such possession to "any civil enforcement officer of the state or of any city or county." On Saturday, May 29, 1954, Allan Graskamp, Robert Burkart, David Rabinovitz, and Max Raskin had met with Wisconsin Attorney General Thompson and were advised that, in his opinion, a chief of police or a village may *not* possess tear gas or machine guns. In questioning the propriety of a deputy's acquiring tear gas and ammunition, the union representatives asked, "Does this mean that any lodge or labor union or any factory who happens to have a deputy, whether as a production worker, an office worker or of supervision, could they possess the items of tear gas, guns, automatic guns, riot guns or machine guns?"

The Wisconsin District Attorneys' Association, at its annual conference in June, 1954, adopted a resolution calling for an amendment to the state law so that village law-enforcement officers would be included among those who could possess tear gas and weapons. The Wisconsin legislature defeated the controversial "machine gun bill" by a vote of 70-25. But the debate over the legality of village law-enforcement officers possessing machine guns continued. Union attorneys continued to press the attorney general for more definitive interpretations. Finally, in January, 1956, Edwin M. Wilkie, executive counsel to Governor Kohler, who said the machine-gun issue had been referred to him for legal study, wrote Rabinovitz: "It seems to me your contention that Section 164.20 prevents village officials from possessing or using either automatic weapons or tear gas may be seriously questioned." He said village officers are duly constituted peace officers with responsibilities and duties in enforcing law, and as such, cannot be reasonably set apart from city, county or state law-enforcement officials so as to deprive them of means to enforce the law. The union was advised that it was entitled, however, to present facts of its case to any magistrate in Sheboygan County, who may issue a warrant if he concludes there is probable cause to believe a crime has been committed.[27]

The Capital Times [28] of Madison, Wisconsin, commented editorially:

> . . . Wilkie . . . is the candidate of the special interests who control the Republican party in this community as well as throughout the state . . . As a legal aid to Governor Kohler, he recently wrote an opinion that [it] is legal for the Village of Kohler, controlled by the Kohler Co., to possess tear gas and machine guns. Why should Kohler have machine guns and tear gas if not for use in labor controversies? What other village keeps such an arsenal?

A New Use for "Civilian Defense"

Kohler Police Chief Capelle, with the co-operation of the company, had organized an expanded "special police" force under the guise of a civilian-defense training program in 1952. The "civilian volunteers" selected by the chief of police were to assist regularly appointed police officers in the discharge of police duties in emergencies arising from "fires, floods, earthquakes, or other natural causes, or any destructiveness resulting from enemy attack, sabotage, or other hostile action."

Albert Braun, one of the special police, testified at a hearing in the Justice Court, Sheboygan County, before John Schneider, Jr., Justice, on April 30, 1954,[29] that he was told he would go on full-time duty "in the event that a strike was to take place." He got his special-police badge when he took the oath in the village hall. Lee Blandin, another Kohler employee who started work for the company in 1949, was sworn in as a special-police officer in a unit called "civilian defense" in the summer of 1952. Questioned by the NLRB Trial Examiner about the procedure he went through to be hired by the Kohler Police Department, he replied, "Well, it was assumed that if there would be a strike that we would be called full-time as police officers."

Ralph Feudner, one of the special police who lived in Kohler and had worked for the company for fourteen years, gave a statement to the union's attorney concerning his experience with the "civil defense" program in which he said:

. . . that he was given a badge that said special police; that they had speakers on civil defense and fellows with short wave radios and everything was on the up-and-up; that sometime in February, 1953 a special meeting was called at the Village Hall of the civil defense group, at which there was a display of tear gas guns and other weapons; that Capelle gave a little talk and said, among other things, "I imagine you fellows know what this meeting is for. I want to talk to each one individually and Herbie Klein will instruct any of you fellows in the use of this stuff"; that some of the fellows jumped up like little kids playing cowboy; that the men were called in to the Chief one by one, and finally he was called in; that the Chief said to him, "Ralph, there is no secret about this thing. You know what this meeting is for. It looks like we are going to have a strike and we need you fellows to help along." That he told the chief he belonged to the Union and was told that that made no difference; that he said it made a difference to him though; that the Chief said if a couple highschool kids came through the village and threw a rock through a window the union would be blamed for it and they had to protect that sort of thing. . . .

Lee Blandin described his experience in the "civil defense" unit in an affidavit, as follows:

. . . he attended a special meeting in February, 1953 and this was a meeting of all the members of this civilian defense group; that they were not sure whether the contract would go through or not; that sidearms were issued to the group that he was in; that he continued as a member of the civilian defense group after the contract was signed in 1953 and attended meetings and had pistol practice out-doors and indoors; that regular meetings continued even after the contract was signed; that the manner of the meetings was changed somewhat in that they had more talks and movies on atomic attack and disaster; that in the summer of 1953 a sub-machine gun was in use and was in the arsenal after the strike started . . . We all real-ized the use of tear gas, machine guns, riot guns, tear gas, billy clubs was not necessary for training under atomic defense and that it was in connection with a possibility of a strike. The instructions by Capelle were all made in connection with a picket line or riotous mob.

Blandin worked as a special policeman from April 5, 1954, the first day of the strike, until the beginning of August. He joined the UAW-CIO in September, but continued to live at the American Club in Kohler until January 1, 1955, when he received notice from the company to vacate. Between 1952 and 1954, Blandin partici-pated twice a month in special training programs which involved the use of firearms, tear gas and machine guns and viewing special movies.

Local 833 UAW and the union's attorney, David Rabinovitz, both contacted Ralph Olson, Director of Civil Defense for Wiscon-sin, and were told that the state does not "authorize the use of civil defense personnel for this duty. No state or Federal funds have been authorized for police in connection with this strike." Ray-mond Porter, a retired Air Force officer and Director of Civil Defense for the city of Sheboygan at the time, was subpoenaed by the charging party in the April 30 hearing and stated under ques-tioning that to his knowledge, civil defense had nothing to do with training for use of firearms; that the emphasis was on providing first aid in the event of emergencies; but not on the use of side arms, machine guns or tear gas. Edmund J. Biever testified to the purchase of 12-gauge shotguns and ammunition and 75 rounds of tear-gas ammunition, ". . . when I bought it I was a deputy sheriff which permitted me to have this material, and after my commission as a deputy was revoked, I turned it over to the other police officer."

By the time the strike started in April, 1954, Chief Capelle had enlarged his force to 90 men. Seven or eight of the special deputies who were members of the union quit the force at that time. "I felt there was quite a bit of unrest . . . ," Capelle had reasoned, "and if we were going to have trouble, I thought it would be better to prepare for it."

Federal vs. State Court Jurisdiction in Mass Picketing

The issue of mass picketing was a bone of contention between the adversaries for many months as the question was taken from court to court, eventually to come before the top tribunal of the country. Ten days after the strike started, the company, before the WERB, charged the UAW with illegal mass picketing. The union argued that, because the company was involved in interstate commerce, the NLRB had jurisdiction in this case; but on August 30, Judge Arold F. Murphy ruled that the WERB *did* have jurisdiction.

On November 29, 1954, the UAW-CIO then sought an injunction from Milwaukee Federal Judge Robert E. Tehan on the WERB ruling.[30] If there was mass picketing and violence, the union maintained, these could be controlled by invoking the state's police powers, but not by use of the WERB's powers under the Wisconsin Employment Peace Act.* The union also appealed Judge Murphy's decision to the Wisconsin Supreme Court, which, on May 3, 1955, upheld his ruling.[31] The union took the case to the United States Supreme Court, which ruled, June 4, 1956, that the Wisconsin Employment Relations Board had jurisdiction in the matter of mass picketing and home demonstrations. Said the Court, in part:

* A law restricting union activities and repealing the Wisconsin "Little Wagner Act" which was enacted in 1939; the Wisconsin Council of Agriculture sponsored the Wisconsin Employment Peace Act and industry supported it.

The dominant interest of the State in preventing violence and property damage cannot be questioned. It is a matter of genuine local concern. Nor should the fact that a union commits a federal unfair labor practice while engaging in violent conduct prevent States from taking steps to stop the violence. . . . The States are the natural guardians of the public against violence. It is the local communities that suffer most from the fear and loss occasioned by coercion and destruction. . . .

Chief Justice Warren and Justices Douglas and Black dissented, stating:

. . . We disallowed that duplication of remedy in *Garner v. Teamsters Union*, 346 U.S. 485. In that case we held that a state court could not enjoin action which was subject to an unfair labor proceeding under the federal Act. . . . Of course the States may control violence. They may make arrests and invoke their criminal law to the hilt. They transgress only when they allow their administrative agencies of their courts to enjoin the conduct that Congress has authorized the federal agency to enjoin. We retreat from *Garner* and open the door to unseemly conflicts between state and federal agencies when we sustain what Wisconsin has done here.[32]

Governor Kohler Proposes Arbitration

In late June, 1954, Harvey Kitzman decided to contact Governor Kohler, for assistance in settling the strike. Kitzman suggested that the governor name a fact-finding panel to study the situation and make recommendations. Governor Kohler told him, Kitzman recalls, that "he was no longer officially connected with the company and that they had booted him out and that maybe his intervention would be more of a hindrance than good."[33] Fearing lest the governor might expect the union to ask for some pro-union members on such a panel, Kitzman hastened to say that the union would abide by any findings of a panel composed of such persons as Harold Storey, corporation attorney for the Allis-Chalmers Company; Ward Rector, a former justice of the Wisconsin Supreme Court; and anyone the governor might name as the third member. "Well," observed the governor, "that is hardly a group of CIO organizers."

Several days later Governor Kohler called Kitzman to tell him he had failed in his mission; Storey and Rector had refused, telling him, ". . . if this were a sane situation, they would probably move into it, but the kind of situation that existed, they did not want to do anything about it." Governor Kohler, however, decided to see what he personally could do and sent the following letter to Herbert V. Kohler, president of the Kohler Company, and to Allan W. Graskamp, president of Local 833:

Gentlemen:

Throughout the current dispute between Kohler Company and Local 833, UAW-CIO, I have hoped that the issues would be speedily resolved. Recently, however, I have become increasingly concerned at the lack of progress in negotiations.

As you know, I have no financial interest in or other connection with Kohler Company. However, as a lifelong resident of Sheboygan county, I have a deep interest in the welfare of the community.

Moreover, as governor, I would be negligent if I were indifferent to the serious economic consequences to Wisconsin arising from a prolonged controversy such as that existing at Kohler.

Obviously, these consequences are staggering. The losses entailed by the company, the employes, the community and the state can never be regained. It should be the desire of all parties, and certainly would serve the interests of all parties, if the questions at issue were promptly resolved and the strike ended.

It had been my hope that these issues might be resolved before now at the bargaining table. It became obvious last week, however, in conferences with representatives of the company and the union, that broad areas of disagreement still exist on many of the principal issues. Negotiations appear to have reached an impasse, and little prospect exists that these disagreements can be speedily resolved through collective bargaining procedures.

It would appear, therefore, that unless new methods are applied in the dispute, this prolonged strike will continue until a contract is imposed upon one side or the other through the sheer force of economic pressure. Such a contract is apt to be a bad contract under which one side or the other would be restive and dissatisfied and would be good neither for the company nor for the union.

This fact, coupled with the serious economic consequences of a prolonged dispute, impels me to propose that, the remaining issues in the dispute be submitted to arbitration and that each party agree to accept the findings of an impartial arbitrator.

Arbitration, while not the usual procedure in contract negotiation, nevertheless would be by no means unique. Similar action in other extended disputes has produced amicable settlement of differences between labor and management, and I see no reason why that should not be the case in this instance.

There is, certainly, great virtue in submitting the respective merits of the dispute to an impartial arbitrator detached from the heat and bitterness engendered in conflicts such as this. Charges and counter-charges, recriminations and counter-recriminations, breed emotional attitudes which are not conducive to composed and objective analysis, and the merits or demerits of the original points at issue are lost. Submission of the issues to an impartial arbitrator can restore dispassionate consideration of the fundamentals originally involved.

I need not tell you how disturbed I am over the severe personal hardship being endured by those who are unemployed because of this dispute. Extension of the conflict is good for neither the company nor the union. It is emphatically not good for the community nor for the state.

It is my hope, therefore, that both parties will agree to submit the remaining issues to arbitration, and I am happy to offer the facilities of the Wisconsin Employment Relations Board in the selection of a qualified, impartial arbitrator.

In considering this request both the company and the union should bear in mind that refusal to submit the issues to arbitration undoubtedly would be interpreted by the public as indicative of a lack of desire to see the strike at an end, and a lack of confidence in the merits of its case by the party which declined.

I shall look forward to an early response to this request.

> With good wishes,
> Sincerely yours,
> (signed) Walter J. Kohler
> *Governor*

Herbert V. Kohler sent the governor a sharply worded three-page reply the next day, and mailed copies, with a letter reiterating the company's position, to Wisconsin manufacturers and businessmen. Salient parts of the letter to Governor Kohler follow:

We are fully aware of the economic consequences of the strike at Kohler Co. It was the Union which called this strike and must bear the responsibility therefor.

The economic and other consequences have been greatly aggravated by the fact that for eight weeks the plant was closed by an illegal mass picket line which by coercion and violence prevented employees who desired to come to work from doing so. . . .

We are concerned not only with the immediate consequences of the strike, but with the long term effects upon the economic welfare of the company, the community and the state, were we to submit to an improvident settlement under the pressure of illegal coercion. Such a settlement would —

1. Impair the ability of the company to compete successfully and, in the long run, be to the detriment of its employees, the community and the state.

2. Insure that illegal violence and coercion would continue to be concomitants of strikes. We are convinced that so long as violence in connection with a strike is rewarded by favorable settlements, it will continue. . . .

Our wages, including our present offer to the union, exceed the average for Sheboygan, where the plant you head is located,* by 43.4¢ per hour, and by $23.30 per week.

Experience has shown that arbitration of the terms of a labor contract, or of wages, leads to settlements based on "peace at any price," which promote further labor unrest and do not result in any permanent solution. . . .

We will not grant to anyone, having no experience with the business and no responsibility for it, the ultimate authority to prescribe such vital elements of cost as wages, working schedules, fringe benefits, etc.

One of the major demands of the union is for the union shop.

We have refused to coerce our employees to join a union against their will and will continue to refuse.

We will not give anyone the authority to order us to grant the union shop or other form of compulsory union membership. . . .

We will not yield to any pressure to make a "peace at any price" settlement. This would assure that the union, having been rewarded for its rash and illegal conduct, would continue it and that we could look forward to continued trouble in the future.

The practice of bailing labor unions out of impossible positions in which their own rash demands and conduct have placed them, has increased labor disputes, not decreased them.

We do not accept your suggestion that we turn the making of a contract and the decision as to wages over to an arbitrator.

You are so far wrong in your suggestion that our refusal to let

---

* This reference is to the Vollrath Company in Sheboygan, manufacturers of enamelware.

an arbitrator write a contract for us will embarrass us before the public, that we shall see to it that the stand we have expressed in this letter gets the fullest publicity.

"Unconditional Surrender"

The Union had requested that negotiations be resumed on July 23 and H. V. Kohler replied that the company would attend a meeting on August 4, but warned that there would be "no point in further long and protracted meetings" if the union's bargaining proposals did not vary substantially from its end-of-June position.

A week after bargaining had resumed the union cut its wage demands in half and changed its demand for a union shop to a maintenance-of-membership clause that provided for a self-renewing dues checkoff. It continued to ask for a noncontributory pension plan; making discharge subject to arbitration; layoffs based on seniority; and a 4-per-cent lunchtime allowance for enamel-shop workers and pottery dry finishers working in continuous three-shift operations.

On August 13, the company called the union's demands "virtually the same" as in June, varying "in terminology rather than in substance" from prestrike demands. Kohler again offered the 3-cent-an-hour increase with no extra increase for skilled workers and rejected the proposal for noncontributory pensions and layoffs based on strict seniority.

Harvey Kitzman asked if the company's letter constituted its final offer. When Conger said it did, Kitzman stated that the strike could not be settled on that offer, and commented that it amounted to asking for "unconditional surrender" from the union. Conger agreed that that was correct.[34] The union could not view this as an idle threat. The second week in June, Herbert V. Kohler, extremely annoyed that pickets had interfered with the progress of his car at the office entrance, had told the men, "When I get through with you, you'll come crawling back on your bellies, begging for jobs!"[35]

The Newspaper Ads

As during collective-bargaining hassles in previous years, the company bought full-page ads in *The Sheboygan Press*, setting

One of the Kohler Company "Pay Day at Kohler" advertisements which were intended to undermine strikers' morale.

forth its views on strike issues. The union replied, via the same medium, with arguments concerning wage differentials, company possession of tear gas and machine guns, and the ability of the union to win. A favorite public-relations ploy of the company was the calendar with "Today is Kohler Pay Day," and detailed listings of vandalism incidents in the community.

A UAW full-page ad on June 7, 1954, expressed typically, the feelings of the strikers:

Let's wash the ring out of the bathtub! For years we made good bathroom fixtures at Kohler Company. The basins and bowls were as good as any in the industry. The wages and working conditions were not. Into each tub we made went a lot of workmanship, and

Will The Good People Of Sheboygan Show Courage To Help Settle The Strike?

We, the undersigned officers of Local 833 and -ike committee, strongly resent the attacks on r good friend Emil Mazey.

Our fellow citizens who have parroted the hler Co. propaganda line in these attacks have t served the best interests of the Kohler strikers of organized labor in Sheboygan.

Instead of standing up forthrightly and de- anding for the good of our community that hon- t collective bargaining take place, they have wardly attacked Emil Mazey and tried to divide r union.

We have waited patiently for those outside of ganized labor to speak up in the name of the mmunity for fairness in the Kohler strike.

The very people who should take the leader- p in bringing both sides together now crouch hind the Kohler Co.

This strike has taught us who our real friends .

Countless union brothers and sisters through- t America have generously sent us money from ir own pockets to help us carry on our struggle.

Over $2,000,000 has been contributed from the rd-earned cash of ordinary workingmen and men to minimize hardships during our long fight.

Our International Union, and particularly Emil zey, have not hesitated to come to our assis- ce whenever we have needed it.

When Kohler Co. selfishly and thoughtlessly cancelled our hospital insurance, the International Union provided us with the best full-coverage hos- pital insurance in the city.

We cannot forget such friendship. Neither can we forget those who are taking sides against us by attacking such devoted friends as Emil Mazey.

Those who sincerely want to settle the Kohler strike cannot afford to become tools of Kohler Co.

They must now speak up for the good of all in Sheboygan or lose whatever respect they once held among the working people of Sheboygan.

Silence on the important issues that have locked Sheboygan citizens in battle is imprudent and is harmful to the community.

This is no time for timid souls to wring their hands on the sidelines, but rather a time for cour- ageous people to speak boldly for the issues re- maining in dispute to be settled honorably and peacefully.

Will the good people of Sheboygan show this kind of courage now so that democracy may come to Kohler Co.?

The Kohler strikers have vowed they will not be slaves to their employer. Will those outside the ranks of organized labor show the courage of their convictions?

ALLAN GRASKAMP
PRESIDENT

E. H. KOHLHAGEN
RECORDING SECRETARY

ARTHUR BAUER
VICE PRESIDENT

ohn Stieber	Bernard Majerus	Kenneth Klein	Leo J. Prepster
enneth Nitsche	Gordon Majerus	Elmer Oskey	William E. Rawling
eo J. Brierather	Curtiss Nack	Edward Kalupa	Elmer Gross

LOCAL 833 EXECUTIVE BOARD and STRIKE COMMITTEE

JOBS ARE PERMANENT AT KOHLER CO.

The UAW-CIO has untruthfully spread the word that employees presently being hired by Kohler Co. will be discharged when the strike is settled.

The union has stated in advertisements: "When the strike has been settled Kohler Co. will discard the few strike breakers who violated the picket line."

That is a deliberate falsehood.

The many men and women newly employed at Kohler Co. are hired as permanent employees.

Kohler Co. will continue to hire qualified men and women who come to the plant seeking employment . . . on a permanent basis . . . with full participation in the many benefits which include life insurance, hospital and medical and surgical benefits, pensions, and paid holidays.

KOHLER CO.

The argument between union and company was also conducted in the Sheboygan Press *during the first year of the strike as these November, 1954, advertisements show.*

little invisible rings of resentment — resentment against the atmos- phere of fear . . . against second class contracts we got for making a first class product. The layers of that resentment kept piling up . . . why are our ranks still intact in the tenth week of the strike? The answer is easy. Those rings of resentment were piled up pretty thick.

The company's reply next day was another appeal to the pocketbooks of the strikers and the community:

The UAW strike by the end of this tenth week will have cost the employees $3 million in lost wages — long lost purchasing power. There has been nearly one-fifth of a year of unemployment. While we regret that among those of us who suffer the consequences are . . . many innocent people, it is our conviction that not in the interest of the company, but of its employees and the community at large we have continued in this stand we have taken.

Close to a hundred full-page ads were placed in *The Sheboygan Press* by the Kohler Company, first, in a campaign to keep the KWA from affiliating with the UAW; and, after the strike began, as a device for enticing former and new workers to take jobs in the plant. Other ads were designed to win community support away from the union and promote the company's own economic philosophy — *i.e.*, right-to-work laws, and so on. The union, with a smaller "advertising budget," replied to every third or fourth ad, with arguments against company policies.

Home Demonstrations

The frustrations mounted as attempts to negotiate the strike during the summer of 1954 failed. There were defections from the strikers' ranks as men who felt economic pressures returned to work in the plant and men and women from surrounding rural areas, seeing in the strike situation a chance for a source of income, took jobs at Kohler. The strike bulletins kept a running account of individuals who crossed the picket lines and the acid tones of the "personals" were a clue to the growing resentment and bitterness.

Like Father Like Son . . . B—— M——, son of H—— M——, . . . gave up his job at the Wisconsin Power & Light Co's Edgewater plant to follow his father's footsteps across Kohler picket-lines. . . . The junior scab tried many times before to get a job at Kohler. . . . This clearly indicates how desperate the Company is.

C—— W——, a Kohler scab, as he paused at the Gate 7 stop sign one morning was asked by a picket if he would rather have self-respect or money. . . . W—— snapped back, "Money!" He certainly is losing one to get the other.

It Will Be A Scabby Merger. . . . V—— O—— . . . recently quit her job at Vollrath to scab at Kohler along with her fiancé. . . . We hear the scabful wedding will be held in the very near future.

Lists of workers crossing the picket lines were published in the strike bulletin. Strikers who knew these individuals were asked to try to convince them not to work; the "persuasive" discussions grew in July and August, from gatherings of half a dozen to occasionally several hundred persons at homes of nonstrikers returning

A crowd assembled on a Sheboygan street at a home demonstration. Officer at right center is Police Lieutenant Clarence Zimmerman, who testified at the McClellan hearings. (Sheboygan Press *photo*)

from work. This action was similar to the "escorts" provided workers by the striking molders' union in 1897, but much more extensive. The "greetings" involved name-calling and occasional obscene gestures, but there was no violence.

Termed "home receptions" or "home demonstrations," these shouting, ridiculing assemblages of strikers, women, children and the merely curious were demoralizing to nonstrikers. Company officials denounced the demonstrations, claiming that they were deliberately planned and led by the union; the union maintained that the presence of company photographers snapping pictures of the crowd and taking down names, pointed to company "inspiration" of the demonstrations. The police were sometimes called by fearful workers or their families, or were tipped off and sent to the site of the sidewalk gatherings.

On August 17, 1954, Captain Steen Heimke and his officers arrested eleven persons on North 21 Street. Orders had been given to arrest ten. One striker, Elmer Zittel, was arrested at his home a few doors away, although he had not even been at the scene. Others arrested maintained they were only bystanders and one of them was an elderly man whose son insisted on accompanying him to City Hall. All were charged with "unlawful assembly" and represented in Municipal Court by Attorney David Rabinovitz.

The trial began on August 21 with attempts to select a six-man jury. The available jury list provided only four persons considered disinterested enough to serve. The clerk of municipal court prepared a new jury list of three hundred names from which the remaining two jurors were finally chosen after considerable argument. The hearing got under way before Municipal Court Judge Randall H. Miller on August 30 and after two full days of testimony, five of the eleven cases were dismissed and the jury found the other six not guilty. The five whose cases were dismissed all testified that they had been on the scene merely as curious bystanders. They had read or heard about the gatherings and had gone to the area when the police-patrol wagon appeared and they were placed under arrest. Paul Jacobi, a Kohler photographer, had been at the scene and testified as to the remarks directed at him and others in his car, "Go back to Denmark, you knuckle-headed foreigner," "dirty scabs," et cetera.[36]

The number of home demonstrations dwindled after Judge Murphy granted the WERB's enforcement order on August 30.

Judge Murphy Attempts Conciliation

The home demonstrations became the grounds for an injunction suit against the union by the WERB. The hearing took place in the 20th Judicial Circuit Court of Wisconsin where Arold F. Murphy had been designated by the chairman of the Wisconsin Board of Judges to preside in place of Judge Schlichting. The hearing was held on August 30. Murphy at that time was in the middle of his fifth six-year term as Circuit Judge and before that had been elected district attorney of Marinette County on the Republican ticket for four two-year terms.

Judge Murphy granted the injunction requested by the WERB and then immediately decided to see what he might do to help settle the dispute. He told the bailiff to notify the attorneys for both sides to keep their seats for a while. Those present were Beatrice Lampert, the assistant attorney general representing the WERB, Max Raskin, counsel for the union, and Lyman Conger and L. P. Chase, lawyers for the Kohler Company. Raskin favored Murphy's effort to mediate the dispute; Judge Murphy described Conger's position thus:

> Mr. Conger said he would not refuse to meet, but he thought any further meetings would be futile. I recall my reply was that, of course, anybody entering the meetings with the idea that the meetings were futile would make them futile. That conversation was not very long, and it was quite quickly agreed, maybe a matter of 5 minutes, that meetings would be resumed.
>
> I inquired of Mr. Conger whether Mr. Fleischman [Fleschman], who was the chief Federal conciliator who had presided at previous mediation meetings should not be contacted, and Mr. Conger said he thought that was only proper, and he agreed at my request to notify Mr. Fleischman, which was obviously done promptly because the meetings resumed within a matter of 3 days, I believe, or maybe it was 2 days.

During the mediation sessions held early in September, 1954, many of the same issues in dispute were restated by both sides. Kitzman authorized Murphy to propose a 7-cent wage increase and on his own initiative, he even told the company he thought the union might settle for 5 cents. There were seven hearings during September, but no agreement was reached. Judge Murphy made the remark that his voluntary efforts bore nothing but "goat feathers." He acknowledged that there were two issues in dispute: the matter of wages and the matter of rehiring the discharged strikers — an issue he did not get into. On this issue Mazey maintained, "Every worker should return to his job," and the company insisted there were about 50 of them who they felt had so conducted themselves in the strike that they would not take them back.[37]

Violence, Vandalism, Convictions and Hoaxes

The strike at Kohler was remarkably free of violence when the antagonisms of a long, bitter strike, involving several thousand people are taken into account. "I am opposed to violence, but it isn't so mechanically easy to see to it that every human being acts as though he has wings in a situation where people are provoked and there are irritations and emotionalism," observed Walter Reuther at the McClellan Committee hearing. Hostility and resentment on the part of strikers and nonstrikers were evident in the shoving, threatening, name-calling and some fist-swinging that took place on the picket line, but there were no serious beatings; neither was there destruction of plant property by strikers, nor use of weapons by the special deputies as in the '34 strike.

The first violence during the second strike occurred on the third day. Five men tried to sneak into the Kohler plant through a back field east of the plant on Wednesday night, April 7, but were detected by several strikers. Three managed to get into the plant, but Dale Oostdyk and Herman Miesfeld were tackled like football players and forcibly taken to the strike headquarters. Oostdyk, who had learned from his brother that the union was going "to pull the plug" on Monday morning, had gone to work on Sunday evening. Monday night was his National Guard meeting, so he had left the plant to attend. When he tried to get back into the plant on Wednesday evening, he said he was "jumped on," "kicked" and "dragged" to the soup kitchen.

Later, in response to a question by Robert Kennedy, at the McClellan hearings, Oostdyk said, "Before I got there, they had sent a runner back to let them know that they had caught a scab. . . ." He told about being detained for about forty-five minutes and related, "Every time I got up to use the phone, they grabbed me and threw me down on a chair. Right after they kept me seated on the chair they put a card in front of me and told me to put my name and my clock number on the card and where I worked." Oostdyk stated he was a deputy sheriff at the time, but was not wearing his badge because he was trying to get into the plant. He refused to sign up with the union.[38]

Miesfeld, the other captured "scab," had an easier time of it. He did not put up any resistance and was drinking coffee in the union strike kitchen when Oostdyk arrived. He testified, "At that particular time they asked me, I would either sign up in the Union or get beat up, so I signed up." Senator McClellan asked him whether they (the persons in the strike kitchen) had "anything there present to indicate that they meant what they said about beating him up?" Miesfeld replied, "Well, the determined looks on their faces."[39]

Away from the picket lines, strikers and nonstrikers came in contact at pool halls, taverns, bowling alleys and filling stations, and the bitter feelings of the strikers toward the "job thieves," who did not respect the picket line, exploded on several occasions – to the detriment of the union's image in the community. Although the union, as an organization, was not responsible for individual acts of violence, it was blamed for those which occurred. Many instances of vandalism reported were also laid at the door of the union, in spite of the fact that nearly all cases remained unsolved.

Several assaults during the summer and fall of 1954 which received widespread publicity, played into the hands of the company, and cost the union some of the support it had in the community during the first months. On the night of June 18, twenty-seven-year-old William Vinson from Briggs Local, Detroit – six feet, three and a half inches tall, weighing 230 pounds – beat a non-striker, Willard Van Ouwerkerk, a much smaller man, at Sopetto's bar in Sheboygan Falls. There are conflicting explanations as to what prompted the assault. Vinson is quoted as saying: "As I came out of the restroom, I heard somebody say, 'Let's get the hell out of here; there are too many union people here.' So I lost my temper and I hit him."[40]

Circuit Judge Schlichting, who heard the case, sentenced Vinson to the Wisconsin State Prison for not less than one or more than two years, of which he served thirteen and a half months. The UAW International and his own local each gave $50 a week to support his wife and family, and paid the court costs.

Walter P. Reuther, asked about the Vinson case in the course of the McClellan investigation, said he did not condone violence, but when a man got into trouble, the union had an obligation to support the family, who were in no way responsible, just as the Kohler Company paid for damages resulting from vandalism. In this case, the company had paid Van Ouwerkerk's hospital bill.

John Gunaca, also from Briggs local, together with Nick Vrckovic and an unidentified person, drove into a Sheboygan Falls filling station on the night of July 4, where William Bersch, Jr., a nonstriking Kohler worker, was on duty. Vrckovic asked about fixing power brakes, but Bersch said he was busy. Some words about scabbing at Kohler followed. Bersch went into the station to phone the sheriff's department and was followed by Gunaca, who tore the phone receiver off the wall and struck Bersch, knocking him to the floor and kicking him. William Bersch, Sr., who had come to the station to visit his son, came to his defense with a child's baseball bat and he was also knocked down from behind and beaten. The elder Bersch, age sixty-five, sustained a broken vertebra and when he died a year and a half later, it was alleged by company spokesmen that the beating contributed to his death, even though the Bersch family doctor recorded the cause of his death as a heart attack.[41]

Gunaca went back to Detroit, and when a warrant was issued for his arrest, Michigan Governor G. Mennon Williams granted Gunaca's attorney's request not to extradite him to Sheboygan until strike tensions had eased, on the grounds that he could not get a fair trial in that community. *The Chicago Tribune*, among others, made much of the governor's refusal to sign extradition papers. Gunaca finally returned to Wisconsin for trial, pleaded *nolo contendere*, was found guilty and sentenced by Judge Clarence E. Rinehard, Chippewa Falls, to three years in prison on each of two charges to be served concurrently. He served eighteen months at the Wisconsin State Prison. Rinehard, in handing down sentence, said:

> . . . Now, doesn't the Court have a duty, when cases like this are presented in their stark reality, to also create an example — an example to others?"[42]

Union people felt that Vinson got a "stiffer" sentence than would have been the case had he not been involved in the strike situation. Judge Rinehard's statement suggests that he felt the sentence imposed should act as a deterrent. There had been a number of character witnesses on Gunaca's behalf and he expected to get the ordinary penalty in this assault case.

Vrckovic, also involved in this incident, was fined $250 and sentenced in October, 1959, to six months in the county jail under the Wisconsin Huber law, which permits a person convicted of a misdemeanor to work outside the jail during daytime hours to help support his family. Vrckovic's appeal to the Supreme Court was denied.

One other instance in which strikers became involved in disputes with nonstrikers and were convicted of assault, occurred on October 15, in a tavern in Chilton, Wisconsin, in the neighboring county of Calumet. Here four strikers, after several drinks, came around the bar to beat August Miller, who had gone to work at

Kohler about a month before. They also pleaded *nolo contendere;* two were sentenced to five months at hard labor in the county jail; two received three-month sentences. The Calumet sheriff, unable to find work for the men, transferred them to the Sheboygan County jail so they could earn a livelihood for their families under the Huber Act, at $50-a-week jobs provided by Local 833.

Lesser infractions of some law or ordinance, on the part of strike-connected persons, included such violations as the following:

Jess Ferrazza, April 7, was charged with disorderly conduct. Fined $15 and costs on April 19.

James Fiore, April 7, was accused of operating a sound truck in a manner violating the village ordinance. Case heard on April 23. Found guilty and fined $50 and costs. Case appealed and never brought to a decision.

Emil Mazey, April 8, charged with violating Village of Kohler sound ordinance when he addressed pickets in front of plant over a sound system in the union's station wagon. Mazey was found guilty and fined $50 and costs in Justice of the Peace Court on April 23. Case appealed and Circuit Judge Russell E. Hanson upheld decision. Mazey paid $50 fine and $14.25 costs.

George Klauser, April 11, a striker, was charged with disorderly conduct and preventing people from going to work. Case tried April 30. Found not guilty.

Edmund Biever, the company's plant manager, was arrested on May 4 for failing to yield right of way to a pedestrian (Roger Fredericks, a picket) at a sidewalk crossing. He was fined $15 and costs. Biever appealed but Circuit Judge F. H. Schlichting upheld the finding of guilty.

Paul J. Kasberger, May 11, a picket captain, charged with disorderly conduct on the picket line. Case dismissed by District Attorney.

Joe Burns, May 17, 1954, was charged with disorderly conduct and preventing people from going to work. A trial was held on July 29 in Justice of the Peace Court. He was found guilty on disorderly conduct charge and fined $25 and costs. The charge of preventing people from going to work was dismissed. The disorderly conduct charge was appealed to Circuit Court where he was again found guilty and the fine was paid.

Franklyn Schroeder, May 25, a striker, was charged with disorderly conduct arising out of a fist fight with Leland Dykes, a nonstriking Kohler worker. Found guilty on July 22 and paid $25 and costs. Dykes, a leader in the "back to work" movement, was also arrested in this fist-swinging episode, but found not guilty on August 19.

Frank Stallons, Jr., June 22, charged with disorderly conduct and preventing people from going to work. On October 8 he was found guilty of disorderly conduct but not guilty on the other charge.

Gordon Sommerfeldt, October 7, a striker, was charged with willful destruction of property. It was alleged that he blistered the paint on a nonstriker's car by throwing acid on it at the picket line. He was fined $25 and costs on May 16, 1955, but the case was appealed to Circuit Court and Judge Henry Detling dismissed the charge on January 11, 1956.

Albert Gore, NLRB counsel at this time, now in private law practice in Chicago, pointed out to the author that much of the evidence produced by the company was in the form of pictures taken by cameras with telephoto lenses, many feet from the picket line, and that when a three-dimensional scene is reduced to two dimensions, it is often impossible to determine whether bodily contact actually took place.

The Harold Curtiss Case

A shotgun blast was fired through the living-room window of the Harold Curtiss * home, Sheboygan, the evening of June 28. The incident was reported to Kohler Village police, rather than to the county sheriff.

The following morning, the Company came in [to a bargaining session] and didn't even open their briefcases. They said, "This is it. We are not negotiating under such conditions as these," and they walked out.[43]

Ewald Guske, a striker, when interrogated by Senator Curtis of the McClellan Committee, stated:

. . . We were on picket line No. 1. A few people . . . said, "Let's go out, drive out, and take a look at that accident." So we drove out. We drove past the building very slow . . . between 10 and 11 o'clock, and there was Mr. Kohler and Mr. Beaver [Biever]

---

* On August 16, 1955, Curtiss, a nonstriker, was charged with disorderly conduct and later admitted in an NLRB hearing that he had threatened Mrs. Robert Treuer, wife of a member of the union's publicity staff.

standing in the house, looking at the shot, laughing and cheering. I don't know what was to laugh about, because it was just another incident to break off the negotiations.[44]

Emil Mazey announced on July 2 that the UAW-CIO was offering $1,000 reward for the apprehension and conviction of the vandal in the Curtiss case. The Kohler Company also offered a $500 reward. No one was apprehended.

In a conflict situation, such as the Kohler strike, it was natural − in fact inevitable − that each party would try to make the other appear in as bad a light as possible, but the responsibility for the overwhelming majority of vandalism cases was never established.

It was extremely frustrating for the union leadership to have so much adverse publicity and community sentiment building up against the union. In the course of the strike, a number of rewards were offered for the arrest and conviction of the guilty parties, but none were ever claimed. These included offers by the company, *The Sheboygan Press*, a law-and-order committee, a contractors' association, the UAW-CIO, the Sheboygan local of the Newspaper Guild, and individuals.

Although this chapter deals with the first year of the strike, it seems appropriate to summarize here the vandalism cases which occurred in Sheboygan County from 1954 until the McClellan investigation in 1958. The Kohler Company blamed the strikers and their leadership for provoking and committing 836 incidents of vandalism. The sheriff's department and the Sheboygan police also had their lists. The union leaders denied connection with, or responsibility for these acts and were convinced that the company's policies encouraged vandalism. The Kohler Company hired a private detective agency which, in its reports to the company, stated:

Captain Heimke of the Police Department [Sheboygan] . . . will immediately notify the writer of anything suspicious found. In accordance with a request from Captain Heimke he was furnished a list of the stewards of Local 833 who are presently on strike. He requested this list inasmuch as he wanted to concentrate his efforts on some particular individuals and attempt to tie in the source of vandalism to some starting point.

Police Chief Walter H. Wagner of Sheboygan, on orders of

Mayor Rudolph J. Ploetz, appointed 11 special-police officers on April 22, 1955, to help check the growing wave of vandalism accompanying the protracted strike. The action came after several automobiles belonging to nonstrikers had been dynamited. *The Milwaukee Sentinel* (April 23, 1955) reported:

> Not a single person has been arrested in connection with the vandalism. The Sheboygan County Sheriff's department previously hired additional deputies in an effort to cope with acts perpetrated in the area it patrols. . . .

Some of the 836 cases recorded by the company during the period, April 7, 1954, to January 29, 1957, were serious, but most were of the nuisance type, intended as harassment. The 53 incidents which occurred during the first three and a half months of the strike — April 5 to July 18, 1954 — can be classified as follows:

Stone or paint thrown at home or through windows	12
Assault	11
Acid, paint or paint remover thrown on auto	8
Damage to auto tires	7
Paint or tar on garage	3
Sugar or sand in gasoline tank	3
Air let out of tires	3
Coerced to join union	1
Threatened with bodily injury	1
Object hurled at auto going through company gate	1
Shotgun blast at house (Curtiss)	1
Wire netting torn from mink sheds	1
Shrubs torn out of ground	1

Herbert V. Kohler issued a memo on July 19, 1954, to company employees:

> The union claims to know a great deal about production and about working conditions in the plant.
> If it does, the union is lying in its radio programs, its advertisements, its strike bulletins, and in its weekly newspaper.
> I think it is time you should know the facts.
>> 1. Men returning to work are being given jobs, the same or comparable with jobs they formerly held, in the departments in which they were employed.

2. The average hourly wages and the average weekly wage are higher than before the strike.
3. The company is producing ware and is shipping ware. As it was prior to the strike and always has been, the amount of production is confidential, but I can tell you that it is impressive. This I attribute to the splendid morale, which has never been higher.

These facts are a flat contradiction of union statements.

The union's statements are made in a desperate effort to keep employees from returning to their jobs, and are as ridiculous and unfounded as the union's statements that the company is about to capitulate to union demands.

Financial losses suffered during a strike are never made up, either by the company or the employees. However, I can assure you that those employees who have returned to work are finding their financial burdens eased by fat paychecks.

Since the company discontinued bargaining and offered a reward for information leading to the apprehension and conviction of guilty persons, vandalism has stopped. I cannot promise that there will be no more vandalism. However, you might be interested to know that the company has indemnified and will continue to indemnify employees for damage done to their property in all cases where it is not covered by insurance. . . .

After the company publicized that it would pay for vandalism losses suffered not covered by insurance, the incidence of vandalism increased by about 3-fold during a similar time period, rather than stopping as Mr. Kohler predicted. From July 19 to November 5, 151 cases occurred as compared with 53 during the preceding 3½ month period:

Damage to cars — writing "scab" on car, scratching, stoning, splashing paint remover or paint, etc.	53
Window-breaking — homes, garages, or trailer	28
Damage to tires — letting out air, cutting valves, slashing tires, or strewing nails	24
Throwing paint at homes — usually in light bulbs	18
Assault on persons — fights in taverns, beatings, etc.	15
Damage to farm machinery — usually corn choppers	5
Shotgun blasts at homes	2
Injuries to livestock	2
Other — paint on sidewalk, cutting trees, etc.	4

The explanations given for the increase ranged from a company spokesman's statement that "law enforcement officials turned their heads the other way" while "goons" from Detroit crossed Lake Michigan by boat, committed their misdeeds and sped back again, to "the Union was determined to make the Company pay plenty," or "some people wanted a new paint job or a new set of tires, as long as the Company would pay for it anyway." Certainly the damage was not usually the kind on which one could make money. Probably the most important factor was the social climate of a bitter strike situation which encouraged some individual strikers and scabs, as well as non-strike-connected persons — the youthful pranksters and the cranks of the community — to give vent to their hostility. Elmer A. Madson, the company's former detective, and several law-enforcement officials emphasized that without plaintiffs who would press charges, or witnesses willing to testify, arrests and convictions were not possible.

The union compiled its own list of 36 vandal attacks against union members:

Damage to cars — Acid, paint, or paint remover thrown
    on car   8
  Damaged with sharp instruments or bullet, windshields
    broken, top slashed   7
  Sugar, asbestos or gravel in gas tank   6
  Tires slashed   3
  Egg thrown at car   1
Damage to buildings — Windows broken, paint spattered,
    grease and garbage thrown against house   4
Other — Roofing nails or tacks in driveway   3
  Eggs thrown at striker   1
  Striker threatened with knife   1
  Sabotage on sailboat   1
  Graskamp hung in effigy in plant, with knife in back
    (October 9)   1

Assistant Counsel Jerome Adlerman of the McClellan Committee summarized three categories of statistics on vandalism for the committee: the company's own count of such acts, Sheboygan Police Chief Heimke's list of strike-connected complaints on file with his department, and the one compiled by Adlerman, based on records in the Sheboygan police department and the sheriff's de-

Paint thrown on the Arthur Hedstrom house on September 6, 1954. Arrests were made but no conviction was obtained. This type of vandalism occurred more frequently than any other during the strike. (Sheboygan Police Department photo)

partment. Heimke's list, from the beginning of the strike until the day he was subpoenaed in March, 1958, totaled 930 complaints, of which 572 were from nonstrikers, 58 from strikers, and 300 from "third parties." Heimke's list included 13 cases of name-calling and the case of one harried worker who "asked us to protect his home while he was getting married."

Adlerman's list totaled 838, of which 636 were from the city police (1954 through 1957) and 202 from the sheriff (1954 through 1956). Of the 838 complaints, 439 involved actual acts of vandalism; the balance included phone threats, prowlers, suspicious cars and unwanted merchandise sent to homes. Adlerman reports that of the 838 acts listed by the company, only 105 had been reported to the Sheboygan police. The sheriff's complaint records did not contain names. Adlerman concluded that among the victims of vandalism and violence, the ratio of nonstrikers to strikers was about 8 to 1 and that about two thirds of the acts took place within the city limits of Sheboygan. As to the statistics presented by the company, Gerard Desmond, Kohler attorney, testified that in 832 of the 833 acts of violence and vandalism listed, no culprit had been apprehended. In the one incident, where the store owned by the mayor of Sheboygan Falls had paint hurled at it, two brothers were found guilty. *Neither of them was a Kohler striker or nonstriker.* Of the 930 strike-connected complaints calculated by Heimke and on file with the Sheboygan police, 53 arrests had resulted. Of these, 16 had been withdrawn or dismissed, and 25 were still pending; 8 of the other 12 had resulted in verdicts of not guilty and 7 in guilty verdicts. These 7 included the conviction of William Banonse, a Kohler worker who had become "fed up" with being called a scab by the strikers, had gotten drunk and paint-bombed a striker's car. (See page 215.)

"Mutilated Cows"

The rural area surrounding Sheboygan and Kohler was viewed as an important battleground by company and union. The company had always recruited some of its labor force from the farms and once the plant was struck, this source supplied a still greater percentage of workers. "Many of the new Kohler employees came from the farm and fresh out of high school," reported *The Sheboygan Press* of December 17, 1954, and according to E. J. Biever, "they had learned fast and were producing excellent work." The union, on the other hand, realized that its success in the strike would be greatly helped or hindered in proportion to the number of rural people who refused to take jobs at Kohler.

Two incidents of injuries to dairy cows on nearby farms in October, 1954, were exploited by the company in its campaign against the union and against the re-election of Sheriff Mosch. Not until October 25 — two weeks after the incidents — did *The Sheboygan Press* carry the story that county authorities were investigating reports about "malicious mutilation of cattle in the town[ship] of Holland" on October 6 and 8. Undersheriff Lawrence Schmitz had visited Earl Bernisse, in Oostburg, and learned that Bernisse did not call a veterinarian or report the incident to the sheriff's office but had the cow butchered.

Bernisse stated that he did not associate the incident with the Kohler strike until some time later when an attorney from the Kohler company came to his farm and suggested it was the work of Kohler strikers, due to the fact that his brother is employed at the Kohler company. . . .

Of the other "slashing," the *Press* reported:

. . . The Sheriff's department was first notified of this slashing incident on . . . October 10th . . . when Mrs. Hopeman called to say that one of their cows had been cut sometime Friday or Saturday evening. Officer Gannon immediately drove to the Hopeman farm to investigate, and according to Gannon, Hopeman at the time said he thought the cuts were made by barbed wire.

Hopeman admitted to the author * that representatives of the company had come out to see him three times in connection with the alleged "cow slashing."

People, the newspaper published at Kohler, then printed an indignant editorial on October 27th:

A New Low:
*Cows Slashed and Cut
By Sneaking Hoodlums*

Instead of throwing paint bombs, acid or rocks, the paper declared, the hoodlums "directed their vengeance against animals." The paper reported that one animal had been destroyed and that another was saved by "quick action on the part of a veterinarian." How could "anybody in his right mind even think of such a crime," the editorial asked, "much less actually carry it out."

Harold Kroll, Mosch's opponent in the election for sheriff that fall, used these episodes as a campaign issue, and "mutilated cows" figured heavily in the campaign propaganda, particularly in rural areas.

Said Mosch, in a political advertisement in *The Sheboygan Press,* on October 26, 1954:

---

* The author, who grew up on a Wisconsin farm and operated a dairy farm near Madison, Wisconsin (1941–1951), doubts that anyone, especially a stranger, could get near enough to a cow in an open field to inflict injuries with a razor.

He has seen cows torn by barbed wire in a way which might lead an urban resident to suspect vandalism.

I . . . proceeded to investigate and find there is no evidence upon which one could claim that such mutilation was done by a human being and most likely, was caused . . . by a barbed wire fence. . . . I ask my opponent, and his chosen friends, to explain how it is physically possible to mutilate a cow in an open field as is the case here, and particularly how it would be possible for any stranger to slash the cow a second or third time as my opponent would have you believe.

The Joyce Hoax

On January 6, 1955, *The Sheboygan Press* carried a story about a Henry Joyce who had just started working on Monday at the Kohler Company being:

> . . . visited early Wednesday morning by some person apparently bent on destroying the Joyce car. Awakened by his dog at 2:30 A.M. . . . Joyce slipped a shell into a 12 gauge shotgun and slipped into the yard. . . . He noticed that the door to the machine shed, which houses the family car, was opened and he saw a shadowy figure at the door. Joyce said he fired once, heard the man shout a curse, and then saw the man run to a nearby parked car. Joyce is uncertain as to whether he injured the man, but he said the man had a definite limp as he ran to the car. . . .

Kohler Company representatives went to the Joyce farm to investigate, but could find no signs of any shotgun pellets imbedded in the machine shed. They had Joyce fire another shot in order to determine the pattern it would make at the distance of his alleged shooting.[45] District Attorney Weber and Sheriff Mosch * investigated the case thoroughly, and, in brief, there was agreement among law-enforcement officers, as well as Kohler officials, that this had been a hoax. Mrs. Joyce had given a statement in the presence of District Attorney Weber and Police Officer Walter Gannon that she was sure she would have heard it if a shot had been fired; and that he did not tell her about the shooting until he had arrived

---

* In an interview with former sheriff Mosch, November 28, 1964, the author was told that shortly after the Joyce incident, James Gannon and Harry Smith, a County Board member, contacted Mosch to ask him why he "spirited the injured vandal by plane to Detroit," Michigan, for treatment, inferring that the shotgun blast had seriously wounded a striker who was trespassing on the Joyce property, and that the "injured" man had been removed to evade identification and arrest. Mosch told the author, "I was hardly able to believe my own ears!"

home from work late Wednesday afternoon with three men from the Kohler Company. A lie-detector test also indicated that no shot had been fired by Joyce.

Private Detectives

The services of a labor detective agency from New York were engaged by the Kohler Company from the time the strike began. The choice of the Schindler Agency came about, according to Lyman Conger, because Raymond Schindler had addressed the Kohler Women's Club on one of their distinguished speaker programs, "so I kind of thought of him." Schindler's services, Conger said, had been enlisted simply to find out who "kidnapped" Dale Oostdyk. When nothing was turned up, the company then employed Elmer A. Madson and V. Allen Adams (both former FBI agents) of the Madson Detective Agency of Green Bay, Wisconsin.

The Schindler arrangement was not altogether open and aboveboard. Documents obtained from the McClellan Committee showed that a statement was rendered the company by a "Briggs Supply Company, New York City," merely listed on Invoice No. 6053, "services and necessary disbursements – April 21–May 21, 1954," in the amount of $3,736.18. The Schindler Bureau of Investigation in turn issued a check to the Inter-state Detective Agency, Inc., Chicago, to reimburse it for detective assistance. Documents also showed that E. J. Hammer, Conger's assistant, met Schindler's detective at the airport in Milwaukee three days before the strike started and drove him to Kohler for a conference with Conger at the American Club.

The subpoenaed reports of the Schindler Agency operators "371" and "487" provide some insight into the company tactics in the strike. A few brief excerpts dealing with the pursuit of the alleged Oostdyk kidnaper, "Butch," are given here:

April 25, 1954. . . . On Monday a round of the known tavern spots was again made and continued into the night. Peterson's is, of course, the most active. . . . Butch's identity will be given tomorrow.

Many of the men at the various hangouts made remarks . . . that they wished the whole thing could be called off and that they could get back to work. Those who spoke in this way were chiefly the more stolid, German-speaking type of good citizen laborers.

April 29, 1954. . . . In the opinion of both ops, practically any bartender has the information desired but none of them is expected to part with it until complete confidence is gained.

May 1, 1954. . . . Bars in the vicinity of Miesfeld's residence are being well covered. . . . It is to be noted that there are 144 taverns in the town of Sheboygan. . . . Most of these are being frequented. It is believed that here a fortunate break could well ensue. . . .

May 6, 1954. . . . Correction on the previous data is in order on the subject of John (Butch) Haynes. . . . This is not the Butch who boasted of the beating of Oostdyke.

May 7, 1954. . . . A complete survey of all hangouts today failed to bring out anything of additional importance.

May 15, 1954. . . . At Smerke's Tavern today considerable time was spent in the company of Henry Turk . . . and a companion. . . . Through them the op was able to make entry at the Peterson's back room headquarters. Here in the combination kitchen and office a number of organization men of the higher ochelon [sic] were met for the first time. There was no sign, however, of Butch the picket captain. . . . Op was invited to take part in the picket line . . . this should also present opportunities.

The month-long round of Sheboygan taverns ended for "ops" 371 and 487 when the company discontinued their agency's service. Their final report concluded:

A survey of taverns within a reasonable distance disclosed no sign of the subject [*i.e.*, Butch]. . . . This afternoon approximately twelve taverns were visited, but no evidence of the picket captain was found.

The Madson Detective Agency collected a more substantial sum — $40,114.23, according to Conger's testimony before the committee. An examination of the agency's expense statements submitted to the company reveals that Madson and Adams spent much time in travel between Green Bay and Kohler and its environs, but other trips took one or both men to Milwaukee, Madison and Fond du Lac, Wisconsin; to New York City and Syracuse, New York; to Toledo and Cleveland, Ohio; Detroit, and so on. Investigation time was $50 for an 8-hour day, but time often came to 12 to 16 hours per day. Included were such items as:

January 2, 1955	William Seery (New York City)	50.50
	Informant Cummings	50.00
	" "George"	50.00
	" Wiley	15.00
January 7	John E. Holmes, Gratuities	50.00
January 9	To informant (Gratuities)	15.00
March 3	Meals (Lunch D.A., Sheriff, subj.)	7.90
	Meals (Sheriff and wife for dinner)	11.85
June 28	Gratuities to informants	40.00

"George," an informant on Burkart in Ohio, offered to tell everything they wanted to know for $50,000 and a lifetime job. This was whittled down until he told "all" for $350, minus the lifetime job.

Some of the entries in the detectives' reports told the company that anti-Kohler and anti-Conger feelings had been discovered at striker hangouts, and occasional expressions of sentiment for ending the strike.

A notation for January 27, 1955, states that Adams conferred with Kohler attorneys, Desmond and Chase, about a spectograph analysis of a fluid used in "bombing" the Gosse farm near Six Corners; that tests indicated a "very close resemblance" to a ditto ink used by the Kohler Company.

Madson and Adams plainly felt they had an "inside track," not only with local law-enforcement officers, but with the State Crime Laboratory at Madison * as well, and therefore were entitled to supply, and be supplied, with "information" at all law-enforcement levels. Like a thread running through the voluminous reports to the company, is a complete identification with officials of the city, county and state departments. The names of Police Chief Walter Wagner, Captain Steen Heimke, police detectives Frank and Janssen of the Sheboygan police department; police chiefs Billman of Sheboygan Falls, Zimmerman of Plymouth, and Capelle of Kohler; sheriffs George Lemieux of Fond du Lac County; Les Nichols of Manitowoc County; and Vic Jordan of

* The detective agency reports subpoenaed by the McClellan Committee recount that the Crime Lab was anxious to keep the liaison quiet so that it could not "be generally known to law-enforcement officers in this state that this agency had an inside track at the Wisconsin State Crime Laboratory." Charles Wilson, superintendent of the Crime Lab, in an interview June 1, 1965, told the author that the Madson Agency got the same weekly listings of vandalism as were supplied to law-enforcement officials in the area.

Winnebago; the Sheboygan district attorney, David Weber; and Wilson and Wilomovsky of the State Crime Laboratory at Madison, appear frequently in the reports in most co-operative roles.

Sheboygan County Sheriff Mosch, who, following the advice of District Attorney John Buchen, had taken nonstrikers "up to the picket line," but had refused to use force to get them through, was not taken into the detectives' confidence to the same extent as the other law-enforcement officers. Mosch asked the detectives, they reported, why they had not contacted him, and they told him they had reasons to believe he was sympathetic to the union and not doing all he could to apprehend the vandals. Yet, even Mosch co-operated with the agency at many points. Madson reports:

> Theodore Mosh [Mosch] definitely committed himself in that [he] introduced the writer as being a deputy [a ruse] from Oshkosh to Kalupa [a local 833 steward and strike leader]. It was felt that if the Union finds out the exact status of the writer that Mosh will be in disfavor with them. . . .

Investigations by Madson and his partner, Adams, where vandalism was involved, started with the assumption that strikers were the perpetrators. They "surveilled" homes of suspects and conferred with police detectives Oakley Frank and Gordon Janssen, whom they described as "very cooperative." They were not above plying one of their "leads" with alcohol (which they humorously referred as "liquid lie-detector"). This occurred at taverns on the way back from Madison where they had taken him for polygraph tests. They left the fellow in a Fond du Lac jail to sleep it off. At one point, together with officers Frank and Janssen, they combed through the "albums" (spy files) which the company kept on strikers; out of them they selected "approximately two" who, they thought, "would furnish information regarding vandalism if they were furnished enough money." Officer Frank thought he could "operate with a five thousand dollar figure . . . to obtain all the information necessary to break all the acts of vandalism in Sheboygan County."

Although Conger declared that the initial purpose of hiring detective assistance was "to get the evidence of criminal acts of violence and vandalism," the agency reports did not focus on this phase of their task until several months after the agency was hired.

Their earlier efforts were concentrated on gathering evidence on the fact that Robert Burkart had once been a member of the Socialist Workers Party, a Trotskyist organization, in Toledo, Ohio, and that he was separated from his wife and was frequently seen at the apartment of Grace Chilson in Milwaukee before he married her. The morals squad of the Milwaukee Police Department arrested Burkart and Grace Chilson in her apartment * at midnight on April 7, 1955, on a tip-off to Lieutenant Harry Kuszewski who was in charge of the squad. Charges of disorderly conduct were brought and Max Raskin, their attorney, paid fines of $10 and costs for each.

The language in the Madson report suggested that the detectives may have been the ones who informed Lieutenant Kuszewski. On April 20, the report states that attorney Max Raskin "had gone so far as to go directly to Chief of Police Polcyn of the Milwaukee Police Department asking for the name of the complaining witness . . ." and that Kuszewski assured Madson that, "as yet, Polcyn has obtained no information regarding the actual complaints."

It was illegal, under the Taft-Hartley Act, for an employer to commit "surveillance," *i.e.,* spy on an employee. Conger viewed the detectives placing a woman in the strike kitchen as a "paid informant" as a distinction from employment of a spy by the company in that she reported to the detective agency and not to the company itself. Conger admitted that Burkart's mail and long-distance calls were checked in a co-operative project between the police and the detectives, which he did not regard as illegal because "I believe that any police officer can check up on what long-distance calls are made by anyone."[45]

Robert F. Kennedy, Chief Counsel for the committee, queried Conger as follows:

> *Mr. Kennedy:* Interference or tampering is explained to be any taking of confidential information off a letter or from the contents of a letter. Do you know anything about that?
> *Mr. Conger:* No, sir, I do not.

* The company detectives and the Sheboygan police department detectives did not display the same fine moral sensibilities when they arranged "briefing sessions" to school a prostitute for securing a job in the strike kitchen as an informer. The reports refer frequently to the "female informer" in the strike kitchen, but the information they got was merely general scuttlebutt about strikers' complaints about strike benefits, et cetera.

Mr. Kennedy: Did you disapprove of this mail checking?

Mr. Conger: It was all done before I ever got notice of it.[46]

Conger, who at other points in his testimony had criticized the Sheboygan city police for slack law enforcement, felt that for co-operation with the detective agency they deserved credit for a job well done. In response to Counsel Kennedy's comment that if the police, co-operating with the detectives, had turned over confidential information obtained through a mail cover, they had "violated their trust," Conger replied, ". . . it seems to me that there has been a great deal of to-do made about possible breaches of ethics by police officers who were sincerely trying to do their duty and quell this violence and this reign of terror. . . ."[47]

It is difficult to see how the kind of evidence sought and gathered on Burkart had any connection with a "reign of terror," the cause of which and responsibility for which has never been established in the overwhelming majority of cases cited. Conger estimated that during the investigations of the Madson Agency, which lasted over four years and "covered quite a bit of territory," some 12 to 15 informants had been hired. He saw nothing wrong with this. He said, "We take the position that we have a right to employ a detective to catch a criminal, particularly when law enforcement officers are tolerating an open reign of terror."

Senator Pat McNamara of Michigan asked Conger: "Did this employment of the private detectives and their surveillance of the union headquarters bring about the discovery of any criminals?"

Conger replied, "No; I think they came very close a couple of times."

As to the second broad purpose * of the Kohler Company's employment of detectives, Walter P. Reuther, president of the UAW, labeled this "an improper practice, contrary to the spirit of the law that requires good faith collective bargaining."[48] Reuther then enumerated for the committee some of the Kohler-endorsed activities as follows:

> . . . they spied on the activities and background of a Government attorney [Gore] while he was involved in the processing of a case before the National Labor Relations Board involving this company

---

* Spying on union-connected personnel to discredit them publicly.

in this dispute. I personally think it is a sad day in America when a company employs spies to shadow Government officials while they are carrying out the provisions and their constitutional obligations under the law. That is precisely what they did. They spied on union activities at our strike kitchens, on our picket lines, and they attempted to improperly get information at the hotel where some of our people were living. They interfered with the U.S. mail, as their reports will indicate. They kept track and invaded the people's privacy by finding out about long-distance telephone calls. They spied on the personal lives of strikers and international representatives and union officials. On one occasion their paid spies posed as a law-enforcing agent in an attempt to secure information, under false pretenses. These are some of the things they did.[49]

Company investigations had also been made of Emil Mazey, secretary-treasurer of the UAW, Frank Wallick and Robert Treuer of the union's publicity staff. Information was primarily sought, Conger said, "about any subversive background or connection that we could use as a defense in our NLRB case."[50]

Our purpose was to bolster our defense which, by the way, is still in the picture, that the union was not bargaining in good faith because it was being represented by people who were trying to overthrow all industry, not only the Kohler Company, but all industry.[51]

The report on Mazey, Conger testified, was "pretty much negative" as was the one on Treuer. The check on Wallick showed that he was resigning to take a job with a Democratic congressman. The final report of the McClellan Committee [52] records:

Another project of the detectives employed by the Kohler Company ranged less far afield than Milwaukee, concentrating, indeed, right in Sheboygan. As Steen Heimke, then captain of police in Sheboygan, recalled it —

two Madson men asked me where the union stayed, and I told they [them] they stayed at the Grand Hotel. They said, "Do you know what part of the building?"

I said, "I don't know. What difference does that make?"

They said, "Well, we would like to find out what is going on in there."

That is all I heard.

Under questioning, however, Heimke remembered a bit more of the conversation. The detectives had told him that they wanted to put a tap on the room used by the UAW people as their headquarters; he replied, he said, that he didn't know what room the union was in, what the capacity was for tapping, and that "that was their business, but we weren't going to be involved in that."

Heimke, who asserted that he had "good, clean, law enforcement," and that his police had never tapped a line or bugged a room, was asked why in that case he had seemed so willing to be helpful to the detectives and why they had come to him at all. Heimke replied that Madson and he had been friends for 20 years.

John F. Kennedy, then senator, expressed his amazement at Heimke's idea of a law-enforcement officer's proper duties:

If bandits came along and asked you the location of the First National Bank and how to get in there, what the guards were, and the conversation took 2 minutes, and the bank was later robbed, do you think you would be a party to that illegal act?

Mr. Heimke: There is no comparison.

Senator Kennedy: Why isn't there?

Mr. Heimke: Elmer Madson, a former member of the FBI and with a nation-wide detective agency, I have the greatest confidence in his ability, and if he could be of some assistance to us without our department becoming involved, that was — he was hired to do a job.

Senator Kennedy: Chief, that is the strangest statement of responsibilities of a law officer of Wisconsin or any other state that I have heard. If your sensitivity to illegality is so dull that you did not see that you were a party to an illegal act, it puts in question many of your actions in the whole strike.

Mr. Heimke: First of all, the act has to be committed for it to become illegal.

Senator Kennedy: Do you know whether it was committed?

Mr. Heimke: To my knowledge it was not committed.

Senator Kennedy: Are you ready to say whether it was committed?

Mr. Heimke: I do not know for sure. Elmer Madson is the only one that would know.[53]

Walter H. Wagner, who was then Sheboygan chief of police, and who revealed that it was on his recommendation that Conger had hired the Madson Agency, testified that he introduced Madson's associate, Al Adams, to the manager of the Grand Hotel, and that Adams "was pointed out where the union officials had their office."[54] Wagner would not say that the introduction was arranged so that Adams could bug the room, but conceded that it was for at least a "discussion" of bugging. To his best information, he declared, the room was never bugged.

At one point the Madson report states:

> . . . upon recontacting Mr. Conger, no further action is being taken at this time regarding this matter, which is not being explained fully here, inasmuch as Mr. Conger is aware of the same and has requested that we hold this line of investigation in abeyance pending the outcome of the NLRB hearing in Sheboygan during the week of February 7 through February 12.

The McClellan Committee revealed that the union hall "just around the corner from the Grand Hotel," was by Conger's admission, also under scrutiny of the detective agency:

> . . . I have no doubt that they did watch the comings and goings at the Union hall, particularly after dark, and I know they collected some license numbers of some cars around some of the union hangouts, and tried to get whether those same license numbers were going to appear some place in connection with vandalism.
> *Senator McNamara:* Don't you think that this is at least verging on the employment of labor spies and is that not an illegal act under the Taft-Hartley Act?
> *Mr. Conger:* No, I believe it isn't even close to it, Senator. I believe we have a right to hire private detectives to catch a criminal at any time, whether he be a union member or a nonunion member.
> *Senator McNamara:* Then does this imply that all of these people around the union hall were criminals, and therefore it was legal?
> *Mr. Conger:* No; it implies that they were logical suspects . . .[55]

In addition to professional detectives, the Kohler Company delegated to Gerard Desmond and some 12 to 15 of the company's staff the responsibility for compiling a "strike incident" file of detailed information, strike-related or not. Items were gleaned from newspapers, strike bulletins put out by the union, affidavits and informers. The "spy file" grew to fill four large alphabetized books, cataloging the activities of 742 strikers. Conger told the McClellan Committee that the purpose of this project was "to get evidence to use before the WERB" in the company's efforts to "stop mass picketing . . . the violence and vandalism" and later, that the records were used "to justify before the NLRB the discharge of people that were discharged."[56]

Entries record such events as a twelve-year-old son of Carl Gorr, Jr., "molesting" a five-year-old and flicking his finger in her eye; a picket, dressed as Abe Lincoln, having his picture along with five others in *The Milwaukee Journal;* another "trespassing" on company property to retrieve a ball; that a striker "looked menacingly" at a nonstriker bowling at a recreation hall; others who shouted "scab" at nonstrikers, or turned up at home demonstrations. Senator Ervin joked: "Whoever kept those records was more thorough, I hope, than the recording angel." The files were supplemented by hundreds of photographs made by company photographers who, with telephoto lenses, movie cameras and recording devices, covered picket lines from dawn to dark, appearing at the home demonstrations, sites of vandalism and at strikers' gatherings.

Women in the Strike

No account of the Kohler strike should — to paraphrase the popular cliché — underestimate the power of the women — the wives, daughters, mothers and sisters who peeled potatoes and vegetables and made sandwiches in the "soup-kitchen," poured coffee for the picketers, walked on the picket line so that the men might attend union meetings, and stumped cities in and out of the state, urging consumers not to buy Kohler products.

Catherine (Babe) Gelles, UAW-CIO International representative in charge of the women's auxiliaries, came to Sheboygan to assist the ladies' auxiliary, which was organized in 1952 and became the largest auxiliary in the UAW. They poured their energies into helping with clerical work of the union, distributing strike bulletins, supervising recreational activities for the teens, the children, and for the women themselves, since strike-benefit checks could not possibly be stretched to include movies, outings and the normal diversions of family life. Auxiliaries in other parts of the country raised funds for strikers' families — for shoes, layettes and maternity clothing.

"Personals" in the strike bulletin reflected the strikers' belief

The women walked on the picket line when their men attended union meetings. (UAW photo)

that wives, unable to put up with the exigencies of month-after-month without a pay check, were often back of a man's decision to leave the picket line and return to a job at Kohler. The emotional strains on the women were great; Sheboyganites recall that some of the most abusive and unprintable language heard during the strike was uttered by women — both by indignant wives who denounced those who crossed the picket lines to "take" their husbands' jobs and by women strike breakers and wives of nonstrikers.

The survival problem of the families of men on strike is an acute one. When strikes wear on, as did the one at Kohler, imposing years-long hardships and bleak prospects for settlement, the endurance of the union men *and* women becomes a testimonial to the quality of their morale and their conviction that their cause is just.

Joe Burns, International representative of the UAW Community Services, administered the strike-benefit program, supported by the union's strike fund. Strikers and nonunion members who would not cross the picket line were eligible for support. In addition to a $25 weekly cash allowance, vouchers were given for groceries and, where a need existed, such items as rent and utilities were also included. The dependence of families on the strike benefits is illustrated by an item in the August 13, 1954, *Strike Bulletin* which related:

> . . . A woman came to the Strike Assistance Headquarters the other day and asked for her husband's voucher. . . . After checking the books, she was asked if her husband was picketing or what, as no record could be found of him. . . . She replied, "No, no, he's working in the plant, but it'll be four weeks before he gets a check and we figured we would get a voucher to tide us over." . . . Needless to say, they are still waiting.

Labor Act Violations

The NLRB was involved in many phases of the dispute at Kohler; the involvement of the board was based on two sections of the National Labor Relations Act which provide:

1. *Rights of Employees*, Section 7. Employees shall have the right to self-organization, to form, join or assist labor organizations, to bargain collectively through representatives of their own choosing, and to engage in other concerted activities for the purpose of collective bargaining or other mutual aid or protection, and shall also have the right to refrain from any or all of such activities except to the extent that such right be affected by an agreement requiring membership in a labor organization as a condition of employment as authorized in Section 8(a) (3).
2. *Unfair Labor Practices*, Section 8(a). It shall be an unfair labor practice for an employer —
   (1) to interfere with, restrain, or coerce employees in the exercise of their rights guaranteed in Section 7; . . .

   (3) by discrimination in regard to hire or tenure of employment or any term or condition of employment to encourage or discourage membership in any labor organization. . . .

   (5) to refuse to bargain collectively with the representatives of his employees, subject to the provisions of Section 9(a).

This section presents only a summary (as recorded in the brief prepared by the United States Court of Appeals for the District of Columbia Circuit) of the main charges in dispute, which arose from actions taken by the company before the strike began and during the first year of the strike.

Before the strike started:

The Company was two months late in furnishing incentive-in-equity wage information requested by the Union, over a period of 10 months, and never did furnish about 35% of the information requested.

During the first year of the strike:

The Company on June 1, unilaterally and without notice to the Union, instituted a 3-cent wage increase — at the same time, according to the testimony of president H. V. Kohler, kept in effect the old contract terms. [The NLRB ruled that this act converted the strike from an economic strike to an unfair labor practice strike on that date. A later ruling (see Chapter 9) of the board found the strike to have been an unfair labor practice strike since its inception. Kohler concluded that if the increase had been given on April 5, it could not logically be considered a refusal to bargain, so the 3-cent increase was made retroactive to that date. It should be noted that since the plant had been closed because of mass picketing until May 28, making the 3-cent increase retroactive did not cost the company much.]

The Company, on July 1, transferred 29 temporary employees from the Shell department who were not on strike, to other jobs and fired 53 employees from the same department who were on strike. [Such strategy, calculated as it was to punish the Union supporters and reward the strikebreakers, necessarily tended to arouse resentment among the strikers.]

The Company hired the Schindler detective agency in April and the Madson Detective Agency in July. These agencies were found to have engaged in surveillance and anti-union espionage, which is clearly illegal under the Act. [Company detectives resorted to checking Burkart's mail and telephone calls, placed an informant in the union headquarters, discussed plans to "bug" the union's headquarters at the Grand Hotel, etc.]

The Company evicted 8 striking employees from the American Club and 2 from Company-owned homes, but served no eviction notices to nonstrikers. [Even club residents who did not work at the company were not asked to move.]

Kohler's bad faith in post-September bargaining was manifest by its action in rebuffing the attempts of third parties, such as Judge Arold Murphy, to settle the dispute. [Based on the Board's findings, the Court observed: "Moreover, reflecting on its 'studied procedure planned to give the mere appearance of bargaining,' is Kohler's persistent re-offer throughout this period of the already implemented 3 cents on condition that the union capitulate completely on virtually all other issues. . . ." It is difficult to believe that the company with a straight face and in good faith could have supposed that this proposal had the slightest chance of acceptance by a self-respecting union, or even that it might help the negotiations by affording a basis for discussion; rather it looks more like a stalling tactic by a party bent upon maintaining the pretense of bargaining.]

Alois Forstner had been employed by the Company for 14 or 15 years and had developed great skills as a color mixer which very few men possessed. In June, 1954, his foreman, Fred Nack, came to his home in St. Cloud and persistently solicited Forstner to return to work, saying he could work as many hours or days as he wanted to – a liberty he had never enjoyed before the strike. Nack also urged Forstner's wife to have her husband return to work.

Attempts at Settlement

The numerous controversies which flared up during the first year of the strike – the mass picketing and home demonstrations, the presence of the "arsenal" in Kohler Village, the extensive vandalism, the extravagant claims and counterclaims via press and radio, together with preparations for "siege" and the espionage system undertaken by the company – did not create a climate for a quick and easy resolution of the differences which had brought on the second Kohler strike.

Most labor-management agreements, including those of firms much larger than Kohler, have been settled in far less time. The NLRB, Judge Murphy and others judged the company's bargaining as mere "surface" bargaining in which it went through the motions of meeting, hoping thereby to place itself in "technical compliance" with the National Labor Relations Act. Over and over, company representatives repeated that their prestrike offer was all they were prepared to give and that they were not going to be stampeded or worn down by long sessions.

Meetings were held on forty-four days during the first year – 41 of them during the first five months of the strike. The only session in April took place on the nineteenth. Four meetings were held in May, but in two of these the company refused to participate. Twenty-two sessions took place in June after the mass picketing

*When negotiations got underway, June 1, for the longest and most
intensive period of the strike, the principals were photographed at the
Foeste Hotel. Left to right: Allan Graskamp, Arthur Bauer, E. H.
Kohlhagen, William E. Rawlings (standing), Group 5 chief steward
Edward Kalupa (standing), and Robert Burkart, representing the
union; L. E. Gooding (WERB), Glenn C. Fleshman (Chicago, Federal
conciliator and chairman of the negotiating sessions), Virgil Burtz
(Milwaukee, Federal conciliator), and James A. Despins (Green Bay,
Federal conciliator); Kohler management committee members — Mar-
tin Hollander, L. L. Smith, Lyman Conger, W. J. Ireland, E. J. Hammer (standing) and Edmund J. Biever. (Sheboygan* Press *photo)*

ended and the company resumed partial operations; one meeting
was held in July, six in early August and, after Judge Murphy offered his services, seven took place in September. There was no session in October, one in November, two in January and none in
February or March of 1955. Most sessions lasted six to eight hours,
although twelve ended in two hours or less.

One to three of the Federal conciliators — Fleschman, Burtz
and Despins — attended every meeting held during the year; Gooding of the WERB sat in on twenty-three of the sessions.

The Grand Hotel in Sheboygan was selected for most of the
meetings, although the September sessions with Judge Murphy
took place in the county board room at the courthouse; one con-

vened in the regional office of the FMCS in Chicago; and one session was called at the United States Department of Labor in Washington, D.C.

The Kohler Company team usually consisted of Conger, Biever, Hammer, Hollander, Howe, Ireland and L. L. Smith, although Born attended nineteen and Ebert fifteen sessions. The usual spokesmen for the UAW Local 833 were Graskamp, Bauer and Kohlhagen, but they were sometimes joined by Breirather, Arthur Fox, Kenneth Klein, Kalupa, Gordon Majerus, Elmer Oskey, William Rawlings and Attorney Rabinovitz. Spokesmen for the International Union were Burkart, Ferrazza, Kitzman, Raymond Majerus, Mazey, Rand, Sahorske and Attorney Raskin. Others who attended one or more meetings were Charles Baker, Reginald Barber, Paul Held, Treuer, Wallick and Attorney Arthur Goldberg.

One of the events of the first year, which made headlines, was the proposal by Sheboygan clergymen that both sides declare an Easter truce from Good Friday to Sunday — a proposal in which the union concurred, but the company did not.

Victor Reuther, administrative assistant to his brother Walter, was speaker at a big strikers' rally on August 1; Brendan Sexton, education director of the UAW, and J. F. Friedrick, veteran labor leader from Milwaukee, were speakers at the county Labor Day picnic.

A first-class furor was created when Emil Mazey went to Sheboygan in November for a meeting of Local 833, and in a statement criticized frankly the prison sentence meted out to William Vinson by Judge F. H. Schlichting. Mazey asked that strikers' grocery orders be withdrawn from the Piggly Wiggly stores in which the judge held shares of stock. Professional organizations, clergymen and the business community loosed a flood of public statements condemning Mazey for "an attempt to influence a judicial body" of the community.*

At one point, Senator James Murray (Montana) wired H. V. Kohler for information about the strike in order to determine if a Senate inquiry was warranted. On March 1, 1955, the company fired ninety strikers, including the union's executive board and five of its six chief stewards — the entire leadership of the union. The

* See Chapter 10.

union contested this action and eventually the NLRB ordered the majority of the ninety reinstated. The company won a point when the United States Circuit Court of Appeals, in Chicago, upheld the NLRB's ruling of April 14, 1954, approving the action of the company in discharging 12 enamelers, whose dismissal was one of the factors which brought about the strike. The Court, however, ordered the company to reinstate one former employee.

As the strike approached the first anniversary, much had happened, but little to suggest when a reconciliation might take place.

6

THE STRIKE CONTINUES

"KOHLER STRIKE is One Year Old; Hope for Settlement Virtually Nil" — was the way *The Milwaukee Journal* appraised the situation on April 5, 1955, as the strike at Kohler entered its second year. Strikers and many in the community wondered how long it would last; no one could foresee that only in the next decade would the final settlement be reached. Some of the strikers had broken ranks and returned to work at the Kohler Company, yielding to, the economic pressures of sustaining their families; others had moved to such distant places as Colorado and California. But the majority of strikers stuck with their union despite the year-long struggle in which no progress toward agreement had been made. Their solidarity was possible only because of the extensive support of the UAW International Union once the strike had begun.

All mutual respect and confidence between the company and the union had been dissipated in the name-calling and impugning of motives on both sides during the first year of the strike, and, to a lesser extent, for years before it started. The company was confident that it could hold out longer than the union, but the union, too, did not intend to capitulate even though it did offer to reduce its demands in the hope of achieving an honorable settlement with which its membership could live. The strike had become, in many ways, a war of attrition in which the union's strike weapons and tactics shifted from mass picketing to a boycott and reliance on legal proceedings, in the expectation that eventually the NLRB would rule favorably on the union's charges of unfair labor practices. The company resorted to measures it hoped would attract enough workers to keep the plant operating efficiently and win enough sympathy and support among antilabor segments of the wider community to provide a market for its products.

Just one day before the first anniversary of the strike, attorneys Raskin and Rabinovitz argued before the Wisconsin Supreme Court that U.S. statutes supersede the Wisconsin Labor Peace Act, that the NLRB had been in the case first and that this barred the state board from interfering. Raskin said:

> The WERB, blind to what is happening before the NLRB, stamps us with guilt at the very time when a national agency is attempting to stamp guilt on the employer. If the company desires a remedy, let them file a complaint before the NLRB. . . .

More Vandalism and Violence

Although there was some ebb and flow in the emotions of the strikers and those who had gone to work at Kohler, feeling continued to run high on both sides in the embattled community. Charges and countercharges continued unabated, but few vandals were caught and still fewer convictions were recorded. The company list of vandalism acts perpetrated after the first year of the strike and filed with the McClellan Committee [1] included such items as:

No.	Name	Affidavit Date	Date of Incident	Description
133-A	Leslie Pike	7/8/55	4/7/55	Aerial broken on car and fender skirts removed
134-A	Adolph Riehl	4/15/55	4/9/55	Flat tire, southeast gate, oversize tack with ½ inch head
135-A	Victor F. Balnaitis	4/13/55	4/11/55	Flat tire, oversize tack; 10 flats not reported
136-A	Herman Grams	4/14/55	4/11/55	Lead pellets hit house
137-A	Frederick Domke	4/19/55	4/12/55	Flat tire, northeast gate, roofing nail

Descriptions of other incidents included:
> nails in driveway at home
> tire cut causing blowout
> glass jar of bluish waxy substance thrown through window, damaging interior of home
> flowers, shrubs and plants trampled on, cut and damaged
> acid thrown on car
> sugar in gas tank

Interior of auto belonging to Fred Yurk of Sheboygan, a nonstriker, which was dynamited on April 12, 1955. (Sheboygan Police Department photo)

> car dented by pickets at northeast gate
> word "scab" painted on front door of nonstriker's home
> dynamite exploded under car of nonstriker, causing extensive damage

Between April 5, 1955, and January 29, 1957, a total of 312 such incidents — some serious and others trivial — were recorded by the Kohler Company.

The antagonism between strikers and those who had gone back to work or who had taken a new job at Kohler was deep-seated and widespread. It was no joke to be called a "scab" or "job-thief," but neither was it fun for strikers to see their years of seniority lost to strike "replacements." It does not require a trained sociologist to understand the means of expression given to the resentments which grew out of the conflict. What some individual strikers and nonstrikers did does not necessarily reflect policies of the union or the company. Moreover, the heat and passion of the strike situation encouraged pranks and hostile and mischievous acts on the part of individuals totally unconnected with the strike, who knew the prime suspects would be the strikers and nonstrikers, and they themselves could thereby escape detection. Here are some of the incidents that aroused the community:

A "Kidnapping"

On May 18, 1955, *The Milwaukee Sentinel* and *The Sheboygan Press* reported that law-enforcement authorities were investigating the mysterious disappearance of a nonstriking Kohler employee. James Bucholtz, thirty-one, had left home for work on Saturday morning and his wife reported on Tuesday that he was missing. A Brown County traffic officer had spoken to Bucholtz when he was found sleeping in his car in the Town of Preble, Brown County, at 6:30 A.M. Monday. He told the officer that he would start immediately for work at Kohler, but instead disappeared. He was later convicted and sentenced on a breaking and entering charge entirely unrelated to the strike.

The Banonse Paint-bombing

On October 10, 1955, *The Sheboygan Press* reported that William P. Banonse, a nonstriking Kohler worker, admitted hurling jars of paint at two cars, one belonging to a Kohler striker and the other to a commercial fisherman, whose father was a striker. District Attorney Weber recommended that the court assess the maximum fine of $200 and give Banonse an opportunity to make restitution. Banonse told police he had been drinking quite heavily and wanted to "get even" with the men for their insults to him when he returned home late that night.

The Holub Hoax

On July 18, 1957, Sheboygan radio station WHBL reported that Frank Holub, a nonstriking Kohler worker

was assaulted on a Sheboygan street in front of his home about 1:30 this morning. . . . Holub went to the Kohler Company first aid

office this morning for treatment of a gash on the back of his head
and a severe bump on the forehead. Kohler police were summoned
who later notified Sheboygan police. Holub reported that when he
came home from work, three men approached him and asked, 'Are
you a Kohler scab?' and when he said 'yes' he was slugged over the
head with a 'filled hose' or 'black jack.'

Holub broke down after questioning the next day and con-
fessed that his story was a hoax, that he had fallen while drunk
and injured his head.

"According to police," the station reported, "Holub was
afraid he might lose his driver's license if it was known that he
drove while drunk." He also told police that he thought the
Kohler Company would "take care of" his medical bills if he said
he was assaulted for working at the company. He pleaded guilty to
"disorderly conduct" and was sentenced to thirty days in jail.

The "Dynamite Cache"

A glaring 5-column lead story and pictures appeared in the
April 29, 1955, *Sheboygan Press* announcing:

Arrest Four Strikers
At Cache of Dynamite

One Was In Act of Getting Explosive From
Hiding Place When Officers Make Arrests

Four members of striking Local 833, UAW-CIO were arrested
this morning as they walked directly to a well-hidden supply of
dynamite and blasting equipment about three blocks north of the
strike kitchen and headquarters in the town of Sheboygan.

A joint statement, issued today by Sheriff Ted Mosch and Chief
of Police Walter H. Wagner, whose departments cooperated in the
investigation leading to the arrest revealed that the arrests may clear
up the wave of terrorism that has gripped the city and county in
recent months. The capture of the four men was the result of a tip
to Sheriff Mosch, the closest of cooperation between the police and
sheriff's department plus the unceasing surveillance of the cache of
explosives since Sunday. A 24-hour watch, despite severe rainstorms
that made the task almost unbearable, was capped with the arrests
today. . . .

The story of the trap which was sprung this morning began at

Deputy displays the cache of dynamite "found" about 3 blocks north of picket gate, 8 and ¾ miles east of the Kohler plant. Looking on are officers and deputies, with Police Chief Wagner of Sheboygan (wearing hat). (Sheboygan County Sheriff's Department photo)

noon Sunday. Sheriff Mosch received a tip from an unidentified person who told the sheriff about the cache of dynamite. Sheriff Mosch, accompanied by Deputy Carl Herman, checked the scene and discovered the explosives. A second trip to the scene included Mayor Rudolph Ploetz.

The site of the cache was about three blocks north of the union's strike kitchen, in a field and carefully hidden in the thick brush. A total of 29 sticks of dynamite, a box containing about 20 blasting caps and six feet of dynamite fuse were all found on the scene. The blasting equipment was in plastic bags and was laying on some waterproof paper. The entire collection was covered by pieces of an old coat, giving the appearance of some old rags laying under the brush. . . .

Sheriff's deputies and police officers were assigned to watch the "discovery" from ravines about 100 feet away. Upon apprehending the four men, law-enforcement officials were careful, however, not to release their names until they had statements from them, even though they were described as members of Local 833. The four men were questioned throughout the day and released for lack of evidence after they all had agreed, independently, to take lie-detector tests. Arrangements were made by Sheboygan County district attorney, David Weber, for the administration of voluntary lie-detector tests at the State Crime Laboratory at Madison, Wisconsin, to Philip Pinekenstein, fifty-six; Daniel Regan, forty-one; Ignatz Kastelic, sixty-four; and Paul Frederick Gibeault, thirty-one. The District Attorney reported that tests lasting 1½ hours completely exonerated Pinekenstein, and that partial tests had been given the other three. In a letter to Pinekenstein, Weber wrote:

> It gives me great pleasure to address this letter to you today. The cooperation which you displayed in appearing for polygraph or lie detector tests at Madison was wonderful.
>
> As you know by this time the results of the polygraph test have completely vindicated you from association of any sort in the dynamite matter.
>
> It may please you to know that Charles Wilson, the director of the Wisconsin State Crime Laboratory, made the comment upon the completion of this test that this man, referring to you, Philip Pinekenstein, knew less about the dynamite located in Sheboygan County, than he, Charles Wilson, himself knew. . . .[2]

The oldest of the four arrested strikers was Ignatz Kastelic, who had come to the United States from Yugoslavia at the age of nineteen and started working at Kohler in 1925. He gave this version of how they happened upon the cache of dynamite, the arrest and interrogation:

> I was in a shanty at gate No. 8 until 7:00 A.M. laying on an old couch. I heard someone outside say, "Let's take a walk, it's too nice a day to waste." I said, "Wait a minute, I'll go along with you."
>
> We started walking north from Gate 8 alongside the gravel pit. There are some wild cherry trees at the end of the gravel pit. I have some cherry trees of my own at home and I grafted some branches onto the wild cherry trees. I told the fellows I was getting old so that when cherries would be getting ripe, I'd show them where they could get some. We walked to the trees and I showed them to them.
>
> From the cherry trees we continued going north through the

brush and woods. I said, "I hunt rabbits. If I can find a rabbit's nest, we can have some fun." After walking a way, the other three turned east and I kept going north. As I was walking I came to a big bush. I had to either go one way or the other way around. Then I noticed something underneath the bush, something black. It looked like some old rags or coat, or rug. It looked funny to me so I lifted a corner of it. I saw something wrapped up with white paper what looked like a sausage or something, thicker than a broom handle. I dropped the rag or rug and I called out to the other guys who were about ten yards away, "Hey, you guys, look what I found here!" They came over and I picked up the corner again. I asked, "What is this?" One fella said, "I don't know." Just then there was a shot from a rifle. We all looked up. Two guys were standing north of us, holding rifles on us. They told us to start walking towards two other fellas on the hill in the cemetery. They took us to the cemetery and they put us in a car. They told us nothing. They took us to the city hall. All four of us went into one room. They asked me how I found this, how I got there, etc. The questioning was only about 15 minutes.

Then they put me in a cell. I was in there about one-half hour to 45 minutes. During this time they never asked me if I wanted to see a lawyer. I had just about fallen asleep when they told me the sheriff wanted to see me. They took me to a room and told me to sit there. The sheriff said, "Ignatz, you are an old man, almost as old as me. Are you going to tell the truth?" I said, "Sure I'm not going to tell you a lie." He said, "Raise your right hand and say you put the dynamite there." I said, "I'm never going to say that I put the dynamite down there even if you hang me up. I found it, that's all." On further questioning I told them that in the old country, I used dynamite and caps when I worked for the railroad [forty-five years before]. They questioned me about fuses, caps and dynamite, but I told them I never saw any dynamite or caps in this country and I don't know how they use it here.

The chief asked me if I knew how to dynamite cars. I told him, "No, that's a foolish question. I always go to bed at 7:00 P.M." He also asked me if I had ammunition in my house. I told him I had a 12-gauge pump shot-gun for hunting. They took that. They also asked me if I had any paint. I told them I did.

At five o'clock they took me home and searched my garage, car and house. That's when they took my gun.

I told them I'd take a lie detector test. They said if I'd take the test and State Crime Laboratory found I lied, I could be put in jail the rest of my life. I said I wasn't afraid of that, but because of my heart, I couldn't take any more shoving back and forth from the chief's office to the jail and back all the time.

When they asked me if I wanted my name in the paper, I told them I didn't care — so did my picket captain, Dan Regan.[3]

Gibeault's story was similar to Kastelic's. He recalled being shown the tree grafts and Kastelic's continuing in a northerly direction "looking for rabbits" while the others headed northeast; that they were called to look at what Kastelic found in the bushes; that they heard shots fired and were taken to the city hall and courthouse for interrogation, fingerprinting and "mug shots."

Dan Regan stated:

> They questioned me whether I had anything to do with it, whether I knew it was there, whether I knew the person or persons who put it there, whether I knew it was there before the chief told me. One question was put in a vague way — whether I knew the dynamite was there *until* the chief told me. I told him to re-word the question. He did — he substituted "until" with "before." I answered "no." The wording always bothered me until the wording was changed. This probably showed up on the machine [lie detector]. After they were through, they called Paul and me back in and told us they weren't quite clear and satisfied, and asked us to come back again Thursday [about a 125-mile trip]. We said we would. After we got back to Sheboygan we decided — three of us, Phil didn't have to go back — not to go back. We decided enough is enough.[4]

The law officials' report on the strikers' arrest was spread in screaming headlines in area newspapers. *The Milwaukee Sentinel* gave it front-page, 8-column headlines in 1½-inch block type: "Free 4 Kohler Strikers Seized Near Dynamite," and the pictures in *The Sheboygan Press* were 3-column-wide cuts of photographs taken at the site of the "discovery." The fact that the charges were dropped rated much more modest headlines on a 2-column story in the *Press*, May 5.

Statements of the four men indicated the strain and anxiety to which they were subjected in the hours following their arrest. None of them was advised that he could call a lawyer. Requests to be allowed to phone home were put off throughout the day with "We'll see," and between questionings, the men were held in cells without being told why they were arrested. Late in the afternoon, they were taken to their homes where officers conducted a search of house and premises. Lie-detector tests were urged upon them by the authorities on the ground that it "would clear us [the strikers] with the public."

District Attorney Weber had concluded his letter to Pinekenstein:

> It is always a source of inspiration to this office when citizens of your high calibre cooperate so fully with the law enforcement agencies of the county. On behalf of all law enforcement agencies in the county I . . . thank you for your cooperation. . . .[5]

Seven automobiles were dynamited in Sheboygan and vicinity between February and April, 1955. The community was apprehensive and law-enforcement officers were understandably eager to find the perpetrators. They were spurred on by charges, made by the company over the months, that both city and county law enforcement were not doing enough to try to apprehend vandals. The "stake-out" on the dynamite cache was made a joint venture, with two sheriff's deputies on each of two night shifts and two Sheboygan police officers on the daytime shift, even though the cache was outside the city limits. When the four strikers were picked up, *The Sheboygan Press* carried 3-column pictures of the police chief, sheriff and the deputies at the dynamite cache.

In an interview with former Sheriff Mosch, the author learned that an employee of a Sheboygan firm[6] had reported the find of the dynamite. One story was that the man had been looking for mushrooms. *The Milwaukee Sentinel* reported he had been looking for black dirt (on a very rainy weekend) and the informant himself told the author he was merely out for a walk. When Mosch inquired of the informant (January, 1965) about the circumstances under which he had discovered the dynamite, he wanted to know why the question should be raised again ten years later. Sheboygan police officers, the former mayor and the former sheriff all recalled that it was raining so hard the Sunday the find was reported that the creek nearby was overflowing when they visited the scene, and Police Lieutenant Clarence Zimmerman remembers falling into the swollen creek as he tried to cross on a log that lay across the stream.

The author talked with the police officers assigned to the day-time shift — Leroy Hotz and Robert Nitsch — and learned that other strikers had been seen walking through the gravel pit north of Gate 8 on several occasions during the week, but there had been no indication they knew the dynamite was there. When Kastelic picked up the old coat covering the cache, the deputies, under orders to arrest anyone who came to the cache, moved in. In Sheboygan two men were taken to the city jail and two to the county jail, apparently so both departments could share credit for the arrest and apprehension.

The circumstances raised enough doubts in the author's mind about whether the four men deserved the adverse publicity they received so that he visited the Gibeault, Pinekenstein and Regan families and found that the men did not deviate in any essential point from their affidavits, even though ten years had passed. (Kastelic had been dead for some time.) The traumatic experience had left a lasting impression on them all. The author also talked with Elmer Madson, then head of the detective agency employed by the Kohler Company, now chief of police in Green Bay, Wisconsin. Madson said the stake-out had been "badly handled"; that many knew the dynamite was there; and that "they never got the right guys." Charles Wilson also had the impression that people, generally, knew about the dynamite before the men were arrested. Wilson said there had been a report that — by accident or design — a gun had been discharged by a stake-out guard, which might have tipped off the perpetrators that the cache was under surveillance. This implies, of course, that pickets hearing a shot (if there was one) would know what it signified. This also suggested that Wilson believes there was a possibility that one of the stake-out guards intended to alert the strikers in the area. Had this been the case, it would have been even less likely the men who were arrested were guilty, for surely no one involved with the dynamite would go near it while it was under surveillance. No evidence was found that any-one heard or knew that a gun had been discharged while the cache was under guard, but apparently some strikers wondered what the law-enforcement officers were doing near the creek. At one time, the officers even used a fishpole to obscure the reason for their being there.

Philip Pinekenstein, whom the district attorney exonerated,

told the author that he was firmly convinced, even though he felt cool toward the union, that none of the men arrested at the cache had anything to do with it.[7] Under economic pressure, Pinekenstein returned to work at Kohler in 1957. He believes there was a miscarriage of justice because the informant, who was not publicly identified by the law officials, had not been submitted to a polygraph test as the men had been. So strongly did District Attorney Weber feel about the men completing the lie-detector test, Mrs. Gibeault said, that he became very angry with her on the phone when he learned her husband would not go back to Madison. Several officials mentioned that the union attorneys had advised the men not to complete the tests and that they had then gone to Milwaukee to consult about what they should do. Asked about this, Gibeault and Regan [8] maintained that they had independently made up their minds on the way back from Madison that "enough is enough." "We went to Milwaukee, all right," Gibeault said, "but it was to discuss with Max Raskin if we had grounds for suing for false arrest," for they all felt their rights had been violated by the way the law officials went about holding them, without counsel or even a chance to phone their anxious wives.

Excerpts from the Madson Detective Agency reports of May 3, 1955, made to Lyman Conger, disclose their eagerness to apprehend someone at the dynamite "plant," and the intimate relationship they had cultivated with law-enforcement officers and officials.

Further interview with Chief Walter Wagner . . . April 28th and 29th revealed information to the effect that the plant on the dynamite previously mentioned in this report is going to be continued until Saturday or Sunday, depending upon the circumstances, at which time they are going to take photographs of the plant, its location and of the dynamite and coat covering it. According to Wagner, he believes that even though no one went directly to the dynamite in question that there should be enough to at least pick up ———— and that from him the names of the other individuals who were in the area be obtained, and pick them up for interviews as to the dynamite plant. Chief Wagner feels that no results will come from the plant but rather than give it up at the present time, he is going to continue it for at least a couple of days more. Chief Wagner advised that he feels that an arrest of ———— or an interview with ————, together with pictures of the location of the dynamite, particularly with reference to its close location to the strike headquarters . . . would be indicative to the general public of the owners and users of the dynamite in question. Chief Wagner intends, even though the interview is negative to release all the facts regarding its location and substance, and to let the people of Sheboygan draw their own general conclusions based primarily on the fact that five strikers were in the area [another group of strikers who went for a walk near picket gate 8, other than the 4 arrested on Friday morning] . . . Chief Wagner advised on Thursday, April 28th, that he would immediately notify Mr. Adams or Mr. Madson [of the detective agency] when the surveillance was discontinued or when arrests were made. . . .[9]

Albert Gore, NLRB counsel, was in Sheboygan when the dynamite cache was publicized. He met with Police Chief Wagner to discuss the matter, in the presence of Adams and Madson, whom he had been led to believe were local Sheboygan detectives. The Madson reports to Conger quote Gore as saying, ". . . if an act of vandalism is proven against strikers, *our* case goes out the window."

Gore was greatly concerned about the incident, for the NLRB staff had the responsibility to investigate the facts for the NLRB General Counsel, and under the law, either labor *or* management may file charges of unfair labor practice. Detective Madson prepared an affidavit in which he stated that his colleague, Adams, asked Gore if any conclusions could be drawn from the fact that "all the acts of violence were against non-strikers." (This is not borne out by facts.) Madson quoted Gore as replying that he had made a search of court cases in 48 states and "found only one lower court case in Florida substantiating this [that NLRB would be required to withdraw from a case when all the acts of vandalism had been committed against nonstrikers]." Even so, as Gore explained to the author, a number of Federal Circuit Courts of Appeals had ruled against the Florida decision. This incident, as company, union, NLRB and law officials were well aware, was "loaded." Whether the cache was genuine or a "plant" has never been determined.

Gore recalled that he made a general reference to the famous Mohawk Valley Formula (see Appendix) which suggests that, at times, employers have blamed unions for violence they did not commit. The detectives apparently were not familiar with this "formula" because Madson refers to comment by Gore in these terms: ". . . they had information that a Mohawk Valley group had hired private detectives to do acts of violence against non-striking employees to make it look as though the Union strikers were doing it. . . ."

The Kohler Humane Society

It has been recorded for posterity that John M. Kohler, founder of the company, was a charter member of the Sheboygan Humane Society. On June 7, 1955, a Humane Society chapter was organized in the Village of Kohler with Waldemar G. Capelle, A. J. Aschenbrenner, attorney, and five other nonstriking residents as incorporators. There was a reference made by the incorporators that they had "some problems with cats and dogs" in the Village.

Graskamp, Local 833 president, charged (June 27, 1955) that the Kohler Humane Society chapter had been formed for the purpose of legally possessing machine guns and called it a "sneak play" because "it [the Company] thinks this will give them legal leeway to keep their . . . guns."* Several days later the Wisconsin Humane Society asked that the charter of the new Kohler chapter be revoked if it was not organized to carry out the traditional functions of such a society.[11]

Testifying before the McClellan Committee, Police Chief Capelle said the training of the initial 45 special police consisted of "regular basic, police training" including the fundamentals of village ordinances, State statutes, operation of squad-car radio and foot-patrol techniques. In addition, there was "training and target practice in the use of guns that we have, which include revolver, shotgun, submachinegun and gas guns."[12] Ultimately, Capelle said, there was "quite a bit of ado" about the machine guns and tear gas. On the village attorney's advice, the humane society was set up "for prevention of cruelty to animals," and Capelle was selected as chief officer — making him a state official confirmed by the governor. This move afforded "added protection," it was explained, "to insure the legal right" of village police to possess the weapons.

* A quirk in the Wisconsin laws, it was discovered, made it legal for Humane Society Officers to possess machine guns. Article 3 of the Society's Articles of Incorporation provided, "The purpose shall be aiding the *enforcement of the law* for the prevention/or punishment of cruelty to animals, children, women, aged or dependent people or criminals."[10]

Seven men carrying violin cases paraded before the Kohler village hall on June 8, 1955, to call public attention to the machine guns in posses-sion of village authorities. Talking with Chief Capelle is Robert Treuer of the UAW. (Milwaukee Journal *photo*)

On June 7, 1955, some strikers decided to dramatize the ma-chine-gun issue in Kohler Village. Seven pickets marched back and forth before Kohler village hall, carrying signs calling for the re-moval of illegal machine guns from Kohler, and toting empty violin cases.* There were very few spectators in the village and only after the demonstrators had been arrested and pictures taken, was the machine-gun story picked up and carried in major Wis-consin papers.

The Clay Boat Incident

One major event of the strike involved not only union, com-pany and community but the wider Great Lakes area as well. Be-cause of it, the cities of Milwaukee (Wisconsin), and Muskegon (Michigan), and Montreal (Quebec) all had a taste of the strike

---

* A violin case with a machine gun inside became a symbol of the gangster-ism of the Prohibition era.

at Kohler; the governor of Wisconsin was asked to intervene, by calling out the National Guard, if necessary; President Eisenhower was requested by Mayors Rudolph Ploetz of Sheboygan and Frank P. Zeidler of Milwaukee to provide more assistance in settling the dispute; the FMCS was asked to play a more active role, and the NLRB sent 25 people — most of its regional staff — to Sheboygan County to obtain affidavits as to what happened and who was responsible [13] in this major episode in the strike.

Referred to as the "clay boat incident," the altercation over the M.S. *Fossum*, loaded with special ball clay from England for the strike-bound Kohler Company, remained in the headlines for months. This event became a major issue in the strategy of company *vs.* union, each side calling public attention to the activities of the other in the hope of making some gains in the stalemated industrial warfare.

Mayor Rudolph Ploetz was apprised by a letter (June 28, 1955), from G. A. Desmond of the Kohler Company's legal department:

In our discussion some time ago relative to police protection when our clay boats are unloaded at the Hildebrand dock in Sheboygan, you requested that you be advised as soon as we have information concerning the date of arrival of the vessel.

We have been informed that the "S.S. Fossum" departed Montreal, Canada, on June 26, and is expected to arrive in Sheboygan on the morning of July 1, 1955.

On July 1, Desmond wrote Mayor Ploetz that the "S.S. Fossum is now expected on Saturday, July 2nd." On July 2, he wrote to Ploetz:

. . . Certain statements were made by Local 833 UAW-CIO in its radio broadcast over radio station WHBL at 6:30 P.M. on July 1, 1955, in an obvious attempt to invite a large number of their members to be present during the docking and unloading of the boat.

This is notice that we demand adequate police protection to prevent any mob or riot interference with the unloading of the boat and the transportation of the clay, and in case such protection is not provided and damage results we intend to hold the city of Sheboygan and you personally liable under the provisions of Section 66.01 of the Wisconsin Statutes for any damage, including demurrage, which may result.

The radio broadcast referred to was one of many broadcasts prepared and given by Robert Treuer during the strike. Treuer, radio commentator for the union, had said in his July 1 program:

. . . Also in the news, a clayboat — loaded with clay for the Kohler Company, is expected to dock in Sheboygan Harbor some time Saturday or Sunday. It is expected of course that a number of people will be on hand to meet and greet this clayboat when it arrives. Information is that the sailors on board the ship have been contacted by CIO brothers before the ship has even approached Sheboygan, and have been told the full story of the Kohler strike. . . .

Two days later, July 3, Treuer's WHBL broadcast reported:

. . . Saturday the *SS Fossum*, a ship of Norwegian registry, pulled into Sheboygan harbor with a load of clay for the Kohler Company. As the boat approached Sheboygan harbor, a little armada . . . little speedboats with outboard motors, went out to greet them. The Kohler strikers in those three small boats carried signs in Norwegian, German and English, announcing the fact that the clay on board the *SS Fossum* was consigned to the strikebound Kohler plant. No effort was made, of course, to detain the boat or to interfere with it in any way — rather the effort was made only to advertise the fact that a labor dispute exists at the Kohler Company. It must be understood that the sailors, who are mainly Norwegians and Scandinavians, on board this ship, are prevented by law from refusing to handle this cargo or bring it in. So of course, no effort was made to even ask them to do such a thing.

Radio station WHBL carried numerous newscasts and bulletins between 9 A.M. and 10 P.M. about the events at the unloading dock on July 5.

The first report announced: ". . . a report received a short time ago tells of several thousands of union men and their families milling around the boat."

At 12:15, the newscast read in part:

. . . An explosive situation is developing along the Sheboygan river at the foot of Pennsylvania Avenue where a Norwegian clay boat, loaded with clay for the Kohler Co., is docked. The clay boat — M.S. Fossum — was scheduled to be unloaded this morning according to Kohler Co. Atty. Lyman Conger. Conger said drivers for the Buteyn Trucking Co. of Sheboygan were to have begun unloading operations this morning, but that a threatening mob prevented them. Several hundred members of striking Kohler Local 833 have been picketing the boat since early this morning. Shortly after nine o'clock this morning a car driven by Kohler Co. time-study man Joseph Born had difficulty leaving the dock area through a driveway because of numerous persons milling in front of the driveway. Police parted the crowd long enough for the car and its occupants to drive through. . . . Other passengers in the auto aside from Born were Kohler plant manager Edmund Biever, Paul Jacobi, the Company photographer, and Company attorney Gerard Desmond.

Treuer's evening broadcast on July 5 gave a further account of the harbor situation, reporting that "the S.S. Fossum is still not unloaded as tempers flared along the waterfront . . . angry Sheboygan citizens crowded the dockside to give vent to their strong feelings of disdain for the Kohler Company."

Reports and investigations agree that the crowd was not just Kohler strikers, but others from the community — employees of other plants, closed for the July 4th holiday; young people, professional and white-collar workers, and curious townspeople. A retired member of the police force told the author, "The Company knew they couldn't unload that boat over a holiday, so why did they have to bring it in and let it set there and get everybody riled up?" Treuer also commented on the appearances of Edmund J. Biever:

> The Kohler Company, in its usual blundering fashion, almost set off a serious riot at least twice when — deliberately or accidentally, we don't know yet — it sent one of the most hated individuals in the long strike situation to the scene in person. This was none other than Edmund Biever, the long-missing plant manager who failed to answer seven subpoenas last week to appear at the NLRB hearing but *did* show up this morning at the clayboat dock. Nothing could have been more coldly calculated than Biever's appearance to provoke an incident. . . .

The union's feelings were stated, quite bluntly, by Robert Burkart when he participated on the union's daily radio program, July 6:

> . . . After the company representatives angrily walked out of the meeting,* Mayor Ploetz determined that the meeting should be held

* Called by Mayor Ploetz to attempt to resolve the clay boat unloading altercation.

anyway, and sat and talked with the union representatives who were present. We told the Mayor that we would cooperate with him and with the authorities in every way to keep peace and order in the community. We told him that our organization (and this is contrary to some things that appear in the *Press* tonight, especially the items appearing immediately under the pictures) that our organization did not promulgate this thing at the foot of Pennsylvania [Avenue. It was] a spontaneous community reaction to the vicious anti-labor policies of the Kohler Company's industrial relations department. Allan Graskamp . . . this morning . . . pointed out how difficult it was for other workers in Sheboygan to come to agreements with their employers because on so many occasions these employers are saying, well, let's wait until this Kohler thing is settled.

An examination of 281 pages of documents — letters, newspaper stories from *The Sheboygan Press*, *The Milwaukee Journal* and *The Milwaukee Sentinel*, radio scripts and affidavits, leads the author to this interpretation of what happened and why:

July marked the beginning of the sixteenth month of the strike. There were no signs of its being close to a settlement. The company was operating somewhere between half and full capacity with non-strikers and new employees and was making no effort to reach an agreement with the union. The union had undertaken a nation-wide boycott against Kohler Company. While it was having some effect on company sales, it was not as successful as the union had hoped, and some of its staff members were looking for ways to dramatize and call attention to their plight. Robert Treuer took upon himself the decision to get together a small "UAW Navy" to go out to meet the M.S. *Fossum*. Treuer later told the McClellan Committee:

> We thought . . . if we could get any publicity to the effect that the strike was still going on, it would be to our benefit. . . . We were going to have six small rowboats with outboard motors . . . go out and meet the clay boat and . . . escort it in. These little boats would have people . . . carrying signs, saying, "This clay is for the strikebound Kohler Company," and "This strike is still going on." It didn't quite work out that way because, of the six boats, sir, three foundered before they . . . got too far away, and one of the fellows got tired of waiting and he went fishing. . . .

Don Rand, an International representative from Detroit, working on the boycott, apparently agreed that a large turnout at the unloading dock would indicate support for the strike and he hoped he could persuade Buteyn Brothers, who were to unload the clay, that their co-operation could contribute to an earlier settlement of the dispute.

The local executive committee of the union knew that Gerard A. Desmond of the Kohler Company had written Mayor Ploetz, demanding "adequate police protection to prevent any mob or riot interference with the unloading of the boat. . . ." Committee members apparently had ambivalent feelings about the net effect of a mass demonstration at the dock because all the testimony of local officers indicates that they did not endorse any demonstration, yet did not object to individuals going down on their own initiative. "Eggie" Kohlhagen, secretary of Local 833, stated under oath:

> . . . we made an unofficial decision to do nothing about the clay-boat, to establish no picket lines and to make no attempt to stop the unloading of the boat. However, we did not want to publicize the decision because it would tip our hand to the Company; this is a war of nerves and we didn't want the Company to know ahead of time what we would do. . . . We did, however, make an effort to tell our membership about this decision through the grapevine — through the strike kitchen and the picket lines. We told them that the Union would do nothing with respect to the clayboat, that anyone who went down to the dock went as an individual spectator responsible for his own activity. . . .[14]

The news stories and radio broadcasts created much interest and curiosity regarding the arrival of the boat. Spectators, including strikers, began gathering near the dock at five o'clock in the morning. By nine o'clock the crowd was estimated at a thousand, including many women and children, perhaps a third of whom were Kohler strikers, the rest coming from other plants in Sheboygan and also including business and professional people.

The Buteyn Brothers' trucks and unloading equipment came early in the morning and parked in a line on Pennsylvania Avenue. Police Chief Wagner told the author that he asked Peter Buteyn and several of the drivers, "You want to get in here? I'll open up for you," and that two of the drivers said, "I ain't crossing any picket line," and then the trucks and equipment were pulled out by Buteyn.

A crowd estimated at 2,500 milled around the Kohler Company crane brought in to unload the clay boat, Fossum. *Tires were deflated by persons in the crowd to prevent moving the equipment into the dock area of Sheboygan. (World Wide photo)*

Arrangements were then made by company officials to borrow a Buteyn truck to bring in the company's loading crane, which arrived midmorning. The company car with Biever — and later with Born, Desmond and Jacobi — made several trips in and out, having considerable difficulty with the crowd, who moved in, shouting and rocking the car. There was an incident in which a woman threw herself, or was pushed or shoved, on the hood of the Kohler car and shouts went up, "Biever's done it again!" The emotions of the crowd were intense, but the Kohler officials left the area, and allowed the crane and truck to stand on the street.*

Air was let out of the tires of the truck carrying the crane; a gas line was pulled out of another truck; and the stalled equipment

---

* Wagner told the author that Biever came into his office afterward and said, "As long as we can't unload, we'll let that crane set there."

became a drawing point for the milling crowd. When Mayor Ploetz prevailed upon Peter Buteyn to come down and move the crane out of the area, the crowd amused themselves by letting air out of the tires as fast as Buteyn got them repaired. He threatened to quit unless he got some help, so Ploetz got a sound truck and loud-speaker and asked the people to permit the truck to be repaired so the equipment could be moved out.

The worst thing that happened, in the opinion of several law-enforcement officers, was that a nonstriking Kohler worker, Roman Gruenwald, received a broken nose. The crowd had identified him as a strikebreaker and he was chased into a nearby tavern and "roughed up." Windows were broken in the house of a nonstriker who lived near the dock; one car was overturned. Several police officials felt that the Kohler crane had been brought in "for effect" with no intention of actually unloading the clay. After the crane and truck were removed, police dispersed the crowd and the dock area became relatively quiet.

Mayor Ploetz was annoyed that the Kohler Company had not even replied to his requests for a meeting to discuss what might be done to bring about a settlement in the strike, yet had demanded an immediate reply to its letter demanding police protection for the clay boat. Ploetz and a majority of the Sheboygan aldermen, elected with labor support in the spring of 1955, were considered to be in sympathy with the strikers. Alderman Carl A. Mohar of the 5th Ward charged during the strike that the previous city administration had been "puppets of special interests," and, at one time, presented a prepared statement to the city council which said in part, ". . . All the clay in England and all the truck tires in the U.S. are not worth one human life, be it one of my people from the 5th Ward or a citizen from the first Ward. . . ." The sheriff and mayor both feared a possible repetition of the violence of the 1934 strike.

On July 6 Mayor Ploetz ordered the police department not to allow unloading within three blocks of the dock because after the disturbances on July 5, "My primary concern," he said, "is for the protection of the people of this community." He called a meeting that morning in his office of representatives of the company and union, but Lyman Conger and other Kohler officials walked out within two minutes after the meeting began, objecting to the presence of Dan Nero, an Associated Press photographer.

The company blamed the near-riot situation on July 5 on the union and the mayor. The union continued to place the responsibility for all local labor unrest on the Kohler Company's "refusal to sit down and bargain a decent American contract."[15] That night the *Fossum* sailed for Milwaukee, about sixty miles south of Sheboygan. Milwaukee unionists and the state president of the Wisconsin CIO, Charles Schultz, contacted Mayor Frank P. Zeidler, asking that the city refuse to unload the clay. A city-wide strike of all CIO union members was threatened. Schultz told the Associated Press that he received assurance from Mayor Zeidler that the *Fossum* would not be unloaded there "until the Mayor receives a legal opinion."[16]

Municipal port director, Harry C. Brockel of Milwaukee, called an emergency meeting of the city harbor commission for the next morning (July 7) to determine policy, saying, "The port of Milwaukee serves hundreds of shippers in midwestern states. We have always recognized valid and legitimate labor disputes and have refused to handle strikebound ships from other ports."

Schultz disclosed that a "Union boy" had been aboard the *Fossum* as a passenger as it went through the locks at Buffalo, New York. (The locks are at the Welland Canal, Ontario.) He asserted that "this ship is a propaganda instrument to sharpen public opinion against us. We can't permit it to be unloaded here without doing something about it. . . . There is no reason why the city of Milwaukee should 'aid and comfort' Herbert Kohler. Let him do his bargaining in Sheboygan."

The Milwaukee city attorney's staff advised Mayor Zeidler that the city was obligated to handle "legitimate cargo if the city has the facilities with which to handle the cargo," *but*, the opinion continued, "if the city employees will not unload the ship, the city is placed in the position of not having the facilities to handle it." Mayor Zeidler said his immediate reaction was to ask the owners of the cargo to send the ship back to Sheboygan.

Anthony J. King, business manager of Plumbers Local No. 75 of Milwaukee, wired Mayor Frank P. Zeidler:

The officers and members of Plumbers and Gasfitters' Union No. 75 AFL hereby register opposition to the attempt of the Kohler Company and others who seek to justify the unloading of clay cargo on the boat "Fossum" docked in the Milwaukee harbor. The un-American labor policy of the Kohler Company should satisfy all fair-minded people that this firm does not subscribe to accepted conventional procedure in dealing with labor unions. The Kohler Company merits no assistance from the citizens of this community.

By Saturday morning, a week after arriving in Sheboygan, the clay boat was scheduled to sail for the harbor at Montreal, Quebec. From there it was expected that the clay would be transported by train to Kohler, Wisconsin.

On July 11, Mayor Zeidler wrote President Eisenhower an 800-word airmail letter requesting the President to give the Federal Mediation and Conciliation Service "whatever additional help or prestige it needs to continue its efforts to effect a settlement." Meanwhile UAW regional director, Harvey Kitzman, said that all ships attempting to unload clay for the Kohler Company would be picketed. A second Norwegian freighter, the *Divina*, was already en route with clay to Milwaukee.

The Chicago Tribune reported (July 11) that "opposition by organized labor and labor-dominated officials of this city to future unloading here of foreign ships carrying clay for the Kohler Company collapsed tonight (July 10) in the face of threatening lawsuits." Labor leaders changed their position with the explanation that the change was due to Mayor Zeidler's appeal to the President. This short-lived truce collapsed when a Kohler Company spokesman indicated that the company was not "interested in anybody trying to do something to settle the strike,"[17] thus stiffening the attitude of organized labor.

Lyman C. Conger characterized Mayor Zeidler's request to the President as another attempt by the union to get out of "an impossible situation." He said, "The practice of government agencies trying to bail unions out of impossible situations caused by their own recklessness has served to increase strikes and not to reduce them."

On July 12, Governor Walter J. Kohler, Jr., announced, "I will make certain there will be no unlawful interference with lawful commerce." Asked if the National Guard would be called out in event of future disturbances, the governor replied, "We'll cross that bridge when we come to it."

On the same day, Kohler Company attorneys accused three NLRB attorneys of "flagrant abuse" in processing 11 union complaints of unfair labor practices and alleged that the NLRB counsel had "openly acted, not as governmental officials but as the *alter ego* of the union." The NLRB hearing, in recess since July 1, was scheduled to resume July 20 in Sheboygan before NLRB Trial Examiner George A. Downing, of Washington, D.C.

Wisconsin State Federation of Labor president, George Haberman, told the Milwaukee common council that, "Milwaukee should not accept lake cargoes that are diverted here because of labor difficulties elsewhere." Harbor commissioners were strongly divided on what position the city should take.

President Eisenhower ordered the Federal Mediation and Conciliation Service "to intensify in every way possible" its efforts to settle the strike.

The Milwaukee harbor commission said it could find no legal basis or precedent for refusing the cargo. The owners of the *Divina* had in the meantime decided not to send their ship to Milwaukee but to dock at Montreal. O. S. Hoebroeckx,* attorney for the charterers of the M.S. *Fossum*, announced on July 14 that his firm was preparing lawsuits, asking damages of between $50,000 and $100,000 from the cities of Milwaukee and Sheboygan.

On July 18, members of the Independent Longshoremen's Association, Montreal, advertising that the clay was bound for the struck Kohler Company, decided not to cross a union picket line. The day before, Kitzman had telephoned the Canadian Congress of Labor with which Canadian UAW locals were affiliated, informing them that the clay on the *Fossum* and *Divina* was destined for a UAW-struck plant. UAW pickets appeared on the dock in Montreal the next morning with signs. Donay Bibeault, ILA representative, stated that his union would not cross the picket lines as "a matter of union principles," and a UAW representative said pickets would remain on the dock as long as the two clay boats were in the Montreal harbor. Harbor police ordered the pickets from the dock area and on the nineteenth unloading of the boats proceeded.

On July 20, five prominent Sheboygan businessmen — a corporation lawyer and the presidents of a dairy, a shoe manufacturing firm, a coal company and department store — formed a "law and

* Formerly attorney for the Wisconsin Manufacturers Association.

order unit," the "Committee of Five," to protest the violence that had occurred in connection with the strike. *The Milwaukee Sentinel*, one of the Hearst newspapers which was more against the union and against the mayor of Sheboygan than was *The Sheboygan Press* or *The Milwaukee Journal*, editorialized about the five-man committee:

> . . . The thousands of other God-fearing, law-abiding Sheboygan residents who are sick and tired of the alien-directed reign of totalitarian terror in their city will do well to rally about this sound nucleus of aroused citizenry. . . .

U.S. Secretary of Labor James P. Mitchell told an industrial relations institute in Madison, Wisconsin, that the 15-month-old Kohler strike was "deplorable" and that management and labor ought to sit down as quickly as possible to settle their dispute.[18]

On July 23, Charles Schultz, Wisconsin CIO president, met with Governor Walter J. Kohler, Jr., to discuss the prolonged and violence-marked strike. The NLRB hearing on 11 unfair-labor-practice charges against the company was recessed, while the union agreed not to interfere with clay-boat unloading.

Three Federal mediators were assigned to a new negotiating session with union and company representatives. Arthur Goldberg, at that time national counsel for the CIO, Allan Graskamp, Harvey Kitzman, Emil Mazey and Max Raskin, Milwaukee, Wisconsin, CIO counsel, represented the union; Lyman Conger, L. L. Smith, company vice president, William F. Howe, Washington, D.C., attorney, and E. J. Hammer were the Kohler spokesmen.

On July 26, the Muskegon (Michigan) city commission asked the Grand Trunk Western railroad not to use the city's railroad or port facilities to handle the clay consigned from Montreal to the struck Kohler Company, after the AFL municipal dockworkers refused to unload the clay when CIO pickets appeared. National Maritime Union leaders also hinted that NMU crews aboard Great Lakes car ferries might not handle cars loaded with Kohler clay. Eight clay cars were switched into the Kohler plant grounds with supervisory personnel of the Northwestern Railroad operating the diesel locomotive. Pickets and strike sympathizers gathered along the railroad tracks shouting threats and catcalls, but did not follow through with action. Most of the Sheboygan police force and a

Following the departure of the Fossum, *a token picket line was at the railroad crossings as the first cars loaded with clay for the Kohler plant were moved through the city of Sheboygan.* (Sheboygan Press *photo*)

dozen sheriff's deputies were on hand as the train passed intersections in Sheboygan.

Subsequently seven boxcars of clay were delivered to the Kohler Company "with even less excitement than attended the delivery of the first eight carloads," reported *The Milwaukee Sentinel* on July 29.

On July 31, the *Sentinel* reported that Governor Walter Kohler found himself in the position of an "umpire" who had "to call 'em as he sees 'em" when he announced he would call out the National Guard, if necessary, to preserve order.

On August 1 the Northwestern Railroad said it would seek an injunction against any further picketing, claiming that this was "unlawful secondary boycott activity." Union attorney Max Raskin was sure there were no grounds for suit. A crew of train men refused to transport freight for the Kohler Company past striking CIO pickets; supervisory personnel of the railroad piloted the train into the Kohler plant.

August 3, twelve labor organizations were charged with violating the Taft-Hartley Act by interfering with shipments of clay to the struck Kohler Company plant. Attorneys for owners and shippers of the clay filed charges with the regional office of the NLRB in Chicago. The attorneys said that the Kohler Company had requested a delay in the filing of these charges, while Federal mediators, negotiating in Chicago, attempted to end the strike. The talks failed on August 1. "It now appears that relief under the Act * is essential to enable our clients to fulfill their contractual obligations," the attorneys said.

The Sheboygan Central Labor Council (AFL) wrote Mayor Ploetz, supporting his stand in the clay-boat incident: "Your consideration for the health and welfare of the people and their safety should be highly commended rather than condemned by the so-called representative committee of business men. . . . It is apparent that the true and hidden meaning of the committee [the five-man committee mentioned under the incidents of July 20] is to support the Kohler Co. as against the Kohler Strikers."[19]

On August 5, Clarence Leverenz, president of the Leverenz Shoe Co. and member of the "Committee of Five" denied emphatically that he had urged the Sheboygan chief of police to use clubs on Kohler strikers. Mr. Leverenz said that the quote attributed to him by Mayor Rudolph Ploetz "is not correct." Ploetz, speaking at a special meeting of Local 833, had quoted Leverenz as telling Police Chief Wagner, "Don't your boys carry billy clubs? Well, let's start swinging them and lay them down like cordwood and maybe the boys will come to their senses." Leverenz said the mayor had placed his own interpretation on any statements he [Leverenz] had made, but he would not reveal what, if anything, he *had* said to Wagner.[20]

The Wisconsin Chamber of Commerce, meeting in Madison, said it had asked the state legislature (when it reconvened on October 3, 1955) to review what the chamber called "intimidation, force, boycotts, vandalism, property damage, and labor bosses' monopolistic tide." The chamber's letter stated:

Currently in Wisconsin, growth of union monopoly — attained through picketing, "hot cargo" clauses, secondary boycotts, with the losses they bring to the employer's business and workmen's jobs — is being carried out under the guise of "freedom of speech." Wisconsin citizens have just cause for alarm. . . .

* Referring to the National Labor Relations Act, as amended.

The letter also commended Montreal officials for providing police protection in unloading the clay boats and continued:

> . . . However, in the sad tale of two cities, Sheboygan and Milwaukee, weak public officials, acting under the dictates of labor bosses, who threatened the loss of labor's votes, refused to rule that there was no local labor dispute. . . . Until Wisconsin citizens arouse themselves against these indefensible union practices, there is going to be chaos.

August 8: Three aids of the NLRB arrived in Milwaukee to begin an investigation of secondary boycott charges against 12 unions which allegedly interfered with clay shipments to the Kohler Company. Meanwhile 11 more boxcars of clay, bringing the total to 70, entered the Kohler plant, brought in by trains manned by supervisory personnel.

The unions named in the investigation were: Wisconsin State CIO; Wisconsin State Federation of Labor, AFL; UAW Local 833; International UAW-CIO; Milwaukee County CIO; Milwaukee District Council 48 of American Federation of State, County and Municipal Employees (AFSC & ME); Local No. 2 of the AFSC & ME, representing Milwaukee Dock Workers; AFL Operating Engineers No. 139 (Milwaukee Crane Operators); Milwaukee Federated Trades Council, AFL; International Brotherhood of Longshoremen at Duluth, AFL; AFL Maritime Trades Council, Duluth (Lake Superior Dock Workers); CIO National Maritime Union of Luddington, Michigan (where the boxcars from Montreal, loaded with clay, were put on ferryboats for Milwaukee). Later in the day, the investigators drove to Sheboygan.[21]

On August 9, Sheboygan Police Chief Walter H. Wagner submitted his resignation, effective October 1, to the city's Board of Police and Fire Commissioners. Police Captain Steen W. Heimke, forty-two, was named acting chief. Wagner, sixty-two, who had joined the police department in 1917, had asked for an indefinite leave about two weeks earlier because of ill health. He told reporters he was resigning "entirely on my own volition" because of a "highly nervous condition" (obvious to newsmen). Wagner recalled that he had been ready to retire two years earlier, but that Mayor Edward C. Schmidt and later Mayor Ploetz had insisted he continue.

In a letter to the Police and Fire Commission, Mayor Ploetz had charged Heimke with insubordination and recommended his demotion from captain to sergeant. He wrote that Heimke "devotes 75 per cent of his time to non-police activities . . . and that much of the time nobody in the department knows his whereabouts . . . I could write a book on what's been told me," Ploetz remarked.[22]

The police department had been under criticism ever since the strike began and especially after the clay-boat incident. Mayor Ploetz quoted Wagner as saying he was "fed up with all this." Wagner, referring to the appointment of Heimke as "a damn silly thing," said, "It shouldn't have come up in the first place . . . it was a lot of political maneuvering." Heimke, contacted later, said Ploetz's charge of insubordination is "the end result of a planned plot for the last two years," adding that "stooges of the chief have been spying on all my activities."[23]

August 10: *The Sheboygan Press* editorially commended Chief Wagner for his exceptional ability, for the recognition he received by being elected president of the Wisconsin Chiefs of Police Association for two terms, and concluded with:

. . . We earnestly hope that relief from the heavy burdens of office will quickly restore Chief Wagner to full health and that he will live many more years as one of this community's most respected citizens.

August 15: Before a jam-packed Sheboygan City Council chamber, Alderman Carl Mohar, in a prepared statement, renewed his attack on the previous city administration and the "Citizens' Committee of Five," stating that "instead of going to Madison [Wisconsin] to get an escort for the clay boats, they should have gone to the root of the problem, 3½ miles west of Sheboygan [Kohler]." Alderman Hugh A. Dales commented: "We have just heard criticism of our most respected citizens and I think it's childish, asinine and ridiculous."[24]

October 11: Mayor Ploetz told *The Sheboygan Press* that he had conferred with the officers of Local 833 and had been "assured again, as I always have in the past, that they wish to settle the Kohler strike in an amiable and peaceful manner." He said he had conferred with Police Chief Heimke and Sheriff Mosch and had been given assurance that "their departments could handle any situation that might arise in connection with unloading of further clay boats."

October 13: Allan Graskamp made the following statement:

Although we had hoped to be able to ignore the subject of the clay boats altogether, daily front page stories in the press and news items on the radio concerning the expected arrival of one or more clayboats in Sheboygan have forced us to make this comment:

"In accordance with the federal court stipulation entered into in Milwaukee some weeks ago, we will not picket nor otherwise interfere with the unloading of clayboats here. We have asked our membership to stay away from the unloading area, and we are asking all other citizens to do likewise, since the union might be blamed for whoever congregates at the dock. We wish to point out that this union was not responsible for the demonstrations last July and we will do everything in our power to prevent a recurrence."[25]

Governor Kohler issued a statement saying, "Very substantial units of the Guard have been alerted and will be ready for any emergency."[26]

October 17: A claim for damages as a result of the City of Sheboygan's alleged failure to provide protection for the unloading of a clay boat in July was rejected by the common council in a 13 to 3 vote. Buteyn Excavating Co. had asked for $2,335.19 in damages. City Attorney N. S. Heffernan had ruled that the council was barred from considering the claim because it had not been brought to the council by the judiciary committee within the 60-day period provided by law.[27]

October 24: Further complications developed in the city council, stemming from conflicting interpretations on proper legal procedure to be followed in processing damage claims.[28]

November 7: A second claim, filed by the Hildebrand Lumber and Supply Co. for $698.40 in damages stemming from the riot at the Sheboygan waterfront in July, was disallowed by the Sheboygan Common Council.

November 28: The Sheboygan Common Council voted down a resolution introduced by Alderman Mohar calling upon the Buteyn Excavating Co. to reimburse the city for police protection accorded its equipment when unloading clay for Kohler. He charged that the Buteyn equipment had been under "constant surveillance" by the police department over a period of weeks and that "never before had the city accorded that kind of protection to the equipment owned by a private party on private property." Police Chief Heimke had argued that "this is not a normal situation" in justifying the constant surveillance.[29]

December 29: The Kohler Company filed a claim for $60,516 in damages against the City of Sheboygan in connection with violence at the unloading docks in July. The firm said the largest item in the claim was $46,722 for moving the clay overland. It also listed $11,509 in legal fees and expenses to the importers.

January 4, 1956: A claim for $54,625.95 in damages, growing out of a failure to unload clay for the Kohler Company, was filed against the City of Milwaukee by Attorney O. Stanley Hoebroeckx on behalf of the clay importing firms. In Sheboygan a fifth claim was filed against the city, this one for $5,949 by a nonstriking Kohler employee, Roman Gruenwald, who alleged he was "severely beaten, bruised and injured by a concerted effort and conduct of many persons who participated in riotous conduct" on July 5. This brought claims against the City of Sheboygan to a total of $89,844.[30] Buteyn Brothers eventually were paid $2,000 by the City of Sheboygan on itemized damages of $2,355.92 on February 2, 1959.

The City of Milwaukee, on January 27, 1959, paid $43,039.88 to Paper Makers Importing Company to settle the damage suit involving the refusal to unload the *Fossum* and *Divina*. On March 4 of that year, it also paid $19,000 damages to ship owner Frederik Hoyer. The Sheboygan City Council authorized payment of $6,024.80 to the Kohler Company December 7, 1959, on its demand of $60,516.10 arising out of claims under Sec. 66.091 of Wisconsin statutes, relative to "the inability of the Kohler Company to unload or have unloaded certain vessels carrying clay to the Sheboygan harbor during the 1955 shipping season."[31]

The Bowling-Alley Incidents

Root's Recreation in Sheboygan, where a bowling tournament was in progress during February, 1956, became a place where there was severe friction between strikers and nonstrikers, resulting in charges against some strikers, which caused the NLRB later to uphold their dismissals by the company. The bowling-alley incidents received considerable attention, but the same feeling of antagonism found expression in taverns, department stores, gas stations — wherever strikers and nonstrikers, or their families, happened to meet.

Kohler had entered a team in the tournament and the team and its supporters included supervisory personnel from the company. Strikers and sympathizers gathered to jeer and shout in language the NLRB described as "particularly vile." From insults, it was only a step further to physical "roughing up." On February 6, 1956, John Nisporic, one of the hecklers, shouted, "Down with the rest of the dirty scabs!" and struck Robert DePagter in the ribs. The same evening, on the way out of the recreation hall, Paul Jacobi — a Kohler time-study man and company photographer who had made many entries against strikers in the company's "spy files" — was kicked several times by Ralph Sabish.

Two nights later, a crowd again gathered at Root's, jeering the Kohler bowlers and indulging in what *The Sheboygan Press* termed "hoodlumism." Police were called and 10 officers were dispatched to escort the Kohler team from the hall and hold back the crowd. Next day the Kohler Company announced it was withdrawing its team from the tournament. Three men — all of them strikers — and a woman, the wife of a former striker, were charged with disorderly conduct.

Witnesses testified that 100 to 150 people crowded the lanes; that hooting, name-calling and beer-throwing were indulged in by both men and women. Company attorney Desmond, who accompanied the Kohler team the evening of February 8, testified that Al Burkhard had remarked to him: "If the lights go out around here, there'll be a dead lawyer." In the hearings, the names of some of the better-known strikers were mentioned as being in the crowded lanes that evening and there is no doubt that the presence of company officials escorting the Kohler team helped draw the lines for a skirmish between the opposing factions.

The Quasius Case — A Mystery with Political Overtones

A destructive paint-bombing took place at the Quasius Brothers' contracting firm office in Sheboygan during the early morning hours of August 31, 1956. The incident set off a bitter round of ac-

The full-page advertisement in the Sheboygan Press, *August 31, 1955, inviting the public to see the vandalism damage at the Quasius Brothers contracting firm's office.*

cusations and counteraccusations, which provided ammunition in the campaign for sheriff that fall.

Quasius Brothers had begun work on a $300,000 construction job to build locker rooms, washrooms and a lunchroom for the enameling and shipping departments at Kohler. The firm employed about 60 building-trades-union workers, of whom only 5 agreed to work on this job. The $100 fines imposed by their union for crossing a picket line were paid by their employer.

According to *The Sheboygan Press* and police reports, 4 rocks and 5 jars filled with red paint were hurled through windows and a glass entrance door of the office, splattering walls, floors, chairs, desks and office equipment with paint and glass. One jar was not broken. Police Chief Heimke told the *Press* that the premises had been checked at 2:00 A.M. and the damage discovered at 7:00 A.M. when Leslie and Ray Quasius arrived at the office. The *Press* ran a 3-column picture of the exterior of the building and the story was headlined: "Quasius Bros. Inc. Object of Vicious Attack by Vandals." A *Press* employee, in view of the unsensational front-page picture, wondered why the paper had not used pictures of the inside paint damage.

The same edition contained a full-page ad, explaining that it was being run as a "public service" and depicted "before" and "after" scenes. The public was invited to visit the offices that evening and all day Saturday. According to the firm, over 7,000 accepted the invitation, and needless to say, this incident became the talk of the town, most people again assuming that one or more "union vandals" were the perpetrators.

The Sheboygan Press ran an editorial entitled, "Shocking Vandalism" and offered a $1,000 reward for information which would lead to the arrest and conviction of "the individual or individuals who are guilty of this barbarous act." Sheboygan builders, contractors and individuals added to the reward offer until it totaled nearly $10,000, none of which was ever collected.

Even before the local paper was printed, stories about the incident were in editions of the Milwaukee papers. The next day the same pictures of the paint damage were used in handbills distributed at the Sheboygan County fair, urging the election of Harold Kroll for sheriff. The handbills were sponsored by the Republican county campaign committee of which L. P. Chase and Carl J. Kohler of the Kohler Company were members.

The Sheboygan Builders' and Traders' Exchange held a meeting and voted "to conduct a program of public information on labor strife arising out of the Kohler strike and to promote the use of local-made products in an effort to help the economic situation in this area." They pledged themselves to work for "peace and harmony and prosperity," and to do away with "bickering" and "hatred." They commended the Sheboygan Board of Education for insisting on the installation of Kohler fixtures at one of the local schools.

The response was an ad sponsored by the Sheboygan County Central Labor Council on September 6 which asked:

1. why the State Mobile Crime Laboratory had not been called in immediately to investigate the paint bombing;

2. why the local police department did not call in the most experienced photographer in the county;

3. why the police did not rope off the area, rather than allowing 7,000 people to trample and destroy possible evidence;

4. why incidents of vandalism usually happened just before an election; and

5. why news articles always suggested that labor was connected with such acts, when court records showed the only conviction for vandalism had been that of a Kohler employee.*

"Let's Keep Our Eye on the Ball" the *Press* replied editorially, and quoted extensively from a union broadcast by Treuer and Graskamp, taking these two speakers to task for their charges as to how quickly the pictures had to be developed and the printing done for the full-page Quasius ad. This could not have been done if the *Press* had enforced its 48-hours-in-advance rule for ad copy, the union spokesman said. Exceptions had been made for the union, too, the *Press* retorted.

The Builders' and Traders' Exchange, on September 14, expressed their views further in a quarter-page ad in the *Press:*

The self-respecting citizens of Sheboygan know that outsiders have brought shame to the Sheboygan community where the tradition of *gemütlichkeit* . . . is yet the dominant influence. . . .

Either all decent residents . . . determine to rid themselves of the professional saboteurs and hatchet men using the Red hammer and sickle tactics . . . or they cave in to the diabolical will of the LAW-LESS guerillas. . . . Outsiders have planned, organized and perpetrated the crimes against persons in the Sheboygan community. . . . It is the duty and responsibility of Sheboygan residents to cooperate with the local police officers to apprehend and bring the GOONS to justice. . . .

In these advertisements, the Quasius case and vandalism were deliberately linked to the acid-blinding attack on Victor Riesel, newspaper columnist of New York City. Later ads emphasized

* There were also two men convicted in Sheboygan Falls who were neither Kohler workers nor strikers.

that the union's boycott must be defeated "UNTIL people can select the firm of their choice to install materials or products of their
choice . . . UNTIL this is a FREE COUNTRY."

Curiosity concerning a number of details connected with this
incident impelled the author to attempt to check further. The more
people he talked with, the more questions arose. Police-department
logs show that 4 men were off duty on the rainy, foggy night on
which the paint-bombing took place; a fifth man was sick, and a
sixth man on vacation, so that there was about a 35-per-cent reduction in the force. The Quasius families, according to Mrs.
Badtke, office secretary and sister of Ray and Leslie Quasius, who
appears in the ad pictures, were out of town that night for a family
anniversary get-together. These factors, together with the neighborhood in which the office is located — opposite a large shopping-
center parking lot, no homes within a block on either side — made
a combination of circumstances in which a bona fide vandal, or
someone politically-inspired, could commit the damage with little
danger of being caught. Records show that the police checked
out in detail, "tips" turned in throughout the neighborhood and that
these yielded nothing.[32]

In an interview, Ray Quasius said he came to work about 7:00
A.M. on August 31 and did not notice the broken glass in the door
and windows until he put his key in the lock. He phoned the police, as records show, about 7:15 and officers Winkel and Zimmerman, who patrolled that district during the night shift, stopped
by to make notes and pick up the stones, paint jars and paint samples which they took to headquarters.

In the Quasius office, the author was shown a collection of
photographs of the damage. Some of the photos had detailed information, dittoed in purple ink, pasted on the back. One — "Number: 1673–0831/56LC" — which was given the author, shows a
broken glass desktop and a Venetian blind hanging over an office
machine; it is labeled "8 to 9:00 A.M." and taken by "L. Charling."
The Sheboygan County Directory listed a Louis Charling as a
Kohler photographer.

The composing-room foreman at the *Press* estimated it would
take 2 to 3 hours, after receiving the photoengravings of the pictures, to make up the full-page ad. The fact that the ad did appear
shows that it *was* possible to produce it for publication in the after-

noon *Press*, but it is obvious that everything clicked with unusual precision to meet the deadline. Even the "before" pictures must have been readily available.

An examination of 296 pages of reports by the company's detective agency from July 5, 1954, through 1956 failed to turn up any mention of their being asked to investigate the Quasius case.

Ray Quasius seemed to have no idea who did it and he said he held no hard feelings toward anyone. He did not think any of his employees were responsible. Insurance covered the loss and his business, he said, increased following the incident. Had someone, the author inquired, perhaps reached through the broken glass to open the door from the inside? Quasius did not think so; he had seen no footprints on the glass-and-paint-splattered floor.

Several law-enforcement officers, who did not wish to be quoted, said that they considered it a "political" rather than a "vandalism" case and one said he was glad he "was not involved in that one." Former Mayor Ploetz told the author that he had gotten a phone call from the Quasius Company about 10 A.M. to inform him of the damage. He went first to the police department and then to the Quasius office where he found Hugh Dales, first ward alderman, "acting like the master of ceremonies." When Ploetz asked why the premises had not been roped off for investigation of clues, et cetera, he got no satisfactory answer. Quasius' offices had been campaign headquarters for Harold Kroll in an unsuccessful bid for sheriff two years before.

Although, as of now, it is not public knowledge who did the paint-throwing, it does *not* seem to be a simple case of some disgruntled union member attempting to damage a contractor who worked for the Kohler Company. That the incident was effectively used in the campaign to elect Kroll and that much of the community suspected some union members or sympathizers committed the act, was obvious. Perhaps someone, someday, will "spill the beans" about who committed the most expensive single act of vandalism in Sheboygan.

The Boycott

A consumers' boycott is one of the weapons used by organized labor from time to time, when it is not making progress in direct negotiations. A consumers' boycott is a concerted effort to with-draw, and to induce others to withdraw, from any business dealings with a given employer. A *primary* boycott involves withdrawing patronage from the employer and getting members of organized labor to cease dealing with or buying from him where a labor dispute exists. A *secondary* boycott, one directed against a neutral employer through his employees, is illegal under the Taft-Hartley Act. Gitlow [33] observes that a *primary* (or consumers') boycott is usually not effective in the case of manufacturers whose customers are business firms (wholesalers or retailers) rather than individuals. The truth of this statement was to be borne out with the passing years of the second Kohler strike. After the union had spent about $10 million in strike benefits without approaching a settlement, it, in effect, admitted defeat on the picket line and resorted to a massive boycott campaign against Kohler products. It got considerable support from many public bodies such as city councils, county boards, et cetera, but it could not generally persuade architects and builders to refrain from using Kohler ware. In fact, those who were opposed to unions often specified Kohler fixtures in building plans, so that the boycott became a double-edged sword.*

Boycott campaign literature prepared by Local Union 833 used language highly critical of the company. The union appealed to the public with leaflets saying in part:

DON'T BUY KOHLER PLUMBING WARE
IT'S MADE BY STRIKE-BREAKERS!!!

Thousands of years of seniority — years of artisanship and know-how — are represented on the Kohler picket lines today. . . .

Strike-breakers have been hired to take some of the regular Kohler workers' jobs. These newly hired strike-breakers lack industrial experience and have none of our artisanship and know-how in making top-notch plumbing ware and other Kohler products. . . .

We ask you *"not to buy"* Kohler products now, because your purchase would only prolong the strike. If possible, delay your pur-

---

* The name of Kohler often came up in Oklahoma when that state was arguing the pros and cons of a "right-to-work" law in 1964. Proponents of the law in the construction industry openly urged the use of Kohler products because the company symbolized their philosophy of labor-management relations. On the union side there were reports of "careless handling" of Kohler fixtures by members of other unions. Toilet bowls were damaged when installed in public buildings and dropped when loaded on ships for overseas markets.

Bathtub Baron

by Hank Weber, a Kohler Striker

Be Union — Boycott Kohler — Win The Strike

UAW Local 833 on strike since April 5, 1954. Support the Kohler Boycott. Write for further information to: Kohler Strikers Boycott, 729 Center Avenue, Sheboygan, Wisconsin

chase until there is a just settlement. If you cannot delay your purchase, we recommend the union-made products of Kohler Company competitors such as Universal-Rundle, Briggs, Standard, and Crane. . . .

As to "How can you tell it's Kohler?" the union offered the public these directions:

Crates and cases bear the trade letters K of K. This stands for all sorts of things, but the company means it to represent Kohler of Kohler. You know, like some of the old-fashioned German titles . . . Herbert *von* Ober und Under. The pieces themselves have the same lettering on it — in faint blue — K of K. This means the same thing to the company, but all sorts of other things to the union.

To other union workers, the strikers made an appeal to join the battle:

Has your boss been exposed?
Have the germs of Kohlerism touched your employer?
    STAMP OUT DISEASE before it spreads
BEAT KOHLER   KOHLERISM
    BOYCOTT KOHLER   threatens *you* too!
        WIN THIS STRIKE
            The Bathtub Baron Spreads the Disease

LIKE TYPHOID MARY, Herbert V. Kohler continues to tour the country exhorting other employers to follow his example of strike-breaking and union busting. . . .

In an 8-column printed sheet entitled "How to Boycott Kohler" the *UAW Local 833 Reporter and Kohlerian* outlined an action program to implement the strike and told how one community, Racine, Wisconsin, a strongly unionized city, organized "the AFL-CIO Committee on Struck Goods." It reported:

> Among the big building projects in Racine where the Committee has successfully kept out Kohler are a $1 million library, $1 million County Hospital addition, $1½ million Junior High School, a $1 million Grade School and $3 million Elmwood Plaza Shopping Center.

St. Luke's Hospital in Milwaukee was picketed for months in an effort to keep out Kohler fixtures.

The efforts to keep them out of public institutions in Sheboygan did not meet with such success. Two thousand citizens signed a petition asking the school board not to install "scab Kohler ware [in the Lyman School in the summer of 1956] until the strike is settled and the firm has redeemed itself in the eyes of the law." Joseph Born, one of Kohler Company's top personnel, was a school-board member whom the union felt "obviously [is] representing the Kohler Company better than the taxpayers of the Sixth Ward." Despite protest meetings, picketing and petitions, Kohler fixtures went in. Two Catholic parishes were wracked by dissention over the issue of installing Kohler equipment usually offered to Sheboygan religious institutions at a reduced price. One priest resolved the problem by putting in a Kohler fixture, then one of another make, then a Kohler fixture, and so on, in "easy stages."

Boycott support by the sympathetic plumbers' union was a prickly problem. In a column entitled *"Can Plumbers Boycott?"* the local's paper states:

> Many union people have asked: can't the plumbers boycott Kohler? Well, the plumbers can and do engage in a legal primary boycott of Kohler — they don't buy the stuff. But when a customer insists on Kohler, the plumber has to install it. If the plumbers' union were to refuse to install, it would be a violation of the Taft-Hartley Act's secondary boycott provision.

Harvey Kitzman (left) and Emil Mazey inspect a Kohler boycott display at the AFL-CIO national merger convention, December 5, 1955. (UAW photo)

A plumber as an individual, can refuse to install Kohler. If he gets fired for it, there is nothing his union can do for him.

The Plumbers' Union has passed a resolution supporting the Boycott Kohler campaign, and has given full support to the Kohler strikers as far as the law will permit.

A 32-page 3-color booklet, published by the UAW International Union, and Local 833, entitled *The Kohler Worker's Story*, carried a picture of a youngster in rompers with the caption — "All my life my Daddy's been on strike to make my future better." This booklet reviewed the early years of the second strike from the union's point of view.

An article in *The Wall Street Journal* of August 9, 1956, by Ray Vicker, a staff reporter, described the extent to which the UAW organized its "business-like boycott" and got support from much of the labor movement. Here are parts of the article:

KOHLER BOYCOTT
UAW Lines Up Unions,
Cities in Drive to Cut
Sales of Struck Firm

———

Union Offers Anti-Company
Ties, T-Shirts: Boycott
"Salesmen" Tour the U.S.

Preview of a Potent Weapon

———

Sheboygan, Wis. — On a bulletin board in the United Automobile
Workers Union Local 833 headquarters here, a pin-studded map of
the United States is divided into 15 territories.

At first glance it might be mistaken for a business sales map. Actually, it is a battle map tracing a U.A.W. boycott offensive aimed at
throttling Kohler Co. — the U.A.W.'s adversary in one of the bitterest and the longest labor disputes of the postwar period. . . .

Each pin on the map represents "the enemy," a Kohler sales outlet.
Tiny flags show the location of U.A.W. agents who are "on the
road." The 15 territories represent zones covered by these special
representatives in drumming up support for the boycott.

"This is the most comprehensive boycott ever organized by labor
because we now have the full weight of the combined A.F.L.-C.I.O.
with us," says Don Rand, husky 37-year-old U.A.W. international
representative who heads the boycott. "We've put this program on a
highly organized, business-like basis with this as a central office."

U.A.W.'s boycott has implications which go far beyond this tree-
studded city of bratwurst, bock beer and sauerkraut. Since it is a
boycott which could only be effectively waged through a combination of the A.F.L.-C.I.O., it provides business with a preview of a
powerful, souped-up weapon which has been placed in labor's hands
by that merger.

Mr. Rand shakes his head as he leans against a huge "Don't Buy
Kohler!" placard in the U.A.W. office and says, "It seems to me that
it is almost sinful to have any labor dispute degenerate to the point
where this one has — where we actually have to wreck the company.
That's what we're doing, wrecking the company."

U.A.W. hasn't yet succeeded in its goal, though. "We have not
been able to see that the boycott has had any appreciable effect on
our sales or is anything else than somewhat of an annoyance," con-

tends L. C. Conger, chairman of Kohler Co's management committee. . . .

Each representative is making the rounds in his territory much like a traveling salesman with a suitcase full of samples. He appears before local union groups seeking cooperation in the boycott of Kohler products. He appears before city and state groups urging that purchasing departments shun strike-bound articles with emphasis on the Kohler line. He suggests to area plumbers and contractors that they steer clear of the Kohler label. . . .

Original strike issues have long since lost their importance. As the union saw its picketing failing it moderated demands to such an extent that they bear little relationship now to original proposals. Basically, the issue now is whether or not the company should have an outside union in its plant.

This spring . . . the U.A.W. finally admitted defeat on the picket line. It announced reductions in benefits and urged strikers to get jobs elsewhere.

But the U.A.W. wasn't tossing in the sponge. It then focused attention on two points: Fighting the company before the National Labor Relations Board for alleged unfair labor practices, and the boycott.

"Since April, we estimate that over 1,200 of our members have gotten jobs elsewhere," says Mr. Rand. . . .

Not all workers have been so lucky.

"Jobs are scarce in this town," says slim, friendly Bob Bernico, a striking pottery inspector. He is still supporting a family of eight with union subsistence food, rent, and utilities vouchers after 28 months on the picket line. . . .

Chubby Leo Breirather, boycott coordinator, holds up a nylon T-shirt. Emblazoned across the front is the plea: "Boycott Kohler. Win the Strike." A design on the back says: "Don't Buy Kohler. . . ."

To reach sympathizers, the U.A.W. has obtained lists of every AFL-CIO union business agent, local president, secretary and other official in the country.

Says Mr. Rand: "Before the merger such lists were carefully guarded and it would have been impossible to get them."

With the lists, the U.A.W. has been successful in stirring up support from hundreds of locals. In addition, the auto union also has obtained information about union meetings and conventions scheduled throughout the next year. At such meetings, a boycott representative appears to tell his story.

Each such appearance usually results in a resolution being passed by the meeting offering assistance. In many cases, the hat is passed and funds go along with the resolution. . . .

Mr. Conger of Kohler Co. questions the legality of such resolutions since in most cases public works must be let to the lowest bidder according to state laws. Moreover, Kohler Co. has not yet been convicted of unfair labor practices, he points out.

He adds, "There is no question but that the U.A.W. will do everything possible to promote such resolutions, . . . wherever they believe that they can find politicians supine enough to bow to their dictates and to forget their duty to the public."

As for results of the boycott, you get widely differing stories from the union and from the company.

Says Mr. Conger: "Production and employment are not yet quite on the pre-strike basis, but we are operating satisfactorily and on a profitable basis."

The U.A.W. claims to have an accurate count of railroad boxcars and trucks which have left the plant since the strike started.

"Railroad shipments now are 63% of the 1954 pre-strike level while truck shipments are 25% of that level," claims Mr. Rand.

On May 31, 1957, Leo Breirather, boycott coordinator, Local 833, wrote this letter to Ray Vicker of the *Wall Street Journal:*

The Kohler strike and boycott is getting quite a bit of publicity in some of the nation's leading publications, the most notable of late is the May 20 issue of *Life* magazine.

Almost without exception these articles make reference to your article found in the Wall Street Journal of Thursday, August 9, 1956, particularly to the statement that you attribute to UAW International Representative Donald Rand:

"It seems to me that it is almost sinful to have any labor dispute degenerate to the point where this one has — where we actually have to wreck the company. That's what we're doing, wrecking the company. . . ."

I recall very distinctly the conversation which lead to this remark and wish to call your attention to it. The discussion revolved around the nation's labor laws which tend to induce employers to revert to the law of the jungle rather than to induce peaceful strike settlements through the methods of arbitration. My understanding of Don's remarks is that it is almost sinful that a union is required to adopt a program such as the boycott program in order to win justice and an honorable settlement for its members if it at all wants to live up to its responsibilities to its members as in the case of the Kohler strike.

I believe that I can say with all honesty that the aim and goals of the UAW are not to wreck or to tear down any organization which would provide employment for people. The record of the UAW shows and is clear that the main concern of this union is for people and in the case of the Kohler strike the record also shows and is clear that the UAW accepted every proposal on the part of public officials, members of the clergy and other people of influence to settle this dispute on an honorable basis and in a peaceful fashion through the recognized methods of arbitration.

The record is also clear that the Kohler Company not only refused these proposals, but publicly chastized those who, in their opinion, had the audacity to make the proposal.

Vicker replied to Breirather's letter, saying he was sorry to hear that Rand's statement was being misused and it seemed to him there could hardly be any misunderstanding unless "a guy were trying to misunderstand it." He added that quoting out of context was like planting photographers around the plant and "having them wait until a guy has a scowl on his face before snapping a picture," thus making an ordinary Joe look like a Capone gangster.

Company Spokesmen Take to Road and Airwaves

While UAW Local 833 was enlisting support for the boycott of Kohler products among unions and sympathizers, Kohler Company officials did not stand idly by. Commercial and business organizations and clubs in widely separated parts of the country heard the Kohler executives give their version of the strike story. Two speeches by Herbert V. Kohler — one to the Freedom Club of the First Congregational Church in Los Angeles [34] and one to the Economic Club of Detroit — have been cited in Chapter 4.

Appearances of company officials included:

Herbert V. Kohler, company president:

November 3, 1955, Birmingham, Alabama — Associated Industries of Alabama.

December 9, 1955, Chicago, Illinois — Executives Club of Chicago.

March 24, 1956 — National Association of Manufacturers program, ABC Network (which included WHBL, Sheboygan).

. . . We refused, and we still refuse, to yield to extravagant demands which would give union bosses important parts of the operating control of the company. They hope by arbitration to win a part of their demands. We will not let an arbitrator write a contract for us. You can't arbitrate anarchy. Unless the citizens, the professional people and the working people of this country take action to curb lawlessness, they eventually will be little more than pawns of a few union bosses.

October 5, 1956, Chicago Illinois – Central Supply Association.

. . . There are certain unions in this country – not all of them, mind you – with whom violence is a deliberately chosen instrument, and they want that violence legalized. The efforts of Reuther and his kind will not be confined to trying to change the labor laws. They are for bigger governments, . . . more spending, more and more taxes and destruction of state, local and individual rights.

November 15, 1956, Milwaukee, Wisconsin – Milwaukee Advertising Club.
"Failing in attempts at illegal coercion, the union turned to arbitration," said Kohler. He claimed that the union wanted to "save face" and salvage part of the demands by relying on the well-known tendency of an arbitrator to "split the difference."[35]

September 9, 1957, Salt Lake City, Utah – American Mining Congress.
Walter Reuther is a "Moscow-trained socialist."

Lyman C. Conger, company attorney and chairman of the Bargaining Committee:

February 9, 1956 – Wisconsin Club of Chicago.
Policies the striking United Auto Workers were "trying to force on us would eventually destroy the company." Referring to Wisconsin's Governor Kohler: "We have a governor who took no action during the 54 days our plant was shut down by an illegal mob, nor during the reign of terror that followed, but demanded that we let the arbitrator write a contract for us."[36]

January 30, 1957 — San Diego, California.

. . . For example — the ultimate end of yielding to the union demand for strict seniority is that every job will be held by a marginal worker — one who can barely get by on the job — rather than the most efficient worker.

April 11, 1957 — Biloxi, Mississippi — Alabama Cotton Manufacturers Association.

May 29, 1957, Appleton, Wisconsin — Appleton-Neenah-Menasha Personnel Associations.

June 22, 1957, Duluth, Minnesota — Minnesota Bar Association.

June 26, 1957, Bloomington, Illinois — Illinois State Normal University.

August 14, 1957, Randolph Center, Vermont — Vermont Farm Bureau and Associated Industries of Vermont — Farm-Industry Field Day.

. . . We have taken our stand in the firm belief that if this is to remain a free country, unions must be brought to the realization that they are not above the law, that while they have rights that must be respected, they must also respect the rights of others. The attempts of these union leaders to gain political domination of the entire country are not collective bargaining — they represent only sheer arrogance and unbridled lust for power.

September 28, 1957, Atlanta, Georgia — Associated Industries of Georgia.

January 19, 1958 — Manion Forum Radio Program, Weekly Broadcast No. 173.

. . . When we succeeded in getting the mass picket line opened up through an order of the Wisconsin Employment Relations Board, the UAW changed its tactics.

A campaign of terror was instituted at the homes of employees who desired to exercise their rights as American citizens, to determine for themselves whether or not their wages and working conditions were satisfactory.

The vicious home picketing was begun. Men returning home from work were greeted by mobs of 200 to 500 — yelling threats and epithets — and intimidating them and their families.

———

L. L. Smith, company vice president, had started his series of public addresses with a talk before the Industrial Relations Association of Wisconsin in Milwaukee on November 2, 1955, where he said, ". . . The UAW followed a line of thinking like the Communists. The employer is the natural enemy. The employees need a strong hand to protect them from the oppressor. The UAW is that strong hand."

In another speech at the Neenah Club (Wisconsin) he said, "I don't know whether Mr. Reuther aspires to the [U.S.] presidency, but his plans for nation-wide political dominance are no secret."

Lucius P. Chase, the general counsel for the Kohler Company and a member of the U.S. Chamber of Commerce committee on boycotts:

May 14, 1957, Atlanta, Georgia — U.S. Chamber of Commerce.
January 14, 1958, St. Petersburg, Florida — Contractors' and Builders' Association.
February 4, 1958, Milwaukee, Wisconsin — Wisconsin Association of Plumbing Contractors.

. . . A second target for the UAW's secondary boycott has been government itself. By flexing its political muscles, the UAW expected subservient public officials to disregard laws requiring competitive bidding and ban Kohler products from public construction. Fortunately, most public servants have been faithful to their trust. Many journeymen plumbers have refused to cooperate with the boycott. They just don't want to pick up the tab for the auto workers' history of violence and coercion. Journeymen plumbers have profited more from the company, which gives them fixtures to install, than from the UAW. . . .[37]

Lawrence O'Neil, secretary to Herbert Kohler:

January 7, 1956, Manitowoc, Wisconsin — Kiwanis Club.

. . . anything that is not extorted from an employer, anything that might look like an act of generosity or humane consideration of the employees is simply no good in the eyes of the UAW-CIO. If they get it, that's good bargaining. If you give it, that's paternalism. . . .

May 1, 1957, Grosse Point, Michigan — Women's Republican
Club.

. . . We've been told time and time again that we should not only
have a union contract as our competitors do, but we must have one
exactly like theirs. Yet the backbone of our industrial strength in
this country lies in its diversification. Many companies manufacture
the same general product. But they have different designs; different
methods of advertising, selling and marketing; different approaches
to engineering and production. What's so wrong about having a
different concept of labor relations?

The resolution of the conflict, with the passage of time, seemed
more remote than ever as the tempo of strike activity was reduced,
as many strikers sought other employment, and attempts to settle
the strike failed. The clay boat incident had been in national headlines; Congressional committees had been investigating irregularities
on the part of some unions and management; and it came as no
great surprise to the public when the McClellan Committee announced its intention to investigate the strike at Kohler.

7

THE MC CLELLAN COMMITTEE HEARINGS

Origin of the Committee

WHEN control of the United States Senate passed from the Republicans to the Democrats in 1956, John L. McClellan (Dem.) of Arkansas became chairman of the Permanent Subcommittee on Investigations. This committee had received considerable notoriety when Senator Joseph McCarthy (Rep.) of Wisconsin had been its chairman, although investigating improper union activities had at that time been considered the function of the Senate Committee on Labor and Public Welfare. Senator McClellan nevertheless went ahead with labor investigations on the grounds that his committee was concerned with "such matters as government procurement, government operations, violations of our tax law, etc." After some objections from the Senate Labor Committee and from labor leaders, the issue was resolved by the establishment on January 30, 1957, of a Select Committee on Improper Activities in the Labor or Management Field. Four Republicans and four Democrats * were taken from the two rival committees to form the new body, with Senator McClellan, by whose name the committee became known, as chairman. Robert F. Kennedy was appointed chief counsel.[1]

The committee hearings began on February 27, 1957, and in due course covered 253 active investigations. The committee called 1,526 witnesses to testify during 270 days of public hearings which provided testimony to fill 58 volumes (20,432 pages) of records. The testimony on the Kohler strike alone filled nearly 2,000 pages of parts 21 through 25 of the McClellan Committee reports, and over 100 pages of the final summary report.

Robert F. Kennedy, as the counsel of the committee, had come

---

* Republicans: Carl T. Curtis, Nebraska; Barry Goldwater, Arizona; Irving M. Ives, New York; Karl T. Mundt, South Dakota. Democrats: Sam J. Ervin, Jr., North Carolina; John F. Kennedy, Massachusetts; John L. McClellan, Arkansas; Pat McNamara, Michigan. By the time the Final Report of the hearings was prepared, the 85th Congress was in its Second Session and Homer E. Capehart, Indiana (Republican) and Frank Church, Idaho (Democrat) had replaced Senators Ives and McNamara on the committee.

across instances of labor-organization violence and corruption in the course of investigating military procurement contracts. Information about possible corruption within the Teamsters' Union led to some preliminary investigations, which some members hoped would lead to corrective labor legislation, and the McClellan Committee focused its attention on improper activities of the Teamsters, the Bakery and Confectionery Workers, the Operating Engineers, the United Textile Workers, the Allied Industrial Workers, the Carpenters and the Laundry Workers. All of these unions were affiliated with the AFL-CIO at the time of the hearings. The AFL-CIO expelled the Teamsters, the Bakery Workers and the Laundry Workers for failure to comply with the ethical-practices code of the AFL-CIO, while other unions took the necessary corrective action to remain within the Federation. The United Automobile Workers union was investigated concerning the strikes at Kohler and at the Perfect Circle Plant in New Castle, Indiana, but came through "without damage to its reputation for honesty and democracy."[2]

An Attempt to "Get Reuther"

The Kohler strike hearings began February 26, 1958, "after a ten-month struggle within the staff and committee that almost caused its complete break-up," according to Robert Kennedy. After the Dave Beck (Teamsters) hearings had ended, press stories began to appear which quoted unnamed "Republican senators" and "Republican sources" as calling for investigation of the UAW. Kennedy, in his book *The Enemy Within*, says he later learned that many of these stories originated with Senator Karl Mundt of South Dakota.[3]

The implication was that there was doubt whether the committee would investigate the UAW because it was closely identified with the Democrats and "the Kennedy brothers" were "close" to Walter P. Reuther. The fact was that Vern Johnson, one of four committee staff investigators, had been sent to Sheboygan early during the committee's investigations. He reported in May, 1957, that there was nothing new to "add to the millions of words of testimony taken by the NLRB or make another probe worthwhile."

SQUIRREL HUNTER IN BEAR COUNTRY

This cartoon by Orr appeared during the early months of the Mc-Clellan investigations before the announcement of intention to investigate the Kohler strike. (Reprinted, courtesy of The Chicago Tribune*)*

Nevertheless, stories of a political fix became more numerous and when a *Newsweek* article reported: "Counsel Robert Kennedy has ignored continued demands for investigation of Walter Reuther, GOP members say privately," Senator John F. Kennedy called the committee's attention to the story. Republican Senator Ives (N.Y.) denied making any such statement. Senator Goldwater said that all members of the committee, of course, were completely satisfied with the investigations and he had given no statement which even implied criticism of the Democrats or the counsel. "So far as this Republican member is concerned, I'm happy as a squirrel in a little cage," he said. Senator Mundt chimed in, "I too am perfectly happy and I'm happy as a South Dakota pheasant in a South Dakota cornfield." Senator Curtis expressed general satisfaction, but did not compare himself with any form of wildlife.[4]

The impression persisted, however, that the Kennedys and the Democrats were shielding Reuther. At Senator Goldwater's request, the committee hired an investigator and assistant counsel, Jack McGovern, a Republican, who had been the minority counsel for the Lobbying Committee. Senator McClellan placed McGovern in charge of the UAW-Kohler investigation and Vern Johnson was assigned to assist him.

McGovern and Johnson did not make a single report or ask a single question of Chief Counsel Kennedy from July until December, 1957.[5] Kennedy reports that he learned McGovern deliberately avoided reporting to him because he [McGovern] "feared I would turn all the information I was given to the UAW." Needless to say, this irked Kennedy; he learned later that only the Republican members of the committee had been given regular reports by McGovern and Johnson. Senator McClellan received his first report from them in October, 1957; it turned out to be largely verbatim excerpts from the NLRB Trial Examiner's hearings. McGovern had incorporated the parts unfavorable to the UAW into his report, but nothing in his reports was unfavorable to the Kohler Company, even though the trial examiner had found the company guilty of refusal to bargain in good faith and of other unfair labor practices, as well as finding the union guilty of mass picketing.[6]

Robert Kennedy recalls a conversation with Goldwater in which he called attention to McGovern's report; Goldwater then suggested that Kennedy take over the investigation himself, which he was reluctant to do because of the stories which had appeared in the press. "I told him our preliminary investigation had found that the facts were essentially those disclosed in the NLRB report,"

Kennedy said, "and therefore a new investigation was unlikely to accomplish what he wanted and expected, namely to destroy Walter Reuther. . . ." Goldwater remarked in the course of the conversation that he was not interested in calling Reuther before the committee.[7] *The Wall Street Journal* had carried a story that Senator McClellan was reluctant to go into the UAW-Kohler investigation because it would reflect so adversely on the Democratic senators from Wisconsin and Michigan that they might be defeated in the next election and McClellan would lose the chairmanship of the committee if the Democrats lost control of Congress.*

In December, 1957, investigator McGovern told a press conference that he had uncovered "sensational developments" in the Kohler case. This was news to the chairman and chief counsel of the committee, both of whom deemed it highly improper for a staff investigator to air his findings before the hearings began. The reaction of the UAW was to proclaim it had been smeared and to demand that the committee "put up or shut up."[8]

At the suggestion of Senator McClellan, Chief Counsel Kennedy went to Sheboygan on January 3, 1958. At Milwaukee he was met by two staff members, Carmine Bellino and LaVern Duffy; Vern Johnson joined them and drove them to Sheboygan. Here they discovered, as Kennedy describes it, a feeling so intense that he compared it to the all-consuming hatred between Arabs and Jews, which he encountered on a visit to Palestine. "Men on both sides of the controversy were still hurling profane insults at each other four years after the strike had started." On his first visit to Kohler, he carried away a vivid impression of the company's counsel, Lyman Conger:

> . . . His face, his manner and his whole body seemed to tighten at the mention of the UAW. He made no secret of his deep and abiding hate for the union . . . a thing unpleasant to see.
>
> Conger made no bones about the set-up; he was in charge and he was running the company as the company had been run when he was a boy. He would permit no interference by anyone from the outside. Particularly would he countenance no interference by a "left-wing" labor union. It was Mr. Kohler's company and Mr. Kohler or his

---

* In Michigan, Senator Potter, a Republican, was up for election and no matter what the results, that state could not have adversely affected the make-up of Congress for the Democrats.

delegate was going to run it — not Walter Reuther or the UAW. Before giving in on this principle, Conger made it clear, the Company would close down.[9]

Their meeting with UAW leaders Allan Graskamp and Don Rand in the union's Sheboygan office was not particularly cordial either. Rand and Graskamp wanted to know why the committee was picking on the union and not going to the Kohler Company to get at the real source of the trouble. Rand started lecturing them, according to Kennedy, who replied that they had come to "get facts, not a sermon." Kennedy then went out to the Kohler Company. Two hours later he returned for what turned out to be a four-hour session at the union headquarters. He and the investigators heard the union's version of the strike and the union representatives were told, Rand recalled, that "the best thing we could do would be to tell the truth and that we would be given ample opportunity to tell our story to the committee."

The "sensational developments" which McGovern had reported to the press came to light. He had, it seemed, "discovered" $100,000 missing from the union's treasury — an error which Carmine Bellino, the committee's accountant, located while examining the union's financial records. McGovern had looked in the wrong column of expenditures. The union had also spent a sizable sum of money for bratwurst and McGovern and Johnson figured there must be a kickback somewhere to union officials. This suspicion, too, turned out to be unfounded. They simply had no idea how much Sheboyganites relish bratwurst, a German link-sausage.

At an executive session of the McClellan Committee on January 8, 1958, Senator Curtis said he understood that all the committee's incoming mail and complaints were first examined by the AFL-CIO — a statement that shook Robert Kennedy and apparently made him more determined than ever to carry through an investigation to get the facts. Senator John F. Kennedy moved that the UAW-Kohler hearings be the first order of business. Senators Mundt, Goldwater and Curtis hesitated, saying they did not want to rush into the matter.

Robert Kennedy reported that McGovern and Johnson had told him they would be ready to proceed with the hearings by February 1. He tried to pin Johnson down concerning a reported interview with Judge Arold F. Murphy of Marinette, Wisconsin, an important witness in the NLRB hearings, only to find out later that the Judge had never been interviewed by either investigator. Although McGovern and Johnson had been in Sheboygan for some six months and were in charge of the investigation, their reports were far from complete. Kennedy wrote:

> . . . Bellino discovered that the two had overlooked large sums of money that the company had spent to purchase guns and ammunition shortly before the strike started. They also failed to tell us that company officials held target practice at the plant just before the strike, using targets in the shape of human forms. . . .[10]

The activities of investigators McGovern and Johnson became more strange with each passing week, Kennedy remembers. They reported that they had located a Francis Drury who would be a key witness — a man who had been involved in burglarizing a rival union office in Detroit, and who (according to a report James Hoffa gave to Clark Mollenhoff, a Washington newsman) was a "goon" who had done work for the UAW. Drury was located in prison where he had been jailed for burglarizing stamp machines — not union offices. A three-week search for a man named McCluskey, who allegedly masterminded Drury, ended when McGovern and Johnson finally realized that no such man existed. A man named Brotz, who supposedly had made arrangements to bring Drury and other "goons" to Kohler, had died in 1951 — three years before the strike began.

There was also a heated controversy within the committee as to whether or not Walter Reuther would be the first UAW witness. The four Republicans took the position that it should be anyone but Reuther; they feared he would steal the show and that the remainder of the hearings would merely be an anti-climax. The "showmen" won: when the hearings opened on February 26, 1958, Allan Graskamp, Local 833's president, was first to appear.

The hearings took place in the same room in which the Army-McCarthy investigation had taken place in 1954; the same omnipresent TV cameras were there; and who knows how many political "ghosts" were lurking in the anterooms? Senators McClellan and Mundt and Counsel Robert Kennedy were part of the "cast" of the Army-McCarthy hearing, and Senator Mundt, as an

Lyman Conger, accompanied by Ellison Smith, seated before the microphones in the Senate hearing room. Behind the witness table are the press. Television and broadcasting equipment, which were omni-present during the McClellan hearings, are in evidence throughout the room. (World Wide photo)

old "stage-hand," was sometimes carried away by the realization that a vast audience was taking in the whole performance.* At one point, in an argument between Senators Ervin and McNamara, Chairman McClellan had to remind them:

> Gentlemen, we are not going to waste a lot of time with this. You want to get your language in the record, be careful of what you say. This thing is on television and on the air, radio, and whatever you

---

* Mundt (pp. 9171–2) was cross-examining Robert Treuer about the woman who was on the hood of the company car, the day of the clay-boat incident. Treuer said: "I didn't see the incident of how she got up on the hood or what." Mundt argued: ". . . In other words, if she got up there, she had to climb up there, be-cause a car moving at walking speed cannot possibly overcome the law of gravity sufficiently to toss a woman up on the hood of a car. *You know that and everybody listening to this program knows that. . . .*" [Emphasis added.] On another day, Mundt was questioning former Mayor Ploetz as he tried to read an affidavit from Mosch; Mundt interjected: "Mr. Chairman, the reason I thought we should have the affidavit at this point is so it can all be in the same news story."

Television cameras frame members of the McClellan Committee during the Kohler strike investigation. Clockwise from foreground are Senator Ervin, Chairman McClellan, Counsel Robert Kennedy, Senator Karl Mundt, Senator Curtis (hidden), and Senator Goldwater. (World Wide photo)

say, I don't care how you withdraw it, but it is still out there on the air. People are listening to it.

Chairman McClellan did his best to run the hearing fairly and he could be as sharp with the members of his committee as with witnesses who, in his opinion, transgressed. On one occasion, McClellan called to the stand a photographer who had been taking pictures of the committee members and staff under circumstances which aroused the chairman's suspicion. Under oath a United Press photographer explained that he had been told to "make pictures of Mr. [Joseph] Rauh [UAW counsel] whenever I could." Mr. McClellan demanded to know if it were true that Conger had made special arrangements to have pictures taken of committee members talking to representatives of the union. Conger said no, he hadn't, but McClellan pursued the question with respect to George Gallati, public relations man for the company. Conger admitted that Gallati had made the picture-taking arrangement. Gallati was called to the stand.

"Have you made any special arrangements to have pictures made of members of this committee talking to union members?" McClellan wanted to know. Gallati, seizing upon the word "special" said, "Not any special arrangements, no."

McClellan pressed on: ". . . What arrangements have you made?" and Gallati asked to "speak to the Counsel" (Conger).

"Now, you would know," Robert Kennedy nudged Gallati.

". . . You are both under oath," McClellan reminded him. "I want to know the facts. If you did it, say so, and if you didn't, say you didn't." Finally, the chairman got the information that a UP photographer had indeed been asked to take pictures of *any* of the committee seen talking with Mr. Rauh. Senator Mundt opined that he didn't know what it was all about, but he didn't mind someone taking pictures of him talking with anybody. McClellan was not put off: "I have no objection on earth to taking my picture at any time, but to hire a photographer to come up here especially to try to get a picture to lend some color of truth to what otherwise is intended to get something to smear members of this committee, in my book, it is pretty low. It is pretty rotten."

Of the 77 witnesses called up to testify concerning the Kohler strikes, 9 were company officials and 22 were nonstrikers who supported the company's contentions of mass picketing, vandalism and violence, et cetera. On behalf of the UAW, 7 from the International and 9 from Local 833 were called upon to testify. Others who appeared were law-enforcement and public officials — former Sheriff Mosch, former Mayor Ploetz, Undersheriff Schmitz, Police Chief Capelle, former Police Chief Wagner, and officers Heimke, Frank and Zimmerman. Others came from the teamsters' union, contracting firms and the plumbers' union, and one citizen was sent by the Sheboygan County Contractors' Association to plead that "the interests of our community have been lost in the . . . crossfire of charges and counter-charges between the two parties to the dispute." Many were on hand who were never called to testify. Among those subpoenaed, who did not take the witness stand, were the detectives for the company.

The Sheboygan Press sent its own reporter, Carl Fiedler, to Washington to cover the hearings. He wrote: "There are so many prospective witnesses from Sheboygan who have taken up temporary residence in Washington that a long distance operator

*UAW counsel Joseph Rauh glanced up to see the reaction of the Koh-
ler legal staff (William Howe, Lyman Conger and Ellison Smith) as
Leo Breirather read the affidavit in which John Deis said he recognized the Kohler deputies who shot him in the 1934 strike. (World
Wide photo)*

wondered if there was anyone left at home." He reported, the day
before the hearings began, that Lyman Conger was "closeted all
day," working on Herbert V. Kohler's statement, "preparing for
any eventuality." As it turned out, Kohler, as well as Reuther, was
called by the committee during the final days of the hearing.

Perhaps the most tense and dramatic moment of the hearings
came when Leo Breirather read John Deis's statement, in which he
said that on the night of the July 27, 1934, riot at Kohler, he recognized four company deputies with guns, who — after an exchange
of words — shot him as he bent down to pick up his coat. Lyman
Conger rose in furious anger to claim the witness stand and deny
the accusation, calling it "complete and utter fabrication" which,
"if made under oath . . . [was] perjury."

Emil Mazey, along with Don Rand and Robert Burkart of the
UAW International union, bore the brunt of the cross-examining
until Reuther was called before the committee. Often, Mazey's opposite number from the company, Lyman Conger, was brought

into the cross-questioning and vice versa, so that the discussion
became what could be called lively and heated, for the differences
of attitude and opinion were wide and deep. Much of the time, the
International union witnesses had the task of trying to explain background and perfectly legitimate and long-standing union practices
which were completely foreign to the committee members, even
those basically sympathetic to organized labor. The members who
were most critical of labor * often appeared to be "coached" in the
questions they pursued, giving the impression that on such matters
they were "dumb like a fox."

The Kohler strike had been described variously as a "battle,"
a "conflict," an "industrial war," and "a fight to the finish." Mazey's view of this came up in some leading questions about his strong
interest in civil rights and minority rights. Mundt's question —
somewhat abbreviated — for Mr. Mazey was:

> One of the basic premises [of AFL-CIO civil-liberties and civil-
> rights committee and the civil-rights committee of UAW in which
> Mazey had just admitted membership] . . . is that minorities have
> rights?
> *Mazey:* Yes, minorities have rights. . . . I will agree with you.
> *Mundt:* Now will you explain to me how in the world you can
> arrive at this conclusion on a minority worker . . . [when] . . .
> the only thing wrong with him is he doesn't quite agree with the
> fellow who joins the union as the best way in which he can advance
> himself . . . as a worker in the company . . . where do his rights
> come in if you are going to dub him as a traitor and deny him his
> right to work . . . and call him a scab?
> *Mazey:* We went through a very costly war [World War II] just
> a short time ago and over 30 percent of the Kohler workers took
> part in that struggle. . . . Now if we had people that were op-
> posed to participating in the war, and if they were aiding the
> enemy, we certainly would call them traitors, wouldn't we?
> Well, this struggle against the Kohler Company was a struggle for
> the same kind of freedom and decency we were fighting for all
> over the world, and anybody that was impeding our efforts in try-
> ing to win that freedom and that justice that some of the workers
> [in] the Kohler plant deserve, is in the same category as someone
> who would be fighting against the interest of our country in a war.

* Goldwater, Curtis and Mundt.

Further questions as to whether or not a majority of the workers at Kohler had voted to strike, and whether or not a nonstriker might be considered a "conscientious objector" to the union, followed. Mazey said:

I don't think there is any comparison of the two things. I think, Senator Mundt, if you ever worked in a sweatshop plant and you were fighting for decent working conditions and for seniority and better wages in order to improve the status of you and your family, you would have a different attitude on this question. It is awfully hard to explain these things to people who haven't had a struggle for a livelihood in these sweatshop plants around the country.

On the Witness Stand

Although references to testimony at the McClellan hearings appear throughout other chapters of this book, some of the statements by company spokesmen, union members and nonstrikers, as well as members of the committee and staff, are included here to provide further insight into the nature of the "thirty years of conflict." The page numbers refer to the published committee reports.

On "Organizing the Garden of Eden"

Senator Ervin: But it takes reasonable men on both sides of the bargaining table to take and reach a reasonable agreement. It has to be from both sides. If you have unreasonable men, either on the side of management or on the side of labor, you are not likely to reach a current conclusion, are you?

Mr. Kitzman: That is correct, Senator. I want to point out to you in this situation that even after this strike started, I made a number of efforts, by meeting with 1 or 2 people, in trying to bring about a settlement in this strike. When I was told point blank, not on one occasion but on several occasions by that management, "Look, Kitzman, we didn't start the strike. The union started it and we are going to teach this union a lesson." That is a far cry from reasonableness at a bargaining table.

We have to remember that you cannot organize a plant, and I have a number of them in my union, you cannot organize a plant, no matter how many organizers you have on it, where there is real reasonableness on the part of managements. You cannot organize a plant in the Garden of Eden. It is conditions that organizes unions. . . . (p. 8562)

On Controversy in the Enamel Shop

Processes involved in the enamel shop required working at high temperatures. Graskamp testified that even when the KWA represented the Kohler workers, the men in the enamel shop "had the courage to sit down and not work" and were given the 6-hour day with overtime for more than 6 hours and overtime for over 30 hours per week. (p. 8366)

He explained that with the department running on a 24-hour shift, there was no room for overlap and that is why the union had asked for a 4-per-cent increase in pay for the enamelers.

Conger testified:

. . . On April 21 and 22, illegal work stoppages occurred in the enamel shop. In dispute over a grievance, notice had been given to the company that the men would not complete their shift if they felt sick unless their grievance was satisfactorily adjusted. On April 21 and 22, in accordance with the scheduled notice, many of the enamelers blamed illness and discontinued work. Strangely enough, all these men became "sick" at exactly the same time and in accordance with the scheduled notice to the company.

They were examined by company doctors and those found not to be sick were ordered back to work. Twelve who refused to return to work were discharged. (p. 9487)

Graskamp presented this version of the same incident:

Senator Kennedy: Did the company negotiate the matter of the enamel plant with you?

Mr. Graskamp: No. They made no offer. This was just put into effect, and you take it. On top of that, they always had fans to blow the heat away from the man. The fan was in back of the man, and this blew toward the furnace, and when they took the tub out and the man was there the heat blew the other way. Then they turned the fans off, and that is what led to the discharge of the 12 enamelers in 1952. With the fans off, the people, from the heat, got dizzy, and some got sick. It so happens that some of them that went to the medical department got sent home, but the most active UAW guys didn't get cards to go home, but were told to go back to their jobs, and they were the ones that were fired in 1952.

Senator Kennedy: They not only increased the hours, and cut out the lunch hours, but also turned off the fans, in order to get rid of your members?

Mr. Graskamp: That is right. (p. 8366)

Mr. Conger explained turning off the fans as follows:

Mr. Kennedy: Were some of the fans turned off?

Mr. Conger: We have what is called a barrel fan, sort of a colloquial expression. It is a large fan which simply circulates air, the same as a desk fan does, only it is much bigger. Some of these furnaces were equipped with these. At the time we had the 12 enamelers' case, some of those were turned off as an experiment. It was suspected that they [the fans] were kicking up a lot of dirt that was getting into the enamelware.

Mr. Conger came back to the question of the lunch period. Robert F. Kennedy had some questions:

Mr. Kennedy: You say that the men can put equipment in the oven, then they can step back and eat their lunch during that period of time. How much time is there then before they have to do some more work?

Mr. Conger: From 2 to 5 minutes depending on the piece.

Mr. Kennedy: So you feel they can step back from the oven and take off their mask and have their lunch in 2 to 5 minutes?

Mr. Conger: Mr. Kennedy, they have been doing it for 36 years, to my knowledge. I am sure they can do it.

Mr. Kennedy: Did you work in the enamel shop?

Mr. Conger: Yes, sir. That was my first job.

Mr. Kennedy: And you feel as long as they were doing it 35 or 36 years ago, they should still be able to do that?

Mr. Conger: Not necessarily, but they are doing it. I don't think anybody can come along and say it is impossible to do what a man is doing.

Mr. Kennedy: There have been, I guess, some improvements in working conditions in the United States in the last 35 years. (p. 9525)

On Pregnancies

Another category of workers who were treated unfairly, from the union's viewpoint, were the married women who became pregnant. The union attempted to have management grant maternity leave. Leo Breirather told about a woman who worked up to 2 days before giving birth, but was refused her job back with the statement (attributed to Lyman Conger but denied by him) that the company was not responsible for her pregnancy. Company president Kohler pointed out that those who return are granted full seniority rights, but he did not guarantee a job on their return:

> *Mr. Kennedy:* Can the girl always get her job back within 2 years? Is that written in the contract?
> *Mr. Kohler:* No we don't guarantee her job. We will try to take her back.
> *Mr. Kennedy:* But there is no guarantee of that?
> *Mr. Kohler:* No, sir. (p. 9950)

On Mass Picketing

The reason so large a group turned out to picket at Kohler was explained by Mazey and Kitzman on three grounds. First, they said, the Kohler strikers remembered the fateful 1934 strike and felt that there would be "safety in numbers"; second, they wanted to give the lie to management's claim that the strikers did not represent the majority of its employees; third, in Mazey's words: "They were probably out there to persuade the people from going in." (p. 9057)

Testimony that the pickets' techniques were considerably more vigorous than described by the union was offered by Lawrence Schmitz, who was, at the time, undersheriff of Sheboygan County. On one occasion when he and his officers escorted some nonstrikers to the picket line, Schmitz recalled, three of his men, two in uniform, were knocked down and he, himself, was dropped to one knee by a method he outlined thus:

> . . . this pushing, which would start, the depth at times, I would say might be 10 or 12 or even 15 men, one behind the other. The men in front were actually not doing any pushing. The ones that were pushed against us the day we were knocked down had no choice in the matter. The weight in numbers behind them were forcing them on top of us. (p. 8472)

Schmitz characterized the pickets' behavior in general on the line as "quite orderly, although they were determined also." (p. 8467) He testified that to his knowledge there was no damage to the Kohler plant and that the disorders mainly took place when the nonstrikers came across the street to go into the plant.

The most vivid report on the mass picketing was provided by Lyman Conger:

> Whenever any nonstrikers would approach the picket line to enter, the pickets — led by union officials and imported goons — would go out and meet them and block their path while those who remained would lock arms, stop marching and completely blockade the entrance. Shouts of "hold that line," "nobody gets in," "we shall not be moved," "yellow scab" and similar epithets would arise from the picket line or be chanted in concert. Employees attempting to enter the plant were slugged, kneed in the groin, kicked, pushed, and threatened. No one except supervisory or office employees or those having a pass signed by a union official was able to pass through the picket line. (p. 9493)

Mazey expressed his viewpoint on mass picketing as follows:

> *Senator Ervin:* . . . I think mass picketing is engaged in . . . for these purposes: To convince management that a substantial or very substantial number of the employees . . . are favoring the strike; second, to convince the other workers that a substantial number are in favor of the strike; and, third, to convince those who are not convinced of the righteousness of the strike that they would be very foolish to attempt to enter the plant.
>
> *Mr. Mazey:* Senator Ervin, in most of our strike situations, the companies do not attempt to operate the plants. For example, the last time we had difficulties with General Motors in 1945–46, the company did not attempt to operate any of its plants. Ford and Chrysler do not. The late [last] Chrysler strike was in 1950, 8 years ago. The last Ford strike was in 1949. Most of the companies realize that the sensible thing to do is not to create a situation in which emotions can be raised and problems developed.
>
> In this case, I pleaded with the Kohler Co. I made a speech on the picket line on April 8 or 9 from a sound truck, and incidentally, I was arrested for violating a newly-enacted sound-truck ordinance. . . . The reason we had difficulty here is that this company, unlike most companies when a strike takes place, refused to bargain with us. (p. 9063)

Reuther held the opinion that the social point of view of the group should transcend the position of the individual:

Senator Mundt: Which is that, the minority member, the fellow who doesn't decide to strike, who wants to work, has as much right to go into the plant and work as a man has to stay out on strike?

Mr. Reuther: Legally there is no difference between their rights [striker and nonstriker].

Senator Mundt: How about ethically, morally, spiritually? He [nonstriker] is a free man. Does he lose any of his rights of freedom as a member of the minority block because he has to work with his hands as a laboring man, or does he have it ethically as well as legally?

Mr. Reuther: I think [that] philosophically, I think that every member, every human being in a society has the same rights, the right to choose to go in, the right to choose not to go in, but I say that the human family was able to crawl out of the jungle of the past and to build a civilization because we began to recognize that there are areas of human relationships in which somehow there has to be a social point of view in which the position and the problems of the group transcend the position of the individual.

Otherwise, we would all be living in caves yet, seeing who could get the biggest club to beat the other fellow's skull in. We got to the point where human civilization was possible only by recognizing that the total of the human family, whether it was a village or a state or a nation, and ultimately the world, that the whole of society has problems that we can resolve only by common decision, and that the individual has to be bound by those decisions. I think a worker who goes into a plant after a democratic decision has been made to strike the plant is wrong. He is morally wrong. . . .(pp. 10098–99)

On Vandalism

Fifteen nonstrikers and 3 strikers testified before the committee concerning vandalism or violence directed at them. Most of the destruction involved damages to their cars, or houses — acid-throwing, paint-bombing and dynamiting. There were also telephone threats and 5 assaults.

Fred Yurk testified that he had worked for the Kohler Company since 1929. He did not join the UAW and returned to work when the mass picketing ended. Robert F. Kennedy did the questioning:

Mr. Kennedy: Now, on April 12, 1955, you were at home, on one Tuesday evening, watching television?

Mr. Yurk: That is right.

Mr. Kennedy: And did your wife then come running in the house?

Mr. Yurk: Yes sir.

Mr. Kennedy: Would you relate or recite what happened?

Mr. Yurk: She came into the house, and said a car passed in front with the lights out, and someone opened the door and threw a lighted object under my car, which was parked in front of the residence at the time.

My son was with me at the time, and I said, "Well, possibly it could be a cigarette," and she said, "No, I don't think so." So my son went out to investigate with a flashlight, and I went part way with him, but he hollered at me then and said, "Get back to the house. It is a stick of dynamite."

So, in the meantime, my wife went to the telephone to call the police department, and while she was talking to the police department the stick of dynamite went off and exploded. (p. 8716)

James J. Holsen, who used to live in Sheboygan, moved out to Kohler Village after his house was stoned during the clay-boat incident. He had gone to work at Kohler in August, 1954. He told of harassing phone calls, of being called a scab, and of his car being sprayed with acid.

Mr. Kennedy: So you received the telephone calls, and paint remover or acid was thrown on your automobile on two separate occasions. Your automobile was dynamited and then wrecked at the time of the clayboat, and you had stones thrown through the windows of the house where you lived; is that correct?

Mr. Holsen: That is correct.

Mr. Kennedy: Anything else?

Mr. Holsen: Well, nothing except the usual name calling in public places, sometimes, and on the street.

Mr. Kennedy: Was there great bitterness between the strikers and nonstrikers?

Mr. Holsen: Very much so, sir.

Mr. Kennedy: Was there particular bitterness toward those who the strikers felt had come in to take their jobs?

Mr. Holsen: I expect they would be bitter; yes. (p. 8721)

Gilbert Moede testified that he had worked at Kohler since 1926. He did not favor the UAW and went back to work when the mass picketing ended. He told about receiving threats on the streets and about going to his cottage near Oshkosh on Christmas

day to find it in a "mess." He presented pictures to the committee
to show how vandals had used acid to damage "boats, motors and
everything else." Acid had also been thrown on a Bible, bedding
and furniture in the cottage.

> *Mr. Moede:* The week before I came [here], I worked for $10,
> so I could make along. But the farmers are all good around there
> by me, and when I had a chance to come here to testify, well, I
> didn't know what to do. The Mrs. said, "Here is your chance to
> stand up and fight for our rights, what we are fighting for."
> *The Chairman* [Senator McClellan]: Do you feel you are fighting
> for your rights just as much as the union men are fighting for theirs?
> *Mr. Moede:* Well, here is the Constitution. Take the Constitution
> and the Bill of Rights. It gives me the right to earn my living. If
> I can't work, how am I going to exist?
> *The Chairman:* I agree with you. I think it is one of the highest
> civil rights we have, the right to work.* (p. 8726)

Ewald Guske, one of the strikers on the picket line who had
worked for the Kohler Company for 18 years, related one of his
experiences:

> *Mr. Kennedy:* Did you receive any property damage?
> *Mr. Guske:* Yes. My car was sprayed on August 28 . . . 1956.
> *Mr. Kennedy:* What happened?
> *Mr. Guske:* I was picketing on Gate 7 and when the Kohler
> workers came somebody opened the window and looked through
> the window and hollered, "You goldarn goon, you can walk here
> until doomsday, we got your job, we got a nice job. You can walk
> until doomsday," and they pointed something at me.
> It looked to me like it was a spray gun, a water pisol or some-
> thing. My car was parked right alongside the road. After a while,
> when the crowd was out, about 10 or 15 minutes later, I walked to

---

* In this connection, the author would like to point out that whoever is out
of a job, understandably feels insecure and treated unfairly, whether that unemployment results from discrimination because of race or creed; because of dis-
placement by automated machines; because of imports; or because of a strike. We
still have millions of unemployed in America. Yet most people are not greatly
concerned about what Senator McClellan calls "the highest civil right we have,
the right to work."

Actually our society does *not* guarantee a right to work — much less the right
to work in a particular factory or firm. Workers have jobs as long as employers
can profitably employ them. Since the advent of unions, workers have tried to
spell out some job rights through seniority systems, but unions are also limited in
what they can do to provide jobs.

the car and I seen the whole car was sprayed with acid. It looked like a checkerboard. (p. 8704)

On Support for the Strike

Senator Mundt did some friendly quizzing of Mr. Conger to help create the impression that only a minority of the Kohler workers favored the strike. Then Mr. Kennedy spoke up:

Mr. Kennedy: On this point, there is this newspaper clipping that was brought in, I believe by Mr. Mazey, in the Sheboygan Press which said, "Kohler Strike Continuation Voted 1,571 to 21." That is dated November 18, 1954 [7½ months after the strike started]. Do you know anything about that meeting?

Mr. Conger: I don't know anything about that meeting, and I don't know whether that vote was taken by ballot or by show of hands, or how it was taken. I may say that at that time probably some people went down to that meeting and voted to continue in order to get strike relief they were getting from the union. That was a factor. (pp. 9573–4)

On Guns for Recreation

Mr. Biever: Kohler Co. conducts an extensive recreation program, including bowling, basketball, baseball, band and chorus, card playing, photography, archery, horseshoe pitching and similar activities. Since at least 1917, the recreation program has included rifle and pistol shooting, both large and small bore and an outdoor and indoor ranges. . . . (p. 9456)

Mr. Kennedy: It appears to be more than a coincidence that on May 11, the employees of the plant voted to affiliate and on May 13 you start buying guns and ammunition, and that continues through 1952, 1953, and 1954.

Mr. Biever: The guns that were ordered in 1954, the shotguns and the buckshot were ordered because there was a threat that the village police were about to be disarmed. The union made every attempt to disarm the police.

Mr. Kennedy: When was that?

Mr. Biever: That was about in June of 1956.

Mr. Kennedy: June of 1956? or 1955?

Mr. Biever: 1955. Excuse me.

Mr. Kennedy: That is why you bought the 12 riot guns?

Mr. Biever: Yes sir. Most of the ammunition was used for police training, for recreation purposes, as I read to you out of the statement.

Mr. Kennedy: Are riot guns recreation for the people at the Kohler Co.?

Mr. Biever: Riot guns? No sir, but they could readily be converted.

Mr. Kennedy: To recreation?

Mr. Biever: They could be.

Mr. Kennedy: Have they been used for recreation?

Mr. Biever: They have not, not one has been used.

Mr. Kennedy: According to the pamphlet that comes with them, they are to be used against mobs and groups of people.

Mr. Biever: Not one of them was ever used. (p. 9469)

On the Right to Work vs. Union Shop

Mr. Kohler [Herbert V.]: There is no so-called right-to-work law against the union shop in Wisconsin, although by way of contrast we do have a law which my brother signed as Governor years ago, outlawing yellow-dog contracts.* We have not questioned the union's right to make such a union-shop proposal or demand.

But we believe it is also beyond question, that the company was right to reject the demand, in view of our convictions on this subject.

Wisconsin does have a law against the use of mass picketing, force and coercion to prevent people who desire to go to work from doing so. . . .

The union argument seems to be — and it has been openly so expressed — that in a strike situation, the company has no right to operate, nonstrikers have no right to work, and the union's view as to the merits of the dispute is conclusive and binding upon everybody. . . . (p. 9934)

* The "yellow-dog contract" was an epithet applied to the practice employers sometimes used before 1932, requiring a worker to sign a statement saying he was not a member of a union and would never join a union while working for that employer. Union members said you had to be as "low down as a yellow dog" to sign such a statement. The Norris-LaGuardia Act outlawed such practices by Federal legislation in 1932.

In an interview October 7, 1965, the author was reminded by Herbert V. Kohler, Jr., that his uncle, Governor Walter J. Kohler, Sr., had signed a bill outlawing yellow-dog contracts in Wisconsin, several years before the Federal law was enacted.

On Detective Agents

Mr. Kennedy: Did the detective agency use a minifon at all?

Mr. Conger: Yes there was.

Mr. Kennedy: It says on one of these reports that there was a purchase of a minifon [a miniature recorder that can be concealed].

Mr. Conger: Yes there was a minifon used. We had a report from one of our guards that Mr. Donald Rand had tried to bribe him [the guard] to turn information over to him [Rand] on what was going on in the plant, and also a strong suspicion that he was to be bribed to commit some sabotage in the plant. We equipped that guard, and when I say "we" I mean the detective agency equipped that guard, with a minifon, and the conversation with Mr. Rand, purportedly with Mr. Rand, was reported to me. The minifon didn't work very well, and the conversation was pretty sketchy. After we had thoroughly checked it out I came to the conclusion that there wasn't too much to it and we never did anything about it. (p. 9563)

Ray Majerus and Harvey Kitzman made the following comments about the minifon episode in a taped interview conducted by the author in Milwaukee:[11]

Majerus: The union offered a $1000 reward, along with rewards offered by the company. No one ever came forward that was able to offer any clues — and this despite the fact that they [the company] put their agents into the strike kitchen, on the picket line and in the union office.

Kitzman: This is one of the strong points as far as the union is concerned, because for months before we knew it, they had spies working — in the strike kitchen, on the picket line, sitting around the union hall and attending union meetings. If the union would have been guilty of any of these things, these guys couldn't help but learn it.

Majerus: The detectives did two things: one, they "sicked" a good-looking gal on Rand at the Foeste Hotel to try to get him to go up to the room with her, and two, they "sicked" their own security guard out of the plant with a minifon attached to him to try to get him [Rand] to agree that he [the guard] could take some sabotage material into the plant, and showed him the layout. . . . This kid called us [Rand and Majerus] up and he said, "Look, I've got some real, good information for you on the guy who rides the midnight patrol." He said, "I can *tell* you some things and I'm willing to *do* some things for you. I'm willing to go and sabotage the powder in the enamel shop or in the pottery."

The Company came into the McClellan Committee hearings and said, "We feel pretty bad that we have to play these recordings because Rand used some obscene language. . . ." This guy wanted us to agree and would do it [sabotage] for "X" amount of dollars. Then they could come in and knock out our NLRB case. We told this guy that we had a good case and that we were going to rely on the law. . . . We knew the guy was wired. He was an amateur, as well as some of the detectives. He proposed to meet us on 14th Street by the Lakeland plant, in the alley. He talked with us in a way that we were quite sure he had a microphone. No guy calls you up out of that plant and says, "For a thousand dollars, I'll blow the plant up." We baited the guy along. We said, "Look, you go in there and you tell us exactly what you can do, what you want to do, get your program, get your price all set up." This they never played back, you see. They said, "In deference to the ladies we won't play the language Rand used." We told the guy to come back and let us know who he'd have to work with — and we never heard no more from the guy.

We used to get these calls three to five times a week. *Every* guy was going to settle the strike. *Every* guy knew how to do it. They all had "hot" information right out of the plant. . . . Then he would come out with some fantastic cock-and-bull story.

We subpoenaed the detectives to the hearing. In came two men — one from Green Bay and another man came in from Oak Park, or Skokie [Illinois], or near there. He didn't even look like a detective and in *that* respect he was a very good detective. This little guy comes up there that morning and says, "Hey, I've got a job. I'm working . . . I've gotta get back home. Can I get these things taken care of? I've got these records!"

So we said, "Who are you?"

He said he was operator "371" or one of the operators [Schindler Agency]. So we said, "Well, look! Let's see what you have. Let's see your records."

The fellow I talked with said, "Look, I'm a friend of yours — I'm a union member — I'm a steamfitter. I don't have anything against you. Everything I got is an open book. Here's all my papers!"

I said, "If you're a union guy, why did you get involved in this?"

He said, "Well, I needed a job. A man from the Interstate Detective Agency said to me one day, he knew I was out of work and I needed a few dollars — I had some sickness in the family — so he told me I could make a few bucks and expenses and live like a king."

He said they made him a proposition to go to Sheboygan. All he was supposed to do was tour the bars [taverns] and the soup kitchen, the picket line and make friends. His *primary* instruction was to make friends. So he said, "Hell, I wanted to pick up a few dollars. I wasn't going to hurt nobody! I didn't see much wrong with it. They told me how to put the money in my shoe . . . how to make reports, etc."

Here with all the money they [the company] spent, they had some poor little guy who really didn't know what he was doing, trying to pick up a few dollars! And he really was a member of another union!

The Madson detective reports discuss meetings with Conger concerning a plant guard, N——, who was in touch with Rand and who had allegedly been offered money by Rand, if he would furnish information about whether plant guards carried guns, how many were on duty, et cetera. Obviously, the company management hoped they might catch a potential "saboteur." The guard may well have been playing up to "both sides of the fence." After 27 days of playing a cat-and-mouse game with Rand (and Majerus), during which time N—— got one poor recording on the minifon, the detectives concluded that their man ". . . is not the type of individual who can be effectively used for the purpose previously reported due to the fact he appears to be slightly unstable, a person who drinks to excess and also an individual who is having marital problems with his wife."

When the McClellan investigation turned to a discussion of the detectives' actions connected with shadowing union activities, the following exchange took place:

Senator Kennedy (To Mr. Herbert V. Kohler): I know you have given Mr. Conger wide latitude . . . but are you prepared to tell me whether you know . . . the detective agency did more than find out whether your wires were being tapped?

Mr. Kohler: The reports were not made to me directly. . . .

Senator Kennedy: Did you know about the surveillance of Mr. Burkhart, the head of the union, and that the detective agency was responsible for securing a policeman to raid Mr. Burkhart's home?

Mr. Kohler: I did not know that, sir, until after it happened.

Senator Kennedy: . . . but you left those matters to Mr. Conger?
Mr. Kohler: Yes, sir. (pp. 9946–47)

Conger then related how their detectives, working in co-operation with the police department, put a "mail cover" on Burkart, as
well as checking the telephone calls he made. Mr. Kennedy pointed
out to Mr. Conger that, even if it had been the police who got information about Burkart, they violated their trust by turning it over
to a private individual.

Mr. Conger: No, they did not violate their trust. We were co-
operating with the police department to try to solve these things,
and these individuals in the police department who were sincerely
trying to solve these crimes. As Mr. Wagner testified the other
day, he was the one that recommended this private detective agency
to me, and assured me that they would cooperate fully and he would
cooperate fully with them. . . . (p. 9565)

The testimony of Herbert V. Kohler and Walter P. Reuther
came at the conclusion of the hearings. Mr. Kohler appeared first,
read a 5-page statement for which the committee waived a 24-
hours-in-advance rule for filing statements, and presented the company's well-known positions concerning compulsory unionism,
vandalism and violence, and the boycott. The chairman then inquired further about what, specifically, Mr. Kohler considered to
be other union violations of the existing laws which should be
prohibited by law. Mr. Kohler thought of mass picketing, home
demonstrations, vandalism and violence, and the boycott.

The chairman tried to be helpful. He said, "Three is vandalism and violence, and four is boycott. Is there any other that you
would regard as an improper practice . . . on the part of the union
. . . either the local or the international, or both?"

Mr. Kohler consulted with his counsel, Conger, and came up
with the "importation of goons."

Said the chairman, "That's five. Is there any other?"

"I think that covers it, sir," said Mr. Kohler.

The chairman again inquired if these were all. The witness
conferred with the counsel and replied, "Yes Sir."

Would Mr. Kohler, the chairman wanted to know, be willing
to sit down and bargain with the union to try to reach a settlement?
The witness again conferred with counsel. Senator John F. Ken-

nedy appealed to the chair, saying, "Mr. Chairman, it seems to me that Mr. Kohler could give an answer to that. He is the head of the company. . . . We have already heard from Mr. Conger. . . . Does he have to have advice of counsel in answering that question?"

"We have been very generous here in letting them consult counsel," Mr. McClellan thought.

". . . We will go to a bargaining table with open minds," Kohler said, "But I will not give you the answer now."

Weeks of hearings had elapsed when Senator Goldwater came up with the suggestion that there was really no reason to bring in Walter Reuther, but this McClellan would not buy. Reuther admitted that the violence was a problem, and some of the things the union did were a mistake. On the question of whether

> . . . they [the strikers] should have kept people [nonstrikers] out, we have no argument. I think that was an improper activity. The question is, picket lines are not formed in vacuums. . . . I think if I were sitting here today and if you said to me, would you do that again, I would have made a trip to Wisconsin to see that it did not happen . . . (p. 10006)

Robert Kennedy, in *The Enemy Within*, describes Reuther as "a smart, confident, articulate witness," for whom the Republican senators were "no match." Toward the close of three days' testimony and examination by the committee, Reuther commented on one of the aspects of the investigation in this way:

> . . . I don't think it is fair for a member of a congressional investigating committee to draw conclusions publicly 6 months before you begin to investigate someone. That is what I think is unfair.
>
> I love this country and I would do anything in my power to preserve it as it is. But I am worried. I am worried that America will [not] be equal to the challenge in the world of a Communist conspiracy that will stop at nothing. I am worried because we dissipate and we weaken the basic structure in the unity of our country in this kind of a period of unnecessary vilification in the public prints, by unnecessary namecalling.
>
> I don't like to call Senator Goldwater names. I feel sad. I feel as though I am not clean when I do it. But you look at the record, just look at the record, and for every time I have said something nasty about Senator Goldwater, he has trucked it in by the bale.
>
> That doesn't justify it. I plead to you, gentlemen, fight your

political battles, stand up in the market place of free ideas in America, and fight for what you believe in. But fight for what you believe in and try to sell it on its merits, and not by trying to characterize the other fellow as disloyal, dangerous, un-American.

This weakens America and only helps the Communists. If you think my economics are cockeyed, say so. If you think my political philosophy is cockeyed, say so. But prove it is cockeyed based upon its demerits and not based upon I am more dangerous than the Communists, or I am against the free-enterprise system. This is what is wrong.

I say to you I have unlimited faith in free men. This is a faith not drawn out of academic discussion. I lay in the cellars in Berlin when the Nazis were shooting people in the streets. I saw the Communists in Russia. I worked there. I know something about what it means to have a knock on the door at night with the secret police to take a woman's husband away, and then have breakfast with her the next morning and she has not even asked what happened to him. I lived this.

I have faced the gangsters of the Ford Motor Co. I have taken all the abuse because I believe inherently in the worth and the dignity of each human individual created by God. When we destroy the basic unity of America because we lack the maturity to discuss our respective points of view on their merits in the free market place of ideas, when we have to hide behind nasty words, when we have to challenge the motive and the loyalty of people in order to try to discredit the things they stand for, we are hurting America.

And when you hurt America, you hurt the cause of human freedom in the world. I plead with you, let us wage our political differences. You advocate what you believe in, and I shall advocate what I believe in. If I can't take your arguments apart and show that my point of view is superior, based on the facts, then I ought to lose and you ought to win the argument, and the same thing should be true in reverse.

I think that this is the great problem of America: Finding a way to demonstrate that democracy is in depth so sufficiently that we can argue the differences without namecalling. This is my plea. (pp. 10250–51)

Some of Robert Kennedy's observations in *The Enemy Within* are worthy of note:

. . . to put a union official on the witness stand and debate with him on general subjects in the hope of embarrassing him, without

"Sweetiepie, Tell Us Little Old Judges In Your Own Words What A Scoundrel That Reuther Is" — Herblock in The Washington Post.

proof of wrongdoing, can be disastrous. I think Senator Mundt and Senator Goldwater both came to learn this lesson at the hands of Walter Reuther. . . .

The first witness, Alan Graskamp, president of Local 833, was an unpretentious but curiously impressive man who spoke intelligently in simple, short, easy-to-understand sentences as he described his union's problems with the company. He made no pretense, he just told the truth. . . .

Never at any time during the five weeks of hearings did Senators Mundt, Goldwater or Curtis ask questions critical of the Kohler company, or questions that would elicit a reply unfavorable to the company point of view. Apparently it never occurred to them that there were two sides to this controversy.

As might be expected, the committee found itself in disagreement in the conclusions reached. Senators McClellan, Kennedy, Ervin and Church said,

> . . . unlike other committee hearings, there were no charges of personal corruption or evidence presented of racketeering within the union . . . [and] no evidence of misuse or misappropriation of union funds . . .

was discovered in reviewing the finances of both Reuther and the UAW. As to the strike, they concluded:

> The committee was able to discern accord between the Company and the UAW only on such unarguable items as the date of a particular event. . . . On just one other score was there any semblance of unanimity: The struggle has left indelible scars on the once-placid community of Sheboygan . . . This has been a classic example of labor-management relations at its worst. . . .

Senators McClellan and Ervin wrote a supplementary report in which they said:

> In view of the fine contributions made by the Republican members to the progress and effectiveness of the work of the committee, in many instances, we deeply regret that they have now made, in their separate views, statements derogatory to Democratic members of the committee and of the chief counsel and staff . . .

and they concluded by praising the work of chief Counsel Kennedy and the staff.

Senators Kennedy and Church emphasized in a joint statement that the strikes at Kohler and Perfect Circle plants "highlight the necessity for good faith collective bargaining and the importance of speeding up NLRB procedures so that critical cases can be resolved before they fester and make good faith bargaining impossible." Senators Curtis, Goldwater and Mundt concluded that "we do not contend that the Kohler Co. was wholly blameless . . . but it is clear that the violence which took place there was not in response to any company misconduct" but "that it was solely attributable to the UAW method of operation. . . ."

A union editorial writer expressed his opinion of the performance thus:

> . . . The whole spectacle is so doltish . . . Ah for the days when the Republicans had a Taft to speak their labor piece! We disagreed utterly with Senator Taft but we respected the integrity of his person and his logic. The antics of . . . Goldwater . . . the bumbling of . . . Curtis . . . dismay us. . . . Will the Republican party please send professionals into the ring?

The McClellan Committee's activities ended after the Landrum-Griffin (Labor-Management Reporting and Disclosures) Act was passed in 1959. Robert F. Kennedy resigned as chief counsel on September 6 of that year. In his book, *The Enemy Within*, Kennedy relates that, after his resignation, Senator Goldwater in statements to the press said that he [Kennedy] had "run out on the Reuther investigation." Kennedy called the senator to ask if the statements had been made by him, and the senator replied that although he had not expressed it just that way, he had not been satisfied with the way the case had been run. Kennedy inquired what the senator thought he might have done, to which Goldwater protested, "I want to get back to Arizona . . . I don't want any more hearings." Kennedy asked why the senator had said what he did, and the Senator from Arizona replied, "That's politics."

8

ATTEMPTS AT SETTLEMENT
— THE ROLE OF GOVERNMENT
AGENCIES AND INDIVIDUALS

WALTER J. KOHLER, JR., who heads the Vollrath Company in Sheboygan, recalled with amusement that during the time when the 1954 strike seemed unresolvable, a young fellow came to see him to talk about what might be done to settle it.

"After so many prominent, well-known people have tried to settle this thing and failed," Walter Kohler said, "why should you want to get involved in something they haven't been able to do?"

"If I can settle this strike, which is the longest in the history of the United States," said the youth earnestly, "I'll be a hero."

Dozens of individuals became involved in attempts to resolve the second strike at Kohler. In addition to the company and union spokesman there were the representatives of the Federal Mediation and Conciliation Service, mayors of several cities, a county board, a city council, members of Congress, local and national spokesmen of the major religious faiths, a judge and a real-estate man who tried their hand at ending the dispute.

There were some who hoped that somehow Walter Reuther and Herbert V. Kohler, as top spokesmen for the union and the company, might be able to reach an agreement. On Christmas Eve, 1955, Reuther wired Kohler to join him in "a face to face negotiation on Christmas Day. . . . Yours is the cold distinction," Reuther said, "of having the nation's longest industrial dispute at your gate. If you are willing to, I am willing to meet you . . . in Sheboygan or any place of your own choosing."

Kohler ignored the invitation. On New Year's Day, Reuther wired again, repeating his offer to negotiate. Even though the NLRB Trial Examiner's recommendations were somewhat disappointing to the union, Reuther told Kohler, he was willing to go ahead on that basis.* But like other attempts, Reuther's offer got nowhere.

* Emil Mazey told the author that he appeared on a Milwaukee TV program shortly thereafter and was asked why Reuther was willing to "sell out" the strikers on the basis of the recommendation of the NLRB Trial Examiner.

An uncounted number of individuals approached the UAW and others with ideas for settling the strike; meanwhile the union was doing everything it could to find a way to reach a settlement. The strike had worn on about three years, one UAW official recalled, when he was invited to the home of a Milwaukee businessman on a snowy winter night "to talk about this Kohler thing."

"The same invitation must have gone to the company because when I walked into the house, a Kohler official walked in right behind me," he said. The host, a teetotaler, served whiskey to both his guests, and after several drinks, suggested that all three get on their knees and "say a little prayer" for the settlement of the strike. The guests looked at each other in utter astonishment; the Kohler official recovered first and excused himself and left, followed by the UAW man.

Between February 2, 1954, and December 31, 1957, a total of 80 negotiating sessions were held; the FMCS was involved in 59.

Role of the Federal Mediation and Conciliation Service

The FMCS, which had already been involved in the 1952–53 negotiations prior to the strike, was called to assist in resolving the differences that existed between the company and union after the strike started, but without avail. The 44 meetings FMCS held during the first year of the strike are described in Chapter 5. The first negotiating session during the second year of the strike was held at the regional headquarters of FMCS in Chicago on April 21, 1955. Mediators Fleshman, Burtz and Despins were on hand for a session which included 6 company and 8 union spokesmen. No agreement was reached and no further meetings were scheduled until about three months later, when, three weeks after the clay-boat incident, a series of sessions were held on July 28, 29, August 1 and 2 at the Palmer House in Chicago, 150 miles from the scene of conflict. Robert H. Moore and Charles Alsip replaced Burtz and Despins in the later meetings.

Only one meeting between company and union representatives was held during the entire year of 1956 — at Chicago on March 19.

An analysis of the time FMCS spent on the Kohler case, prepared sometime during late 1955, indicated that the equivalent of one and a half man-years was spent on this dispute:[1]

	Hours
Commissioners' time away from official station (from the travel vouchers)	2,592
Formal conference time with company — joint and separate (from company records)	485½
Separate formal conference time with union (estimated)	200
Related conferences with Governor, Mayor, NLRB, WERB, publishers, judges, civic leaders and others (estimated)	76

One hundred ten telephone calls totaling 420 minutes were made in connection with the dispute and 64 reports were prepared for the Washington office of FMCS. Since the agency was also called upon for further assistance later in the case, these figures are only illustrative of the extensive involvement of this mediation agency.

Several Senators Offer to Help

On June 3, 1955, Mazey, Kitzman, Conger and William Howe, company attorney, appeared before the U.S. Senate Subcommittee on Labor and Public Welfare, which was then holding hearings on a bill related to government contracts. Senator Irving M. Ives of New York (Rep.) urged Conger to "sit down here" and "negotiate a contract." Conger refused, saying he had come to Washington to testify and not to negotiate and that he did not have the other members of his company's negotiating committee with him. Nevertheless, there was some discussion of the issues involved in the dispute and, at one point, Howe complained that the union alluded in negotiations to three of Kohler's major competitors, but failed to mention Universal Rundel Corporation, another competitor with whom the UAW-CIO had recently signed a contract which "incorporates practically what we have offered the union and they have refused for a year to take. . . ." Kitzman replied that "we will take the same agreement in the Kohler Company word for word, including the union security we have in the Universal Rundel Corporation, and adopt that lock, stock and barrel." The NLRB Brief, prepared by General Counsel Stuart Rothman, points out that "Conger and Howe executed a hasty retreat with statements emphasizing the differences between Kohler and its

competitors and 'the basic fallacies of trying to ape competitors.' "
Later, when Senator Pat McNamara of Michigan (Dem.) and
Senator Ives suggested arbitration, Conger repeated the company's
position that it would not let an arbitrator write a contract.

The Clergymen Try Their Hand

Observers have commented on the comparative silence of the
clergy of Sheboygan during the 1954 strike. But few were more
aware of the disastrous effects of a strike upon the community than
the clergymen, some of whom had lived through the 1934 strike
and did not wish to see it repeated.

They felt the pressures from both sides in the 1954 dispute,
but chose not to take an active role in the combat. Most of them
believed that if they were to fulfill the traditional role of the
Church as a conciliator, they would have to try to remain "above
the battle." Moreover, their congregations and parishes were
divided and they felt that their duty lay in ministering to them all.

Although the union felt there were few crusaders for their
cause among the Sheboygan clergy, a number of local ministers
took the initiative at the time of the union strike vote in 1954, and
went to representatives of the company to see what could be done
to avert the strike. They felt strongly that the community should
be represented at the bargaining sessions of the union and the
company and pressed for open hearings. The company official
most approachable was L. L. Smith, an active layman in the Congregational Church. He took the view that the community, as such,
was already represented by the Federal mediators. As for open
hearings, Conger insisted that these would only prolong the strike.

The deeply concerned clergymen — among them a Congregational and a Methodist minister, a rabbi and a Catholic priest —
started writing letters to the *Press* and preaching Sunday sermons
aimed at bringing some flexibility and reasonableness into the situation. Novenas for a settlement of the strike were conducted at the
local Catholic churches throughout the first couple of years. The
strike bulletin often carried announcements urging people, regardless of their faith, to attend.

Long before three national clergymen were invited to Sheboygan, Dr. T. Parry Jones, Rabbi Nathan Barack and Father John

Seen from left to right, Reverend Cameron Hall and Father John F. Cronin confer in Sheboygan with UAW representatives Bauer, Kohlhagen, Conway, Kitzman, Rand, Graskamp and Majerus on April 27, 1957. (Milwaukee Journal *photo*)

Carroll met with both company and union officials. They found the union was agreeable to negotiation but the company was not. Feeling that "the damage to the community was compelling," they got plans under way to bring in outside clergymen, representing different faiths, to see what they could do.

The strike was almost three years old and settlement seemed more remote than ever when the three nationally known clergymen came to Sheboygan in February, 1957, to see if they could help clarify the issues in the hope that an agreement could be reached.* Reverend Father John F. Cronin, assistant director of the department of social action, National Catholic Welfare Council, came from Washington, D.C.; Reverend Dr. Cameron P. Hall, executive director of the department of Church and Economic Life of the National Council of Churches, and Rabbi Eugene J. Lipman, director of the Social Action Commission of the Union of American Hebrew Congregations, came from New York City. Joint

* Reverend Charles Webber, long active in religious and labor affairs, had an important role in arranging these meetings.

meetings were held on February 15, 20 and 21, March 21 and April 25 and 26.

All three clergymen-negotiators made clear from the start that they had no vested interests; they were careful not to discuss any substantive issues with reporters, lest it should be another impediment to reaching agreement. They made every effort to avoid fixed positions by asking that both parties pledge to submit no formal documents during the first stages of the discussions. However, the company, at the February 20 meeting, did submit a proposal for settlement, which was later withdrawn.

The meetings, which ended on April 26 with the rejection by the company of the union's four-point offer, had marked the resumption of talks after a stalemate of more than eleven months. As it turned out, this was the last meeting for more than five years. The clergymen met separately and jointly with company representatives Conger, Hammer, Hollander and Hall; Kitzman, Rand and Majerus, representing the UAW International Union;* and Graskamp, Bauer and Kohlhagen from Local 833. At the very first meeting, February 15, 1957, Father Cronin, an old hand at arbitration, suggested that he would like to achieve clarification rather than bargaining, pointing out that it was necessary first to establish a framework so that details could be hammered out later. When it was learned that *Time* magazine was preparing a story on the Kohler strike, even though interviews had taken place long before the meetings with the clergy were planned, Rabbi Lipman suggested that for the sake of the success of the meetings, it might be proper to have the story "killed." Kitzman thought that such an attempt would merely make reporters "dig further" and make an even bigger story of it. At a meeting six days later, with the full contingent of union and company representatives present, Father Cronin observed that there seemed to be "a lot of pulling back on both sides" and that the press was largely to blame for creating an atmosphere which subjected both sides to pressures. He said:

> We came in here, not only to do what we could to help get the strike settled, but to help the community as well. Even after the strike is settled, there will be a terrible problem in this community.

* Jack Conway, administrative assistant to Walter Reuther, participated in the last 3 of the 6 meetings with the clergy.

Without settlement, the problem will be even worse. The bitterness
will last several generations.

Although the talks had begun in an atmosphere which Father
Cronin termed "one of conciliation" in which he sensed a mutual
willingness to negotiate, the major stumbling block was the question of whether strikers were to be reinstated after a settlement was
reached, if it should require laying off the nonstrikers who had been
promised steady jobs by the company. The Kohler Company had
repeatedly stated it would not lay off workers hired during the
strike to make room for strikers. Its contention was that these
promises of steady jobs had been made after the union put ads in
the papers charging that jobs at Kohler were temporary, pending
settlement of the strike. The union claimed the company made these
job offers because it wanted to be in a strong position to keep these
employees should any legal dispute ensue.

Father Cronin asked Conger and Kitzman to serve as a subcommittee to discuss with him the problem of reinstatement. The
other union and management representatives met with Rabbi Lipman and the Reverend Dr. Hall as conciliators to try to arrive at
acceptable language for a clause on seniority. The latter spent most
of the time discussing the fairness of the company's proposed
10-per-cent deviation formula, which the Kohler representatives
argued was a very limited deviation. Union spokesmen insisted that
any deviation from whatever type of seniority system was agreed
upon would undermine the basic principle of seniority when it
came to layoffs and rehiring.

On the issue of rehiring strikers fired for strike activities,
Conger first insisted that none would be taken back. During the sessions with the clergy, Father Cronin had urged taking back most of
this group* and at one point the company did offer to put most of
them on a "preferential hiring list" but said it would not take back
officers Graskamp, Bauer and Kohlhagen; those found guilty by
the WERB's final order of November 23, 1954; those guilty of
contempt of court on June 10, 1955; four convicted of felonies, et

---

* The union often referred to the 90 discharged men as 90 additional issues
in dispute. This number was later put at 77 because thirteen had been involved in
various law violations. After years of litigation, the NLRB on September 29, 1964,
ordered that 57 of these strikers, including all but one of the union's executive
board, be reinstated.

cetera. The union spokesmen doubted whether there was any assurance that strikers would actually get their jobs back by being put on a preferential list. As for the 3 top officers of Local 833, the company spokesmen suggested that prior to any announcement of a settlement they be given jobs elsewhere — preferably on the union's payroll. The reason given was that they "feared for the safety and very lives of these men."[2] The union felt strongly that it could not accept any agreement which would eliminate so many of its leadership. *The Reporter and Kohlerian* said:

> The three clergymen who joined the long list of interested parties who have previously tried — and failed — to settle the Kohler strike: Federal Conciliators, a Federal Court Judge, the Governor of Wisconsin, a Circuit Court Judge, and a Congressional Labor Sub-Committee . . . had the toughest assignment of all the conciliators. . . . The longer a strike runs, the more difficult mediation becomes. . . . There can be no greater tribute to their honest and sincere attempt to bring the long and bitter Kohler strike to an honorable conclusion than their expressed willingness to "stand by" and offer their service again "if a change in circumstances warrant it."[3]

The Continuing Role of the NLRB

The National Labor Relations Board was involved extensively throughout the duration of the dispute at Kohler. Unlike the FMCS, the NLRB was empowered by law to investigate, to take testimony, and to pass judgment as to whether labor and/or management complied with the law the NLRB had been designated to administer.

When the Kohler Company, ten days after the strike started, turned to the Wisconsin Employment Relations Board (WERB) for relief from mass picketing, and so on, the union turned to the NLRB with charges of unfair labor practices leveled against the company. Although the WERB was granted jurisdiction to rule in regard to the mass picketing and home demonstrations, the NLRB was the agency empowered to hear charges of other violations. The union brought to the NLRB a long list of unfair practices charges, some of which dragged on for years before decisions were reached. Eventually the charges were upheld by the board, but in the meantime many Kohler strikers had sought work elsewhere, some had died, others had retired, and therefore did not benefit from the fight the union had made on their behalf.

The NLRB hearings, which had commenced on February 8, 1955, came to a close on January 9, 1959, after 116 days of testimony, which filled an official transcript of 20,414 pages — exclusive of exhibits — the longest, most voluminous case in NLRB history. Counsels' assistants (company, union and NLRB staff) carried load upon load of documents and exhibits in and out of the hearing room, day after day.

Tedious and repetitious as the testimony often was, the Sheboygan County courtroom was frequently filled to overflowing. Throughout the long period, attorneys Albert Gore and George Squillacote handled the case for the NLRB; David Rabinovitz, assisted by others, was attorney for the union; while Lyman Conger, as chief counsel for the company, was its legal spokesman. Desmond, Hammer, William Howe and Ellison Smith were also on the Kohler legal staff. Otherwise wearying proceedings were often enlivened by Conger's shouting "I object!" and quick leaps to his feet. At one point, near the close of the hearings, Trial Examiner George A. Downing granted a recess so that Rabinovitz could examine subpoenaed reports of the detective agencies. Rabinovitz asked Ray Majerus to help him and together they began paging through the exhibits. Conger rushed across the room, shouting to Majerus, "You keep your paws off those reports! . . . We paid for them and we have something to say about who's going to look at them!"

Majerus, Conger's shaking finger beneath his nose, told the irate counsel, "You gave me your last order on April 21, 1952, Conger [the day Conger fired Majerus, a Kohler company enameler in the enamel shop controversy] and I don't have to take anything from you now."[4]

A hurried call by a company attorney brought Downing back to the hearing room; he ruled that Rabinovitz could ask anybody he pleased to help him check the reports, except newspaper or publicity men.

Gore and Squillacote, working out of the Chicago office, spent much time on the Kohler case, especially during the first two years of the strike, as did Joseph Cohen, field examiner for the NLRB. It was Cohen who tried, on 7 occasions during the weekend of

July 4, 1955, preceding the clay boat incident, to serve a subpoena on Kohler plant manager, Edmund J. Biever. Albert Gore told the author that practically the entire regional NLRB staff of about 25, sent to Sheboygan immediately after the clay-boat incident, had obtained more than 200 affidavits in a matter of 3 days, and that seldom during those hectic days did he get more than 3 hours' sleep a night. He indicated that, under the law, the NLRB might have been compelled to withdraw from the case and discontinue hearings on the union's charges of unfair labor practices against the company had there been evidence that the clay-boat riot was instigated and promoted by the union.*

A summary of the NLRB's actions prior to handing down its first major decision in the Kohler case in 1960, appeared in *The Sheboygan Press:*[5]

The original complaint was issued by the NLRB general counsel, Oct. 26, 1954, alleging violations of the Taft-Hartley Act. Amendments alleging additional violations of the act were added as the strike continued.

The hearings before Downing [Trial Examiner] were interrupted over a four-year period by numerous vain attempts by federal and state officials and private individuals to settle the costly strike. . . .

In the first of three reports on Sept. 12, 1956, Downing urged dismissal of the union's complaint on grounds that its trustees had not filed non-Communist affidavits when the complaint was issued.

The Board reversed this ruling [sic] on Feb. 8, 1957, holding that the trustees were not "officers" of the union and therefore not required to meet the affidavit filing requirements of the Taft-Hartley Act.

In his second report, on Oct. 9, 1957, Downing said all rank and file strikers whose jobs had not been filled before June 1, 1954, should be reinstated upon application, or when the strike ended. . . .

The new matter brought out before the Senate Committee (McClellan), Downing concluded in his third report on March 5, 1959, "simply supports and confirms the former findings both in the

---

* Based on this investigation, Gore was convinced that most of the crowd at the Sheboygan dock on July 5 gathered as a consequence of the WHBL newscasts, and, to some extent, the union broadcasts by Treuer and his publicity stunt of the "UAW Navy." Once at the docks, the crowd became engulfed in the anti-Kohler feelings which existed in the community and which were intensified when Biever, who had evaded the NLRB's attempts to subpoena him for the hearings (this had been given extensive publicity in the press and radio), appeared on the scene.

respects where unfair labor practices were found and where they were not found."

After long and arduous work by the NLRB general counsel, the NLRB legal counsel and field examiners, the voluminous testimony gathered in the field was presented to the board. Four of its five members held, after extensive hearings, that what had begun as an "economic strike" became an "unfair labor practice strike" as of June 1, 1954, when the company unilaterally and without notice to the union gave a wage increase to nonstriking employees though it had failed to do so during negotiations. The fifth board member, Joseph Jenkins, Jr., held that it had been an unfair-labor-practice strike from the beginning and cited what he called a long-standing "fixed intent" by the company "to precipitate a situation which would enable it to rid itself of the union." The board ruling, handed down August 26, 1960, held the company guilty of unfair labor practices and ordered dismissal of any workers hired on or after June 1, 1954, if necessary to restore the strikers to their old jobs or substantially equivalent positions with full seniority and other privileges. (Under the Taft-Hartley Act, strikers may be permanently replaced only in the event that the strike is held to be an economic one with no unfair labor practices engaged in by the company — thus the June 1st cutoff date.)

Arthur Bauer, acting president of Local 833, and legal counsel Rabinovitz were elated by the ruling. Bauer said, ". . . the vindication of the union for striking the Kohler Co. is now complete. . . . Even though we experienced keen disappointment by the board's failure to clear all of those strikers discharged by the Kohler Co. for strike activities basically caused by the company's designs to break the union, we are pleased with this concrete ruling favoring the cause of the Kohler workers."* He said he hoped that the company "will accept the decision of the board and work as hard as we can to bring an end to this unfortunate affair." Local union officials estimated that at least 2,000 strikers would be entitled to get their jobs back on request or when the strike ended. Seventy-seven members, the NLRB held, had been lawfully fired by the company for "engaging in or directing and controlling strike misconduct."

---

* In reaching its decision, the NLRB had studied 20,408 pages of testimony, almost 6,000 feet of motion-picture film, 1,900 exhibits and Downing's 156-page intermediate report.

Examiner Downing recommended that 35 of the strikers fired for "misconduct" were entitled to reinstatement, but 3 of the 5 NLRB members held them to have been legally discharged. Downing told the board, "This strike is only one phase of an unedifying industrial conflict — more typical of a bygone era of labor relations — which has been fought simultaneously on several fronts with constant bitterness and frequent fury."[6]

Emil Mazey promptly announced that the union would proceed to apply collectively for reinstatement on behalf of the more than 1,700 workers still considered to be on strike and he urged them also to apply individually. L. L. Smith, Kohler Company vice president, announced within 90 minutes after the decision was received that the company would appeal the ruling. He expressed satisfaction that the board had sustained the company's position on discharging the 77 strikers for misconduct, among them the officers and members of the union's executive board, but said that "on many important questions of law, the decision is, in our viewpoint, incorrect. . . . We think it is our duty, not only in our own interests, but in the public interest, to seek a review of the findings by a higher authority." The company had stated repeatedly that it would not lay off new employees to make room for strikers should the strike end. This became a principal issue in the dispute, despite the fact that the NLRB had ruled in other cases that strikers involved in strikes caused or prolonged by unfair labor practices were entitled to return to their jobs.

On August 26, therefore, both the company and the union moved quickly to file appeals from the NLRB decision, and sought reviews of the case before two different Circuit Courts of Appeals. Each wanted a review of that part of the ruling adverse to it. The UAW filed its petition in the District of Columbia Circuit Court at 10:35 A.M. Eastern Daylight Saving Time; the company filed a petition with the 7th District U.S. Circuit Court of Appeals in Chicago at 10:10 A.M. Central Daylight Saving Time. Under Federal law, where two or more proceedings with respect to an order are filed in different courts, the one first instituted has jurisdiction. Stuart Rothman, general counsel of the NLRB, agreed with the technical point raised by the UAW and ruled that the case be heard in the District of Columbia Court because the UAW petition, due to time zone differential, had been filed there 35 minutes ahead of the company's appeal in Chicago. The 7th Circuit (Chicago) agreed that the case should be heard in Washington, D.C.

Headlines in *The Sheboygan Press* on September 2, 1960, announced that "The 'endless' Kohler Company Strike ended late Thursday." Termination of the strike did not imply a mutually acceptable settlement; but it did establish a date from which the company would be legally liable for providing back pay for strikers. It left the door open to resumption of negotiations on a new contract.[7] Pickets were immediately withdrawn from the plant gates, indicating that the union was calling off the strike. The union also took steps to insure that the members' rights to collect back pay — dating from five days after reinstatement — were protected. On September 14, the Kohler Company sent letters to about 1,400 striking employees who had not gone back to work during the 6½ year strike — about 400 less than the union claimed were eligible to go back — offering to reinstate them and requesting they make application by October 3. While the company declined to reveal how many had accepted reinstatement, a union spokesman estimated the figure to be "approximately 1,000."

Because the company wanted to retain as many of the men it had hired during the strike as possible, it cut the work week from 40 to 32 hours to make room for returning strikers. This, in effect, amounted to a 20-per-cent (less tax deductions) cut in weekly earnings.

The union claimed this discouraged many men from leaving 40-hour jobs to return to Kohler and the board initiated contempt proceedings against the company for failure to comply with the court decree. The union also claimed that some strikers were reluctant to go back into the plant until the company agreed to the union's request to resume bargaining. E. H. Hammer, acting chairman for the Kohler management committee, wrote the UAW (September 28, 1960) that the firm could not bargain collectively "without thereby conceding the validity of the NLRB decision and order."

On October 7, 1960, the UAW asked the NLRB to proceed immediately to seek an injunction ordering the Kohler Company to comply with the board's order of August 26. The union claimed that the company was not complying because it had not made an offer of reinstatement to more than 300 strikers included in the board's order. A union spokesman pointed out that under Section 10(e) of the Taft-Hartley Act the board can seek an immediate injunction even though an appeal has been made. "We want relief now, not two or three years from now after the appeal has been ruled on," said Ray Majerus.[8]

On January 26, 1962, the U.S. Circuit Court of Appeals, District of Columbia, enforced all of the remedial portions of the board's order. It also concluded that the grounds on which the board had found the strike not an unfair labor practice strike at its outset, were inadequate. The Court further concluded that the board should have followed the doctrine of the Thayer case (see Chapter 9) and weighed the misconduct of the 77 dischargees against the respondent's unfair labor practices, in determining whether their misconduct was sufficient to disqualify them for reinstatement. Accordingly, the Court remanded the case to the board for reconsideration as to the causation of the strike, and the question of the discharge of the 77 strikers.[9]

Cases Heard before U.S. Circuit Court of Appeals

Three cases were taken before the U.S. Circuit Court of Appeals:[10]

No. 15,961   With the UAW Local 833 as Petitioner and the NLRB as Respondent and the Kohler Company as Intervenor.

No. 16,031   With the NLRB as Petitioner and the Kohler Company as Respondent.

No. 16,182   With the Kohler Company as Petitioner and the NLRB as Respondent.

The pleadings of the NLRB are bound in five volumes of a Joint Appendix totaling 2,317 pages. The board also prepared a 142-page brief summarizing these three cases. Cases No. 16,031 and No. 16,182 were combined in the brief. The issues under consideration in Case No. 16,031 were:

1. Whether the Board has exceeded its statutory authority in issuing any order against the Company, since the trustees of the International Union had not filed "non-Communist" affidavits pursuant to Section 9(h) of the National Labor Relations Act.

2. Whether the Board properly concluded that the Company violated Section 8(a), (5) and (1) of the Act by refusing to furnish the Union wage information to which it was entitled, by unilaterally granting wage increases, and by otherwise refusing to bargain in good faith.

3. Whether the Board properly concluded that Kohler Company violated Section 8(a), (5), (3) and (1) by its treatment of the Shell Department employees. . . .

4. Whether the Board properly found that the Company, by violating Section 8 (a), (3) and (5) occurring on and after June 1, 1954, prolonged the strike which had begun in April 1954 and converted it into an unfair labor practice strike.

5. Whether the Board properly concluded that the company violated Section 8(a)(1) of the Act (a) by statements of supervisory personnel to an employee, (b) by soliciting an employee to return to work, (c) by serving eviction notices on and thereafter evicting certain striking employees who were then residents or tenants in company-owned properties, and (d) by engaging through hired detectives in acts of surveillance over the union and anti-union espionage.

6. Whether the Board's order is valid and proper.

On these cases, the NLRB's conclusions included the following evidence:

1. unilaterally putting a 3-cent wage increase into effect on or about June 1, 1954;

2. unilaterally discharging 53 temporary Shell Department employees who were on strike while transferring nonstriking employees from the same department to other jobs;

3. not supplying pertinent wage data requested by the union;

4. adhering to an adamant position of no wage increase when negotiating with the union — its determination to "teach the union a lesson";

5. rebuffing attempts of third parties to settle the dispute, resorting to the use of detectives for surveillance of union activities, evicting striking employees from Company-owned residences and trying to induce a valuable employee to abandon the strike.

Case No. 15,961 dealt with these issues:

1. Whether the Board properly concluded that the Strike of April 5, 1954, was economic at its outset and was not initially caused by any unfair labor practices of Kohler Company.

2. Whether the Board properly concluded that Kohler's March 1, 1955, discharge of each of the 77 strikers because of his conduct during the strike was not unlawful.

3. Whether the Board properly concluded that the Company did not violate Section 8(a)(3) of the Act by serving eviction notices and evicting certain striking employees. . . .

4. Whether the Board erred in failing to conclude that the Company violated Section 8(a)(5) of the Act by failing to negotiate with the Union respecting the discharge of 77 employees for conduct during the strike.

5. Whether the Board should have ordered backpay for the striking Shell Department employees beginning November 22, 1954.

This board, serving toward the end of the Eisenhower administration, ruled on Case No. 15,961 that the strike was started as an economic strike and had become an unfair labor practice strike on June 1, 1954. It also ruled that the company was justified in dismissing the 77 strikers, including all the union's officers and executive board members, stating that they ". . . by their mere presence in these incidents contributed to their coercive and intimidatory effect." Since this board held that the strike did not start as an unfair labor practice strike, it contended that the strikers' mass picketing, et cetera could not be viewed in the light of the Thayer Doctrine, which called for weighing the seriousness of the company's unfair labor practices against the seriousness of the strikers' misconduct in determining what was just. The NLRB brief contended that "the extent of the misconduct of the 77 dischargees was of such gravity, both in character and scope, as to result in a forfeiture of their right to reinstatement, even in light of the equitable considerations expounded in *Thayer*."

Under the Kennedy and Johnson administrations, Frank W. McCulloch, chairman, Gerald A. Brown, John H. Fanning, Howard Jenkins, Jr., and Boyd Leedom served on the National Labor Relations Board. Many students of the governmental process have observed that the general philosophy of political appointees to boards and administrative agencies tends to reflect the philosophy of the dominant political trend at the time. While there is usually some lag, this is to be expected. To have it otherwise would indicate that these agencies were not responsive to the "will of the people." Whoever is at the receiving end of an adverse ruling often will argue that the ruling was political, but such complaints never come from those in whose favor a ruling is made.

The National Association of Manufacturers in the fall of 1963, campaigned for legislation to curb the powers of the NLRB. With this suggested change, Boyd Leedom, a Republican and a frequent dissenter to decisions of the majority of the board, did not concur. Speaking to the Long Beach (California) Chamber of Commerce in December, 1963, Leedom said that the men appointed by President Kennedy were excellent selections, who had sought to carry out the law to the best of their ability and with complete honesty. He denied that the board decisions had been "pro-labor." Leedom, who had served as chairman of the NLRB during the Eisenhower administration, stated that the fact that he was a frequent dissenter did not mean that the board was biased toward labor any more than the Eisenhower board was. "I believe, on balance," he said, "the changes made by the Board have been far more acceptable to labor than management. But those who disparage the board now as 'pro-labor' would have to label the board on which I served as chairman under the Eisenhower administration as 'pro-management.' Neither charge withstands scrutiny. The swing of the pendulum merely reflects honest difference of opinion."[11]

U.S. Supreme Court Sustains Union — Bargaining Is Resumed

On June 4, 1962, the United States Supreme Court rejected the company's appeal for review of the District of Columbia U.S. Circuit Court's decision which upheld the NLRB ruling of August 26, 1960. This action by the Supreme Court led to a resumption of negotiations later in June of that year and finally resulted in a new union contract — the first in 9 years.

Collective bargaining sessions were resumed on June 27, 1962, by the Kohler Company and Local 833 — after 5 years, 2 months and 2 days away from the bargaining table. Negotiations had intermittently occurred between 1954 and 1957. The strike had been formally terminated on September 1, 1960, but the company would not resume serious bargaining until it exhausted all its legal rights to appeal to higher courts.

Seated around table at first bargaining session in more than five years, union and company officials gathered at the YMCA in Sheboygan: (from left) Kitzman, Mazey, Rand, Majerus, Marshall Hughes (Detroit), Andrew Willadsen, Julius Siech, Arthur Fox, Ray Frescarri (Detroit), representing the union; and Marvin Messner (assistant to Ireland), Martin Hollander (assistant to Conger), Walter Ireland, Sr., George Gallati, James L. Kuplic, L. L. Smith, Conger, Howe, Gray Castle (associate of Howe), Hammer and Charles Pagnucco (Kohler training director). (Sheboygan Press photo)

The '62–'63 Agreement

On June 28, 1962, *The Sheboygan Press* carried a 3-column picture of Emil Mazey and Lyman Conger (both smiling) over a caption: "Conciliatory Air Pervades Kohler, UAW Negotiations." The words "friendly" and "hopeful" were used to describe a 2-hour exploratory session held at the Sheboygan YMCA. Mazey said, "We have not formulated our demands. I think it is in the best interests of the company and the union that we get a fair and equitable agreement as soon as possible." Conger said it was too early to speculate whether the company will be able to meet on a day-to-day basis until agreement is reached. The company's bargaining team of 11, headed by Conger, included L. L. Smith, executive vice president; attorneys Howe and Hammer; Ireland, the personnel director; and J. L. (Les) Kuplic,* successor to Edmund Biever, as plant superintendent. Mazey's associates included Don Rand, Harvey Kitzman, Ray Majerus and Marshall Hughes, administrative assistant to UAW vice president Duane (Pat) Greathouse, and three Kohler plant stewards: Andrew Willadsen, Arthur Fox and Julius Siech.

The UAW had had a one-year contract with the company during 1953-54 and now, eight years later, was seeking a second contract. Mazey asked for resumption of negotiations and immediate representation for the purpose of handling grievances and in-plant problems. During these negotiations the company agreed that the grievance procedure contained in the 1953 contract would be followed until new terms were agreed upon. This was a significant step forward for the union because it meant that the union was officially recognized for dealing with grievances.

The union did not present a specific proposal to the company but suggested that they start with the 1953 contract and submit proposals for changes and improvements. This procedure was acceptable to the company and proved to be most helpful in negotiating the new agreement. The atmosphere was similar to that which prevailed in earlier bargaining sessions, with one big difference — the company's willingness to reach an agreement. Both parties were conscious of the long struggles which were behind them and both still hoped to win the cases pending before the NLRB and the courts. Even though never mentioned across the bargaining table, these were "strong arm" considerations in the minds of the negotiators.

There was little rehashing of earlier differences. The company agreed to a check-off of union dues with very little discussion and no reference to the bitterness which prevailed in 1953. A mutually acceptable agreement on leave of absence for pregnancy was also worked out with little difficulty.

* J. L. Kuplic was named president of the Kohler Company, succeeding Herbert V. Kohler, Sr., in July, 1962.

The union negotiators concentrated on improving the fringe benefit provisions of the contract before turning to a wage increase. When they came to this issue, the company pointed out that fringe benefit improvement agreed upon already amounted to 13.7 cents per hour. Union spokesmen pointed out that while there had been some wage increases during the strike period, there had been no adjustments in fringe benefits from 1954 to 1962. Company spokesmen then argued that 1960 and 1961 had not been a very good period for the company's business.

When negotiations on a new contract began, Emil Mazey, secretary-treasurer of the UAW, pointed out that he had not participated in bargaining talks since March 19, 1956, and that he had "a lot of catching up to do." He said, "We hope we can achieve a contract comparable to contracts we have with Kohler Company's principal competitors. We are not seeking to place the Kohler Co., at a disadvantage with its competitors."[12]

An agreement was finally reached after 3½ months and presented to a membership meeting of Local 833 for ratification on Sunday, October 7. After a 3-hour meeting attended by about 700 members, a "disappointing" contract was approved by a vote of 411 to 45, a vote that represented about a third of the union's claimed membership. Harvey Kitzman, the UAW regional director, pointed out that the new contract provided for 13.7 cents per hour in increased fringe benefits, although there was to be no cash wage increase. One of the gains for the union was an improved medical plan that provided up to $10,000 surgical and medical care, with the company paying 80 per cent of the increased cost. Lyman Conger stated in a prepared release that the contract "does not grant the UAW a union shop or any other form of compulsory unionism. . . . this is a contract that we arrived at after thorough discussion at the bargaining table. We feel it is fair to everyone concerned. It is our hope that it will prove to be a workable agreement."[13] Donald Rand told the union members that questions of back pay and reinstatement were to be decided by the NLRB.

When Kitzman was asked whether the strike was worth it, he replied, "Only the years down the road will tell." He noted that five wage increases, totalling from 28 to 46 cents per hour, had been instituted by the company since the strike started in 1954. Others who spoke at the meeting included Ray Majerus, Don Rand, Charles Heymanns and Attorney Rabinovitz.

Duane H. (Pat) Greathouse told the members at the meeting that he was convinced that the new contract signified "the time that unionism came to the Kohler Co." He said unionism did not come to Kohler the year the union won bargaining rights (1952) or the year it negotiated the first contract. "I happen to believe," Greathouse continued, "that in the negotiation of this agreement, for the first time the Kohler Co. accepted the union. I am convinced that this is the important thing in this contract." He said the company did not agree to the contract "because they like you or the union any more now than in 1954 . . . they have learned that they have got to live with a union."[14]

Attorney David Rabinovitz told the Sunday meeting that investigators for the NLRB from Chicago and Washington would be in Sheboygan within a week or two to interview persons regarding reinstatement and back pay. Rand insisted that hundreds of people were refused reinstatement by the company . . . so it looked as though more trouble and conflict was ahead, even though a new contract had been signed.

On October 8, 1962, *The Sheboygan Press* ran a 4-column story, comparing the 1953–54 contract with the newly negotiated 1962–63 agreement. It summarized the significant changes as follows:

Checkoff: The new agreement honored check-off cards for dues signed both before and after the agreement was executed — with the 30-day escape period provided by law. Under the former agreement cards were good for only one year and then only if signed after the effective date of the agreement.

Arbitration: The arbitration clause defined the jurisdiction and scope of the arbitrator and included discipline and discharge cases as well as other grievances. The Company had insisted that discipline and discharge were not subject to arbitration under the earlier agreement.

Seniority: Under the new agreement employees who were laid off could retain their seniority rights for as much as 2½ years as compared to 90 days under the old contract.

Layoffs: Under the old agreement the Company claimed they could lay off anywhere in the seniority listing, using the 10%

deviation formula in the agreement, even laying off the man with most seniority if they so chose. The new agreement called for laying off men with the least seniority after the Company had exercised its 10% deviation right.

Transfers: The old agreement was "silent" on many details on transfers which gave no protection to union stewards against transfer, nor did it provide for upgrading to better jobs, based on seniority. The new agreement provided for a consideration of seniority when other factors were equal and protected union stewards from transfer out of their department. Transfers to avoid layoff became subject to arbitration.

Leaves of Absence: The new contract provided for arbitration to settle disputes involving illness or injury. The Wisconsin Industrial Commission was designated as the agency to name an impartial physician to arbitrate such cases. Under the old agreement the Company had held that a refusal to grant leaves of absence were not subject to arbitration.

Lost Time for Stewards: The old contract provided for the Company's paying 70% of list time for the first 1500 hours devoted to dealing with grievances during the year, 60% for the second 1500 hours and 40% of the third 1500 hours. The new agreement raised the percentage the Company would pay to 80%, 70% and 60% respectively.

Holidays: Paid holidays were increased from 6 to 7.

Shift Premiums: Premium pay for working the second or third shift was increased from 7 to 8 and from 10 to 12 cents.

Insurance: $2,000 additional life insurance was added with no cost to the employee. Sickness and accident benefits were raised from $30 to $50 per week. Hospitalization benefits for employees and dependents were substantially increased.

Pensions: The waiting period was reduced from 5 to 3 years and retirement became possible at age 62 instead of 65. Full vesting was provided at age 40 after 10 years of service as compared with 15 years after 55 or 25 years service at any age. Pension "floor" provided for $2.50 per month for each year of credited pension service up to a maximum of 30 years.

The new contract also provided for some improvement in the time allowance on rates in the enamel shop and stated that working schedules could not be reduced below 32 hours per week without the mutual consent of both parties, except for major breakdowns.

While the contract did not provide for a general wage increase, it did contain a clause for a quarterly wage re-opener, and in April, 1963, a three-cent across-the-board wage increase was negotiated for the workers. This amounted to about eight cents per hour for a total of 21.7 cents improvement for the year.

The '63–'64 Agreement

The first year under the new contract turned out to be fairly peaceful, although legal battles were still being fought in the courts and before the NLRB. The relationship between the company and the local union had become quite friendly, and more grievances than before were settled in the plant at the departmental level. Historically the company had refused to commit itself to any future wage increases, thus the contract provided for quarterly wage re-opening.

The union proposed a hospitalization program for retirees and such changes in the contract as it felt were indicated based on the first year's experience, and a new agreement was negotiated which was estimated to cost the company about eleven and a half cents per hour.

Among the terms agreed upon were:

Wage Increase: A three per cent wage increase for all incentive rate workers and a four per cent increase for all day workers, effective April 8, 1964.

Adjustment of inequities: Fifty-three day work classifications had their maximums increased and a total of 510 incentive job classifications had their base rates increased, some as much as twenty per cent above the base rate.

Health and Accident Insurance: The seven-day waiting period was eliminated for confinement to a hospital due to illness. Families had to pay only the first $150 in medical expenses rather than the first $50 for every member's illness.

Coverage for retirees: Employees who retired could convert their major medical plan into hospital and surgical insurance with the company paying half the premium for retiree and his wife.

The contract also provided better terms for persons permanently and totally disabled; an additional paid holiday, eight in all; thirty instead of 90 days' waiting period for eligibility for insurance coverage; preservation of time records for use by stewards when disputes arise; tools and equipment used at work to be furnished by the company, as well as an increase in its contribution toward purchase of safety shoes from $1 to $2. The contract alo provided that a steward may go directly to the foreman without any prior request from an employee when the steward has a claim that the foreman violated any provision of the contract. The steward was also given the right to report the settlement of a grievance to the employee or employees involved, in addition to the right to investigate and present grievances. An additional 1,500 hours were allowed for investigating and processing grievances for which the company paid 60 per cent of the lost time.

The '64–'65 Agreement

By the time the second one-year contract came up for renegotiation, UAW Local 833's representatives in the Kohler plant were functioning in much the same way as those in other union locals — handling grievances and participating in the discussions they were entitled to, under the terms of the contract. Plant supervisors at Kohler had generally accepted the presence of the union and much of the "arm's length" attitude had disappeared. Most decisions were being made at the department level.

Without any mention of them, the unresolved issues still played a role at the bargaining table. Away from the bargaining table, during this time, the company and the union were still busy pleading their cases. Judge DuQuaine at Green Bay, Wisconsin, was conducting extensive hearings on the question of whether or not the company was, in fact, complying with the orders of the NLRB.

The September 29, 1964, ruling of the National Labor Relations Board, calling for a reinstatement of 57 dismissed strikers — with back-pay provisions — slowed down negotiations for a new contract and prevented reaching agreement by October 7, 1964, the expiration date of the contract. The company had announced it would appeal the NLRB decision, but negotiations continued until an agreement was arrived at early in December. The life of the contract was extended until a new agreement was reached about two months later.

After a 2-hour meeting in Sheboygan on December 6, about

one-fourth of Local 833's membership voted 230 to 24 to accept the new contract terms which had been worked out with the company representatives by Ray Majerus, Local 833 administrator,* and a committee of the local union.

The bargaining committee of the union had prepared a written report for the membership meeting which listed a number of contract improvements:

A general 3% wage increase, with an additional 2% increase for certain classifications of skilled workers;
Increases in job maximums and in shift premiums;
Increases in group medical, hospitalization, health and accident insurance;
Changes in procedure in connection with dismissal warnings;
Written notification of special rates;
Changes in holiday pay eligibility and in overtime recess;
Bereavement and jury pay (both new).[16]

Ray Majerus conducted the meeting and told the members assembled that the agreement would mean 7.7 cents per hour in wage increase and 0.6 cents in fringe benefits for a total of 8.3 cents gain. The wage increases were scheduled not to go into effect until April 12, 1965 — a provision which drew critical comment from several members on the floor.

One additional improvement in the new contract, according to Majerus, was a provision that the union receive a copy of *any* kind of "warning which is incorporated in written form in his [the employee's] employment record" rather than only the final warning as provided in the old contract. The company also agreed to permit the union to "submit a written statement of its position and its statement of the facts which it claims to be applicable." Such state-

---

* On December 14, 1960, after the resources of Local 833 had been largely dissipated by the long strike, the UAW International Union, acting on a request from the local, voted to put the union under an administrator "to assure continued existence." Harvey Kitzman, the regional director, was named and he, in turn, delegated most of the responsibility to Ray Majerus, his assistant. By the summer of 1965, Local 833 had enough members employed in the plant to provide the income and leadership to run its own affairs; the administratorship was dissolved on July 17. Kitzman formally installed the following newly elected executive board members:

Charles W. Conrardy, Jr., president and shop chairman; Julius E. Siech, vice president; E. H. Kohlhagen, recording secretary; Bernard Majerus, financial secretary-treasurer; John W. Schaefer, Ervin J. Neese and Clarence P. Huibregtse, trustees; Leo J. Schmitt, sergeant-at-arms; and Richard J. Bertschy, guide.[15]

ments were to be made a part of the employee's employment record and made available in case of future arbitration on the discharge of the employee.

Donald Rand, administrative assistant to UAW Secretary-Treasurer Emil Mazey; Harvey Kitzman, director of UAW region 10; and Charles Heymanns, AFL-CIO regional director for Wisconsin, all spoke at the meeting. In a 30-minute speech, Rand, who came from Detroit to attend the meeting, stated that the union had offered to meet with the company in October "to determine whether or not it is possible to find a solution to all of the matters that are pending as a result of decisions of the National Labor Relations Board." He reported that Mazey had written to J. L. Kuplic, Kohler Company president:

> I believe that it is in the mutual interest of the company and the union to avoid further litigation.
>
> The union is interested in finding a sound basis in which we can live together and with which we can resolve our problems on a fair and constructive basis.
>
> I am confident that an early meeting between representatives of the company and the union would produce a basis for mutually satisfactory settlement of all our difficulties.

Mazey's letter was prompted by the September 29 decision of the NLRB, ordering a reinstatement of 57 strikers who had been dismissed for alleged misconduct. Kuplic responded to Mazey's letter by saying: "It is my understanding that, once the NLRB takes jurisdiction of a matter, only the board can negotiate or agree to a settlement of it. . . ."

Rand claimed there were many cases where the two parties to a dispute had worked out a settlement and then gone to the board for approval. He also criticized a public statement, issued immediately after the NLRB decision on September 29, in which Conger had charged that the decision "rewarded the union for violence, mass picketing, flagrant and open unlawful conduct and its long reign of terror over an entire community, in violation not only of law, but all rules of morality and decency." He claimed that Conger used two standards: one to judge the union and another to judge the company. He had just learned, he reported, that former Police Chief Steen Heimke of Sheboygan, dismissed as chief for false swearing in connection with the investigation of his handling of policemen's retirement funds, had been hired as assistant head of the Kohler engine and electric plant.[17]

Kitzman recommended union member approval of the new contract. "When you make a little progress and when you have no strength because the company is living in violation, you have no alternative but to accept their offer."[18]

The company and the union are again in negotiations for a new contract as this is being written. The expiration date of October 8, 1965, has just passed, and a 30-day extension of the contract has been agreed upon. Even though the grievance procedure has been working fairly satisfactorily under the contract, the atmosphere at the bargaining table is still cool, and, at times, antagonistic. Too much has happened during the last fifteen years to make either party feel comfortable in the give-and-take of bargaining. Both parties are aware of cases still pending before the courts and NLRB — a factor which makes them less free to "lay all the cards on the table." Lyman Conger told Majerus, early in October, that the union was in no shape to strike — a statement which may well be a fact, but which does not improve the negotiating climate, and tends to make the union look to the government for help in its struggle with the company.

9

THE EFFECT OF COURT DECISIONS
ON LABOR-MANAGEMENT RELATIONS

STATE and national labor boards and the courts, to which their decisions may be appealed, have had a strong and far-reaching impact on the course of labor-management relations in the United States. Some view this fact with equanimity or approval; others insist that labor, management and the country would be better off if there were less regulation of the collective-bargaining process. What many would prefer, of course, is a lifting of restrictions imposed on their side and the imposition of more regulations on the opposing party.

Throughout the history of this country, laws and amendments to laws have been enacted when a sufficient body of the citizenry demonstrated an interest or need, and then exerted enough political pressure or support to make a new law a part of the rules for living under our government. Near one end of the continuum, are such persons as Sylvester Petro, Professor of Law at New York University, and Milton Friedman, Professor of Economics at the University of Chicago, who insist that we have too many regulatory agencies taking away certain liberties. Toward the other end are found such diverse organizations as the AFL-CIO and the National Association of Manufacturers, who do not agree, however, on the kind of regulatory legislation which ought to be adopted. When there are no strong drives for enacting or repealing labor legislation, it can be assumed that the majority of citizens who are affected prefer, or at least accept, the *status quo*. The coal strike of 1946 was one of the factors credited with generating the support for the amendment of the Wagner Act by the Taft-Hartley Act, and the 1958 McClellan Committee investigations into the activities of the Teamsters and several other unions led to the enactment of the Labor-Management Reporting and Disclosure Act of 1959 (known as the Landrum-Griffin Act). In an earlier day, employer practices contributed to the passage of the Norris-LaGuardia Act of 1932 and the Wagner Act in 1935. The strong voter support for the

Democratic party candidates in the 1964 election caused the pendulum to swing in the opposite direction and revived labor's demand for repeal of Section 14(b) of the Taft-Hartley Act which gives to the states the power to outlaw all forms of "union security," including the union shop.

Decisions of courts and boards are not always unanimous; their interpretations reflect to some extent the sentiment of the majority of their constituents. Some NLRB rulings have gone unchallenged for years and have thus acquired the force of law. Two U.S. Circuit Court of Appeals rulings, *Rubin Brothers* and *Thayer*, one of which provided a basis for the company's contentions, while the other gave support to the union's claims, were frequently cited in the Kohler company-union legal struggles.

Economic vs. Unfair-Labor-Practice Strikes

If a strike is economic in nature, an employer is free to hire permanent replacements — but not temporary strikebreakers — and is not obligated to reinstate strikers after the dispute is ended. If, on the other hand, the strike is ruled to be an unfair-labor-practice strike from its beginning, the employer may be compelled to dismiss strike replacements and may be subject to back-pay penalties under certain circumstances.

As noted earlier, the union contended that, under the meaning of the act, the strike had been an unfair-labor-practice strike from its inception. One of the five NLRB members, Joseph A. Jenkins, was of this opinion when the board ruled in 1960 that the strike had started as an economic strike, but had turned into an unfair-labor-practice strike as of June 1, 1954, thus making all strike replacements hired after that date subject to dismissal, if necessary, in order to re-employ strikers. When the District of Columbia U.S. Court of Appeals remanded the question of economic *vs.* unfair-labor-practice-strike back to the NLRB, it gave new hope to the union that its position would eventually be vindicated. This is a crucial issue for an employer in deciding whether to try to reach a settlement of a dispute, or to hire strike replacements and hope that they will eventually be numerous enough to vote the union out of his plant.

The Rubin Brothers Footwear Case

In a dispute involving the Rubin Brothers Footwear, Inc., of Waycross, Georgia, and the United Shoe Workers of America-CIO, the question arose whether or not the employer must present evidence that employees had engaged in misconduct before he could dismiss them. The NLRB ruled that evidence was required, but the case was taken to the U.S. Court of Appeals (Fifth Circuit) which ruled, April 13, 1953, that all that was necessary on the part of the employer was "good faith belief" there had been misconduct.[1] The decision emphasized that:

> Labor law affords protection against discharge only where it is established that discharge is because of union activity: *and employer discharging employee for brawling was not required to assume burden of showing that employee actually had engaged in fighting* . . .

Judges Hutcheson and Holmes held that, "there was no reasonable basis in the record for the Board's finding of unfair labor practices."

Circuit Judge Rives dissented, saying (in part):

> I do not think that the Board laid down a rule that membership in a union guarantees the member against discharge in its carefully enunciated statement as follows:
>
> "We are now of the opinion that the honest belief of an employer that striking employees have engaged in misconduct provides an adequate defense to a charge of discrimination in refusing to reinstate such employees, unless it affirmatively appears that such misconduct did not in fact occur. We thus hold that once such an honest belief is established, the General Counsel [NLRB] must go forward with evidence to prove that the employee did not, in fact, engage in such misconduct. The employer then, of course, may rebut the General Counsel's case with evidence that the unlawful act actually did occur. At all times, the burden of proving discrimination is that of the General Counsel. . . . It merely places an employer's honestly asserted belief in its true setting by crediting it with prima facie validity."

Burnup and Sims Case

The "good faith belief" ruling by the Court of Appeals set a legal precedent which the NLRB generally followed for over a decade. It is true that rulings in one circuit do not necessarily have the force of law in other parts of the country, but court rulings are usually not ignored. If U.S. Circuit Courts of Appeal in different districts — twelve in the U.S. — reach opposite conclusions, the issue can be taken to the U.S. Supreme Court for a determination. Issues can also be appealed to the Supreme Court by either contending party or the government agency involved. The Supreme Court decides whether it will hear or review a case.

In another labor dispute involving alleged misconduct, the *Burnup and Sims, Inc.* case, the same Fifth Circuit Court of Appeals, as late as August 22, 1963, held that:

> . . . discharge of employees motivated by employer's honest belief that men had threatened to dynamite employer's property was not discriminatory. . . . If employer has good faith belief that employee has engaged in misconduct such as threat to damage employer's property, employer may dismiss employee even though misconduct did not occur and threat was made while employee was engaged in activity protected by the National Labor Relations Act.

> . . . If the employer can establish that he had a good faith belief that an employee has engaged in misconduct such as here, it need not appear that the alleged misconduct in fact occurred. The burden of proving that an employer has discouraged union membership by discriminating in regards to terms and conditions of employment is on the General Counsel.[2]

The Trial Examiner's Intermediate Report prepared for the U.S. Court of Appeals read in part:[3]

> Although putting on its case under the *Rubin Brothers* doctrine, Respondent also announced that it would present evidence that in many cases, the [un]lawful conduct had actually occurred. Indeed, Respondent held for surrebuttal only a small portion of the evidence on which it relied to rebut the General Counsel's [and the Union's] evidence that the unlawful conduct did not occur. . . .

> To establish good faith belief, Respondent put up Conger during its case-in-chief, who identified and who testified to a mass of reports, affidavits, photographs, and other materials on which Respondent had purportedly relied in determining to discharge the individual strikers. [By written order of January 19, 1958, the Examiner received such material in evidence solely on the issue of Respondent's good faith belief, but held it to be inadmissible and

without probative weight on the question of whether alleged misconduct in fact occurred.]

What the entire evidence showed was that Conger originally
submitted to the group [H. V. Kohler, Howe, Hammer, and Des-
mond] a list of some 150 cases with a tentative recommendation for
discharge, presenting the cases *seriatim*, somewhat in the role of a
prosecutor. Several dozen cases were eliminated during the discussions of the individual cases, and the list was reduced to something
over 100 employees. On Kohler's suggestion that they go through
the list again, the final figure was reduced to 91, with all participants
concurring in the decision in each case. As to those eliminated
Conger testified that the group decisions convinced him that his
original recommendations were not sound. . . . [The company discovered that it had erred on one man, and the number was reduced
to 90.]

The company built its case on the good faith belief doctrine,
accepting the conclusion of the original board decision. It reviewed
the careful and thorough way in which Attorney Gerard A. Desmond, under Conger's supervision, carried out his assignment "of
investigating and accumulating information and evidence of anything he deemed of importance, without attempting to weigh or
evaluate the information from the standpoint of a labor lawyer."
Desmond testified that in following his instructions, he preferred to
err on the side of providing excessive rather than insufficient information.[4]

Supreme Court Rules on "Good Faith Belief"

The National Labor Relations Board was not satisfied with the
Circuit Court of Appeal's ruling on the *Burnup and Sims* case and
took it to the U.S. Supreme Court. On November 9, 1964, Justice
William O. Douglas delivered the opinion of the Court that "good
faith belief" on the part of the employer that an employee was
guilty of misconduct, was not enough grounds for discharge.

The Court of Appeals had refused reinstatement of two employees, holding that since the employer acted in good faith, the
discharges were not unlawful. The Supreme Court granted the
petition for *certiorari* because of a conflict among the Circuits. The
Court's opinion stated in part:

. . . Over and again the Board has ruled that Section 8(a)(1) is violated if an employee is discharged for misconduct arising out of a protected activity, despite the employer's good faith, when it is shown that the misconduct never occurred. See, e.g., *Mid-Continent Petroleum Corp.*, 54 N.L.R.B. 912,932–934; *Standard Oil Co.*, 91 N.L.R.B. 783, 790–791; *Rubin Bros. Footwear, Inc.*, 99 N.L.R.B. 610, 611.* In sum, Section 8(a)(1) is violated if it is shown that the discharged employee was at the time engaged in a protected activity,† that the employer knew it was such, that the basis of the discharge was an alleged act of misconduct in the course of that activity, and that the employee was not, in fact, guilty of that misconduct.

That rule seems to us to be in conformity with the policy behind Section 8(a)(1). Otherwise the protected activity would lose some of its immunity, since the example of employees who are discharged on false charges could or might have a deterrent effect on other employees. Union activity often engenders strong emotions and gives rise to active rumors. A protected activity acquires a precarious status if innocent employees can be discharged without engaging in it, even though the employer acts in good faith. It is the tendency of those discharges to weaken or destroy the Section 8 (a)(1) right that is controlling. We are not in the realm of managerial prerogatives. Rather we are concerned with the manner of soliciting union membership over which the Board has been entrusted with powers of surveillance.[5]

Associate Justice Harlan concurred in part and dissented in part with the ruling of the Court. He suggested "a rule which would require reinstatement of the mistakenly discharged employee and back pay only as of the time that the employer learned, or should have learned, of his mistake, subject, however to a valid business reason for refusing reinstatement."

The Thayer Doctrine

While the company relied heavily on the *Rubin Brothers*

---

* The *Rubin Bros.* case made a qualification as to burden of proof. Prior thereto the burden was on the employer to prove that the discharged employee was in fact guilty of misconduct. *Rubin Bros.* said that "once such an honest belief is established, the General Counsel must go forward with evidence to prove that the employees did not, in fact, engage in such misconduct."

† A "protected activity" refers to workers' rights to organize and bargain collectively under Sections 7 and 8(a)(1) of the National Labor Relations Act, free from employer interference, restraint or coercion. It includes picketing and other legal concerted activities aimed at achieving these rights.

doctrine in developing its strategy and justifying its case, the union found encouragement and support in the U.S. Circuit Court of Appeals (First Circuit) decision on the Thayer case. This decision "involved a balancing of the severity of the employer's unfair labor practices which provoked the strike against the workers' misconduct which occurred during the strike."[6]

In 1940, the H. N. Thayer Company had sponsored the formation of a workers' council in its Plant No. 1 in Gardner, Massachusetts, to combat an organization drive of the United Furniture Workers-CIO. In 1945 a similar workers' council was established in Plant No. 2. By 1948, the workers became disenchanted with the "company union" and the CIO United Furniture Workers stepped up its organizing drive. Because of their membership in, and activity on behalf of, Local 154, United Furniture Workers, 17 employees were discharged on January 10–11, 1949.

It is interesting to note the similarities between the Kohler Company and the Thayer Company in the fostering of company unions to keep out an independent union, as well as the similar behavior of the union members in both these disputes. *The American Law Reports (Annotated)*[7] cites this case in connection with a section on "What Constitutes Acts of a Serious Nature." Misconduct on the part of striking employees has been held to be sufficiently serious as to bar employment where

> . . . twenty or thirty men in five automobiles visited the home of a non-striker for the purpose of persuading him to respect the picket-line; three carloads of pickets went to the home of a non-striker to persuade him to join the strike; seventeen or eighteen pickets attacked a non-striker in front of the struck plant. N.L.R.B. v. Thayer Co. (1954 CA 1st) 213 F2d 748, cert. den. 348 US 883, 99 L ed 694, 75 S ct 123.

In this case, the company went to the state's courts and got an injunction against the union which was upheld by the Massachusetts Supreme Court. The injunction completely immobilized the union but did not make it give up its fight. The NLRB took the issue to the U.S. Court of Appeals (First Circuit) which held that a state court did not have jurisdiction to grant an injunction in such a case, and handed down the decision on "balancing" misconduct on June 3, 1954.[8] It ruled that picketing was not subject to injunctive restraint under state law. Said the Court:

> . . . where an employer who had committed unfair labor practices, discharges employees for unprotected acts of misconduct, the board must consider both the seriousness of the employer's unlawful acts and the seriousness of the employee's misconduct in determining whether reinstatement would effectuate the policies of the act.[9]

The General Counsel of the NLRB argued, in relying on certain language in the *Thayer* case, that the Kohler Company

> . . . having provoked, caused and prolonged the strike by flagrant and pervasive unfair labor practices, the Board's power to determine the validity of the discharges and to order reinstatement of the discharges is not limited to the consideration whether they had engaged in unprotected concerted activities.[10]

In an earlier case (NLRB v. Indiana Desk Co. 1945, CA 7th 149 F.2d 987) it was held that an employer was justified in refusing reinstatement to all of the striking employees where it was shown that a method of picketing, by walking in a circle in front of the plant entrance, thereby preventing access to the plant by nonstriking employees, deprived the employer of the possession and use of his property, although apparently no attempt was made to identify specifically any of the strikers as among those doing the picketing.[11] The board continues to adhere to the *Thayer* principle in appropriate cases.

NLRB Orders Reinstatement of 57 Strikers — Company Appeals

A "Supplemental Decision and Supplemental Order" was handed down by the NLRB on September 29, 1964, ordering the Kohler Company to reinstate 57 of the 77 strikers fired for alleged violations. All but one of the 16-member executive board of Local 833 (which included all the union officers) were ordered reinstated. The board also ruled that the company *"caused and prolonged"* the strike and had a *"firm and fixed intention to undermine, weaken and eventually destroy the collective bargaining relationship."* (Emphasis added.) This ruling, by declaring the strike an "unfair labor practice strike" from its beginning, eliminated the grounds or premise on which the company had insisted it would not take back certain strikers or dismiss loyal nonstrikers to make room for strikers. The board ordered back pay (with interest but less any net interim earnings) beginning on January 26, 1962, the date when the Court of Appeals had made its ruling.

The board's decision found the company guilty of violating sections 8(a)(5), (3) and (1) of the National Labor Relations Act because

> . . . it had unlawfully refused to bargain in good faith by unilaterally putting into effect wage increases, discharging certain striking employees . . . without notification to or consultation with the Union, but refused to furnish certain pertinent wage information for purposes of bargaining . . . engaged in surveillance and anti-union espionage, by threatening or promising benefits concerning the handling of grievances by a union steward . . . promising benefits to procure the return to work of a striker, etc.[12]

The company immediately announced that it would appeal the case. The Circuit Court of Appeals ruled that the board's supplemental order should be enforced and the company then sought *certiorari* in the Supreme Court. On December 30, 1964, while the case was still pending, the company offered to take back the 57 discharged employees. The NLRB had refused to order reinstatement of 17 of the 77 "who physically and violently assaulted non-strikers, or threatened members of non-strikers' families." (Three of the 77 had died since 1954.)

In reviewing the record of labor-management relations going back beyond the 1953 period when a one-year contract was agreed upon, the board held that the Kohler Company's provocations created a "climate of desperation and fear among employees, which produced the mass picketing." It ruled that the company's "continued violations after June 1, 1954 — unlawful discharges, transfers, threats, solicitations, evictions, espionage, information refusals — induced the home demonstrations and employment office picketing."

The decision of the board was by a 4 to 1 vote. Those concurring in the ruling were Frank W. McCulloch, Gerald A. Brown, Howard Jenkins, Jr., and John H. Fanning. Boyd Leedom dissented from the ruling and submitted his minority report. Conger called it a case of the NLRB "formally rewarding community-wide violence and illegal conduct."

Conger's statement issued shortly after the ruling, said in part:

> The recent decision of the NLRB rewards the union for violence, mass picketing, flagrant and open unlawful conduct in its long reign of terror over an entire community, in violation not only of law, but all rules of morality and decency. . . . Among those ordered reinstated by the board were officers of the striking UAW Local 833 whom the former NLRB board found had directed and controlled the campaign of lawlessness that marked the strike that began in April 1954 and ended September 1, 1960. . . . It is significant that its present decision, like its former decision of August 26, 1960, was issued on the eve of a national election — after a delay of years.* It is also significant that the majority of the present board has been appointed since the former board's decision. . . . We believe that the present ruling is completely beyond the power of the board and is contrary to the intent of Congress. It is a complete emasculation of provisions of the Taft-Hartley Act. The board's present decision will be appealed.

The Sheboygan Press contacted three union leaders who had been intimately involved during all or much of the strike. Allan Graskamp, former president of Local 833, now a staff representative for the Hotel, Restaurant and Bartender's Union, called it "real good news." He said, however, that he wanted to look at the "whole picture" before deciding whether he would return to work at Kohler, stating: "Maybe a guy can't handle a job he had 10 years ago." Arthur Bauer, former vice president of the local, now sixty-six years of age, said: "This is a decision I have been waiting for, for a long, long time." Bauer is now retired and drawing reduced Social Security benefits because there had been no contributions to his Social Security account during the strike. E. H. (Eggie) Kohlhagen, recording secretary when the strike started and now acting recording secretary, said "naturally" he was very happy about the board's decision and added, "Oh yes, I expect

---

* Conger on one hand alleges that the ruling was politically motivated because it was handed down five weeks before a national election, during a Democratic administration; yet he also refers to a ruling on August 26, 1960, when a Republican administration was in power, as being similarly motivated. He implied that the present board is more sympathetic to labor. Labor used to claim that the majority of the board members under the Eisenhower administration were pro-management.

to go back to work at Kohler." Kohlhagen has been active in Kohler unions, in one capacity or another since 1933.

Emil Mazey, UAW secretary-treasurer, said that the ruling
"completely vindicates the UAW's position — a position we have
maintained for more than ten years." In a prepared statement, he
said:

> We knew that eventually all the facts surrounding this long and
> bitter dispute would be brought to light and put in proper per-
> spective. Our only regret is that this decision did not come sooner.
> As a matter of fact, three of the 77 are no longer living — more evi-
> dence that justice delayed is justice denied. . . . We are currently
> engaged in contract negotiations with Kohler, our third round of
> such talks since the strike terminated. We sincerely hope that the
> NLRB decision will further clear the air and result in more har-
> monious relations between Local 833 and the Company. . . .[13]

Harvey Kitzman, UAW Regional Director, said the ruling
"bears out what I said prior to the strike and after the strike started."
Ray Majerus, UAW representative, said, "Although the struggle
was hard and the hardships have been tremendous, the Kohler
strike was a just one. We knew we were right and we knew what
we had to do, and stayed with the struggle until now, when we
hope, it has reached conclusion. . . . Members of Local 833 are
grateful to the international union, particularly Brother Mazey,
who said 'The international union, would walk the last mile with
the Kohler strikers in order to achieve justice. . . .' "

In a 34-page ruling September 29, 1964, 4 of the 5 NLRB
board members went into great detail, reviewing the history of
labor-management relations at Kohler and enumerating the various
practices engaged in by the company and the union during the long
strike. In finding the company guilty of unfair labor practices since
before the strike started the board relied heavily on the Thayer doctrine where the U.S. Court of Appeals (First Circuit) noted that:

> . . . a determination that an employee is not engaged in a section
> 7 activity does not necessarily mean that, if he is discharged for his
> participating in an unprotected action, the discharge is "for cause."
> That depends on the surrounding circumstances. What is cause in
> one situation may not be in another.

The ruling then notes:

> Thus, while directing or engaging in mass picketing and other coercive demonstrations might indicate, in some circumstances, unfitness for further employment, in the instance case, it revealed only that employees can be goaded into excesses after many years of flagrant disregard for their lawful rights. . . . Indeed, we note that the Respondent reinstated or offered reinstatement to other strikers who engaged in mass picketing, home demonstrations, and employment office picketing.

In summarizing its findings the board said:

> The totality of all evidence establishes that Kohler Company failed and refused to bargain collectively with the union in good faith at all times material herein; and that this unfair labor practice caused the strike — it was an unfair labor practice strike from its inception.

The board found that even though the company had entered into a one-year contract with the UAW in 1953, the company "administered the contract in such a way as to deny employees the benefits they had negotiated." The ruling states:

> . . . during the course of the contract year, Conger frequently disparaged those employees who utilized the grievance procedures by calling them "malingerers and finaglers." Moreover the Respondent consistently manifested such an uncooperative attitude toward the whole grievance procedure that many employees felt it useless to submit grievances, and the union was hard pressed in getting employees to serve as job grievance stewards. Clearly, such evidence leads to the conclusion that the Respondents administered the grievance provisions of the 1953 contract in bad faith. . . .

Excerpts from the NLRB ruling, which review some of the events of the Kohler dispute, are quoted to provide further insight on how the board viewed the bitter struggle:

> . . . The UAW began its first organizing drive in 1950. Following one of the organizational meetings held in his home, Edward Kalupa, a member of the UAW organizing committee, was asked by Superintendent Gavin why he was not satisfied. Gavin went on to say that he hated to see a young intelligent man being misled by some union. . . . The Respondent [company] actively engaged in the preelection campaign against the UAW by various radio broadcasts

and full page newspaper advertisements. The KWA won the election. At the first meeting between the KWA and the Respondent after the election, Conger stated, "We are the ones that won that election for you. We got on the air and put ads in the papers and we are certain that is what changed the picture, otherwise we might be meeting with somebody else right now."

The UAW continued its organizational drive after it lost the election. But, in the summer of 1951, at a meeting attended by President Herbert Kohler, Personnel Director Walter Ireland, and Plant Manager Biever, some of Respondent's supervisors were told to find any individuals that were trying to promote the UAW in their departments, report any infractions of the shop rules by these employees, and if three such infractions were reported "the Company would then have a just reason to discharge that individual. . . ."

On April 29, Herbert Kohler made two radio addresses in which he stated that "a vote for affiliation with the UAW-CIO will be a vote for a strike at Kohler. . . ."

On June 2, Conger made a radio address wherein he charged that dissatisfaction with the KWA was caused by new KWA leaders who posed as "fighters" and "militant labor leaders," who "wanted to see their names in the newspapers," who "used the tactics ambitious men have always used to try to make themselves look bigger than they are," and who "have been aping typical abusive CIO tactics for the past two years." Conger completed his speech by saying that the former KWA officers — now CIO officials — "brought Kohler employees more trouble than benefits in the last two years," and they "are now where they belong." Thereafter, on June 4 and 9, Herbert Kohler made radio addresses in which he indicated that the Respondent was "opposed" to the UAW because it advocated the union shop, straight seniority, escalator wage clauses, and force. He also stated that "should the UAW-CIO succeed in its attempt to organize Kohler Co., negotiations of a mutually acceptable contract would be very difficult. . . ."

Despite the favorable publicity issued by the Union in regard to the 1953 contract, record evidence shows that nothing in the 1953 contract, either in its execution or in its administration, lessened the Respondent's animus against the Union and its leadership. As illustrative of such evidence, in September 1953, during a grievance meeting, union representative Burkart compared the parties' relationship to a marriage, and Conger responded, "You may liken this to a marriage, but if it is, it sure as hell was a shotgun wedding. . . ."

President Kohler testified . . . "I had an idea from the day we signed the first contract that they were going to pull a strike as soon as they could, as soon as they could drench the minds of these people." Again later he testified that the UAW was a very "militant union," which from the very time that it came into the plant was attempting to take the life of the Company. . . . Indeed, it appears that the Respondent administered that contract in "bad faith" with its sole purpose being to demonstrate to the employees that contract or no contract, law or no law — their achievement of a bargaining relationship had little meaning. . . . following President Kohler's labor philosophy that "you don't have to give them anything to bargain," the Respondent rendered the negotiations even more sterile when it offered the Union as the sole basis upon which it would contract, a patently unacceptable proposal which withdrew from the grievance-arbitration system many of the vital matters of great concern to its employees and their bargaining representatives. . . .

. . . it was not just engaged in hard bargaining, but was consciously withholding from the Union a fair opportunity further to engage in the give and take process necessary to such negotiations. Indeed, no other logical explanation appears, for after the strike had commenced, the Respondent unilaterally established a three-cent wage increase while continuing in effect the terms of the old contract — the very combination which the Union was never afforded an opportunity to accept — the very combination which the Union could at least claim as some slight improvement over the 1953 contract. As the Board and Court found, this flagrant violation of the Respondent's obligation to bargain in good faith "disparaged the Union and the collective-bargaining process" and did in fact prolong the strike. However, in our view, such deliberate, calculated unfair labor practice does more than that; it provides "the final insight" into the Respondent's unlawful intent and conduct of the pre-strike negotiations. . . .

In remanding this aspect of the case, the Court directed the Board to follow the doctrine of the *Thayer* case in determining whether the conduct of the 77 dischargees was sufficient to disqualify them for reinstatement. Specifically, the Court stated:

. . . the Board must consider both the seriousness of the employer's unlawful acts and the seriousness of the employees' misconduct in determining whether reinstatement would effectuate the policies of the Act. Those policies inevitably come into conflict when both labor and management are at fault. To hold that employee "misconduct" automatically precludes compulsory reinstatement ignores two considerations which we think important. First, the employer's antecedent unfair labor practices may have been so blatant that they provoked employees to resort to unprotected action. Second, reinstatement is the only sanction which prevents an employer from benefiting from his unfair labor practices through discharges which may weaken or destroy a union.

. . . the record shows that the unprotected activities for which the 77 strikers were discharged fall into four broad categories: (1) mass picketing; (2) presence at or participation in home demonstrations or employment office picketing; (3) organizational responsibility by the 13 strike leaders for their direction and control of the strike from April 5 through May 28, 1954; and (4) individual acts of assault, threats, or other misconduct. The record also shows that all of the misconduct occurred in a context of flagrant antecedent and concurrent unfair labor practices on the part of the Respondent. . . .

In view of these unremitting calculated provocations, it is not surprising that the strikers themselves felt compelled to seek both economic survival and the survival of their collective bargaining agent by a massive and sustained demonstration of solidarity. . . .

While we do not condone the mass picketing of the strikers or the planning and direction of such picketing by the union leaders, we must conclude that such activity is attributable no less to the Respondent which provoked that behavior, than to the strikers and union leaders who accepted the challenge presented by Respondent's open preparations and its complete disregard for its employees' statutory rights. . . .

Viewing the Respondent's violations of its employees' rights and the provocations with which it thereby confronted its employees both before and after the commencement of the strike, it is clear that now to permit the Respondent to discharge with impunity those strikers who succumbed to its provocations would be to permit the Respondent to take advantage of its own wrongdoing. . . .

The board found that most of the incidents involving the 77 strikers could be classified as:

1. actively engaged in halting, encircling, blocking, shouldering and bumping of non-strikers or job applicants during the mass picketing;

2. verbally harassing, insulting or abusing non-strikers at the picket lines, their homes, business establishments, or place of amusement;
3. participating in inspecting railroad cars leaving Respondent's plant, or attempting temporarily to halt certain trucks leaving Respondent's plant; and
4. physically and violently assaulting non-strikers or threatening members of non-strikers' families.

Where evidence that strikers were guilty of the fourth type of activity was presented, the board ruled them ineligible for reinstatement. Seventeen cases involving physical assault were recorded; in a number of these cases the fisticuffs were preceded by name-calling, usually such epithets as "scab," "scum," "dirty scab," and even "yellow-bellied pig." Some of the specific incidents which disqualified strikers for reinstatement were:

Seven incidents (involving 8 strikers) occurred in which nonstrikers or job applicants were struck, kicked, knocked down, spat upon or cursed by pickets at the plant gates or the employment office. Three were attacks upon nonstrikers, accompanied by their wives, at local taverns, and in each case the striker was the aggressor in first launching an argument and then striking his victim. In two of these instances, police were called and the couples escorted home. Threats to "do harm" were made by two other men who called on the wife of a Kohler worker to tell her that her husband would endanger not only himself but his wife and family if he crossed the picket line again. "Ten or 12 beers" figured in still another attack when two men tried to strike a Kohler driver in his truck cab at a Sheboygan coalyard. The driver struck back with his jack handle and tried to pull the horn cord, but was prevented from doing so by one of the men who tried to hit him with a blackjack and broke his window. A chunk of coal flew, but the driver managed to get into the coal-company office to call police. The other men were involved in the disorders at the bowling alley in Sheboygan.

The NLRB put its position thus:

The above described individual, violent attacks upon certain nonstrikers and job applicants as well as the threat of violence provoked by the [company's] flagrant unfair labor practices, were also in part the product of personal vindictiveness or grievances. . . . By engaging in such violent conduct, the strikers have rendered questionable their ability or fitness for future satisfactory service at the . . . plant. We recognize that to bar reinstatement to those strikers will permit the [company] to benefit to some extent from its own unfair labor practices. However, we consider that this is more than offset by the encouragement such misconduct would receive. . . .

Boyd Leedom, the board member who dissented from the majority opinion, stated: ". . . I am no less cognizant than the Court and my colleagues of the Respondent's unfortunate labor relations history," but he adhered to his earlier decision of 1960 that the strike had turned into an "unfair labor practice strike on June 1, 1954" rather than having started as one, and thus he felt that there was adequate evidence to deny reinstatement for all except 4 of the 77. He went on to say that he "could find no warrant regardless of the nature of the Respondent's misconduct, for the harassment of the families of the non-strikers at their homes" or "deliberate striking and bumping which is itself an invitation to further violence." Leedom also took the position that those found to be entitled to reinstatement should get back pay only "from the date of this Supplemental Decision and Supplemental Order."

The Kohler Company again appealed the NLRB decision to the Fifth Circuit U.S. Court of Appeals. On April 20, 1965, that court enforced the board's Supplemental Decision and Supplemental Order of September 29, 1964, in which the board found that the strike was an unfair labor practice strike from its inception on April 5, 1954.[14] The company then filed a petition for *certiorari* with the Supreme Court, which on October 11, 1965, rejected the company's appeal from the government order to reinstate 57 discharged strikers.

Contempt Charges Against Company

Another case which occupied the union and the company during much of 1964, was a civil-contempt case against the Kohler Company, heard by Special Master E. M. DuQuaine, a retired Brown County circuit judge, at Green Bay, Wisconsin. The NLRB had petitioned the Federal Circuit Court of Appeals, District of Columbia, to find the company guilty of contempt for failure to comply with the court-enforced NLRB order of August

26, 1960, which called for reinstatement of the following categories of strikers:

82 releasees who signed termination of employment slips in order to obtain employment elsewhere;

72 retirees who retired during the 6½ year strike;

105 workers who refused to return because the work-week had been reduced from 40 to 32 hours, claiming this was not "their same or equivalent job."

238 workers who refused to go back to work at Kohler as long as the company was not complying with the NLRB order to bargain with the union;

108 dual-reason strikers, who would not return because of the reduced work-week and the company's refusal to bargain.

In addition, 477 strikers had returned under the reduced work-week schedule.*

The District of Columbia Court of Appeals appointed Judge DuQuaine Special Master on November 6, 1963. There followed months of hearings, which covered much of the same arguments heard before by the NLRB, the FMCS, et cetera, although the judge was asked to rule whether the company had lived up to the board's order on reinstatement. Closing arguments were presented by Attorney Jerry Kronenberg, Chicago, for the NLRB; Joseph L. Rauh, Jr., Washington, D.C. for the union; and Lyman C. Conger, vice president and legal counsel, for the Kohler Company.

Finally, on February 1, 1955, Judge DuQuaine ruled that the "releasees" and "retirees" were not entitled to reinstatement, but that the 105 workers who refused to return because of the shortened work-week, the 238 who would not go back because the company had not complied with the NLRB order to bargain and the 180 dual-reason strikers were all entitled to their jobs with back pay. He ruled that the 477, who had gone to work under the short-work-week schedules, were entitled to "the difference between what they earned and what they would have earned, had there been full reinstatement."

---

* Immediately before the start of the second strike, there were 3,301 employees in the bargaining unit. On September 1, 1960, five days after the NLRB order to reinstate strikers, the union made an unconditional application for reinstatement of strikers. At that time 2,444 workers were employed in the bargaining unit, 1212 were "pre-strike" employees (union and non-union) and 1232 had been hired after June 1, 1954.[15]

The NLRB prepared a brief on these issues for the District of Columbia Circuit Court of Appeals, objecting to some and agreeing with other parts of Judge DuQuaine's ruling. On September 2, 1965 (60 LRRM 2049), the Court reversed the Master as to the "releasees" and "retirees," but adopted his other conclusions with some modifications. It remanded the matter to the Special Master to take evidence as to the qualification of the individual strikers for reinstatement with back pay, within each group, in accordance with standards set forth in the Court's opinion. The Master is not to determine the *amounts* of back pay due the individual strikers, but only their *entitlement* to such back pay, and the date it began to accrue — the amounts being a matter for the board to decide.

As of September 15, 1965, it appeared that, failing compromise between the parties, further litigation of significant proportions lay ahead. The Master must conduct hearings involving hundreds of strikers on their individual entitlement to back pay and reinstatement. His Report and Decision will then be subject to further Order of the Court of Appeals. A back-pay hearing to determine the precise amounts of back pay due the strikers will then be necessary, subject to Board decision and possible appeal to the Courts. In its decision of September 2, 1965, when the case was remanded to Judge DuQuaine, the Court of Appeals said, "This is an extra-inning game, even by modern judicial standards. Unless the parties step out of character and achieve a compromise, it appears that many innings lie ahead."

Briefs were filed with the Supreme Court by the National Association of Manufacturers, the U.S. Chamber of Commerce and the Wisconsin Manufacturers Association in support of the company's position. Opposing a review by the Supreme Court, the Justice Department brief said that, even though some employees may have engaged in misconduct and thereby forfeited the protection of labor law, "the board may, in appropriate circumstances, order their reinstatement as part of the remedy for the employer's unfair labor practices. Such a provision is often necessary for the remedy to be adequate."[16]

The Kohler Company had said that the National Labor Relations Act "has perverted into a protection of that which it specifically prohibits."

Upon learning of the Court's decision, Emil Mazey said:

For years, the company propaganda pictured the Kohler strikers and the UAW as "lawless elements" and accused us of fomenting violence. Yet we have won every single court decision.*

It is absolutely incredible that 11 years after the beginning of a strike and five years after its termination, Kohler workers still have not completely hacked their way out of the legal jungle created by their employer.

It would appear to any reasonable person that Monday's decision [October 11, 1965] is the end of the road for the company's opposition to the reinstatement of the strike leaders. But we have long ago stopped counting on what appears to be reasonable.[17]

Meanwhile, representatives of the company and the union made plans to meet with Special Master, Judge DuQuaine, at Green Bay, to hear arguments on resolution of the back-pay issue growing out of the strike.

---

* Mazey is correct with reference to all the Kohler strike-related cases brought before *Federal* courts. At the state level, the company won its case before the Wisconsin Employment Relations Board, and was sustained by a Circuit Court judge who prohibited mass picketing and limited pickets to 25 per gate. This ruling was sustained by the Wisconsin Supreme Court.

10

SOCIAL, ECONOMIC AND POLITICAL
FACTORS IN THE STRIKE

Human and Social Costs

A LONG and bitter conflict, existing with varying intensity for more than a generation, permeates the social fabric of a community. Its human and social costs cannot be measured in any quantitative sense.

Craft unions had existed in Sheboygan before the turn of the century, but no significant labor movement was developed until after the enactment of NIRA and the Wagner Act of the thirties. When the Kohler Company, as the largest employer in the county, became involved in the 1934 strike, the community got more than its share of propaganda from both sides. The window-smashing, the shootings, the coming of the National Guard and the boycott kept the dispute in the national spotlight for seven long years. People's understanding of and attitudes toward unions were largely developed in this climate of protracted controversy.

Those who joined unions became partisans of the Kohler strikers, while many of those outside the labor movement identified themselves with the "open-shop" and "right-to-work" philosophy of the Kohler Company. These conflicting biases and, in some cases, prejudices, provided the basis for the acrimonious behavior of the partisans and the identification with one side or the other by most of the community.

One incident indicative of the strike-connected human relations concerns a bartender, who, having learned that he had sold a beer to a "scab," set out for the customer's home and confronting him at the door, handed two dimes to him, and explained unsmilingly, "I don't serve no beer to scabs."

When the author sought community reactions to the strike in the fall of 1964, he found that the advertisements, news stories and editorials in *The Sheboygan Press* had been a significant factor in molding opinions. Radio programs sponsored by the union and the company on Sheboygan's station WHBL also had an important role in conveying facts as well as propaganda about the issues in dispute. Those who had relatives or friends involved on either side of the controversy believed they got their "facts" firsthand. Those who acquired their impressions second or thirdhand often felt just as strongly, but did not have specific facts to bolster their positions. Nearly everyone had heard about the mass picketing, the home demonstrations, the clay-boat incident, the paint-bombings and other vandalism, but few outside the labor movement understood the significance of labor legislation which defined workers' rights to join unions and bargain collectively. The role of the NLRB and the FMCS was understood by only a small proportion of the populace. Many still maintained that, since the employer was the "giver of jobs," he should unilaterally have the right to set wages and determine conditions of employment.

One farmer thought it reasonable that five executives of the Kohler Company and Mr. Kohler's chauffeur should be sheriff's deputies as a "self-help" means of protecting company property. Based on what he had heard and read, this farmer was convinced that Sheriff Mosch was "in the pockets" of the union and could not be relied upon to open the picket lines so nonstrikers could enter the plant. He firmly believed that the sheriff had revoked the deputy badges, six weeks after the strike started, because of union pressure and saw nothing inappropriate in an employer involved in a labor dispute having his own law-enforcement officers in the plant.

Thirty years ago, 80 per cent of the workers at Kohler lived in Sheboygan; now the percentage is less than 50 per cent and many of them commute from surrounding communities. At that time almost 90 per cent of the county's 323,840 acres was in farms, the majority owner-operated. By 1950 about a third of the operators were working off their farms.[1] For some a Kohler job was the second job in the family, thus providing two or more wage earners to pay for cars, furniture, home improvements, recreation, any of a variety of increasing wants of American families. Farms which once supported large families are now too small for adequate income; modern machinery has reduced the hours of labor required to produce livestock and crops; and in rural communities, as everywhere, the cost of living, as well as living standards, have risen.

The union's recognition of some of the interdependencies of

the modern community was voiced in an appeal to the farmers of Sheboygan County in its August 8, 1954, strike bulletin:

> *Strikebreakers are traitors to both of us.* . . . Higher wages, better pensions, and improved hospital insurance — all help to decide the price of milk, butter, cheese and other farm products. . . . A working man spends more money for his family's food than anything else. . . . Falling farm prices are usually traced to falling wages. . . .
>
> *Strikebreakers.* . . . Now recruited by Kohler Co. from among the good farm people of Sheboygan county are traitors to us and to all farmers, too. . . . Kohler workers, like farmers, must stick together to protect and improve their way of life. . . .
>
> *A strikebreaker* who steals our job during this strike is like a robber who steals a prize milk cow or tractor from your farm. . . . The strikebreakers are only hurting the chances for an early settlement of the strike and they are greatly damaging the future prosperity of our community. . . .

When rural workers began to take jobs in the struck plant, they were dubbed "oleo salesmen" by the strikers. The inference was that in the dairy state of Wisconsin, where farmers year in, year out have plumped for increased butter consumption, and state laws discriminate against oleomargarine, strikers were being deprived of their jobs and thus had to use oleo instead of the higher-priced butter.

Incidents of vandalism, such as the sabotage of farm machinery and the alleged mutilation of cows, were exploited by the company and political aspirants among rural and small-town communities.

Lyman Conger told Paul McMahon, *Milwaukee Journal* staff writer,[2] "Most of the new employees fresh off farms or small towns, never have belonged to a labor union and do not feel any sympathy for organized labor." Interviewees told McMahon:

"I don't feel like I'm stealing anyone's job. . . . I believe I should be able to work anywhere I want to work. . . ."

"The people in Marshfield feel different than people do around here. We think $1.50 to $2.00 an hour is good money. . . ."

"Kohler is a place where you can make some money. I can't figure why these guys are striking. . . . I'd like to make enough to pay off the mortgage on my farm and clear some of the stones off the land. . . ."

"I'm 54 and I've worked all my life. . . . I've got nothing against those pickets but I don't think I took a job away from them. . . . I feel they gave it to me!"

The union gathered a file of evidence that persons receiving public assistance in some northern Wisconsin counties were told that they had to seek employment at Kohler during the strike or be taken off the welfare roles. Only if they brought back from the company a statement that there was no work for them could they continue to receive welfare payments.

The Kohlerian for February 17, 1956, published a statement by Calvin Rowell of Oconto County, Wisconsin, who had arrived at the strike-bound Kohler plant on February 13, suitcase in hand, to look for a job. He explained to pickets that the County Welfare Department told him they would pay his room and board if he got a job at Kohler and continue relief payments to his family until he got his first pay check. He said he had been told that, to get relief, he "must have a slip to show I was down here."

Rowell, father of four, had worked for a cement-block company until December, 1955. Unable to find other employment, he applied for unemployment compensation ($31 per week). When benefits were exhausted, he applied for and was given public assistance at the rate of $24 a week.

Charles Pagnucco of the Kohler Company personnel department gave him a memorandum addressed to "Oconto Relief" which read: "Calvin Rowell has made an application for employment. Nothing available at the present time. We will keep his application in our active file."

A representative of Local 833, who contacted the Oconto County Welfare Director, was told that Rowell had not been given instructions to go to Kohler. The union asked for a full-scale investigation.

Look magazine, in an article entitled, "The Strike That May Never End" (November 29, 1955), emphasized the existence of the "battle lines" and the anger and bitterness which existed in the Sheboygan community. Fortunately for Sheboygan, the prediction which concluded the article — ". . . hatred is the daily bread of life. . . . Even if the strike should end tomorrow, its hatreds will not be forgotten when today's children look down at their grandsons" — has not been realized. True, there are grudges and tempers flare, but few incidents occur attributable to the strike. As pointed out before, the battle was removed from the picket lines into the courts and the open warfare of the first strike did not reoccur.

A decision made by the public-school administration in Sheboygan early in the strike may well have had far-reaching consequences in preventing the blighting of children's lives by the parents' battle. An "armistice" on discussion of the strike in the public-school classrooms and grounds was in force for about five years. "It was decided that the welfare of the children came first," said John W. Hahn, principal of South High School. "We agreed that at least we'll have an atmosphere at school where the children will be free from tension and where they can study and learn." There were no incidents of any consequence either in the public or the parochial schools, which involved children because parents happened to be strikers or nonstrikers.

Jack Barbash, in his book, *Unions and Union Leadership*,[3] included an article on Kohler by Saul Pett which gives added meaning to the emotional by-products of this intense struggle.

Kohler and the UAW: All That Remains Is Hate
By Saul Pett

After three and a half years, the sound and fury of the country's longest major strike have subsided into a quiet war of mimeograph machines.

Each side in the strike at the Kohler Company, makers of bathroom fixtures, continues to roll out opposing statements. But the violence — the shouting, the slugging, smashing of windows, and splattering of paint on private homes — has long since vanished.

What remains, among people directly affected, is hate — deep, abiding, stone hate.

Hate Goes Underground

But even hate has gone underground. After so long a time, it becomes pointless to call your neighbor names, to paint "scab" on his sidewalk, to spit as he goes by. You have not moved him, he has not moved you. So you just don't talk and you go on hating each other across thirty feet of lawn. . . .

The striker whose son-in-law went back to work at Kohler still refuses to enter his daughter's home, has yet to see his two grandchildren. The bridge clubs broken by the strike are still broken.

The men who refused to usher together in church still won't go down the aisle together. Old friends who used to drink beer together after work now go to separate taverns.

They Try to Forget

Few people now discuss the strike. Most try to forget it — with varying success. For obvious business reasons, merchants and town boosters shudder every time the national spotlight focuses on Sheboygan as a strike-torn town and study in human tragedy. . . .

People are easy to talk to — about Sputnik, about the Green Bay Packers, or the glorious Milwaukee Braves. But don't mention the strike. People are alive to national and world problems, and in their classroom discussion school kids are urged to debate many issues. But never the strike. . . .

Town Bounces Back

Some merchants along Eighth Street still complain they don't see many Kohler pay checks any more, but generally, says the Association of Commerce, retail sales are back up to their pre-strike levels.

The association also says no major new industry has been attracted to Sheboygan in the past three years, probably because of the strike publicity. Various efforts have been made locally to counteract that publicity.

One was called "Greater Sheboygan, Inc.," a group of community leaders, some sympathetic to the strikers, some not. But all patently were devoted to restoring Sheboygan's reputation for serenity and hospitality. Then the head of the group, a builder, happened to install Kohler fixtures in a new model house. That ended "Greater Sheboygan, Inc. . . ."

People Lose

Statistic and counter-statistic, claim and counterclaim.

In the riptide of opinions, only one element of the whole long strike remains clear — not who is winning, but who is losing?

People are losing. Individual human beings are losing — in suspicion and hate.

Two old friends, both strikers, both good union men, met on the street. One invited the other home for a beer. The second man refused.

Why?

"I hear you have a scab bathtub in your house."

The first man explained. He had bought the Kohler tub long before the strike at a bargain price, had stored it in his garage for future use, had only recently installed the tub in his bathroom. The second man refused to believe him.

They argued. Finally, they went to the man's home, walked down into the basement. With brace and bit, the owner drilled up through the bathroom floor.

With a flashlight, he showed his friend the production date on the under side of the tub. Only then would the friend believe him. . . .

Just a few weeks ago the mother of a large family died.

At the funeral, all her children came — in two clearly divided groups. They stood apart; they did not talk to each other. Some were still on strike against Kohler. Others had gone back. . . .

Then there is the family of Joseph Zaletel, a sixty-seven [year old], gray, thin man with striking blue eyes, who first went to work for Kohler in 1925. Later two of his five sons — Joseph, Jr. and William — joined him in working for Kohler.

Came the strike — all three were out of work. Came the plant reopening in 1954 and only Bill went back. His father and brother refused to speak to him, looked the other way when they met at St. Cyril Methodist Church. Joseph, Jr. changed churches.

For two years, the father refused to see Bill, but according to other members of the family, the mother saw her son "on the sly." Bill brought over a shirt for Father's Day. His father scorned it. "I don't need your money," he said, "I can buy my own."

But time mellowed him — also the fact that he became eligible for social security and would never return to work. He now sees Bill. . . . But Joseph Zaletel, Jr. is still mad at Bill, intends to stay that way. He has seen Bill only once since the later returned to Kohler. Last summer he visited his parents' home and found Bill there.

"All I said was, 'How's my scabby brother.' He just gave me a funny kind of grin — that's all. My father had a picture on the wall showing him and me on the picket line in the early days. I took it off the wall. I told my father, 'That picture don't belong in this house any more. . . .'"

And the strike at the Kohler Company goes on.

A dimension of the conflict which can never be fathomed is the burden of knowledge of wrongdoing which may never come to light. How many among union members, the company management, the citizens and the public officials of the community have undisclosed information about misconduct during the strike, there is no way of knowing, but it seems quite certain that many will take their secrets with them to their graves. The collective burdens of conscience of some individuals on both sides of the controversy must surely be great, as the following episode bears out.

A Confession

Rudolph Ploetz, former mayor of Sheboygan, told the author that a good-sized rock was hurled against his house the week of the clay-boat incident, narrowly missing a large window beneath which his infant daughter was sleeping in her crib. The episode was reported in local as well as Milwaukee and Chicago papers, but no trace of the vandals was found.

Three and a half years later, in December, 1958, a young man came to Ploetz, saying that he wanted to make a confession — that his conscience would not permit him to withhold the information any longer. "Every time I go past your house and see your little daughter playing on the lawn," he said, "I think she might be dead if the rock I threw had gone through the window." The young man went voluntarily with Ploetz to Milwaukee, where a recorded confession was made, the gist of which is as follows:

X, an 18-year-old and his 17-year-old chum, both high-school students, went out to the Liebelt bar at Six Corners * about six miles from Sheboygan, and stayed until closing time. X's buddy, the son of a prominent businessman, dared X to stone the mayor's house. On the way back to town, they stopped to pick up a rock. The lights were still on in the mayor's house, so they drove around the block several times. When the lights were out, they got up enough courage to stop; then with the lights of the car turned off and the motor running, X ran to the house, hurled the rock — it struck just below the window and landed on the front porch — and sped away. After driving without lights for a block or so, they turned them on and went home.

When X's accomplice, who furnished the car and dared him to throw the rock, was confronted with the confession of his "partner in crime," Ploetz recalled, he flew into a rage, shouting at X, "You shut up! You keep your mouth shut! There weren't any witnesses and your word is no better than mine!"

* A "teen-age" bar serving 3.2 beer.

"He was a law student at that time, who was already beginning to apply his legal training," Ploetz added.[4]

Neither of the young fellows was a son of a striker nor connected with the Kohler Company.

The Influence of "Outsiders" and the Press: The Mazey-Schlichting Affair

The Sheboygan Central Labor Council, a federation of AFL unions, supported the strike even before the AFL and the CIO were merged at the national level on December 5, 1955. Charles Heymanns, the AFL Regional Director, who had been a leader during the first strike, gave encouragement and support to the members of Local 833 whenever he could. Even before the AFL and CIO merged, George Meany, president of the AFL, authorized Heymanns to support the union. On April 5, 1955, the first anniversary of the second strike, Heymanns sent personal and fraternal greetings to Local 833, along with a personal check for the strike fund, even though his national organization — the AFL — was still at odds with the CIO. In a Labor Day address over station WOSH (Oshkosh, Wisconsin) that year, Heymanns urged all-out support for the "brave Kohler strikers," saying, "Their cause is . . . noble and worthwhile."

The local Sheboygan paper carried a story on November 10, 1954:

> The UAW-CIO secretary-treasurer, Emily Mazey, announced today that the union will no longer issue food vouchers for Piggly Wiggly and Schlichting Food Markets as a protest over the "obvious bias shown against organized labor" by Circuit Judge F. H. Schlichting in the sentencing of UAW-CIO member William Vinson to a two-year prison term.

The Vinson-Van Ouwerkerk assault incident had aroused much adverse public opinion, but there was no evidence that the union was responsible for Vinson's conduct. It was in the context of this strong community sentiment, however, that the trial took place, and Mazey's statement served to escalate the situation. The *Press* ran several editorials, the gist of which was:

> It is Mr. Mazey's privilege to buy his groceries where he pleases.

It is not his privilege to enter this county and tell us whom we shall have as circuit judge.

Mazey had said,

The sentence handed down in the Vinson trial was the most severe sentence for a charge of this type ever handed down in this county and the conduct of the judge in this case raises a serious question as to whether he is qualified to serve as judge in this community.

The furor gathered crescendo. The following day, November 12, the Sheboygan County Bar Association ran an ad:

We condemn the action of the officers of the UAW-CIO who are attempting to interfere with and influence the courts of this state and county. By doing so they are striking at the very heart of our free and democratic society.

To speak of "officers of the UAW-CIO" and "courts of this state" was, in the interest of accuracy, taking in more territory than was actually involved.

Among the lawyers signing the ad were Conger, Desmond, Chase and Hammer of the Kohler Company. There was an added note that three lawyers (names given) were out of town and could not be contacted, the inference being that any attorney whose name did not appear was a "union sympathizer."

The County Labor Council came forward with a resolution vigorously defending Mazey, saying "the courts should treat strikers and private citizens alike and show no favoritism to rich or poor, union member or non-union member. . . ."

In quick succession, resolutions and statements chastising Mazey came from:

The Catholic clergy, who said, "He has attacked the integrity of a major court . . . and deserves to be called decisively to task for the insolence. . . ."

The Ministerial Association, which said, "It is . . . an attack upon fundamental institutions which undergird our common life. . . ."

The County Medical Society, saying, "We vigorously protest the implication that our judges and other judicial officers must follow the dictates of any particular group. . . ."

The Rotarians, the Sheboygan Common Council, the Manitowoc Bar Association and the Sheboygan Women's Club issued statements all in a matter of about ten days. When a resolution was introduced at the county board meeting by Walter Ireland, Kohler personnel manager, to "censure and condemn," a long, heated debate ensued. A. W. Ramm said, ". . . it is not going to make for peace. All it will do is aggravate a bad situation."

Through the strike bulletin and their radio broadcast, the union asked, "Where were all these people when it was disclosed that the Kohler Company had machine guns and tear gas in the plant?" and the allegation was made that when the Bar Association had demurred on running its ad for lack of money, Kohler personnel in the association offered to make up the difference.

At a rally on November 17, 2,200 union members turned out to hear Mazey, who said:

> Some of these people have been neutral against us. . . . I said that the sentencing of Bill Vinson was extremely harsh, and it was. . . . they'll find that no judge in the history of this County had dealt with an individual citizen as harshly as this judge has. I say that . . . I had a right to cry out against this injustice and I will continue to do so. . . . I'm not seeking a quarrel with the clergy, the bar association, the medical association, the *Sheboygan Press* and all the others who are seeing fit to castigate me . . . but I think it's only fair and proper to ask these gentlemen the following questions: Why were you silent about the disclosures by Herb Kohler that he had guns, clubs and tear gas, and planned on using them, if necessary, against Kohler workers? . . . Why were you silent on Governor Kohler's request that the matters in dispute be arbitrated by an impartial arbitrator?

"The hornet's nest," as the *Press* referred to the controversy, induced Judge Schlichting to sell his Piggly Wiggly stock on November 23, saying that he did so because his associates were suffering losses due to the boycott, and the relations between the union and the business community grew more estranged in the months that followed. The withdrawal of the $13,000 worth of grocery orders a week had come about because wives of strikers objected to patronizing the markets. Joseph Burns, community services department of the UAW, in charge of strike benefits, had found Piggly Wiggly very co-operative and was glad when business could be resumed with the firm at the end of the month.

Mazey was relentlessly cross-examined about this episode during the McClellan investigation, particularly concerning his remarks about the clergy. Judge Schlichtling, a well-liked and highly respected member of the community, was deeply cut by the controversy. Mazey and the union believed that they were justified in criticizing the various organizations which could so quickly and "spontaneously" overcome the lethargy they had hitherto shown toward ethical issues in the strike, to rise to so much public indignation within hours and days in response to Mazey's statement.

The Mazey-Schlichting episode, which involved the clergy, had left scars. The references to the clergy in the strike bulletin, some felt, were "irreverent," "disrespectful" or at least in bad taste. Several clergymen expressed their disappointment in the leadership and the strike-related conduct of the union. A priest, well acquainted with the policies of the company which had tragically affected the lives of some of his parishioners, expressed an expectation that others shared: that a new era of labor relations might come out of the strike and the company might learn a lesson in humility. But it was evident that a double standard was often applied in judging the acts of the company and the union — and some felt that the union had "let them down" by not conducting themselves like Caesar's wife "above reproach," even when the provocation, frustration and impasse imposed by the company pushed them to the limit. Robert Wallace, in *Life*,[5] expressed some insights which remain applicable to this day:

> Some settlement remains to be made between Herbert Kohler and little labor, the decent courageous men who worked in his plumbing factory and struck because their sense of personal dignity demanded it. Such a settlement cannot be made unless Kohler himself accepts a measure of defeat. And there they stand — a partial winner who must take some loss, and a loser who must be given some gain. Neither side can win the strike in any clear-cut fashion. At the moment the company is ahead, but times change. If the strikers cannot be given peace with honor, then the dispute will drag on bitterly, interminably, fruitlessly. . . . A student of Greek tragedy would feel at home in Sheboygan.

The church leadership felt hard-pressed in the heat of the strike. Former Mayor Ploetz recalled that ". . . [the strike] was pathetic from an economic standpoint, from a social standpoint, as far as the church was concerned, and as far as families were concerned. They were split right down the middle — there was no give or take at all. Regardless of what you tried to do, you were branded. . . ."

A number of top personnel at Kohler attended Catholic churches; there was a large Catholic population in the town, many of whom were strikers, and probably for this reason, Catholic clergy became more involved in the conflict than some of the others. Two clergymen involved with the union, were transferred, and although there may have been extenuating reasons, Sheboyganites tend to believe it was because they tried to help the strike situation. Criticism of the clergy's silence appeared frequently in union publications; yet the strike bulletin carried the announcements of novenas to pray for a settlement of the strike. *Milwaukee Journal* reporter Paul McMahon said, "Pastors are extremely reluctant to discuss the strike," and *The Milwaukee Sentinel*, in reporting the coming of the three nationally known clergymen to try to mediate the conflict, said, "Local clergymen, however, have wished to remain in the background."

Mission House College (now Lakeland College) faculty members, feeling the pressures of the tensions, violence and vandalism engendered by the strike, issued a public statement seventeen months after the strike began, which they sent to Herbert V. Kohler, to Allan Graskamp, and to all Catholic and Protestant clergy in the community:

> We call ourselves a Christian community. However, in situations such as the Kohler strike, we come to realize much of our Christianity has become a veneer. . . . Many of our deeds speak against our faith. None of us, therefore, can escape the judgment of God also in our economic life. . . . We will do well to remember that He even wills us to love our enemies, to walk the second mile. . . .
>
> In terms of the Christian faith, we no longer see right and wrong neatly distributed in the present dispute. Many of us are not directly involved. Nevertheless, we are becoming enmeshed in what looks very much like collective guilt, either assuming not enough, or too much responsibility, or none at all. . . . Violence is violence, no matter how much one seeks to justify it with pent up emotions.

On the other hand, those who provoke violence show lack of sound judgment. . . .

It is foolish to stand by when a feud threatens to destroy the peace and order of the community. We believe our community has a right to demand that this labor dispute be settled soon. The insistence on either side that it is prepared to carry on this dispute . . . till doomsday is neither a creative or constructive approach . . . as far as the community is concerned.[6]

In October, 1956, editorials appeared in Wisconsin papers. "How Labor Vandals Hurt Their City," said *The Appleton-Post-Crescent*. *The Green Bay Press Gazette* headed the identical editorial on October 9, 1956 — "Foolish Vandals and Industry." A similar editorial appeared in *The Wausau Record-Herald* under "Sheboygan Pays Price for Labor Violence."

The Sheboygan Press maintained editorially that it was objective and neutral, and in the opinion of Albert Gore, one of the NLRB attorneys, it succeeded fairly well. The pressure upon a community newspaper in such a conflict situation is probably as intense as that upon law-enforcement officials of the beleaguered community. Almost any statement issued by either side, about any strike-related event was news and given coverage. Reporters Carl Fiedler and Chuck Fisher conscientiously reported strike news as it appeared to them. Editorially, however, the *Press* had a more difficult task maintaining an attitude of neutrality. Although edited first by Charles Broughton and then by A. Matt Werner — both Democrats — the *Press* tended to support the "forces of law and order" of the business community in its editorial pronouncements.

UAW Local 833 spokesmen said that the full-page ads they ran in *The Sheboygan Press* during the second strike cost $360 each. The union bought at least several dozen full-page ads; the Kohler Company ran almost a hundred, thereby providing income for the newspaper and grist for the mills of the partisans in the dispute.

The Milwaukee Journal, well known for its excellent reporting, kept its headlines temperate, its editorial policy subdued, if critical. *The Milwaukee Sentinel* took a more sensational approach, but the unvarnished partisan in the fray was *The Chicago Tribune*, whose columnist, Chesly Manly, kept a "blow-by-blow" account of the labor-management feud, which left no doubt as to the *Tribune's* crusade on behalf of management. (See Appendix.)

DICTATORSHIP IN AMERICA

(*Reprinted, Courtesy of* The Chicago Tribune)

Any one who, after reading certain newspaper headlines, may have assumed that the "guilty" had been apprehended in such cases as the dynamite cache, will understand that injustice may be done to individuals and their families when there is overeagerness to pin blame on someone, and create sensational headlines.

Charles Owen Rice, of the Pittsburgh Catholic diocese, wrote a resume for *Commonweal* in which he said:

The general public has not been inconvenienced by the strike, and so . . . has not been stirred by the issues in the long drawn-out battle; and the liberal fringe of society, except for those involved in the labor movement by sympathy or avocation, has shared the apathy of the times and the public. Extreme conservatives, however, have not been apathetic; they have been passionate on the subject.[7]

He expressed the hope that other "willful employers" would "think twice before following the Kohler course of action" and that other unions should be encouraged by the "persistence" of the UAW and its victories in the courts "to stand fast and pursue every remedy at hand, no matter how many years or how great pains are required, when dealing with scofflaw industrial power."

Father Edward A. Keller, University of Notre Dame, thought the stalemate lay in the "glimpse into the future of labor-management relations" which the issues of the strike provided. He wrote for *Human Events:*

Unions increasingly emphasize non-economic issues because they cannot possibly contend, except for propaganda purposes, that the American worker receives subnormal wages. The constant expansion of the scope of collective bargaining beyond the "bread and butter" issues of traditional American unionism is indication of a strong union drive toward co-management.[8]

Both company and union gave widespread distribution to reprints of articles which reinforced their viewpoint. News coverage, in balance, was tipped in favor of the company and both parties were very conscious of how public opinion weighed for and against them.

Radio and TV

News stories, especially about the second strike, were carried via radio and TV throughout the country and two of the major TV networks, NBC and CBS, sent crews to Sheboygan and Kohler as the second anniversary of the strike approached. Dave Garroway featured interviews with key persons involved in the strike as well as on-the-street interviews on his "Today" show in April, 1955; Eric Severeid prepared a background story on the Kohler strike for a CBS news broadcast which was presented during the same month. By far the most extensive coverage came about when the McClellan Committee hearings were televised in the spring of 1958, and took on much of the "show" aspects that had characterized the Army-McCarthy hearings earlier.

*An extraordinary sight in Sheboygan were the camera crews of na-
tional TV networks at work on location near the UAW office for
programs reporting on the third anniversary of the strike. (UAW
photo)*

Commentators Fulton Lewis, Jr., H. V. Kaltenborn and many
others added their opinions — for the most part critical of Walter
Reuther and the UAW — to the fray. The local radio station, however, played a more intimate and crucial role in the second strike
than any of the national hookups. The union maintained a daily
program on which it presented the strikers' side of the story, under
the direction first of Frank Wallick and then of Robert Treuer.
The Kohler Company officials frequently stated their position by
means of radio broadcasts, in and outside the Sheboygan community.* Many people, including Albert Gore, held the opinion
that the Sheboygan station WHBL and its newscaster, Chuck
Fisher, were probably the most important factor in escalating the
crowd gathered at the dock on July 5, 1955, the day of the clay-
boat incident.

Economic Costs

There are no records to indicate exactly how much was lost
by labor and by the Kohler Company because of the two strikes,
but it is safe to say it amounted to many millions of dollars.

* See Chapters 6 and 11.

The first strike, which lasted almost seven years, resulted in the loss of workers' wages and company earnings, as well as in the destruction of company property and human lives. Wages were low during the depression of the thirties and jobs were hard to find. Even so, if one figures $5 per day for only 1,000 workers on strike, this amounts to $5,000 per day. The strike dragged on until April, 1941, although most strikers had taken other jobs by that time and only a skeleton picket crew remained.

In the case of a family-owned corporation like the Kohler Company, earnings and losses do not have to be reported, except on income-tax reports. Wisconsin tax reports used to be open to the public until a Republican legislature changed this policy in 1953. But it is apparent that the company suffered tremendous losses from interrupted production, lower efficiency of new workers, the boycott, et cetera.

The second strike turned out to be more costly because more people were involved and because general wage rates and industrial prices had gone up. It would be a monumental task even to estimate the total economic costs to all persons affected. The costs might be grouped under five major categories:

1. *Losses in Income to Workers on Strike:* Workers never know, when a strike is called, how long it will last. If it is settled in days or weeks, the improvements in wages and fringe benefits may, in a matter of months or a year, pay well for the income lost during the strike. If, however, the strike drags on for months or years, it becomes virtually impossible to recover all income losses. When workers are affiliated with a local union, which is, in turn, affiliated with a large national union able to provide some strike benefits, loss to the workers on strike is reduced. The number of strikers able to find other employment is another factor which affects the total losses they must bear.

If one figured only 2,000 strikers and assumed that they averaged $5,000 a year income, this would amount to $10 million lost wages for a year. A proportion of the loss to the individual workers was offset by strike benefits, but obviously this was only a fraction of the total.

2. *Losses to the Company:* Company losses are equally hard to estimate. Undoubtedly there were losses in production and sales; lower efficiency of operation with new and untrained workers;

cost of staff time spent on preparing advertisements, radio scripts and printed materials; legal work; travel expenses; costs involved in "defense preparation" as well as higher taxes paid to support 90 instead of 5 special deputies in the village, et cetera. On May 4, 1954, the UAW strike bulletin stated: "One of the admissions made by L. C. Conger in court yesterday was that it [the strike] was costing the company approximately $46,000 in profits per day, not including various litigations and general overhead."

3. *Expenses to the Union:* By far the largest single expense item for the union was strike benefits. Workers on strike had their rent and utilities and grocery bills paid and were generally given $25 a week in cash to cover clothing, medical, dental, car and other expenses.

The union's community services director, Joe Burns, reported expenditures for the period of the strike (1954–1957) as $10,188,-961.67.[9] Well over $9 million of this went for strike relief. Newspaper ads, printing, publicity, radio time, prints, photos and signs for the period (1954–1957) amounted to $246,453.43.

The source of the union's income was reported as follows:

From the international union strike fund	$9,814,000.00
From other UAW locals that contributed to the Kohler strike fund	207,579.34
From unions outside the UAW, such as AFL groups, Brewery Workers, etc.	145,559.95
From individual merchants	32,331.19
Donations to the Kohler UAW Chorus	9,238.02

4. *Costs to Government Agencies:* Another strike-related cost is that of expenses incurred by legislative, judicial and law-enforcement agencies. Again, while the exact costs would be difficult to determine, it is apparent that many thousands of dollars were spent to hire extra deputies for the village of Kohler; special police for the City of Sheboygan; and special deputies for Sheboygan County. There were the costs of extra city council meetings, county board meetings, Wisconsin Employment Relations Board hearings, Wisconsin Circuit and Supreme Court cases, and time of the attorney general and his staff. At the national level, there was the work of the FMCS staff, extensive hearings and the voluminous reports of the NLRB, the investigations of the NLRB trial exam-

iners, the work of the U.S. Court of Appeals and of the U.S. Supreme Court, and the weeks involved by the McClellan Committee investigations.

5. *Indirect Costs:* A strike of this magnitude and duration is certain to have a noticeable effect on the economic life of the entire community. While part of the wages were made up by the UAW in strike benefits, the sum did not equal that of the regular payroll checks. The majority of workers were prepared to "endure" the strike in the hope of eventually getting improved working conditions. With reduced consumer spending among the workers and income available for investment by the company reduced, the tax base for the local, state and Federal governments was also reduced.

In a semi-facetious vein, one might suggest that some persons and organizations found an opportunity for employment or financial gain *because of* the strike — printers, newspapers, papermakers and salesmen; lawyers, columnists, proofreaders, private detectives, radio commentators; railroad facilities which moved the English clay from Montreal to Kohler via Michigan and Milwaukee; airlines which transported company and union spokesmen to the far corners of the land to tell their story; special police and detectives who might not otherwise have had jobs, and so on.

Downtown Sheboygan has only recently begun to renovate and rebuild. For years, the downtown business section presented too many dark, vacant store windows, with "For Rent" and "For Sale" placards gathering dust and cobwebs. The attractive lawns, trees and wooded parks could not hide the air of uncertainty, shabbiness and a listless civic outlook that the prolonged economic struggle had produced.

Officials Cannot Please Both Sides

The Kohler strikes, especially the second one, had a pronounced effect on the political campaigns and elections of the community and on the actions of officials chosen to carry out city and county policies. Both the Kohler Company and the union exercised a profound influence on political life in Sheboygan County and the strike cast its foreboding shadows across political fortunes of aspirants to, and incumbents of, public office.

One of the witnesses subpoenaed by the McClellan Committee

was John Deis, a long-time Kohler employee who was among those who went out on strike in 1934 and again in 1954. He had been wounded in the July 27, 1934, riot, and gave an affidavit in 1935 describing how he was shot in the head * and legs that night. He said that four men with shotguns in hand stood on the sidewalk before the shops facing High Street, shooting. In a later affidavit given in 1958, John Deis specifically mentioned the names of Kohler officials who, he claimed, shot him. In the questioning as to why there was this discrepancy between the 1935 and 1958 statements, Deis, in his broken English, tried to explain:

> I lose my job, you know. I told you, the Kohler Co. run the whole Sheboygan County. . . . You have to keep still. My wife told me "You better keep still, or you been out of a job. . . ." I work for the city of Sheboygan this time, and you know when I squawk out on this one, on Mr. Conger or Mr. Biever, . . . then I lose my job sure.[10]

Counsel Robert F. Kennedy, as the interrogation of former Mayor Rudolph J. Ploetz of Sheboygan was drawing to a close during the McClellan hearings, attempted to sum up claims and counter claims of the testimony in this way:

> You have the most confused city, I will say, Mr. Mayor, with the chief of police saying that you are responsible, and you saying the chief of police is responsible, and the result was that there was violence down there. [At the Sheboygan docks where the M.S. *Fossum* was docked.] There is no wonder that there was. . . . It seems to me that is a most unusual law-enforcement program that you have out there.
>
> For instance, in the middle of the strike while these acts of vandalism were going on, and there was this bitter feeling between the strikers and nonstrikers, the sheriff, who is in charge of the whole area, receives a major financial contribution from the union. In the meantime, the chief of police in charge of Kohler Village is working for the village in which Kohler pays 80 percent of the taxes and 2

---

* Deis's testimony moved a reporter covering the McClellan hearings to set down the essence thus:

> D'Kohler company's very kind,
> A fact I gotta mention.
> D'y shot me in the head behind,
> But gave a 12-buck pension.

out of 3 work for the Kohler Co. and therefore his salary is being paid by the company. During this same period of time you are receiving financial support from an organization that is closely associated with the union [the Farmer-Labor Political League].

The deputy chief of police in the city of Sheboygan is having conferences with the representatives of the Kohler Co. about putting a tap on the union telephones, and the chief of police is having another conversation about putting a bug in the room of the union headquarters.

It seems to me that you have five people working out there, and it is not the closest, most amicable relationship that I ever heard of.[11]

To which Ploetz replied, "Well, Mr. Kennedy, if you could have lived . . . in Sheboygan during this time, perhaps you could have a better insight of the story."

The problems of a public official in the strike-torn community are well illustrated by the pressures and responsibilities which inundated Mayor Rudolph Ploetz.

When Ploetz, the labor-endorsed candidate, was elected mayor in the spring of 1955, he sent a letter to the Kohler Company and the union, calling on them to "compromise your differences." On May 3, 1955, Ploetz criticized the company before a city council meeting for failing to reply to the letter, and a heated discussion broke out. Alderman Hugh Dales wanted a grand jury investigation of the strike and denounced Ploetz for not availing himself of "volunteers from the business community to fight vandalism.* There were sharp differences of opinion on the council and stormy sessions took place during the spring and summer of 1955, but at this meeting the council did offer "public facilities free of charge to federal and state officials for mediation."

Mayor Ploetz made a number of attempts at mediation but failed. On June 14, 1955, he appealed (as did Mayor Frank Zeidler of Milwaukee on July 10) to President Eisenhower to use his influence to speed mediation efforts. Two weeks later, June 28, Gerald D. Morgan, special counsel to the President, replied that "The Director [FMCS] assures me that every effort is being made and will continue to be made. . . ." Morgan's reply had been preceded, by one day, by a demand from the Kohler Company for police

---

* In fairness to Mayor Ploetz it should be said that he made repeated efforts to put a stop to vandalism in the community.

protection for the unloading of clay from the M.S. *Fossum* which was expected momentarily to dock in Sheboygan. A second notification letter reached Ploetz on July 1 and the third on July 2. Ploetz talked about the matter with Police Chief Wagner and others and they seemed to have held the opinion that, since two other clay boats had been unloaded without incidents since the strike began, there was no reason to anticipate trouble. As Leo Breirather of Local 833 emphatically told the author: "Nobody thought about that cotton-pickin' clayboat until the Kohler Company started writing letters to the Mayor of Sheboygan!"[12]

But it was obvious that Ploetz felt under considerable pressure from the company to provide police at the dock. From testimony at the McClellan hearings, it was apparent that Heimke did not view the demands of the situation on July 5 in the same light as did the mayor, nor for that matter, as did Chief Wagner. Ploetz felt that the company, in attempting to unload the boat at a time when not only the strikers were on hand, but when workers from other plants also had an extended Fourth of July holiday, was forcing the issue. The company could not have been oblivious of the feelings of the people congregating at the dock. The mayor was caught in the dilemma of either making a show of force at the dock and possibly inciting the spectators at the scene, or falling into further disfavor with the Kohler Company. He did not wish to be placed in a position which could be interpreted as helping to break the strike. It was a sensitive situation in which almost any untoward incident might have turned into a bloody riot. The mayor, the sheriff and the police officers all had memories of July 27, 1934. Ploetz explained to the McClellan Committee: ". . . I was primarily interested not to have anybody injured down there or killed. . . . I was an eye witness . . . to the 1934 episode, when I saw what happened at that time . . . and I would not have been a part of such an act."

Police Captain Heimke, in testimony before the McClellan Committee, had charged that he overheard Ploetz ask Sheriff Mosch at the scene on the day of the clay-boat incident, "How much are you obligated to the union for?" Mosch and Ploetz vehemently denied this. "I charge Steen Heimke with being a perjuror," Ploetz stated. "I never made such a statement that day or any other day." Mosch's affidavit maintained: "At no time did

Mayor Rudolph Ploetz and I discuss what my critics would call 'political obligations.' "

Some of Ploetz's critics in the Sheboygan community distributed a mimeographed publication entitled, *Spotlighting*, which bore no evidence of authorship or financial backing. It referred to Ploetz as "Ruthless Rudolph and his Marxist masters." It was speculated that *Spotlighting* was sponsored by certain businessmen and industrialists in the area who were opposed to Ploetz.[13]

Ploetz's most relentless critic was *The Chicago Tribune* which commented (August 15, 1955) on the roles of Ploetz *vs.* Captain Heimke * in an editorial: "Stuck With a Tough and Honest Cop." On August 27, 1955, the same paper charged editorially concerning the clay-boat incident:

. . . It was a pity the federal courts had to intervene in a situation that should have been handled as a matter of police routine by the cities of Sheboygan and Milwaukee. . . . By its action in renouncing future violence, the union pulled the rug out from under Mayor Ploetz . . . and the union stooges among the Milwaukee councilmen. The claptrap they uttered about placing "human rights" above property rights is now shown to be a simple defence of lawlessness, in violence to their oaths of office.

When Ploetz lost his bid for re-election as mayor of Sheboygan, the *Tribune* announced (April 3, 1955):

[SPECIAL] Sheboygan's union dominated mayor, Rudolph J. Ploetz, who had been accused of betraying his city, was soundly defeated. . . . He was accused of abetting the rioting in connection with the [Kohler] strike.

Editorially the *Tribune* said:

. . . Two years ago Rudolph Ploetz was elected Mayor of Sheboygan, Wis. with the backing of the strikers at the nearby Kohler plant. Several months later he repaid the union by permitting it to stage a riot on the city dock to prevent the unloading of clays (used

* Steen W. Heimke was removed as chief of police of Sheboygan in September, 1964, for false swearing in connection with misuse of funds belonging to the city and to the police pension fund, "having made available to himself without authority, public funds for his sole use and discretion and without accountability thereof to anybody," according to the Police and Fire Commission. Steen W. Heimke is presently employed as assistant manager of the engine and electrical parts division of the Kohler Company.[14]

in the Kohler pottery). . . . He lost the election, carrying only two of the city's 16 wards . . . the voters of Sheboygan have made amends for some of the disgraceful events of 1955.

One of Ploetz's official acts his last month in office was issuing a proclamation for a month of prayer in Sheboygan "for restoration of civic harmony in our community and that we may soon enjoy an honorable conclusion to the Kohler labor dispute. . . ."

The 1954 Campaign for Sheriff

County sheriffs in Wisconsin are elected on a partisan ticket, *i.e.*, Republican or Democratic, for a two-year term. The sheriff may succeed himself only once, but may run again after another sheriff has served for one or more intervening terms. Often the deputy sheriff will campaign for the office when the sheriff is no longer eligible and, depending on how political fortunes turn, a sheriff may be elected again after stepping down to the position of deputy sheriff for one or more terms.

Theodore Mosch, who served as sheriff of Sheboygan County from January, 1945, to the end of 1948, and again from January, 1953, until January, 1957, was the county's chief law-enforcement officer during the early part of the second strike and received tremendous pressures both to open the picket line *and* to leave the picket lines alone. The Kohler strike and the charges and counter-charges made concerning the strike policies of the incumbent sheriff and the other candidates for that office became the most important issue in the 1954 sheriff campaign.

In a taped interview on November 29, 1964, Mosch told the author about some of his experiences in the first days of the strike:

On Saturday, April 3, Walter Ireland [Sr.] called me and said I should come out to the plant. I told him I couldn't come that day. On Sunday they [the Kohler Company] called again and asked me to come out to the plant. I told them that as chief law-enforcement officer of the county, I figured I belonged at the courthouse. I said, "If you want to see me, I'll be waiting here for you."

He said, "Just a minute." So they put Biever on the phone. I told him, "I'll be at the courthouse. How would it look if I come out there the day before the strike as they'll naturally think it's all set." I mean the union would think I had been "bought." So then they put on Conger and he told me I should come out there. I told him "No," and he said, "You'll be out before the day is over."

I didn't go, but they called the chairman of the county board and he called me and told me I should go. But I still didn't go.

I went out on Tuesday morning, the day after the strike started, and what they wanted me to do was to use force. They wanted me to use tear gas; I was afraid to use it because I had only 12 traffic officers and it was hard to find persons who could be sworn in as deputies. I remembered the 1934 strike. If you deputize some and give them a gun, you know what can happen.

You see, when you have a businessman sworn in as deputy and you say to him, "I need you!" he'll say, "Here, take the card; I don't want no part of it." You can't blame them because they're in business and that's what you run into.

Sheriff Mosch recalled that the chairman of the Sheboygan County Republican party, Robert W. Haynes, "came down to the office and demanded that I take these 30–30 rifles and use them at the picket line." I said, "You mean with live ammunition?" and he said, "You better do that!" and I said, "There's the door!"

The stories about "mutilated cows" (Chapter 5) became another main issue in the campaign in the fall of 1954. Sheriff Mosch's opponents seized upon these alleged incidents to underscore their claim that such vandalism had occurred because of less than thorough investigations and vigilance on his part. Mosch's alleged negligence was charged to alleged obligations to the union and it was implied that union members were responsible for most, if not all, of the reported vandalism.

The Sheboygan County Citizen's Committee for Law and Order undertook an active campaign to elect deputy sheriff Harold Kroll as an independent after his defeat in the primary election. The committee sponsored this ad in *The Sheboygan Press* on Kroll's behalf:

How Low Can Men Sink?

Dairy cows on two farms in Sheboygan County have been maliciously and horribly mutilated. The udders of the animals were slit and slashed with razor blades.

"Hoodlumism" in all its forms of violence and vandalism must end.

That is why a "Do-Nothing" Sheriff must be replaced.

That is why we are supporting a candidate who is pledged to and who will support law and order.

A candidate who will break the mob rule directed by Hoodlums.

A candidate who will use his full power and authority to eliminate the cause of fear now haunting the law-abiding and peaceful citizens of this community.

On October 22, 1954, the Citizens' Committee for Law and Order circulated a letter in support of Kroll for sheriff which said:

Widespread violence and vandalism have prompted the formation of this committee to help restore lawful conditions in Sheboygan County. We have been drawn together from all walks of life and all political faiths by our common desire for a peaceful community.

Last April strangers from Detroit moved into this County to handle a strike. They and their local trainees committed acts of violence from the very start. The Sheriff's failure to enforce the law encourages them to go farther and farther. There have been now well over a hundred incidents, several of them almost fatal. Few parts of this County have been safe from vandalism and brutality. The strike issues are none of our business, but the public is entitled to law enforcement, even during a labor dispute.

In September these Detroit outsiders brazenly herded * their followers from other parties into the Republican party to vote for the present Sheriff, whom they consider "safe." Unfortunately believers in law and order split their votes between three other candidates, and so the present Sheriff won the Republican nomination with a minority of votes.†

In response to the Kroll ad, there appeared in the *Press* on October 26, an ad supporting Sheriff Mosch headlined: *"How low can a man sink?"* which stated in part:

. . . My opponent therefore has asked, "How low can men sink?" By his own actions and statements, which have been dictated to him by a chosen few, he has quite well answered the question he has

---

* Citizens in other countries — democratic or totalitarian, would have difficulty understanding this statement. The United States has a secret ballot and no one may accompany voters into the polling booth, much less "brazenly herd" them to vote for a particular candidate. The implication, of course, is that if they vote for the opposing candidate, they are stupid, but if they vote for the espoused candidate, they are intelligent and independent.

† If Kroll had won the Republican nomination over Mosch, with 4 candidates in the field, he would *also* have been nominated by a minority.

asked. . . . The investigation completed by my office revealed that the farmer who butchered the cow and placed the meat in his locker, stated that his loss was very small and he did not call a veterinarian nor report it to the Sheriff's Department. He did not regard it of any significance until he was approached by an attorney for the Kohler Company and was later contacted for a statement by my so-called independent opponent. . . .

The results of the election for sheriff of Sheboygan County, November 2, 1954, were as follows:

Theodore Mosch, Republican   14,124
E. Kallenberg, Democrat   7,204
Harold Kroll, Independent   12,172

Before the McClellan Committee on February 27, 1958, Mosch read a letter from Republican Chairman Haynes:

Dear Ted: You, as the chief law enforcement officer of the county, are responsible for maintaining law and order so that individuals may peaceably go about their business without fear of violence or interference from any other source. In a labor dispute, the law protects the right of individuals either to strike or to continue working. It gives the strikers the right to picket peacefully and to others the right to go to work without being hindered or prevented by threats, intimidation, force or coercion from any source. You have been advised by the district attorney in a written opinion that it is your duty to protect these rights. To date you have taken no effective action.

The executive committee of the Republican party expects officers who are elected under its banner to do their sworn duty according to law without fear or favor. The committee requests a prompt reply from you as to your position and intentions.[15]

Haynes later called Mosch at his office, Mosch told the committee, and wanted to know why the letter had not been answered. "He told me it was about time I opened up that [picket] line. He said, 'You have the authority to use firearms,' he says, 'and use them.' "

During the 1956 campaign Mosch's undersheriff, who was running for sheriff, bought four tickets for a Republican party banquet shortly before the election. When Haynes asked if he intended to bring Mosch and his wife, the undersheriff was told, according to Mosch, "That is out!" Senator Ervin questioned Mosch concerning this:

> *Senator Ervin:* Do you mean to tell me that they refused to allow you to even break bread with the party to which you had heretofore given your allegiance because you would not take the suggestion of the county chairman that you use firearms to open the picket line?
>
> *Mr. Mosch:* I believe that is true, sir, and I stood by my guns. If the Republicans do not want me, perhaps the Democrats will. I don't know.
>
> *Mr. Kennedy:* But you refused to use firearms?
>
> *Mr. Mosch:* That is true.
>
> *Mr. Kennedy:* And that was, again, because of what you knew about the number of people that had been killed and wounded in the strike at the Kohler plant in 1934.
>
> *Mr. Mosch:* That is right.
>
> *Mr. Kennedy:* You received financial assistance from the UAW, did you not, in that election in 1954?
>
> *Mr. Mosch:* I received that later in the fall of the year. We had what they called a Mosch for Sheriff Club, and at that time there was $300 turned over to the club, which was given me from Mr. Graskamp, and I turned it over to the club.*
>
> Perhaps at this time, thinking it over, it might have been improper. But I am here to tell the truth and leave the chips fall wherever they may.

On occasion, officials acted as if they were unaware of the impropriety of their actions, at a time when they should have had many second thoughts as to the course to follow. This time and distance removed, it seems incredible that law-enforcement officials should have been involved in such intimate working relations with private detectives, simply because they were "ex-FBI agents," and that deputies should have fraternized with strikers at the "soup kitchen."

Chief of Police Walter Wagner had served the city of Sheboygan for nearly thirty years when he resigned in the fall of 1955 for reasons of ill health. His successor was Police Captain Heimke.

---

* It should be obvious to the reader that there were few neutrals in this strife-torn community. In the 1956 campaign, L. P. Chase and C. J. Kohler were two of seven members of the Republican Campaign Committee which urged the election of Kroll for sheriff as a "good family man and a devoted member of his church . . . pledged to enforce the laws fairly without fear or favor. . . ."

Chief Wagner was also called to testify by the McClellan Committee concerning vandalism, the clay-boat incident and other matters involving the strike and law enforcement. Robert Kennedy asked the retired police chief:

> I have just one last question. We had Chief Heimke testify that he worked with the Madson Detective Agency who was working for the Kohler Co.
> *Mr. Wagner:* Well, gentlemen, in fact Mr. Conger called me one day and wanted to know of me whether I knew some agency or detective agency, and I am the one that referred the Madson Detective Agency to Mr. Conger.
> *Mr. Kennedy:* Did you work closely with them during this period of time, to try and solve these acts of vandalism?
> *Mr. Wagner:* Well, yes, and in fact they did. They practically came into the police station every day when they were in Sheboygan.
> *Mr. Kennedy:* Even with their assistance and their help, you were not able to solve these things?
> *Mr. Wagner:* That is right.[16]

Although a number of political groups were formed, such as the Sheboygan County Citizens' Committee for Law and Order, the Farmer-Labor Political League and the Citizens' Committee of Five, the majority of business people tried, on the surface at least, to remain neutral.[17] The union generally felt that the community "establishment" was aligned against them. Commercial clubs and organizations publicly criticized the union leadership, both in paid advertisements (*e.g.*, the Bar Association) and in releases to the press (*e.g.*, Kiwanis, Rotarians, ministerial association, Catholic clergy). Therefore, union members generally gave support to those candidates for public office who were most friendly to labor, and as Paul McMahon, a *Milwaukee Journal* staff writer reported:

> The strike has entered the political picture of Sheboygan county, making that aspect of life rougher than it has been in years. Local politics used to be nonpartisan in the city . . . and party labels still do not appear on the ballots, but . . . the strike has helped to crystallize the political efforts of labor through the Sheboygan County Farmer-Labor League. . . . Even the conservative elements in Sheboygan concede that labor has scored repeated successes at the polls since the strike began. . . .[18]

Practically all candidates for public office on both Republican and Democratic tickets receive contributions from friends and special groups who want to see them elected. Usually labor organizations — through the AFL-CIO Committee on Political Education (COPE) — and other liberal organizations, and individuals contribute to Democratic candidates, and businessmen and commercial and professional associations often contribute to Republicans. Some contributions are made more openly than others. Obviously Republican Sheriff Mosch, with the passing months, had developed more sympathy for the strikers than for the nonstrikers, on the basis of what he had experienced, and the propriety of accepting a campaign contribution from a party to the dispute may be questioned. Whenever contributions are made, it may well be asked: "Is this because of sympathy for the policies of the one supported or because of dislike for his adversary?" It has been the author's experience that this question is not usually considered by most citizens. They are usually not interested in the motives and biases of *all* the candidates.

David Rabinovitz, Sheboygan, the dedicated union attorney who labored faithfully for the cause he had been asked to represent over the period covered by both strikes, was ostracized by individuals and groups in the community, and incurred the enmity of some fellow attorneys in the Bar Association. In 1963, when President John F. Kennedy appointed him to a Federal judgeship, the Wisconsin Bar Association vigorously opposed the appointment, claiming that he was unqualified on the grounds that his involvement in labor controversy would make it impossible for him to serve impartially. Although he served nine months as acting judge, he never received the required U.S. Senate approval.[19] Since it is recognized that attorneys usually specialize in some aspect of the law and by reputation become associated with "special interests" of one kind or another, it is fair to ask whether the special fields of service and competency of other attorneys would have received the same scrutiny and opposition from the State Bar Association.

Although political in-fighting within the Democratic party of Wisconsin is generally given as the reason why Rabinovitz did not receive the judicial appointment, there was an interesting coincidence in connection with the Senate judicial committee hearing which turned down the appointment. Even though he did not testify, Lyman Conger, who could scarcely be considered a disinterested spectator, appeared at the hearing.

Frank P. Zeidler, mayor of Milwaukee, kept notes during the clay-boat dispute when the *Fossum* and *Divina* attempted to unload clay at the Milwaukee harbor. These notes, on file in the Milwaukee Public Library, portray in detail the problems and dilemmas of officials and commissions caught in the cross-fire of labor-management battles.

II

EVALUATION AND PROSPECTS

Implications for Industrial Relations

NATIONS, societies and organizations, as well as labor and management, establish goals and policies which reflect the thinking of their majority or dominant group. Today, no country tolerates the entire gamut of public expression of opinion from the extreme left to the extreme right. Before the passage of the Norris-LaGuardia Act in 1932, workers in the United States had very few legal rights as union members, and the unions themselves had little protection under the law. Because many places of employment were no Gardens of Eden, workers turned to collective action to define their employment rights. Unions recognized there were limitations to what they could achieve at the bargaining table and through their national and state central bodies also turned to political action for changes in social and labor legislation.

By 1947, after unions had made substantial gains in membership,* the political pendulum had begun to swing in the opposite direction. The Taft-Hartley amendments to the Wagner Act and the further amendments of the Landrum-Griffin Act in 1959 slowed down the growth rate of union membership.

Although the overwhelming majority of union leaders and members have been anti-Communist, some national and local organizations were captured by Communists during the late thirties and during World War II when Soviet Russia was fighting on the same side as the United States. This proved to be a severe handicap for many non-Communist trade unions. Many conservatives viewed all trade unions — Communist-dominated or not — in the same light; they professed to see no difference between members of the Americans for Democratic Action, Norman Thomas Socialists, militant trade unionists and genuine Communists.

---

* Only about one fourth of American workers are actually organized. While some industries are 80 to 90 per cent organized, others have less than 10 per cent in unions. This is a contrast to the virtual "closed shop" which prevails in the American Medical Association, the Dental Association and the Bar Association.

Having come through a period in which unions were considered "criminal conspiracies" and subjected to injunctions at every turn, unions eventually achieved legal status and developed methods for settling industrial disputes at the bargaining table. In some countries, rival unions may exist side by side in the same plant, each representing those workers who are its members. In the United States, the doctrine of exclusive jurisdiction gives to one union the authority and the responsibility for representing all the workers in the designated bargaining unit. This fact makes practically all union leaders and the majority of union members feel that, since all receive the benefits of union negotiations under law, all workers should contribute toward the support of the organization. Thus the strong drive for the union shop and opposition to so-called "right to work" laws which outlaw the union shop but do not guarantee to anyone "the right to work."

Most major employers deal with unions and accept the union-shop concept, but some persist, on principle, in fighting the union shop in the name of freedom for their workers. The UAW leadership and membership, accustomed to working under union-shop conditions in nearly every place where they have a contract, interpreted the Kohler Company's vigorous opposition to a union-shop clause as a deep-seated antipathy toward unions, which could lead in time to the destruction of their organization. The company viewed the union's aggressive bargaining tactics in the auto industry, and its history of sit-down strikes in the thirties, as an indication of a militant and "power-hungry" movement seeking to take over more and more of the company's prerogatives.

The Effects of Name-Calling

The bitterness engendered by the insults and accusations hurled at their respective adversaries by both sides has been one of the heavy social costs of the Kohler strikes. Psychologically, a person's ego is a relatively sensitive, delicate thing; threats or injuries usually lead to retaliatory behavior.

Empathy — the ability to identify with another or to understand how he feels about an issue — is rarely present in a conflict situation. Partisans frequently attribute the worst motives to the other side and pronounce epithets which are certain to be offensive to those on the receiving end. Who is to determine whether it is worse to be called a "goon," "Communist," "outside agitator," "vandal," "law violator," "outsider," "trouble-maker," "finagler," as a member of the union, or a "scab," "strikebreaker," "spineless," "job thief," "yellow-bellied coward," "midnight worm," "rat," "woodenhead," or "germ" as a nonunion worker? Company officials were referred to as "dictators," "puppets," "field marshals," and "water-front Quislings," while public officials were called "stooges" by one side or the other. With such an extensive list of epithets added to the lexicon of those involved in the industrial warfare, some of the feelings of bitterness and fear engendered by the name-calling were bound to carry over to relatives, friends and the children of the community. Few families escaped the resentments and misunderstandings that grew out of the strike.

The curious thing about name-calling is that sooner or later enough evidence may accumulate to provide some basis for assertions and then the attitudes of righteousness become increasingly deep-seated. Considering the history and cultural background of the Kohler family, it is possible that the Kohlers, who headed the company through the years, firmly believed they were giving the workers all they deserved, and more than many other employers would give. In turn, this might well have led to the conviction that those who did not recognize or admit this were either ungrateful or deliberately trying to foment trouble. On the other hand, workers who had unsatisfactory experiences on the job with piece rates or work assignments, or who were victims of accidents or industrial illnesses, could just as easily conclude that the company was exploiting them and trying to get every "last ounce" of work out of them for as little pay as possible.

During the investigation of these two strikes, the author became very much aware that there was little respect on either side for the sincerity and integrity of the other. The word "dictator" applied to an employer can have a bad connotation, especially when Hitler, Stalin or Mussolini come to mind, just as the word "Communist" offends when applied to a union leader. Anyone living in Sheboygan County could have determined that David Rabinovitz, the union's attorney, was a lifelong resident of the community and had never been a Communist. Yet the company paid detectives to track down a man of the same name in Philadelphia, who allegedly had Communist connections, evidently hoping thereby to discredit Rabinovitz's integrity and diminish his effectiveness as an attorney for the union.

Pressures and Counterpressures

When conflict becomes intense, the inevitable "choosing up" of sides takes place. Senator Ervin (Dem. N.C.) observed during the McClellan hearings:

I think we might get along a little better in this investigation if we all assume that we are intelligent people . . . familiar with some of the facts of life . . . who know that Clarence Darrow was not far wrong when he said that in a strike situation, where some . . . want to go on strike and some do not, where the management is fighting the strikers, a situation builds up in which . . . both sides have something of the spirit that people have in war, in which they yield to the temptation to do things which, as reasonable human beings — uninfluenced by the tensions that surround them — they would never consider doing.[1]

During a strike, as in war between nations, both sides become highly selective in what they see and say. Each looks at the records and performance of elected and appointed public and government officials and decides who is "with us" and who is "against us." Sincere motives may at times be maligned and self-seeking motives may at other times be extolled, but the politician or public official is often helpless to do anything about it.

Once a strike or lockout has been called in a labor dispute, the battle lines are drawn. There is no way to tell when it will be settled and whether there will be a capitulation or a compromise. The situation might well be compared with a case of marital discord. As long as both parties remain under the same roof, there is some hope of conciliation. Once a break has occurred, the relationship becomes difficult to mend.

Abraham L. Gitlow, quoting E. Wight Bakke and Clark Kerr, lists seven requirements for success for the union and for the employer in a labor dispute:[2]

For the union

1. Mold a group of individuals with different degrees of enthusiasm for the strike . . . into a unified, disciplined force of high morale;

2. Maintain the group's unity, discipline and morale as long as required to coerce employer surrender;

3. Win allies and public support;

4. Prevent operation of the employer's plant and employer access to productive factors necessary to operation;

5. Counteract any measures the employer uses to break the strike;

6. Negotiate an agreement successfully concluding the strike;

7. Prepare for peaceful relations between workers, union and employer subsequent to termination of the conflict.

For the employer

1. Undermine the morale, unity and organization of the strikers;

2. Maintain the unity and morale of his own management group;

3. Win allies and public support;

4. Minimize the losses caused by the strike through resuming operations, transferring his orders to friendly concerns, and insuring the protection of the property for which he is responsible;

5. Counteract any union and worker measures which seek to prevent the accomplishment of these aims;

6. Negotiate an agreement successfully concluding the strike;

7. Prepare for peaceful relations between workers, union and employer subsequent to termination of the conflict.

Gitlow adds that the last two requirements for the employer (6 and 7) would be omitted or very substantially altered by one aiming at the destruction of the union and the establishment of the open shop. He continues, "In the struggle to accomplish these objectives, the standards of conduct — of right and wrong — which characterize peaceful relations are significantly altered. Strategy and tactics hinge on the practical question: 'Will it work?' rather than on the ethical one: 'Is it right?' Strikes, like wars, are 'a reversion to dispute settlement by force, a return to the law of the jungle. . . .' "

Since by the very nature of the labor-management relationship the workers are in the position of having to *ask* while the company *gives* or *withholds*, a union could never entertain the thought of omitting points 6 and 7, as Gitlow suggests can be done by a company wanting to get rid of the union.

L. Reed Tripp [3] points out that the right to strike is the ultimate lever available to a union as a bargaining weapon. It involves serious responsibility, since its use deprives the union members of their livelihood for an indeterminate period of time. How the union viewed the pressures from the Kohler Company, as far as recruiting workers was concerned, is reflected in the petition filed with the Sheboygan County Circuit Court on August 21, 1954, by Allan Graskamp, president of UAW Local 833:

> . . . That the Kohler Co. in its back to work movement has recruited workers outside this community and outside the State of Wisconsin and from other plants in this city to engage in strike breaking, and that this pursuit has antagonized and aggravated many working people in this city and the company has frankly admitted the hiring of many new employees in their ads in the Sheboygan Press; that many people have indignant opinions to [sic] this practice and have exhibited their feelings in these neighborhood feuds. . . .

Too Much or Too Little Law

The body of laws governing a democratic society does not remain static or unchanged over a period of time. Laws are enacted, amended or repealed when enough political pressure or support builds up for such action. Legislation governing labor-management relations is always subject to criticism and review. The fact that the interests of workers and those of their employers often diverge leads to a continuing process of accommodation and vying for advantage — one over the other.

The question in the Kohler strike was not one of how *much* law, but what *kind* of law should apply. As pointed out in Chapter 9, each side found support in NLRB rulings and court decisions to fortify its position. Although the union won a much larger proportion of the charges brought before government agencies and courts than did the company, the fact that there was always a possibility of appealing the decision meant that it was years before the final judgments were rendered. It was this situation which moved Emil Mazey and others to claim that "Justice delayed is justice denied." Time itself worked against them. As *America*, a leading Catholic magazine, said editorially in 1960:[4] ". . . Unfortunately, many strikers will never regain their jobs, 126 of them having died since the dispute began. A more powerful argument for speeding up NLRB and court processes can scarcely be imagined."

Union spokesmen contended that the very slowness of the administrative agencies and courts made it possible for the company to continue stalling tactics by appealing every ruling and decision because there was no retroactive penalty if the company was found guilty in the higher courts. When Emil Mazey spoke at a union meeting in Sheboygan on September 11,1960, he said there should be Federal action to penalize the Kohler Company for its "wilful violation of the nation's labor law." He pointed out that the principle of triple damages as it applies to the antitrust laws already exists and he suggested that the labor law be amended to give the worker triple damages from the beginning of an unfair labor practice, instead of simple damages after the board finds the company guilty. Mazey continued, "It is not enough for the National Labor Relations Board to cite spying as an unfair labor practice. The law ought to be amended to provide a jail sentence for any corporation official who directly or indirectly is responsible for hiring spies or stool pigeons to spy on the activities of workers at any time, including periods of a strike."

UAW regional director, Harvey Kitzman, speaking at the same union meeting, called the Kohler strike "the most just battle any group of workers ever fought," but agreed that the NLRB's decision in supporting the union had been too long in coming. He said, *"It took only 29 days for Kohler Company to get an ironclad injunction against its workers and Local 833, but it took the NLRB six years, four months and 21 days to tell the company that it was guilty of unfair labor practices."* (Emphasis added.)

Albert Gore, one of the NLRB lawyers who handled much of the Kohler case for the board, summed up the question of too much or too little law in these words:[5]

There are actually three generally held points of view — the union's, the company's and the public's. . . . I don't think the company has any basis for complaint about too much law, *i.e.,* unless you want to go back to the law of the jungle and have no regulations, as recommended by Sylvester Petro, Milton Friedman and others who would abolish the Interstate Commerce Commission, the Federal Communications Commission, the Securities and Exchange Commission, etc. . . . I must say, though, that regulatory agencies, after a period of time, start giving the stamp of approval to the very problems they were to outlaw. . . . For example, under the Eisenhower administration, coercion by management was given the stamp of approval under the guise of free speech. When you tell an employee you are going to shut down the plant, this is a threat to him and not just a prognostication. . . .

One of the weaknesses of the law is that the only penalty against an employer for non-compliance is a slap on the wrist and an order not to do it again. Even the "I won't do it again" is weak because frequently, when the employer has violated the law and says he won't do it again, the Board is loathe to go in on a contempt case and will merely start a new charge. If you analyze (a) the number of contempt cases the Board has taken, and (b) the number of cases the Board has won, you see that the "I won't do it again" is not a strong deterrent.

I don't think that any person in his right mind can justify the surveillance that was done by the company. No person can condone the invasion of privacy that went so far as to check who attended the cocktail party of a striker's wife, checking the fact that two strikers' wives went to work for another factory where they were then fired. . . .

I disagree with the point of view that a union should be able to use the injunctive process to get pecuniary damages, but I think the law might well be amended so that the NLRB could go to the courts to seek an injunction when it finds a violation to exist. Section 10 (j) provides for a permissive injunction, but the political climate is such that government bureaucrats will seldom exercise this right. Section 10 (l) provides for mandatory injunction under certain circumstances. . . .

When I was with the Board, I had a case in Indiana where I told the company lawyer, "Why don't you settle this thing?" We had the evidence and there was no sense in engaging in extensive litigation. He said, "Well, if I settle this, the union will most likely get ten cents this year, ten cents next year, and another ten cents the following years." He had it figured out in dollars and cents that it would be cheaper to flout the law than to grant the wage increases. When you have a right to flout the law, it seems to me that the whole legal system falls apart. I take the position that there should be injunctive relief in cases where the Board is compelled to move against the union, to go to the courts to enjoin the union in order to maintain the status quo. And the same should hold for companies. I know that in many cases, injunctive relief in effect settles the case. Once the strike is enjoined, you're "dead." The economics of the situation is such that the union has lost everything that it is seeking and must capitulate to the company. If the possibility of an injunction existed for both sides to use, it would have a strong deterrent effect. If Kohler had had the problems of facing injunctive relief, the outcome of the strike might have been different. . . .

The Board should go in for injunctive relief in 8(a)(5) and 8(a) (3) cases and in 8(a)(1) cases when an election is involved. I would permit the union the right to sue for damages for its members and for the union as an institution, just as the employer can sue for damages when a union engages in a secondary boycott. I am less concerned about the injunction than about the damages when a secondary boycott is involved. Damages would serve as a real deterrent. I would not want the injunction used by either union or company, because they could use it improperly for tactical purposes, but the Board should have the power to seek an injunction from the courts when the evidence warrants.

In many cases the law is stronger against the union than against the company. In respect to 8(a)(2), any violation is as much against the union as it is against the company. On the 8(a)(5) refusal to bargain section, both parties can be found guilty. All of the acts for which a company can be found guilty can also be held against a union and, in addition, you have the 8(b)(4) secondary boycott provision. The anti-subcontracting clause is enjoinable as is a jurisdictional dispute, as well as organizational and recognition picketing.

Originally the law was intended to foster collective bargaining. During the early years of the Act there is no question but that the 8(a)(5) refusal to bargain was the most important violation. Basically, the law was designed to get the parties together. Later, under the Taft-Hartley amendments, priority was given to 8(b) (4) cases and then came the Landrum-Griffin Act which placed the emphasis on injunctive relief for the employers and collective bargaining issues now became tertiary in importance.

People violate this law with impunity, as they did the Volstead Act. This law has not really been accepted, in spite of all the hullabaloo. Who knows what a refusal to bargain is? And if so, so what? Three years from now they'll tell you not to do it again.

No, there is not *too much* law on the union side. There is *too little* law on the employer side. There is no law on the employer side that clips him of his economic strength. If this is not done, then you should examine the role of a secondary boycott and perhaps have it made legal. A secondary boycott, if legal, could balance the kind of co-operation that Kohler sought and got from employers. We have reacted to the bad cases, but have not really evaluated the net impact of labor legislation since 1935.

The "Left," "Right" and "Center" at Kohler

On a political or economic scale, most Americans would prefer to be identified as somewhere near mid-center, rather than at the extreme left or right. Yet, realistically, there can be only one hypothetical person or organization exactly in the center — every other is slightly or considerably to the left or right of that position.

If all workers, union, nonunion and management were placed on a continuum from left to right, the majority of workers would be located close to — but to the left of — center; the majority of management would be somewhat to the right of center. There would be very few at either extreme. Franklin D. Roosevelt was certainly to the left of former President Herbert Hoover, but to the right of the La Follettes. The La Follettes, in turn, were to the right of Norman Thomas, the Socialist leader, who was to the right of Earl Browder, the Communist.

Whereas the reaction to prevailing economic conditions during the thirties and forties had swung the pendulum left, the trend to the right set in during the fifties and sixties. In the early fifties, Wisconsin's junior senator, Joseph McCarthy, became the symbol of the new right-wing movement. More than any other individual, McCarthy used the word "Communist" to label indiscriminately, many organizations and individuals from New Deal Democrats to actual Communists. As the pendulum moved to the right, those on the extreme right painted all kinds of liberals and moderates with the brush of communism. Labor unions, co-operatives, the National Council of Churches, and many other voluntary organizations were so labeled by extremists opposed to Social Security, income taxes, civil rights, Federal aid to education and the TVA.

Workers and management at Kohler were also immersed in the ebb and flow of American politics. Most workers, during the thirties, supported the New Deal nationally and the Progressive party at the state level. There were very few Socialists, and even fewer Communists, in Sheboygan County. Most of the management personnel identified with the Republican party during this period, but there was not much political activity on the extreme right. The

Korean War, in which Russian Communists were our enemies and no longer allies as in World War II, and the spread of McCarthyism created a climate in which union leaders often came under attack. Walter P. Reuther played a leading role in 1946 in the defeat of the few Communists who had been elected to positions of leadership in the Auto Workers' Union during World War II. Reuther, who had been a Democratic Socialist — but never a Communist — during the early thirties cast his lot with the Democratic New Deal, seeing in it a more effective mechanism for improving the lot of the workingman. He became an active member of the Americans for Democratic Action, an organization of independent liberals, to the right of Norman Thomas Socialists, practically all of whom supported the Democratic party. In the framework of American politics, most Republicans would naturally consider most Democrats to their left.

As a result of months of study of issues and personalities involved in the second Kohler strike, the author has come to the conclusion that this strike might never have taken place — and certainly would not have lasted as long — if Herbert V. Kohler and the men who counseled him had held a more moderate political and economic philosophy. Instead of recognizing that conditions in the economy and in industry had caused workers to join unions and had brought about a change in the role of government in economic and labor-management relationships, they resisted these trends with vigor and determination. When their conservative views on unionism and the role of government in the economy are understood, it is not too difficult to see why the Kohlers should be drawn into supporting right-wing movements and, in turn, be made the heroes of some of these groups.

Fred J. Cook, in his book, *Barry Goldwater, Extremist of the Right*,[6] says that the original spokesmen for "Americans for Goldwater" were Frank C. Brophy, a retired Arizona banker, and Clarence Manion, former dean of the Notre Dame law school and a member of the governing board of the John Birch Society. Cook goes on to say:

> A complex of right-wing organizations, many of them on the far-out fringe, also joined up in the battle. They included: We, the People; For America; The Wake-Up America Committee; The Anti-Fluoridation League; The Defenders of the Constitution; Pro-

America; and the National Education Program of Searcy, Arkansas, an idea-factory for the Radical Right with an expressed sympathy for the John Birch Society.

Individuals in the supporting cast of sponsors were equally noteworthy for their strong right-wing fixations. They included Herbert V. Kohler, president of the Kohler Company, whose case Goldwater had championed in his futile effort to "get" Reuther; Merwin K. Hart, one of the nation's veteran anti-semites; . . .*

In the fall of 1957, Herbert V. Kohler was scheduled to speak on the Manion Forum radio program. The Mutual Broadcasting System, which had carried Dean Manion and his guests for some time, refused to carry Kohler's speech when he refused to delete certain statements the network termed libelous and slanderous against public officials, as well as allegations against individuals which had not been proven in court. "We've never had any trouble until Mr. Kohler," a network spokesman stated. "Mr. Kohler went a little beyond the bounds of responsible broadcasting in his accusations. . . . We could not subject our affiliated stations to the possibility of libel suits." Manion and Kohler then teamed up and called the MBS part of the "international socialist" conspiracy for barring the speech. Letters appealing for funds to support the Manion Forum went out from Kohler, saying: "We want money – We need money – Fill the Manion war chest with contributions – Give $100 – Give $1,000 or the end will come – International socialism is gradually choking off free speech in the United States – This must be fought to the last ditch."[7]

As late as November 15, 1963, Herbert V. Kohler used company stationery to send out appeals for financial support for the Manion Forum. He is also listed as a sponsor of the American Committee for Aid to Katanga Freedom Fighters; he was a National Advisory Board Member of the Young Americans for Freedom; and, according to *The New York Times*, March 12, 1962, he helped finance the Conservative Party of New York.

The stated purpose of the Manion Forum, according to a *Wall*

* Some observers claimed that a front-page picture in *The Sheboygan Press* during the '64 campaign, which showed Van Pelt (Wisconsin Congressman from Fond du Lac, near Sheboygan) and Herbert V. Kohler applauding Senator Barry Goldwater, helped increase the size of the vote which elected Congressman John Race (Democrat) in that election.

Street Journal article, March 17, 1958, is to wage war by television, radio and the printed page against:

> The confiscatory, Marxist income tax;
> Wanton foreign aid squandering;
> Socialist "public power";
> Destruction of states' rights;
> Futile conferences with Kremlin gangsters;
> Ridiculous budgets;
> Federal aid to education;
> Unrestrained labor bossism.

T. Coleman Andrews, Dan Smoot, Charles B. Schuman, General Bonner Fellers, and Fred C. Schwartz are among those who have appeared on Manion's Forum. Herbert V. Kohler has supported the Forum since it was founded in 1954.

According to reports filed with the Internal Revenue Service and the Clerk of the House of Representatives, the Kohler Company and/or members of the Kohler family have also contributed generously to former General Edwin Walker's campaign for governor of Texas, to "For America," the American Economic Foundation, Americans for Constitutional Action, and the Intercollegiate Society of Individualists, Inc.[8]

Judging by their affiliations and utterances, there is no danger that the Kohlers will be mistaken for liberals or radicals.

It is safe to assume that most Kohler workers who belong to the UAW today identify with the Democratic party. There are no signs of Communist, or even Socialist activity in Sheboygan County. At the national level, Reuther and the UAW have become known for their bargaining encounters with the giants of the auto industry and for supporting improved Social Security, aid to education, civil rights, et cetera. Some of those who have opposed the UAW's "progressive" programs, have not only dug up the past, but distorted it, hoping thereby to undermine that organization's influence in the nation's economic and political life.

It is always wise to consider the source when deciding how seriously to take charges made against any individual or organization, be it management or labor. This means taking into account the knowledge, credibility and probable motive of those who make the charge.

The strike at Kohler was voted by the membership of the local union, but in order to have the financial and legal support necessary to be any kind of match for the Kohler Company, the strike had to be sanctioned by the UAW-CIO. Because Kohler had sales outlets throughout the country, and the strike received national publicity, it was to be expected that the leadership of the national auto-workers' union should come under attack. Some attackers did not like the UAW's collective-bargaining tactics; others resented the union's wholehearted identification with the New Deal and Democratic politics. Michigan's former congressman Clare E. Hoffman read twenty pages of material on the Reuthers and the UAW into the *Congressional Record* in August, 1955, in which he charged that Reuther's purpose was to establish a socialistic government. Fulton Lewis, Jr., well-known for his "rightist" position, said in a radio broadcast (July 23, 1957):

. . . The workers at the Kohler plant have an independent union of their own, with which they are entirely satisfied, and they refuse to join the United Auto Workers, which, in effect, means that this is an outside UAW strike against the workers, which seems somewhat cannibalistic. . . .

This fantastic misrepresentation (the UAW won bargaining rights in the election of 1952) was preceded with a statement by Lewis that:

. . . Officials of the Kohler Company say that they have extensive documentary proof that Walter Reuther himself took a personal interest in the Kohler strike, and they have communications from him in person, in connection with it.

Of course Walter Reuther took an interest in the strike. So did Emil Mazey, the secretary-treasurer of the union, as well as the entire executive board. Once negotiations had come to an impasse and a strike was called, the UAW was committed to help its local affiliate in every way it could to settle the strike as quickly as possible. It did not relish the idea of using millions of dollars from members throughout the country to feed several thousand members in one Wisconsin community. Certainly Reuther and Mazey were interested in getting an "honorable" settlement as soon as possible. There was nothing sinister in that interest, as Lewis implies. Moreover, Reuther had sought a face-to-face meeting with Herbert V.

Kohler on several occasions. There was a feeling in some quarters, both in Sheboygan County and in Detroit, that if Kohler himself could be talked to, issues might be resolved, even though he had said he reposed complete confidence in Lyman Conger and his staff, who represented him at the bargaining table.

Commentator-columnist H. V. Kaltenborn, a native Wisconsinite, succinctly expressed the hopes and fears of some industrialists when he said (November, 1955):

> It is the old story of a big union seeking control of a small-town plant. Similar struggles have usually resulted in union victory. But President Herbert V. Kohler is an industrialist David who was willing to take on the union Goliath. Now it's a fight to the finish. . . . If Walter Reuther wins, it will discourage management everywhere from fighting big union domination. If the Kohler Company continues to win out, it will hearten every plant owner who has so far staved off union control.[9]

Petro – A Company Apologist and NLRB Critic

Sylvester Petro, who was well to the "left" of Albert Gore and George Squillacote of the NLRB when all three were students at the University of Chicago law school in the thirties, has written voluminously in recent years about what he considers to be the principal shortcomings of present United States labor policy. In an article in *Barron's National Business and Financial Weekly*, December 21, 1964, Petro endeavored to show how the NLRB has "rewarded the guilty and punished the innocent." Perhaps the article was written to justify the position taken in his book, *The Kohler Strike – Union Violence and Administrative Law* (1958),[10] which was widely distributed by the Kohler Company and reprinted as one of the John Birch Society's *American Opinion* series. In detailing all of the union's "sins" but none of the company's, Petro argues that the NLRB is the real culprit, using the term "Kangaroo Court" to underscore his point. He does not indicate that he interviewed any union spokesmen, and certainly he made no effort to quote both sides, so the reader could draw his own conclusions from the statements of the parties in the conflict.

As a Kohler Company apologist, Petro says, "It [the company] felt, and still feels, that union leaders do not have a right to make union membership a condition of employment, any more than company executives have a right to insist upon union membership."

The history of labor-management relations is replete with instances of employers' objections to the formation of a union among their employees, but there is no evidence that the opposition to unions stemmed from a concern for the freedom or welfare of the workers. Rather, it was because management wanted the freedom to make unilateral decisions, or because of a paternalistic attitude toward those for whom they provided jobs.

Petro's paperback on the Kohler strike was sent to clergymen, academicians and other thought leaders throughout the country. Monsignor James P. Finucan, one of these recipients at La Crosse, Wisconsin, wrote Mr. Kohler when he received the book:

> I am sorry to know that you are still persisting in opposition to the organization of workingmen. . . . Your vigorous and very intelligent pursuit of this has no doubt been an inspiration to all who agree with you. . . . While I would concede that in many cases the Union was wrong, the Union at least is not wrong in its basic principles![11]

Kohler's reply was a four-page letter in which he said he wished to correct the Monsignor's misconceptions, even though he had no hope of changing his preconceived opinions. He recounted the position he held on vandalism, violence and "hoodlumism" and the danger of Walter Reuther's "socialistic ideologies." He concluded by saying that, if Petro had dealt with the 1934 strike, he would have shown the strike was started by a minority of workers, and that union lawlessness culminated in the riot when "the law of the jungle" was substituted for the law of reason.[12]

Monsignor Finucan defended the moral right of employees to "form associations and bargain collectively. . . . It is quite evident," the Monsignor said, "that our basic disagreement is on the nature of trade unions and the relative importance of money and people." He wrote:

> . . . it is morally impossible for any organization, even of business men, to operate successfully as an organization, if individuals within that organization are going to be free to depart from majority decisions at will and destroy the unity and effectiveness of said organization. Beyond this natural difficulty, there is the added diffi-

culty that a trade union, being an organization of individual men who are selling their labor and their personal skill, men who decide to share the benefits of collective bargaining thereby forfeit their right to bargain individually. They do oblige themselves to participate in the decisions of their union, and this, unfortunately, some of them fail to do. However, the decisions of the union bind them as long as they wish to share in the benefits of organized bargaining.

. . . On your page three, your first point contains a statement that a union has no greater legal or moral right to coerce employees into joining a union than an employer has to coerce them not to join. I disagree. Men have a right which comes from God, Who created them, to form associations and bargain collectively. They have a right to organize such unions and they have a right to a certain amount of moral pressure to get their fellows to join. An employer obviously has no right to coerce employees not to join a union, since it is for their best interests that they have a union. . . . The union is on the side of the Angels in this one, and you are not, Sir.

. . . I say that an employer's right and duty to protect his money does not give him a right to blast the lives of men. The men are more important than the money . . . may I suggest that we Democrats hold out for the right of a rich man to become poor again, as well as the right of a poor man to become rich. You Republicans seem to think of it as a one-way street! [13]

At another point, Petro states that in a strike vote taken on March 14, 1954, only 1,105 voted for it and 148 against. He then speculates that "frequently workers, who do not want to strike but who do not quite dare oppose the union organizers or union leaders openly, stay away when the strike vote is taken." Petro is wrong on three counts because: *one*, on a secret ballot others do not know how you vote; *two*, a local union would be stupid to call a strike if there was uncertainty about whether a substantial majority of the workers would support the strike; and *three*, union members, not union organizers, decide whether or not to call a strike.

In discussing the vandalism which occurred, he suggested that "the count was limited to those who *came forward* [emphasis added] with affidavits." He makes no reference to the active role of the company in seeking out instances of damage which could possibly be listed as strike-connected. Later, he states that "it is clear from the record that the company took not a single step to induce anyone to come to work during the strike . . . the Kohler Co. never once advertised for or solicited employees during the strike. It did not need to do so. . . ." If this is true, the author is at a loss to understand why the company ran so many full-page ads in *The Sheboygan Press* saying, "Another Pay-Day at Kohler," "Wages are Good at Kohler" and "Today is Pay Day at Kohler."

Petro says further: "Matching the UAW's persistent use of intimidation against those who chose to work, the company with equal persistence pursued its legal remedies." On the eviction of strikers from the American Club, he states, "there was a shortage of rooms," although the NLRB found that persons who were not even working for the company were permitted to remain.

In discussing the NLRB's decision of August 26, 1960, when the company was found guilty of unfair labor practices and ordered to reinstate strikers, Petro adds: ". . . the Board's decision in its main thrust amounts to a serious blow to the Kohler Company and a deadly one to a large number of persons who applied for and accepted jobs which the strikers had vacated." This viewpoint, of course, implies that a worker can never withhold his labor no matter what the provocation, without "vacating" the job for someone else.

Another contradiction in the Petro story is his claim that a large number of pre-strike Kohler workers abandoned the strike shortly after it started * — if indeed they had ever taken a voluntary part in it — and that hundreds of others would not be applying for reinstatement because of death, retirement, removal from the area, jobs elsewhere, et cetera. Yet, he says that "possibly more than a thousand" strikers would want to return to work at Kohler, possibly "forcing the Company to dismiss striker replacements in line with the NLRB decision."

Petro wrote his book *before* the U.S. Circuit Court of Appeals sustained the NLRB ruling on reinstatement of strikers and *before* the Board ruled in 1964 that it had been an unfair labor practice strike from the beginning, and that 57 of the dismissed strikers, in-

---

* Out of slightly over 3,000 Kohler production workers, over 2,500 were members of the UAW when the strike started and only about 600 had returned to work at Kohler after the strike had dragged on for six years. Later in 1965, the number entitled to reinstatement rights was still variously reported as between 1,600 and 1,800.

cluding practically all the union's leadership, should also be offered reinstatement.

In justifying the company's hiring of private detectives, Petro says that "the union investigated legal activities [of the company] while the company investigated illegal activities [of the union]; yet the company "suffered the lash of the NLRB's contempt and the force of its 'law' while the union was rewarded."

Writing as a lawyer, and not as an economist, Petro claims,

> As a general rule, the public is the true and ultimate victor when a company wins a strike. Winning a strike means that production is resumed on the basis of the company's offer rather than the union's demands. Whether the strikers themselves come back to work or their jobs are filled by replacements does not matter here. What does matter is that costs are lower and production more efficient under terms offered by employers than under those demanded by unions. . . .[14]

This viewpoint looks at the cost side of the economic equation, but ignores the need for purchasing power and says nothing about the rights of the workers to match their collective strength with that of the employer.

The Human Side

When the 1934 strike was nearly a year and a half old, a small book entitled *The Kohler Strike — Its Socio-Economic Causes and Effects* was published in a modest edition. Its author, who is also the author of this volume, had completed the study of the strike for his Ph. M. degree in sociology at the University of Wisconsin, and because the subject was timely and important, decided to publish the thesis. On the strength of $115 in advance orders from union members, ministers and professors, and a loan from his mother, he ordered a thousand copies printed at Cuneo Press in Milwaukee.

Twenty years later, the second strike controversy was in the courts; and Max Raskin, attorney for the union, submitted the book as evidence at NLRB hearings in Sheboygan. Lyman Conger objected, claiming the book had been financed by the AFL union involved in the 1934 strike — which was not true. The book was accepted by the board, nevertheless, as "rejected" evidence.

Another ten years went by, and one day in May, 1965, the author and Mr. Conger, who was accompanied by Mr. George

Gallati, public relations director for the company, met. In the course of the two-hour discussion, Conger pointed to "the book" and said, "This book was responsible for the NLRB decision against the company in September, 1964." "It would be too dangerous to cooperate with you [in supplying information for a manuscript]," Mr. Gallati interjected. "This would lend an air of objectivity to the book [the present publication] which it does not deserve."

The author had written on November 14, 1964, to J. L. Kuplic, president of the Kohler Company, and to Walter P. Reuther, president of the UAW, explaining that he was working on a manuscript about the Kohler strikes and would appreciate statements from spokesmen on both sides of the controversy, as well as any photographs, documents, etc. which would contribute to an understanding of the events which had occurred.*

On November 27, 1964, the author called at the Kohler Company offices where he had a cordial 45-minute conversation with Mr. Gallati, and showed him a copy of the letter to President Kuplic. Mr. Gallati left the conference room with a copy of the letter and returned shortly. "Forget what I told you about pictures and so on," he said, "They are working on a reply to your letter, and you should hear from President Kuplic in a few days."

The letter from Mr. Kuplic arrived (and since he had not been with the firm during the first strike, it must be assumed that he was "briefed" before he wrote the letter) which repeated Conger's unfounded charge that the union financed the first Kohler strike book, and stated that "this does not give us any confidence that anything more you might write would be from a viewpoint even approaching objectivity."

In the hope of hearing the viewpoint of one of the younger generation at Kohler, the author phoned Herbert V. Kohler, Jr., in October, 1965. He had been graduated from Yale University in June with a degree in industrial management and had been with the company full-time since August. With a talented wife and two beautiful children, he lives in an informal "fairy-tale" chalet in a secluded area near Lake Michigan, adjoining Vollrath Park. He invited the author and Mrs. Uphoff into his house and began to question the author as to the reasons for the interview. After about

* Reuther did not reply directly but asked his staff to make files and documents available to the author.

ten minutes of conversation, the author noticed a copy of his book about the first strike lying on the long table, and next to it, a small microphone leading to a tape recorder at the far end of the table. The young man picked up the book and began asking questions, for which he had apparently been briefed, for the strike had taken place and the book had been written before he was born. The recorder came to the end of the tape and began sending "distress signals" which at first Mr. Kohler attempted to ignore. "Since you are making a recording," Mrs. Uphoff suggested, "why don't you fix the machine and then let's sit around the microphone and talk?" Mr. Kohler explained that he was making the tape recording "for my own protection."

The discussion proceeded in a more relaxed fashion. Henry Ohl's introduction to the book, which had been written at the author's invitation, was offered as evidence that the book was pro-AFL. Mr. Kohler was reminded that Ohl had written:

> From deep delving into factional crevices, he has gleaned facts and opinions that point to injustices so grave and so numerous that might have justified much sharper, more definite and drastic conclusions than those expressed. He has been extremely charitable. His evident desire for impartiality in an academic discussion and his purpose to permit the reader to draw conclusions of his own obviously were restraining factors.

Had not the author at one time been active in Wisconsin politics?

Yes, he had; he had been a candidate for governor on the Socialist ticket when Norman Thomas ran for President. Several Kohlers, the author reminded him, had also taken an active interest in politics.

"I have much respect for Norman Thomas — as a poet," Kohler said, but added that he would not like to see Norman Thomas write a story of the Kohler strike. He, himself, did not object to the whole range of political opinion in this country, including the Birch Society, so long as "they don't pull the trigger." In the course of the conversation he referred to Conrardy, the new Local 833 president, as an able, intelligent union leader who "has the interests of his men at heart."

What does this handsome, fairly articulate young man think

of the future? He looks forward to living in the United States in these times, he said. These are times of tremendous change and challenge.

Change can sometimes be painful, Mrs. Uphoff observed.

True, said Mr. Kohler, but he welcomed it.

Impressions and Interviews

In January 25, 1965, it was announced that, when the traditional gold watches would be given at the next Kohler Company Christmas party to those who had been with the company for twenty-five years, strikers would be included. Among the recipients would be "some former union leaders and members who haven't been on the job for eleven years." "Long Feud at an End?" *Sheboygan Press* headline asked. It was regarded as one of the most notable January thaws the community had witnessed.

The first years of the strike produced much bitterness; friendships, families, choirs, church congregations and fraternal organizations were torn asunder by the partisanship which both sides cultivated in the struggle. Robert Wallace, writing for *Life* May 20, 1957, said:

> An enormous mess, not just an everyday, run-of-the-mill botch, requires good strong men to produce. Weak men lack the courage and tenacity of purpose, the dignity, and above all, the individualism to produce a well-nigh hopeless shambles. Consequently, what is happening in Sheboygan county, and radiating outward from there to all corners of the nation, is a rare thing. Let there be no doubt about it: these men are the salt of the earth, backbone of America, and the mess is a large one.

In the pursuit of the facts in this strike, the character of the people involved proved to be one of the most fascinating and illuminating aspects.

Time has eased the most bitter feelings; a saving sense of humor and restraint, which most people managed to retain to a degree, even in the worst days of the strike, has returned to the union leaders and to most of the townspeople, who can view the struggle with more objectivity now. The remaining "angry men" are those who felt they were "used," whose dignity and self-respect has been diminished and who cannot face the fact that their weakness was their defeat. But who, knowing the pressures to which the

press, the law-enforcement officials and the "third parties" were
subjected, can sit in judgment? Some people interviewed (among
them several law-enforcement officials) went to considerable length
to demonstrate to the author that the Kohler Company did not
dictate to them what they could say or do; it is quite possible that
this attitude is easier to maintain now, in an era of relative peace,
than it was in a state of crisis. Others pointed out that new people
are in positions of responsibility — both in the company and in the
union — and that an attitude of reasonableness is beginning to pre-
vail. Still others stiffened at the mention of the strike and wanted to
know why the whole thing was being opened up. "Forget the past!
We've had enough of that strike!"

With time, both union and company spokesmen have retreated
from some of their militant positions. Emil Mazey pointed out that
when a strike drags on as long as that at Kohler did, one has to ask
himself, "When does a 'scab' cease being a 'scab'? At six months?
One year? Five years?" Now that the strike is officially ended,
strikers and nonstrikers do work side by side and the union hopes
there will be enough forgiveness on both sides to develop a har-
monious relationship in the plant.

Lyman Conger, who told the author there was no point in
writing about the past, is also aware that his employees who went
on strike were not as bad as they were made to appear. The company was not afraid, apparently, that it would be dynamited when
it took back one of the men arrested near the dynamite cache, who
under economic pressure "broke rank" and returned to work. It
was apparently also willing to forgive and forget the mass picketing
activities of those willing to return to work during the early months
of the strike. Only the "77," including all the local union's leadership, were kept on a "boycott" or we-won't-hire list until the
Supreme Court acted.

The entrance to Local 833 headquarters on Eighth Street in
Sheboygan is overshadowed by the Western Union sign and
Friede's on the corner. The sole decorations in the sparsely furnished offices are framed charters of the seven UAW locals in the
area, pictures of President Johnson and John F. Kennedy, and
meeting, CARE and safety-education posters. In the two back
offices, one is likely to find Eggie Kohlhagen or Leo Breirather —
both friendly, soft-spoken men. Kohlhagen has been described by

Albert Gore as "the last guy they could pin anything on," who "made a union newspaper out of a social newspaper" and who was the man most resented by the company because "he was their Benedict Arnold — he was their boy and he turned on them." The battle left no bitterness in Eggie Kohlhagen. He and Leo Breirather, once loyal company men who became disillusioned and then espoused the union cause, can speak of the strike with good humor and remarkable insight. A magazine writer set * down his impressions of Breirather as "at heart a constructive, solid citizen" who "wants to build something, not destroy anything." This was May, 1957, and the description still fits.

Ray Majerus has gone to the regional staff in Milwaukee, but duties as administrator of the local up to the summer of 1965 often brought him back to Sheboygan. Now he is carrying the brunt of new contract talks with Lyman Conger, who fired him from the enamel shop in 1952. Majerus is determined and not easily intimidated by bargaining-table tactics. In size alone, he would make a formidable opponent; his rise as a union leader is perhaps as good an example as any of the men who grew in stature and ability as the stress of the strike tested them. Graskamp, who has gone to work for another union, is, as he says, "pretty much out of things now." Throughout the early years of the strike, he impressed those who came in contact with him as a modest, able, dedicated union man, who dispelled the notion that union leaders are irresponsible, agitating revolutionaries.

Some of the "old timers" from the first strike are still on the scene in Sheboygan. In talking with Rudolph Renn, Charlie Heymanns, Frank Reinthaler, Carl Gunther, Philip Eirich and Chris Leining, one recognizes quickly that these are "the salt of the earth" of which Wallace wrote in *Life*. They are intelligent, literate men, who have in common a spirit of independence and commitment to justice and human dignity. The present union owes a great deal to these men who defied the ". . . Prussian variety of discipline . . . based on fear . . . demanding a sacrifice of personal dignity,"† which persisted into the fifties when another generation of workers rebelled.

As this is written, Dave Rabinovitz, whose life story for thirty

---

* Robert Wallace in *Life*, May 20, 1957.
† Robert Wallace, "A Long Strike's Human Damage," *Life*, May 20, 1957.

Attorney David Rabinovitz in his office at Sheboygan. (UAW photo)

years was the story of the legal battles of the union with the company, has resumed his law practice in Sheboygan. His dedication to the union cause has cost him a great deal in health and income. But he has earned the loyalty and respect of the workingmen, who found him an able and hard-working friend in court during the strike skirmishes and battles.

Despite the intensity and bitterness of the conflict, most of the principals still live and work in Sheboygan and its environs. Ted Mosch, Oakley Frank, Henry Billman, Walter Wagner, Rudolph Ploetz, Clarence Zimmerman, the deputies and officers with whom the author talked, are going about their daily business, mellowing now, able to view the strike events with less pain, and willing to re-evaluate them with someone sincerely interested in getting the facts. For the most part, they count themselves fortunate that the situation never got worse than it did. The feeling of being "caught" between two forces was pervasive. As Donald Koehn, who as justice of peace at Sheboygan Falls presided over a number of strike complaints in his court, said, "people got tired of being subjected to the propaganda and the violence." Resentments built up, directed more often toward the union than the company, although, as Koehn, Billman and others said, "people were acquainted with the working conditions at Kohler."

The clergy of Sheboygan also felt they were caught in the middle, yet they earnestly tried to work behind the scenes, with — it must be added — not much success. Without exception, they recall their dismay as the heat of the struggle rose, then settled down into years of unrelenting "cold war." Had the quiet, early proposals of such men as Rabbi Barack, Fathers Carroll, Knackert and Hoeller, Dr. T. Parry Jones and Dr. Wilford Evans been as acceptable to the company as they were to the union, the community would have been spared much tragedy. Whether or not their decision not to take sides openly, but to minister quietly to their divided flocks was the most effective one, who can say?

Men like Judges Schlichting and Buchen, although *of* the battle, remained above it as their responsibilities demanded. The fairness which is required of a judge is not always appreciated in a fight to the finish where the partisans feel they have to recruit every bystander in order to win.

In talking with those who had the responsibility of law enforcement, the author concluded that most of them — though not all — were very much aware that, only insofar as law and order were kept, could the community survive. Men like Capelle, Mosch and Ploetz, although often accused of being "in the pocket" of company or union, knew that at times they were making "life and death" decisions when any untoward, badly handled incident could have resulted in violence which might have claimed lives. It is to their credit that they weighted their decisions on the side of protecting the lives of men.

The heavy responsibilities and the challenge of the situation developed personality and leadership in some, but the conflict also brought out the worst in others, and these personal tragedies must be deducted from the gains. The enforced idleness and the uncertain future, faced by so many for so long, put strains upon families which some were not able to bear. A wife, in one broken-home situation, explained: "It was the strike. There are others it happened to besides us."

Sheboygan County Sheriff's officers trained in the use of tear gas at riot and mob control exercises with "outdated projectiles" supplied by Kohler Village, according to The Sheboygan Press, June 13, 1964. (Sheboygan Press *photo*)

The same machine guns that were brought out the night of July 27, 1934, are still at the Kohler Village hall "in good working condition." Sheboygan County sheriff's deputies were trained with gas masks and "obsolete tear gas supplied by the village of Kohler" in tactics of riot and crowd control, in June of 1964. In these restless, uneasy times, civil rights demonstrators, students or farmers * might just as well be the objects of such law-and-order tactics as union members on strike. One may well question the wisdom and necessity for such weapons in Sheboygan County, Wisconsin. Only recently did Sheboygan replace a chief of police, who was particularly determined about concentration on shooting-range drill in marksmanship for his men, even though the throngs who take over

* In December, 1964, sheriffs in 18 other industrial counties of Wisconsin were sent a questionnaire, by the author, asking if they held training sessions in the use of tear gas for mob control. Of the 14 who replied, 9 said they did not; 5 indicated they had limited annual or semi-annual programs. One sheriff said: "The recent NFO [National Farmers Organization] actions have brought the demand for better knowledge of the gases although we did not have to use it. It was in the squads on the scene in the field unknown to the pickets."

the city on Bratwurst Day pose the greatest present threat to peace
and order in Sheboygan.

In communities, as well as in international politics, there is an
ever-growing need for an intelligent, reasonable, responsible "third
force" which can bring moral persuasion to bear upon belligerents.
This force, the author believes, will be even stronger when it relies,
not upon tear gas, side arms and marksmanship, but upon understanding the minds and hearts of men, and upon courage to intervene at the propitious moment when the welfare of the community
is at stake, *and* at a time when understanding and moral persuasion
still have a "fighting chance" to succeed.

Speculations — IF

Hendrik Van Loon is credited with the thought that when the
"ifs" of history are contemplated, it opens up a veritable Pandora's
box of possibilities. Complicated events in real life cannot be repeated or duplicated in a social-science laboratory. So many vari-
able factors are at work in these events that it cannot be proved
what might have happened IF something had been done differently,
or IF a different person had played a particular role. Yet, after
reading thousands of pages of articles and documents related to the
strike, and recalling the numerous interviews and conversations
with people involved it is intriguing to speculate what might have
happened IF certain things had been done differently or IF other
individuals had been carrying out certain responsibilities. Some of
these speculations are presented here to indicate how choices and
decisions in a controversial situation might change or alter the
outcome.

> IF the Kohler Company's private detectives and/or the county and
> city law-enforcement officers had identified a substantial number of
> suspects in the vandalism cases reported . . .

A major phenomenon associated with the second Kohler
strike was the great number of incidents of vandalism and the very
few arrests and convictions. Many theories have been presented as
to who was responsible, but the most widely held belief in the community is that union members, who resented the nonstrikers taking
their jobs, committed most of the acts of vandalism. Many union
members, however, believed that the company and/or its agents

had a part in the vandalism — certainly in publicizing and in-
demnifying property damage. They point to the fact that it was
several weeks after the incidents, and only after Kohler representatives had visited them, did two farmers report injuries to dairy
cows. They point to the Joyce incident when company personnel,
together with a Madson Agency detective, went out to a newly
hired employee's farm in an attempt to make a case out of a report,
which a polygraph test later indicated was a complete hoax.

Harvey Kitzman reminded the author that, had the union in
any way been involved in the vandalism, the private detectives
hired by the company would have learned about it, since they in-
filtrated the picket lines and spied in the strike headquarters without the union's knowledge.

Another theory is that because bitter feelings engendered by
the strike made the union highly suspect (for example, the dynamite cache case), law-enforcement officers and editorial writers
seldom looked beyond the union or its members when trying to pin
the blame. Former Mayor Ploetz suggested that this, in effect,
meant that youngsters with an urge to destructiveness had the opportunity for "year-round Halloween tricks" with little risk of being caught.

IF someone other than Lyman C. Conger had been the Kohler Company's chief negotiator . . .

Were participants and observers of the strike to be polled as to
which IF might have made the greatest difference in the outcome of
the long struggle between the UAW and Kohler, this IF would
probably be most frequently mentioned and could be interpreted
in a positive or negative sense. There is no question that Conger's
determination, skill and inventiveness made him a tough adversary.
Albert Gore pointed out that Conger might well have avoided some
of the legal pitfalls which turned out to be costly mistakes for the
company, had he not been quite so "eager." Conger was a self-
made man, a lawyer who passed bar examinations after he had
studied law by correspondence, which earned him the title of
"Sears and Roebuck lawyer" in union circles. Had he taken as
many courses in psychology as he did in law, he might have been
able to empathize and to understand how workers and union members viewed the situation; he might well have done in 1954 what

he eventually did in 1962, 1963, 1964 and 1965 — sit down and negotiate a contract with the union he had called practically every name in the antiunion employer's lexicon. Those close to the situation insist that Herbert V. Kohler was not particularly well informed about labor law or collective bargaining and that it was Conger who "called the shots" on next moves for the company. A more conciliatory person, such as L. L. Smith, might well have averted the 1954 strike.

IF the UAW had assigned some other staff representative than Robert Burkart to Local 833.

Another very if-fy question is whether the Kohler Company might have reacted differently if the UAW staff representative sent in to assist Local 833 had been someone with an impeccable past. Burkart was considered "a very able guy" and "a good trade unionist," but he had, six or seven years earlier, been involved with a Trotskyite group in Ohio. He was also having marital problems. Madson Detective Agency went all out for the Kohler Company in attempting to create the impression that the union was "led" by an "immoral" leader and "Communist." Although it is hard to believe that the company resisted the union so vigorously primarily because of Burkart's past and his personal life, it is obvious that he was vulnerable and, as a result, the union suffered in the eyes of the public.

Hard as the private detectives tried, they could not find anything to detract from the union's attorneys or its other leaders. It is obvious from speeches made by the company spokesmen that they were taking advantage of the hysteria of the McCarthy era in their efforts to defeat the union. Since the Kohler Company signed the third annual agreement with the union in 1964, there have been no further charges that the union intends to take over the company and socialize the entire economy.

IF Mrs. Herbert V. Kohler had lived.

Mrs. Ruth DeYoung Kohler took an active part in the life of the Kohler-Sheboygan community. She had been an editor of the women's section of *The Chicago Tribune* before her marriage to Herbert Kohler; she possessed a feeling for history and a spirit of gracious living which seemed incompatible with an ugly management struggle. Many of the handsome community facilities in

Kohler Village and its well-known Distinguished Guest Artists' Series were her personal projects up to the time of her death in 1953. She founded the Women's Auxiliary of the State Historical Society and the restoration of Wade House, the old stagecoach inn of the previous century at Greenbush was done under her direction. Many workers at Kohler felt certain that, had she lived, she would have used her influence with her husband to reach a peaceful settlement with the union.

IF U.S. Senator Robert M. La Follette, Jr., of Wisconsin, had been re-elected in 1946 and Joseph McCarthy defeated.

Wisconsin voters had alternated between electing liberals and conservatives to public office for many years. Bob La Follette, Sr., had served the state as governor and United States senator and was succeeded by his son when he died. Young Bob carried on in the tradition of his father, first within a Progressive caucus of the Republican party, and then through the Progressive party, which he helped found in 1934. By 1946 it appeared that his chances of continued success as a Progressive at the polls were nil, so he decided to enter the Republican primary campaign. This immediately stimulated Republican "regulars" to look for a candidate to stop La Follette. They endorsed Joe McCarthy of Appleton, who had run in 1944 and in the intervening two years had spent much of his time campaigning.

Many union leaders and liberal editors, as well as Howard McMurray, the Democratic candidate, expended their efforts attacking La Follette because they resented the fact that he had not chosen to enter the Democratic primary; moreover, they naïvely believed they would have a better chance to win against a "bad" Republican than a "good" one.

With the help of some Democrats and some of the state CIO leadership which at that time followed the Communist party line, McCarthy defeated La Follette by about 5,400 votes in the primary election and then went on to defeat McMurray by over 200,000 votes in the November election. McCarthy had an almost pathological urge to win the election; he told fellow Marines in the South Pacific during the war that he intended to become the "first Catholic President of the United States."

McCarthy's intense political ambitions drove him to exploit the anti-Communist sentiment in the country, and to whip up the hysteria known as "McCarthyism" during the early fifties. Many innocent liberals were silenced under the barrage of unfounded allegations McCarthy leveled against many Democrats, labor leaders, editors, clergymen and government employees. If the United States had been spared this era, labor relations at Kohler and throughout the country might well have been conducted with far less suspicion and name-calling, and in a much more tolerant climate.

Kohler and Sheboygan in 1965

In the timbered, high-ceilinged, tile-floored reception room of the Kohler Company's main office are two large murals portraying the manufacture of the company's products — the furnaces, the ruddy-faced, muscled workers, and the tools of their trade. "He who toils here," proclaims an inscription, "hath set his mark." Another states, "To the men whose co-operation has made this organization, this hall is dedicated."

The plant spreads across the level fields east of the village; its three water towers dominate the sections of the factory, which has four principle divisions: the pottery, enamelware, the brass foundry and the engine and electric plant. Visible across the wooded hills to the southeast is the interesting, modern University of Wisconsin Sheboygan Center, which rises above the Sheboygan River. Nearly hidden on the river bank, south of High Street is the lovely Waelderhaus — a nostalgic replica of the ancestral home of the Kohlers in the Tyrol. The white frame village hall stands where Lower Falls Road and High Street intersect; beyond it spread the winding streets and circles, the homes and parks and bridle paths of Kohler. In a secluded bend of the ox-bowed river, south of Lower Falls Road, is Riverbend, the Kohler family mansion. Except for Sheboygan Falls, the village is surrounded by farmland, much of it company-owned and still used for farming purposes. For a time, tenants operated these tracts as individual farm units, but as time passed, large-scale farm operations replaced them, and dairy farms have been supplanted by beef-cattle-breeding projects, with crop-harvesting performed by machines and day labor.

The village population is several hundred below that of a generation ago. The farmlands circumvent its expansion; the owners of homes in the village are growing older and the young families who come in do not compensate for the population loss. Elderly people appreciate the tax advantages; out of 450 homes, perhaps 75 are occupied by lone widows.[15] Kohler Village will probably remain as it is for some time to come — an attractive company town.

A row of little shops occupy part of the showroom arcade on High Street. As one villager put it, having a job in Sheboygan and commuting to the peace and quiet of Kohler to live, is "not a bad deal" at all. The cultural programs, which Ruth DeYoung Kohler was instrumental in bringing to the Kohler Memorial Auditorium adjoining the school, continue under the auspices of the Women's Club, and to this extent the outside world enters the detachment of Kohler Village. Privacy is carefully guarded. The idyllic photographs of the homes and plant which appear on brochures and circulars are made by company photographers and company policy does not generally permit reporters or photographers inside the plant.[16]

Kohler of Kohler is generally ranked second among the plumbing manufacturers of the United States. In addition to the plant at Kohler, there is another at Spartanburg, South Carolina; there are sales branches in 16 states and Washington, D.C.

Today, Herbert V. Kohler is retired, and J. L. Kuplic has been advanced to presidency of the firm. Some of the "old timers" are still there, but only Lyman Conger is "calling the plays" with undiminished vigor. Other Kohlers, with an eye to future industrial developments, have become established in small manufacturing businesses in the area — plastics, precision parts, et cetera. Nonetheless, persons indicated to the author that few new businesses get into the community without the "nod" of the establishment who have been business leaders in Sheboygan for the past several decades — Prange, Garton, Hayssen, Leverenz, Reiss, the Vollraths, and in all probability, the Kohlers, although, as a family, the Kohlers no longer present a united front. Sheboygan is now a city of over 50,000; plans are on the boards for new structures in the downtown area, and a new shopping center out along Memorial Drive.* In the two years during which this book has been "in process," the appearance of the city has picked up to a considerable degree.

* As of February 14, 1966, Sheboygan was optimistic that a $60-million nuclear electric plant facility would be built by the Wisconsin Electric Power Company, just north of the city.

EPILOGUE — 1966

"This is an extra inning game, even by modern judicial standards. Unless the parties step out of character and achieve a compromise, it appears that many innings lie ahead." Thus the U.S. Circuit Court of Appeals for the District of Columbia remanded the UAW-Kohler case back to Special Master Judge DuQuaine on September 2, 1965. Yet, two and a half months later, newspaper headlines across the country announced that all issues in the Kohler strike were settled.

What happened in the interim to produce this surprising turn of events without an "unconditional surrender" on the part of the union or the company?

The Appellate Court had sustained Judge DuQuaine's decision that the Kohler Company violated the NLRB order by offering reinstatement to strikers on a reduced work-week basis, but it overruled his findings that the company had not violated the Board's order when it refused reinstatement to those who had retired and those who had signed a release to obtain work elsewhere. This ruling set the stage for finding the company guilty of contempt of the NLRB order. The Court also asked Judge DuQuaine to hold hearings to determine those eligible for reinstatement. On October 11, 1965, the U.S. Supreme Court rejected the company's appeal to review the Court of Appeals' rulings. It then became a question of what the company would do next.

Although it was not discussed, the significance of the Court rulings was omnipresent when the union and the company met in September and October to negotiate a new contract for 1965–66. It became obvious during the new round of negotiations that contract terms would not be settled by the October 8 deadline and the old contract was extended for thirty days. When the union's proposal for changes in the pension program came up, the parties were face-to-face with the question of what would happen on Court rulings. The company said it would go along with the union's proposal, providing the union and the NLRB agreed that such an agreement would settle all pending claims. At this point negotiations were recessed to permit the union to examine the company offer, and on November 17, 1965, Emil Mazey, UAW actuary Howard Young, Don Rand and Raymond Majerus met in Washington with UAW counsel Joseph L. Rauh, Jr., and John Sillard.

It was decided at that meeting to make an effort to negotiate a settlement of all pending matters on reinstatement and back pay. On earlier occasions, the parties had not been able to reach agreement because there were still unresolved issues in the courts. Since these issues had been decided in the union's favor, the union spokesmen and their counsel decided it was worth trying to reach a total settlement.

On November 29, 1965, Lyman C. Conger, Vice President Edward J. Hammer, and assistant secretary-treasurer, Walter Cleveland, of the Kohler Company arrived at Solidarity House, the UAW headquarters in Detroit, where they conferred with Mazey, Kitzman, Rand, Young and Majerus. This was the first occasion any company spokesman had set foot in a local, regional or international UAW office. The company spokesmen agreed to study the union's proposal and make a counter-proposal. Mazey informed them he would be at the forthcoming AFL-CIO convention at San Francisco, December 6–16, but that he would welcome them in San Francisco if they were interested in meeting during that period.

The 1964–65 contract expiration date had been extended twice in the interim and was nearing the end of the second one-month extension (December 8). Arrangements were made for the same company and union representatives to meet at the Del Webb Town House in San Francisco on December 7–9, and to extend the contract on a day-to-day basis. The series of day and night meetings brought the two parties close to agreement but Conger, Hammer and Cleveland returned to Wisconsin with no definite decision on the final proposition the union had offered through Mazey. Mazey, therefore, instructed Majerus to contact the Kohler Company for their reply to his proposal. On the morning of December 11, a verbal agreement was reached, set down in writing, and signed by the company and the union on December 17, 1965, at the Schroeder Hotel in Milwaukee.*

At the press conference called by Emil Mazey, he sat beside

---

* Walter Reuther had hinted in a speech at the AFL-CIO convention on December 13 that a settlement was near.

While Harvey Kitzman watches, Lyman Conger and Emil Mazey shake hands after the settlement is announced. (Sheboygan Press *photo*)

Conger, and later the two smilingly shook hands. Majerus, who filled in some of the details of the events of December, 1965, told the author that in 1955, when union and company spokesmen were called to Chicago by the FMCS to negotiate a settlement, a reporter asked Mazey if he would shake hands with Lyman Conger. Mazey replied, "I see no point in shaking hands until there is something to shake hands about."

It had been a costly struggle, yet both parties left the press conference in Milwaukee feeling that something had also been gained. The company had agreed to pay $4.5 million in back wages and pension credits to strikers and/or their survivors in return for the union's agreement not to press any further charges on strike-connected events which had transpired up to the date of the settlement. The company could find some satisfaction in the fact that the court settlement might have cost more than $4.5 million and that, for the time being, it did not have a union shop clause in the contract with Local 833. Had this out of court settlement not been reached, it would likely have taken two or three years more to get compliance on the Court's ruling.

Jerry Graf, writing for *The Sheboygan Press*, reported:

> Mazey was asked who won the strike. He said the union won because the workers achieved their goals. The company also won, he added, in that it can now be hoped that better labor-management relations will follow. . . . Attorney Conger said, "This is a complete and final settlement. . . . We had our differences but we managed to work things out. . . . Now we can look forward to going ahead with more constructive things."[1]

J. L. Kuplic, president of the Kohler Company, also said he hoped the agreement would be approved by the NLRB and that the firm was looking forward to focusing its attention on "more constructive matters."[2]

The settlement provided that practically all strikers, with the exception of the seventeen who had been disqualified by the NLRB, be given the opportunity to return to work at Kohler with full seniority rights and privileges. Of the $3 million back pay, $800,000 was specifically allocated for distribution to the 57 dischargees and the 477 reinstated (short work-week) strikers of September–October, 1960. The remainder is to be "distributed to the other eligible strikers in such amounts as are determined by the NLRB." Asked what maximum amount any one worker might expect to receive, Mazey said, "I think one worker will receive $10,000."[3] He estimated that about 1,000 would be entitled to back pay. In some cases, the heirs of strikers who died during the long strike will also get a settlement. The NLRB still has the task of administering the back-pay settlement for each eligible striker, but now has definite guidelines to follow. The settlement meant that the company and the union could now work together under the terms of a new contract without the uncertainties of further court litigation. Judge DuQuaine and the Court of Appeals have been spared many months of work by the settlement.

With the back-pay issue out of the way, quick agreement was reached on the new one-year contract which was submitted to Local 833 membership for ratification. This contract, to run until October 8, 1966, provides for:

> Wage increase: 3 per cent for all day workers
> 2 per cent for all incentive workers
> Ninth paid holiday: the day after Thanksgiving, to be paid retroactively
> 3 days bereavement pay: broadened to include "brother and sister"
> 4th week of paid vacation: for employees with 25 or more years of service

The agreement also calls for improvements in health and accident benefits and insurance coverage. The company agreed to increase its share of cost for lost time in settling in-plant grievances, and added that it will pay for time lost in connection with contract negotiations on the same basis as lost time on grievances.

The news of the settlement came as something of a "bombshell" to those who had been following the strike throughout the years. Radio and TV newscasts spread the news and wire services provided the details to newspapers, large and small, from coast to coast. One former striker who now lives in Boulder, Colorado, received a phone call from his daughter in Connecticut, who wanted to know, "Daddy, how much are *you* going to get?"

The Sheboygan Press, which had given extensive coverage to all the events of the long strike, estimated it had printed 38,000 to 40,000 column inches of strike news since 1954 — enough to fill 225 newspaper pages. The day after the settlement, the *Press* interviewed Sheboygan's mayor, Joseph R. Browne; Arthur Bauer; Attorney Rabinovitz; E. H. Kohlhagen; Charles W. Conrardy, Jr., president of UAW Local 833; John Martin, a steward in the milling room at the Kohler plant; Leo Breirather and former sheriff, Ted Mosch — all were happy about the settlement. Breirather added, "I just don't think you can say too much about Emil's [Mazey's] role in bringing final victory to Local 833." It was recalled that Mazey had promised Local 833 that he would "walk the last mile" with them until the strike was settled.

On January 14, 1966, the U.S. Circuit Court of Appeals for the District of Columbia approved the December 17 out-of-court settlement. Chief Judge David L. Bazelon and Senior Judge Henry W. Edgerton approved; however, Senior Judge Wilbur K. Miller dissented, stating:

> The Kohler Company probably acted wisely in agreeing to pay $3,000,000 to end the troubles which have beset it for some twelve years. But, because I feel strongly that it has been badly treated, I am unwilling to agree to the order approving the settlement, which imposes upon the Kohler Company this heavy additional obligation. I am surprised that Kohler has $3,000,000 left after what it has been through.

The Court ordered that the pending civil contempt proceedings against Kohler Company be "dismissed with prejudice" and that the Board and the Company each pay $100 plus expenses to Judge DuQuaine for services rendered.

The strike settlement has enhanced the standing of the UAW in the community of Sheboygan, and the labor movement as a whole has a more optimistic outlook. Labor in Sheboygan county is more united and more effective in politics and at the bargaining table than before. The present mayor of Sheboygan is a union member; in 1964 Sheboygan county was influential in the election of the first Democratic congressman in many years; the UAW has organized nine plants in the county and has six new locals on its roster. Whatever the short-term effects of the strike, organized labor throughout the country will take heart in the fact the UAW Local 833 not only survived the long, bitter strike, but with persistence and perseverance has achieved a constructive working relationship with the Kohler Company. Had the union been found guilty in the courts, instead of the company, this obviously would have been a different story. Kohler and the Sheboygan community welcomed 1966 with the bright prospect that industrial peace had come at last.

APPENDIX

Chronology of the Second Kohler Strike

TOO many events occurred before and during the second Kohler strike to discuss them all in this book. This chronology traces the important events and decisions which preceded the settlement.

April 11, 1946	KWA won WERB-conducted election over AFL, 1,561 to 716.
December 31, 1949	Kohler Co. refused to extend existing contract with KWA for first time in 16 years. Negotiations bogged down.
March 8, 1950	NLRB conducted all-union shop election; Kohler workers voted 2,570 to 750 for an all-union shop.
June 6, 1950	KWA rejected, 2,549 to 876, a Kohler contract proposal offering union shop but silent on other issues.
July 13, 1950	Company submitted new proposal and withdrew all-union shop offer.
August 27, 1950	KWA accepted new contract with 6–10 cents per hour wage increase and negotiated 5 per cent wage increase retroactive to May 1.
January 1, 1951	*The Kohlerian* became official KWA newspaper and the company issued its own publication, *People*.
February 22, 1951	Company discharged Neuwirth and Schuette, actively organizing in plant for UAW-CIO, for refusing to sign cull deduction slips.
March 13, 1951	NLRB refused to issue complaint in above case because the union's (KWA) charge was not properly documented.
March 28, 1951	KWA won NLRB election 2,064 as against 1,575 for UAW-CIO.
February 4, 1952	KWA filed "failure to bargain" charges against company.
April 15, 1952	KWA rejected company contract offer, 2,888 to 478.

April 21, 1952	Company fired 12 "pro-UAW" enamelers.
April 29–30, 1952	KWA membership voted to affiliate with UAW-CIO 2, 248 to 1,129.
May 2, 1952	UAW-CIO International Union issued charter No. 833 to the new union.
May 5, 1952	Local 833 filed unfair labor practice charges against Kohler Co. for discriminatory discharges of the 12 enamelers and Edward Ertel.
June 10–11, 1952	Local 833 won NLRB election: 1,831 for UAW-CIO, 850 for KWA, and 710 for UAW-AFL; 52 for no union.
June 19, 1952	NLRB certified Local 833 as bargaining agent for Kohler production and maintenance employees.
July 22, 1952	IUKWA, a hurriedly organized minority of 28 KWA members, filed suit against Local 833, seeking jurisdiction over properties and funds of former KWA.
August 3, 1952	Contract negotiations between company and Local 833 were begun.
December 1, 1952	IUKWA v. Local 833 suit began in Circuit Court.
December 22, 1952	Judge Detling dismissed IUKWA case.
January 1, 1953	IUKWA plaintiffs ordered to pay $469.40 court costs.
January 29, 1953	NLRB issued complaint against Kohler Co. for discriminatory discharge of 12 enamelers, discharge of Ertel for union activity, and for interference with employees' rights under Section 7 of National Labor Relations Act.
February 14, 1953	Large turnout at special membership meeting of Local 833 authorized strike, if necessary.
February 23, 1953	Local 833 membership voted to accept first contract with the Kohler Co.
February 24, 1953	Wisconsin Industrial Commission ruled that 12 discharged enamelers were entitled to unemployment compensation. NLRB hearings began on union's charges against company.
May 18, 1953	Local 833 asked for contract reopening on wages.
June 6, 1953	Wisconsin Supreme Court held hearings on IUKWA appeal of Judge Detling's dismissal of case against Local 833.
July 3, 1953	Industrial Commission reaffirmed decision on unemployment compensation for the 12 enamelers.

	Company appealed to Dane County Circuit Court.
July 25, 1953	Local 833 members voted 1,455 to 108, empowering executive board to call a strike, if necessary, to enforce demands for a wage increase. UAW International Union refused to sanction a strike.
August 20, 1953	Local 833 membership accepted company offer of 3-cent per hour wage increase.
October 23, 1953	NLRB trial examiner Eugene Dixon found Kohler Co. guilty of unfair labor practices in his intermediate report.
February 2, 1954	Contract negotiations began.
March 1, 1954	First one-year UAW contract with company expired.
March 14, 1954	Local 833 members authorized executive board to call a strike, if necessary, to enforce the union's demands.
March 25, 1954	Local 833 membership meeting rejected company's "final offer" and set Monday, April 5, as strike deadline.
April 5, 1954	Strike began. Over 2,500 workers appeared on picket lines.
April 14, 1954	NLRB ruled Kohler Co. guilty of unfair labor practices, interference with union organization and discriminatory discharge of Edward Ertel. NLRB found the "12 enamelers were discharged for cause."
April 15, 1954	Company filed complaint with WERB charging union with "illegal" picketing.
April 19, 1954	FMCS conciliators attempted to schedule negotiation sessions. Company refused to attend.
April 28, 1954	Union challenged WERB jurisdiction in federal court.
May 4, 1954	WERB began hearings in Sheboygan on company's charges against union. WERB proposed a truce.
May 5, 1954	Union voted to accept WERB proposal to limit picketing and begin negotiations.
May 6, 1954	Negotiations resumed; no progress; some nonstrikers entered plant.
May 7, 1954	Negotiations continued without progress. Company refused to bargain over weekend.

May 9, 1954	Union voted to resume mass picketing, fearing that if several hundred nonstrikers returned to work, plant would begin operation and settlement would be postponed.
May 10, 1954	Mass picketing resumed. Company negotiators failed to appear at scheduled sessions.
May 11, 1954	Arguments on petition to enjoin WERB heard in Federal Judge Tehan's court, Milwaukee.
May 15, 1954	Judge Tehan proposed truce plan in effort to settle strike.
May 17, 1954	Company rejected Judge Tehan's proposal.
May 18, 1954	WERB hearing ended; H. V. Kohler testified tear gas, guns and clubs in the plant would have his approval.
May 21, 1954	WERB ordered union to "cease and desist" mass picketing.
May 24, 1954	District Attorney initiated John Doe inquiry into charges that ammunition was in the Kohler plant.
May 28, 1954	WERB asked for enforcement of its "cease and desist" order before Judge Schlichting, who proposed day-to-day adjournment dependent on union's compliance with WERB directive and resumption of negotiations.
May 29, 1954	Wisconsin Attorney General ordered confiscation of tear gas at the Kohler plant.
June 1, 1954	Mass picketing stopped. Several hundred workers returned to work but majority continued strike. Lawrence E. Gooding, WERB chairman, entered negotiations which continued most of June.
June 29, 1954	Company discontinued negotiations.
July 2, 1954	Union filed unfair labor practice charges with NLRB.
July 8, 1954	Governor Walter J. Kohler, Jr., Wisconsin, proposed strike issues be submitted to arbitration.
July 9, 1954	Company rejected the Governor's proposal for arbitration.
July 12, 1954	Local 833 membership unanimously accepted Governor's proposal.
August 4, 1954	Federal mediators were successful in obtaining resumption of negotiations.
August 10, 1954	Union reduced its wage demands.

August 15, 1954	Local 833 membership meeting unanimously rejected company's offer, which was substantially the same as its pre-strike offer.
September 1, 1954	Circuit Judge Murphy granted enforcement of WERB interlocutory order limiting picketing activities of union. Judge Murphy entered negotiations.
September 29, 1954	Negotiations were recessed by federal conciliators. No apparent progress.
October 26, 1954	General Counsel of NLRB issued a complaint against company.
November 17, 1954	Local 833, in secret ballot, voted to continue strike.
December 3, 1954	NLRB amended complaint against company, charging "surface bargaining" and attempts to undermine union.
December 30, 1954	Local 833 president Graskamp protested $2 million Defense Department contract for 105 mm. shells awarded to Kohler Co.
January 3, 1955	U.S. Senator Murray, Montana, wired H. V. Kohler for information to determine if a Senate inquiry into strike were warranted.
January 5, 1955	Company and union met in Chicago on request of FMCS. Negotiations failed.
January 28, 1955	Company and union summoned to Washington by Clyde M. Mills of FMCS. No progress.
February 8, 1955	NLRB trial examiner Downing began hearings on complaint against company.
February 11, 1955	Judge Murphy accepted contempt charges against union and 19 strikers and set hearing for March 21.
February 17, 1955	H. V. Kohler rejected union's invitation personally to enter negotiations.
February 22, 1955	Company contended union no longer had majority of its employees and doubted union was still the bargaining representative. (Most of union members were still on strike.)
March 1, 1955	Company discharged 90 strikers, including entire executive board, alleging they were involved in or responsible for violence.
March 4, 1955	NLRB hearings postponed to allow investigation of the discharge of the 90 strikers.

March 7, 1955	U.S. 7th Circuit Court of Appeals found company guilty in Ertel case.
March 21, 1955	Circuit Judge Gerald J. Boileau opened hearings on WERB petition for contempt citation against union and 19 strikers.
March 23, 1955	Judge Boileau took case under advisement, pending Wisconsin Supreme Court ruling on WERB jurisdiction.
April 19, 1955	Circuit Judge Alvin C. Reis, Madison, ruled that 11 enamelers discharged April, 1952, were entitled to unemployment compensation.
April 21, 1955	FMCS called company and union representative to Chicago to resume negotiations. Conger stated effort useless unless union changed position.
April 29, 1955	H. V. Kohler rejected Reuther's invitation to meet him in attempt to settle the strike.
May 3, 1955	Wisconsin Supreme Court upheld WERB's authority in strike. Union appealed to U.S. Supreme Court. H. V. Kohler rejected Sheboygan Mayor Ploetz' proposal to settle the strike for the good of the community.
May 17, 1955	NLRB amended case; four unfair labor practice charges added.
May 19, 1955	Federal Judge Tehan denied union's plea to restrain enforcement of WERB picketing order against union.
May 25, 1955	Circuit Judge Boileau ruled 16 strikers and local union were guilty of contempt but exonerated International Union and three union leaders.
May 27, 1955	NLRB trial examiner accepted four new unfair labor practices against company.
June 3, 1955	Mazey and Conger testified before U.S. Senate subcommittee in Washington; Committee failed to get a settlement.
June 7, 1955	NLRB hearings resumed in Sheboygan.
June 22, 1955	NLRB amended case against Kohler Co. with addition of another charge.
July 1, 1955	NLRB hearings recessed, pending subpoena of Edmund Biever.
July 5, 1955	Mass demonstration and disorder occurred near Sheboygan harbor as company tried to unload clay from M. S. *Fossum*.

July 6, 1955	Clayboat left for Milwaukee harbor.
July 13, 1955	Union and WERB appealed Judge Boileau's ruling on contempt actions to Wisconsin Supreme Court.
July 20, 1955	NLRB hearings resumed in Sheboygan.
July 21, 1955	NLRB hearings recessed to August 4 to permit negotiations to continue.
July 27, 1955	Negotiations resumed in Chicago at request of FMCS.
August 2, 1955	Negotiations broken off when company stated it would not rehire discharged strikers.
August 3, 1955	Local 833 membership meeting voted unanimously to continue strike.
August 4, 1955	Importers of clay for Kohler Co. filed Taft-Hartley violation charges against 12 unions for interfering with clay shipments.
August 23, 1955	NLRB issued a stipulated complaint on secondary boycott charge against UAW-CIO and Local 833. Union agreed to "cease and desist" but did not accede it violated the Act.
August 30, 1955	U.S. 7th Circuit Court of Appeals, Chicago, issued a consent decree enforcing stipulated "cease and desist" order against secondary boycott of Kohler products.
December 24, 1955	Herbert V. Kohler again turned down Reuther's proposal for a face-to-face meeting "to work out an honorable and equitable settlement."
January 10, 1956	Wisconsin Supreme Court upheld conviction of local union and 16 strikers on contempt charges in WERB order limiting picketing and strike activities.
March 19, 1956	FMCS called parties to Chicago for negotiations. Meetings called off when company reiterated its position that it would not rehire discharged strikers.
May 5, 1956	NLRB proceedings ended after 111 days of actual hearings, 19,175 pages of transcripts, 1,163 exhibits, 423 witnesses.
June 14, 1956	U.S. Supreme Court ruled WERB had jurisdiction to act on mass picketing.
October 15, 1956	NLRB trial examiner Downing dismissed unfair labor practice complaint against Kohler Co. on grounds that certain trustees of the International

	Union had failed to file noncommunist affidavits to comply with the Taft-Hartley Act.
February 6, 1957	NLRB reversed trial examiner Downing's dismissal of the complaint against the Kohler Co. and ordered decision on the merits of the case.
February 15, 1957	Clergymen from three major faiths came to Sheboygan for the first of six meetings in attempt to help mediate dispute.
May 14, 1957	McClellan Committee sent investigators to Sheboygan to begin probe into Kohler strike.
October 9, 1957	Kohler Co. found guilty of unfair labor practices by NLRB trial examiner in his intermediate report to the Board.
December 10, 1957	Union and company both appealed the parts of trial examiner's report adverse to them.
February 26, 1958	McClellan Committee began five weeks of hearings on Kohler strike.
December 16, 1958	NLRB trial examiner Downing reopened unfair labor practice case against company on basis of additional charges growing out of McClellan Committee hearings.
March 5, 1959	Kohler Co. guilt reaffirmed in trial examiner Downing's supplemental report to NLRB.
March 15, 1960	McClellan Committee reported findings — Democratic members generally critical of company and Republican members critical of union.
August 20, 1960	Kohler Co. announced a 32-hour work week for enamel and brass divisions.
August 26, 1960	NLRB ruled company guilty of unfair labor practices.
September 1, 1960	Union called off strike, made mass application for return of all strikers and requested immediate resumption of negotiations.
September 14, 1960	Company offered to reinstate about 1,400 out of about 1,800 strikers.
September 22, 1960	Company refused to recognize Local 833 union stewards or to handle their complaints.
September 28, 1960	Company declined to enter into collective bargaining sessions because it did not want to concede the validity of the NLRB decision and order.
October 7, 1960	Union filed non-compliance charges with NLRB.

December 1, 1960	U.S. Court of Appeals in Washington, D.C., assumed sole jurisdiction on appeals of NLRB decision.
March 28, 1961	Union filed additional charges against Kohler Co.: non-compliance with Board order; discrimination against Local 833 stewards; failure to recognize stewards and to bargain; indefinite layoff of 375 employees, et cetera.
April 3, 1961	U.S. Supreme Court rejected Kohler Co. petition for review of Court of Appeals ruling.
April 5, 1961	Harvey Kitzman on 7th anniversary of strike again requested company to begin negotiations for a new contract.
April 19, 1961	NLRB Compliance Division ruled that company had not complied with the NLRB order.
April 20, 1961	Company declined to bargain with the union because it did not want to concede the validity of the NLRB decision and order.
April 24, 1961	Kohler resumed 40-hour week throughout plant.
April 27, 1961	Company filed motion with U.S. Court of Appeals (5th Circuit) to reopen NLRB case stating that it had been denied due process of law in establishing date of the 3-cent per hour wage increase in 1954.
August 17, 1961	Company granted 3 per cent wage increase without negotiations with union. Union charged that the increase was further evidence of failure to bargain in good faith.
September 9, 1961	U.S. Court of Appeals heard oral arguments on various appeals of the NLRB decision. Union argued that the strike should be ruled an "unfair labor practices" strike from its inception and that the company caused and prolonged the strike.
January 26, 1962	U.S. Court of Appeals found company guilty.
February 3, 1962	Union again asked company to begin negotiations in view of the Appellate Court ruling.
February 5, 1962	Company announced it would appeal ruling to the Supreme Court.
April 23, 1962	Company filed petition with U.S. Supreme Court for a review of Appellate Court ruling.
June 4, 1962	U.S. Supreme Court refused to hear Kohler Company appeal.

June 12, 1962	Company offered to begin bargaining for a new contract.
October 7, 1962	Local 833 membership meeting ratified first contract since the strike ended.
May 18, 1963	NLRB filed contempt charges against Kohler Co. with U.S. Court of Appeals.
August 6, 1963	Company filed petition with U.S. Court of Appeals for an "order of discovery" including examination of affidavits and reports of interviews between NLRB staff and alleged complainants, and the appointment of a "Master" to define the issues.
November 20, 1963	Court of Appeals appointed Judge Edward M. DuQuaine as Special Master to determine if company failed to comply with the order of the court.
April 15, 1964	Judge DuQuaine denied union motion to intervene in the proceedings. Union appealed to Appellate Court.
May 12, 1964	Judge DuQuaine began hearings.
May 23, 1964	Appellate Court affirmed Master's ruling denying union intervention in the contempt proceedings.
September 20, 1964	NLRB found company guilty and ruled that the company caused and prolonged the strike with a firm and fixed intention to undermine, weaken and eventually destroy the collective bargaining relationship. The Board ordered reinstatement of 57 of the 77 discharged strikers.
October 21, 1964	Company appealed NLRB ruling on reinstatement of 57 discharged strikers.
November 5, 1964	Contempt hearing before Special Master DuQuaine concluded with oral arguments.
December 29, 1964	Company offered to reinstate the 57 discharged strikers but said it would appeal the back pay order for the 57.
February 3, 1965	Special Master Judge DuQuaine ruled company guilty of contempt and ordered back pay for about 1,000 strikers. He ruled those who signed release statements and those who retired were not entitled to reinstatement or back pay.
February 18, 1965	Company offered reinstatement to 500 strikers without back pay.

April 20, 1965   U.S. Court of Appeals upheld NLRB in its findings of August 29, 1964.

April 21, 1965   Company appealed back pay issue for 57 discharged strikers to U.S. Supreme Court.

September 2, 1965   U.S. Court of Appeals upheld findings of Master that company was guilty of contempt but overruled him on decision regarding retirees and releasees. Remanded case back to the Master for identification of claimants, et cetera.

October 11, 1965   U.S. Supreme Court rejected Kohler Co.'s appeal from order to reinstate 57 with back pay.

December 17, 1965   Company and union agreed on $4.5 million back pay settlement and pension credits, and on terms of 1965–66 contract.

January 14, 1966   December 17 settlement approved by U.S. Circuit Court of Appeals, District of Columbia.

———

Employers' resistance to unions was still widespread in the 1930's. In an article for the League for Industrial Democracy, in June, 1938, David J. Saposs and Elizabeth T. Bliss characterized employers' attitudes and conduct in what has become an industrial relations classic:

The "Mohawk Valley Formula"

Because the "Mohawk Valley Formula," as it is called, has played such an important role in the employers' anti-union offensive, . . . the NLRB summation is reproduced here.

"First: When a strike is threatened, label the union leaders as 'agitators' to discredit them with the public and their own followers. In the plant, conduct a forced balloting under the direction of foremen in an attempt to ascertain the strength of the union and to make possible misrepresentation of the strikers as a small minority imposing their will upon the majority. At the same time, disseminate propaganda, by means of press releases, advertisements, and the activities of 'missionaries,' such propaganda falsely stating the issues involved in the strike so that the strikers appear to be making arbitrary demands, and the real issues, such as the employer's refusal to bargain collectively, are obscured. Concurrently with these moves, by exerting economic pressure through threats to move the plant, align the influential members of the community into a cohesive group opposed to the strike. Included in this group, usually designated a 'Citizens' Committee,' are representatives of the bankers, real estate owners, and businessmen, *i.e.*, those most sensitive to any threat of removal of the plant because of its effect upon property values and purchasing power flowing from payrolls.

"Second: When the strike is called raise high the banner of 'law and order,' thereby causing the community to mass legal and police weapons against a wholly imagined violence and to forget that those of its members who are employees have equal rights with the other members of the community.

"Third: Call a 'mass meeting' of the citizens to coordinate public sentiment against the strike and to strengthen the power of the Citizens' Committee, which organization, thus supported, will both aid the employer in exerting pressure upon the local authorities and itself sponsor vigilante activities.

"Fourth: Bring about the formation of a large armed police force to intimidate the strikers and to exert a psychological effect upon the citizens. This force is built up by utilizing local police, State Police, if the Governor cooperates, vigilantes, and special deputies, the deputies being chosen if possible from other neighborhoods, so that there will be no personal relationships to induce sympathy for the strikers. Coach the deputies and vigilantes on the law of unlawful assembly, inciting to riot, disorderly conduct, etc., so that, unhampered by any thought that the strikers may also possess some rights, they will be ready and anxious to use their newly acquired authority to the limit.

"Fifth: And perhaps most important, heighten the demoralizing effect of the above measures — all designed to convince the strikers that their cause is hopeless — by a 'back to work' movement, operated by a puppet association of so-called 'loyal employees' secretly organized by the employer. Have this association wage a publicity campaign in its own name and coordinate such campaign with the work of the 'missionaries' circulating among the strikers and visiting their homes. This 'back to work' movement has these results: It causes the public to believe that the strikers are in the minority and that most of the employees desire to return to work, thereby winning sympathy for the employer and an endorsement of his activities to such an extent that the public is willing to pay the huge costs, direct and indirect, resulting from the heavy forces of police. This 'back to work' movement also enables the employer, when the plant is later opened, to operate it with strikebreakers if necessary and to continue to refuse to bargain collectively with the strikers. In addition, the 'back to work' movement permits the employer to keep a constant check on the strength of the union through the number of applications received from employees ready to break ranks and return to work, such number being kept a secret from the public and the other employees, so that the doubts and fears created by such secrecy will in turn induce still others to make applications.

"Sixth: When a sufficient number of applications are on hand, fix a date for an opening of the plant through the device of having such opening requested by the 'back to work' association. Together with the Citizens' Committee, prepare for such opening by making provision for a peak army of police by roping off the areas surrounding the plant, by securing arms and ammunition, etc. The purpose of the 'opening' of the plant is threefold: To see if enough employees are ready to return to work; to induce still others to return as a result of the demoralizing effect produced by the opening of the plant and the return of some of their number; and, lastly, even if the maneuver fails to induce a sufficient number of persons to return, to persuade the public through pictures and news releases that the opening was nevertheless successful.

"Seventh: Stage the 'opening' theatrically, throwing open the gates at the propitious moment and having the employees march into the plant grounds in a massed group protected by squads of armed police, so as to give to the opening a dramatic and exaggerated quality and thus heighten its demoralizing effect. Along with the 'opening' provide a spectacle — speeches, flag raising, and praises for the employees, citizens, and local authorities, so that, their vanity touched, they will feel responsible for the continued success of the scheme and will increase their efforts to induce additional employees to return to work.

"Eighth: Capitalize on the demoralization of the strikers by continuing the show of police force and the pressure of the Citizens' Committee, both to insure that those employees who have returned will continue at work and to force the remaining strikers to capitulate. If necessary, turn the locality into a warlike camp through the declaration of a state of emergency tantamount to martial law and barricade it from the outside world so that nothing may interfere with the successful conclusion of the 'Formula,' thereby driving home to the union leaders the futility of further efforts to hold their ranks intact.

"Ninth: Close the publicity barrage, which day by day during the entire period has increased the demoralization worked by all of these measures, on the theme that the plant is in full operation and that the strikers were merely a minority attempting to interfere with the 'right to work,' thus inducing the public to place a moral stamp of approval upon the above measures. With this, the campaign is over — the employer has broken the strike." (*Reprinted by courtesy of the League for Industrial Democracy*)

The Chicago Daily Tribune gave extensive coverage to events in both Kohler strikes. Here as an example of how that paper viewed and reported the conflicts is an article by Chesly Manly, published on November 28, 1955.

Laud Kohler for Defiance of Union Goons

Kohler, Wis., Nov. 27 — Americans in every walk of life have rallied to the support of Herbert V. Kohler, president of the Kohler company, in the 20 month old battle to keep his plumbing ware firm and his workers free from the dictatorship of union bosses.

Kohler, whose company has managed to return to near normal production and show a profit despite the strike and violent harassment by Walter Reuther's CIO United Auto Workers union, has received more than 9,000 letters since the strike began. The letters, coming from every state, overwhelmingly agree with his contention that the issue in his struggle with the union is freedom.

Following are excerpts from typical letters, examined by this reporter:

From a man in Detroit who is putting Kohler fixtures in a new 2½ bathroom house: "Glad to see a company asserts its rights as management. The free enterprise system would not be dying if more firms had the guts not to sell out to the CIO."

From four business men in Peoria: "Millions of people are watching your fight with the CIO goons. We are glad there is at least one concern with the guts to fight the unreasonable demands of the unions. We will buy Kohler products whenever we can."

From the owner of a small manufacturing company in Bellville, Mich. — "I know exactly how you feel. I live in those goons' home town. In 1950 they closed my plant down and put my two boys in the hospital. I told them to go to hell and liquidated the company. I am just starting over again."

From a former employe of the National Labor Relations board, living in Bethesda, Md. — "This letter is to inform you that my family and some friends sincerely appreciate what you and the courageous employes of the Kohler company are doing for us all in standing up against the evil CIO goons. . . . I worked for the NLRB [for four years] and know what evil forces you have to deal with there . . . the vast majority of legal employes are totally brain-washed dupes. . . ."

From a man in the plumbing supplies business in a small Texas town: "Why don't you open a second plant here in Texas? Here in Texas the governor and the Texas Rangers do not allow such law violations by the unions."

From a securities dealer in Glendale, Cal. — "You must remember that your example is helping to firm up other managements in situations you never learn of."

From a plumbing supplies dealer in Pine Bluff, Ark. — "I do know that Arkansas people and Arkansas politicians would not allow such happenings in our state . . . we have different ideas about freedom down here."

From a lawyer in Edinburg, Tex. — "The issue transcends the welfare of your company and extends to the whole system of American free enterprise; and when you battle the union bosses you battle for all Americans."

From an Evanston man who had read about the strike in a Milwaukee hospital — "I believe you are absolutely right in your policies. Others [firms] have forgotten there is a third party — the consumer — and he pays to support the goons."

From a lumber dealer in Itta Bena, Miss. — "We only wish that our country had more good firms like the Kohler company that was willing to stand firm on what they feel and know is right for all concerned."

From a member of the CIO steamfitters union, local 32, in Seattle — "to express my views in a union meeting would be to invite disaster; but I do express my views on the job. I figure I can hold my own there. I have introduced the idea in all arguments that unions don't strike against companies but strike against people. . . ."

From a dealer in rare books and manuscripts in Proctorsville, Vt. — "Frankenstein Deficit Roosevelt is to blame for a large part of our present difficulties. . . ."

From an architect in Mystic, Conn. — "It seems to me that something in the nature of a citizens protective league would be of the order to meet the need. . . . When politics and politicians come to the point where they refuse to meet the issues organized effort must be instituted. . . ."

From a laboring man in Harrison, Mich. — "I only wish that we had 10,000 men like you who are willing to make the sacrifice to protect the rights of the laboring man and the principles of the American business man. . . ."

From a man in Mercer, Wis. — "Wisconsin seems to have the tragic distinction of producing four martyrs — Billy Mitchell, Douglas MacArthur, Joe McCarthy, and Herbert V. Kohler."

From the dean of engineering at a leading Illinois university — "The present tyranny to which the Kohler company is being subjected has called for the indignation of all fair minded people. There must be some way in this land of ours to prevent such goonery."

From a professor at Ohio university — "What sins companies committed before 1900 labor unions now commit. Even as the law stopped corporations so now law should stop unions. . . ."

From an 86 year old woman in Omaha — "It is all one great plot — the welfare state, socialism, communism. It is in our schools, in everything. . . ."

From the president of a Wisconsin college — "This is an epic struggle you are in. You inspire many by your determination to stand for your convictions which in the long run stand for the best interests of your employes. . . ."

From a lawyer in Belle Fourche, S.D. — "It is sickening to see the unions bring large companies to their knees and most heart warming to see smaller corporations such as yours stand up to them and defy them." (*Reprinted by courtesy of* The Chicago Tribune)

Lyman C. Conger was one of the most important figures in the Kohler disputes. Here is a vivid portrait of Mr. Conger's devotion to the company which appeared in *The Washington Star* on March 13, 1958.

Kohler Strikers Hold Conger as Symbol

The way people around Sheboygan, Wis., talk about Lyman C. Conger, you would think he was 46 feet long, breathed fire, and could give St. George the first two falls out of three.

Actually, he is a weatherbeaten little man of 56, who stands about as high as a four-drawer file cabinet and weighs about as much as a keg of Wisconsin beer. But what he lacks in size, Lyman Conger makes up in formidability.

As a pleader for free enterprise and against unions, Mr. Conger sets a record in sharp-tongued fluency. At the bargaining table, he can take a position and stick to it from one year's end to another. He strides briskly through life, leaving in his wake a host of hurt feelings.

And — organizational charts to the contrary — this middle-aged lawyer, whose official Kohler Co. title is "assistant secretary," is the man to deal with at Kohler.

"He runs that joint," says one neutral source. Says another, who has been following the explosive United Auto Workers-Kohler labor dispute for the last six years: "The attitude in Sheboygan is that Conger is the power, and wields considerable influence over (president) Herbert Kohler."

Whatever Mr. Conger's precise position may be, it appears that the Kohler family is getting its money's worth. And Mr. Conger, for his part, can hardly complain over wages. His bosses pay him $55,000 a year for sundry duties, among which is the chairmanship of the Management Committee.

As Management Committee Chairman, Mr. Conger has glowered for six years across the bargaining table at UAW Secretary-Treasurer Emil Mazey. Mr. Mazey, a hot-tempered type, has come to know him so well (and with such hostility) that he publicly reviled Mr. Conger unprintably and berated a Senator for "fronting for that ———."

Mr. Conger took Mr. Mazey's nasty language to be in the nature of a threat, and as such brought it to the Senate Rackets Committee's attention. "He didn't scare me," Mr. Conger added.

To the strikers of Sheboygan, Kohler is just a name and President Herbert Kohler is almost a disembodied figure. It is Mr. Conger who is the living symbol of corporate evil. At the height of mass picketing in 1954, the welkin at Kohler village rang with the chant of 2,000 pickets calling:

"Conger is a meatball."

Mr. Conger, who will be a key witness later in the current hearings, has been in and out of the limelight since the Kohler matter came before the committee late last month. The public got its best look at him to date when he testified briefly yesterday on the 1934 strike riots at Kohler.

In his testimony, Mr. Conger seemed rather more preoccupied with the fact that a large number of windows were broken in the plant than with the fact that 35 people were shot and two were killed. With a businessman's exactitude he denied reports that police deputies guarding the plant had shot the 35 people in the back.

"There were only 20 shot in the back," Mr. Conger explained. (*Reprinted by courtesy of* The Washington Star)

Reverend Clair M. Cook, Th.D., in his column, "Walking Together," published by the Religion and Labor Council of America, wrote an insightful commentary, August 6, 1962, after the second Kohler strike had officially ended:

Out in Sheboygan, Wisconsin, a near-miracle occurred last June 28. The Kohler Company's Lyman C. Conger, major general of its eight-year fight against the United Auto Workers and Local 833, sat down at a table with ten of his associates to engage in collective bargaining. Opposite sat UAW Secretary-Treasurer Emil Mazey and eight union colleagues. As if this were not miracle enough — even though forced by a U.S. Supreme Court decision three weeks earlier Mr. Mazey called the atmosphere in the bargaining room "cordial."

Even as the Hundred Years' War had to come to an end, so has the longest and most expensive industrial strife in American history subsided, to borrow words of the poet T. S. Eliot, "not with a bang but a whimper." In Kohler's last gasp of opposition, the Supreme Court refused to overturn a Court of Appeals decision upholding the NLRB 1960 strike-ending decision that the company was guilty of unfair labor practices. Only by such federal government protection of the rights of workers, together with monumental efforts by the union, has the conflict been forced to its final conclusion. The union's direct cost from its strike fund alone was $12 million.

Most of the action now forced upon the company is no more than restoration of conditions existing in 1954 before the strike began. Seventy-seven strikers fired by the company will have their cases re-examined by the NLRB, before which briefs have already been filed. Other strikers not yet reinstated after the August, 1960 NLRB ruling will have to be taken back with full pay from the date of their application for restoration. Housing will have to be restored to strikers ousted from company-owned Kohler homes.

The tragedy is that, after all the aches of head, heart and pocket-book, after all the bitterest disruption of work force and community, Kohler is now back to its ante bellum status, its surrender at long last gains nothing for anyone, except the chance to begin over after eight years in this new "cordial" climate. Effort to escape the twentieth century was both costly and futile; a contract will be signed after all, with terms about as they would have been without the strike. But there is no compensation for all the suffering of these past years. Perhaps the chief significance now is simply the warning to any feudalistic employer tempted along the same road: "Free unions of their own choosing are the workers' right under the law of the land. The industrial democracy of collective bargaining must not be destroyed." (*Reprinted by courtesy of the Religion and Labor Council of America*)

NOTES

CHAPTER 1

1. Marshall L. Scot, "The Kohler Strike," *The Christian Century*, August 20, 1957.
2. *Kohler of Kohler* (1963), brochure describing the history and operations of the Kohler Company.
3. *Portrait and Biographical Record of Sheboygan County*. S920 P83, p. 676 ff.
4. *Sheboygan Amerika*, No. 143, August 6, 1904 and *Sheboygan Herald*, August 13, 1904.
5. *Die Sheboygan Zeitung*, August 4, 1905.

6. Walter H. Uphoff, *The Kohler Strike: Its Socio-Economic Causes and Effects*. Master's thesis, University of Wisconsin, privately printed 1935, p. 3.
7. *Ibid.*, p. 7.
8. Wisconsin State Income Tax Commission records.
9. *Ibid.*
10. Uphoff, *op. cit.*, p. 11.
11. *Ibid.*, pp. 12–13.
12. *Ibid.*, pp. 4–5.

CHAPTER 2

1. Edward N. Doan, *The La Follettes*. Rinehart & Co., New York (1947).
2. *Portrait and Biographical Record of Sheboygan County*, S920 P83.
3. *Zum Fünfundsiebenzigjährigen Jubiläum-Geschichte der Sheboygan Klassis* (German Reformed Church). Central Publishing House, Cleveland, Ohio (1929), pp. 60–61.
4. Based on telephone interview with J. F. Friedrick. December 29, 1964.
5. Uphoff, *op. cit.*, pp. 14–15.
6. *Ibid.*, p. 14.
7. Don D. Lescohier, and Elizabeth

Brandeis, *History of Labor in the United States, 1896–1932*. The Macmillan Company, New York (1935). Original quote taken from unpublished manuscript.
8. Uphoff, *op. cit.*, pp. 19–22.
9. Brief to National Labor Relations Board on behalf of General Counsel. Case No. 13-CA-1780, prepared by NLRB attorney, George Squillacote, April 19, 1957. Evidence based on NLRB transcript, pp. 3073–80 and 3091.
10. Uphoff, *op. cit.*, pp. 16–23.
11. *Ibid.*, pp. 24–25.
12. *Ibid.*, pp. 25–43.
13. *Ibid.*, p. 44.

CHAPTER 3

Chapter 3 is based mainly on news reports which appeared in *The Sheboygan Press* and the Sheboygan *New Deal*, and were incorporated in the author's thesis. Information was also obtained through personal interviews with participants in, and observers of the controversy.

1. La Follette Civil Liberties Committee Report (U.S. Senate) (1939) Part 15A, p. 5724.
2. Interview with Chris Leining, June 7–8, 1965.
3. *Sheboygan Press*, July 16, 1934.
4. Uphoff, *op. cit.*, p. 49.
5. *Sheboygan Press*, July 27, 1934.
6. Richard S. Davis, *Milwaukee Journal*, July 28, 1934.

7. *Sheboygan Press*, July 28, 1934.
8. *Ibid.*
9. Uphoff, *op. cit.*, pp. 61–63.
10. Uphoff, *op. cit.*, p. 116.
11. Davis, *op. cit.*
12. *Sheboygan Press*, July 28, 1934.
13. *Sheboygan Press*, September 13, 1934.
14. Associated Press report, *Sheboygan Press*, August 2, 1934.

15. *Sheboygan Press*, September 12, 1934.

16. *Ibid.*

17. *Ibid.*

18. Uphoff, *op. cit.*, pp. 104–105, 111–112.

CHAPTER 4

1. Letter from E. H. Kohlhagen, formerly secretary of KWA.

2. Based on interview with Charles Heymanns, Regional Director AFL-CIO Milwaukee, Wisconsin, November 26, 1964.

3. "Kohler's Paternalism Policy," *Business Week*, May 24, 1952.

4. From records of Local 833, UAW-AFL-CIO.

5. George Squillacote, brief prepared for NLRB, p. 6 April 19, 1957. Case No. 13-CA-1780.

6. *Ibid.*, p. 7 (based on NLRB's Counsel's exhibit No. 149-A and Respondent's exhibits 17–22).

7. *Ibid.*, p. 7 (based on NLRB transcripts p. 2354).

8. *Ibid.*, p. 8 (based on Kohler Co., 108 NLRB 224).

9. *Ibid.*, p. 5 (based on NLRB transcripts pp. 259, 951–952, 3109–3110).

10. *Ibid.*, p. 5 (based on NLRB transcripts pp. 2472–2473).

11. *Ibid.*, p. 9 (based on Kohler Co. exhibit 12).

12. *Ibid.*, p. 9.

13. *Ibid.*, p. 6 (based on NLRB transcripts pp. 1111–1112).

14. *Ibid.*, p. 7 (based on Findings, NLRB v. Kohler Co., 220 F. 2nd and 3 [CA 7], 1955, Cert. denied).

15. "Kohler's Paternalism Policy," *op. cit.*, p. 170.

16. Suit brought before Circuit Court of Sheboygan County, Wisconsin, May 15, 1952, against the UAW on behalf of the IUKWA.

17. Members of the IUKWA Constitutional Committee, many of whose names appeared in connection with the violence and vandalism that followed the strike, were: Kenneth Baer, Irving Bawden, Elmer Bueher, Carl Berlin, John Boone, John Elsesser, Harold Froehlich, Carl Gierke, Fred Hammelman, Emil Heinig, Walter Herman, Harold Kohls, Ed Mahnke, Ed Markgraf, Herman Miesfeld, Paul Milbrath, Les Miller, Ruben Nicolaus, Ed Oostdyke, James Van Ouwerkirk, Joseph Pittner, Carl Ruppel, Peter Schurrer, Walter Steffen, Alvin Stricker, Oliver Ter Maat, Alex Yurk, and Walter Zeitler (Source: E. H. Kohlhagen).

18. No. 389 State of Wisconsin: In Supreme Court, August Term, Case 264. Wisconsin 562.59 NW 2nd 800.

19. *The Kohlerian*, February 26, 1953.

20. Based on taped interview with Emil Mazey, Secretary-Treasurer, UAW-Int'l Union, Detroit, Michigan, June 4, 1965.

21. NLRB Case No. 13-CA-1780, p. 12.

22. *Ibid.*, p. 13.

23. *Ibid.*, pp. 14–15.

24. Based on letter from Theodore Mosch, former Sheboygan County sheriff.

25. Testimony before NLRB Trial Examiner, February 9, 1955. Sheboygan, Wisconsin, Case No. 13-CA-1780.

26. *Hearings before the Select Committee on Improper Activities in the Labor or Management Field*. U.S. Senate, 85th Congress, 2nd Session, February 16–March 4, 1958. Part 21, p. 8527 (referred to hereafter as McClellan Committee).

27. *Ibid.*, p. 8528.

28. *Ibid.*, p. 8520.

29. Robert F. Kennedy, *The Enemy Within*, Popular Library reprint, New York (1960), p. 279. *The Congressional Record* – U.S. Senate, March 18, 1958, p. 4109, quotes Senator Paul Douglas (Dem. Ill.) as saying that 32 out of 39 were strikers or strike sympathizers. Douglas adds: "They didn't shoot themselves. Nor were they shot by fellow union members. . . . It is a cruel thing for an untruth to go around the world before truth has time to put on its boots. . . ."

30. *Milwaukee Journal*, August 15, 1955.

31. *Baltimore Sun*, October 24, 25, 26, 1955.

32. Dale Yoder, *Personnel Manage-*

ment and Industrial Relations, Prentice-Hall, Inc., New York (3rd Ed. 1949), pp. 655–656.

33. McClellan Committee, *op. cit.,* Part 24, p. 9631.

34. *Ibid.*

35. *Final Report of the Select Committee on Improper Activities in the Labor or Management Field,* U.S. Senate, 86th Congress, Part 2. March 15, 1960, p. 171.

36. *Ibid.*

37. William L. Blachman, *The Koh-*

ler Strike: A Case Study in Collective Bargaining. Unpublished Ph. D. thesis, University of Wisconsin, 1963, p. 70.

38. *Ibid.,* p. 73.

39. *Ibid.;* p. 81.

40. McClellan Committee, *op. cit.,* p. 8547.

41. Based on taped interview with Albert Gore, NLRB Counsel assigned to the Kohler case; now practicing attorney in Chicago, Illinois. December 29, 1964.

CHAPTER 5

1. McClellan Committee, *op. cit.,* p. 8333.

2. Based on taped interview with Mosch.

3. McClellan Committee, *op. cit.,* p. 8354.

4. Complaint filed with WERB by Kohler Company, Case III No. 5257 Cw-213 April 15, 1954.

5. *Sheboygan Press,* April 27, 1954.

6. NLRB transcripts, Case No. 13-CA-1780, p. 1461.

7. *Ibid.,* pp. 1461, 1507–1508.

8. *Ibid.,* p. 13,238.

9. *Ibid.,* pp. 1505–1506.

10. *Ibid.,* p. 13,107.

11. *Ibid.,* p. 637.

12. *Ibid.,* pp. 641–642, 1692–1693.

13. NLRB transcripts, *op. cit.,* 1464.

14. *Ibid.,* p. 1467.

15. *Ibid.,* pp. 1465–1466, 1509–1516.

16. *Ibid.,* p. 1472.

17. *Ibid.,* pp. 4457, 1409, 1416.

18. WERB Case III No. 5257-Cw-213, Decision No. 3740, May 21, 1954.

19. NLRB transcripts, *op. cit.,* pp. 642–643, 1093.

20. *Ibid.,* pp. 1478, 1495, 1518.

21. NLRB General Counsel, Exhibit No. 40.

22. *Sheboygan Press,* August 18, 1954.

23. Based on taped interview and letter from Mosch. *op. cit.*

24. McClellan Committee, *op. cit.,* pp. 8737–8738.

25. *Milwaukee Sentinel,* May 29, 1954.

26. *Sheboygan Press,* June 4, 1954.

27. *Milwaukee Sentinel,* January 27, 1956.

28. *Capital Times,* Madison, Wisconsin, March 15, 1956.

29. Testimony before John Schneider, Jr., Justice Court, Sheboygan, Wisconsin, April 30, 1954. In Re: *State of Wisconsin* vs. *George Klauser and Robert Woodworth.*

30. *Sheboygan Press,* November 23, 1954.

31. *Ibid.,* May 3, 1955.

32. Supreme Court of the United States, No. 530, October Term 1955. Date June 4, 1956.

33. McClellan Committee, *op. cit.,* p. 8550.

34. McClellan Committee, Final Report, *op. cit.,* p. 217.

35. NLRB hearing, June 15, 1955. Testimony by Robert Dean, Route 1, Adell, Wisconsin.

36. *Sheboygan Press,* August 1, 1954.

37. McClellan Committee, *op. cit.,* p. 8979.

38. *Ibid.,* pp. 8411–8412.

39. *Ibid.,* p. 8423.

40. *Ibid.,* p. 8876.

41. *Ibid.,* pp. 8878–8891.

42. Sheboygan, Wisconsin, Circuit Court records, June 15, 1959.

43. McClellan Committee, *op. cit.,* p. 8633.

44. *Ibid.,* p. 8707.

45. McClellan Committee, *op. cit.,* p. 9564.

46. *Ibid.,* p. 9563.

47. *Ibid.,* p. 9565.

48. *Ibid.,* p. 10,002.

49. *Ibid.,* p. 10,003.

50. *Ibid.,* p. 9547.

51. *Ibid.*, p. 9944.
52. McClellan Committee, Final Report, *op. cit.*, p. 212.
53. McClellan Committee, *op. cit.*, p. 9347.

54. *Ibid.*, p. 9422.
55. *Ibid.*, p. 9572.
56. *Ibid.*, p. 8841.

CHAPTER 6

1. McClellan Committee, *op. cit.*, pp. 8794–8816.
2. *Sheboygan Press*, May 5, 1955.
3. From affidavit given to Attorney David Rabinovitz by Ignatz Kastelic. Statement taken May 2, 1955.
4. From affidavit given to Attorney David Rabinovitz by Dan Regan. Statement taken May 2, 1955.
5. *Sheboygan Press*, May 5, 1955.
6. Arthur Tosten, Jr.
7. Interview with Philip Pinekenstein, December 28, 1964.
8. Taped interviews with Paul Gibeault, June 2, 1965, and Dan Regan, June 5, 1965. Regan died in August, 1965, of a heart attack.
9. From the Madson Detective Agency, Green Bay, Wisconsin, reports subpoenaed by the McClellan Committee.
10. From Articles of Incorporation, Kohler Humane Society, Inc., filed with Secretary of State, Wisconsin, June 8, 1955.
11. *Milwaukee Journal*, July 1, 1955.
12. McClellan Committee, *op. cit.*, p. 8507.
13. Based on taped interview with attorney Albert Gore, Chicago, December, 29, 1964.
14. From sworn affidavit given by E. H. Kohlhagen to Jean Engstrom, NLRB attorney, July 21, 1955.
15. *Sheboygan Press*, July 7, 1955.
16. *Ibid.*
17. *Milwaukee Journal*, July 11, 1955.

18. *Milwaukee Journal*, July 21, 1955.
19. *Sheboygan Press*, August 3, 1955.
20. *Ibid.*
21. *Milwaukee Sentinel*, August 9, 1955.
22. *Sheboygan Press*, August 9, 1955.
23. *Milwaukee Sentinel*, August 10, 1955.
24. *Sheboygan Press*, August 16, 1955.
25. *Ibid.*, October 13, 1955.
26. *Milwaukee Journal*, October 14, 1955.
27. *Sheboygan Press*, October 18, 1955.
28. *Ibid.*, October 25, 1955.
29. *Ibid.*, November 29, 1955.
30. *Milwaukee Sentinel*, January 5, 1956.
31. From records of Milwaukee city attorney, Harry G. Slater, and the comptroller's office, City of Sheboygan.
32. From records of the Sheboygan police department.
33. Abraham L. Gitlow, *Labor and Industrial Society*. Richard D. Irwin, Inc., Homewood, Illinois (1963), pp. 459–460.
34. The Reverend James Fifield, pastor of the First Congregational Church, Los Angeles, is well known for his rightest views.
35. *Milwaukee Journal*, November 16, 1956.
36. *Chicago Tribune*, February 9, 1956.
37. *Milwaukee Journal*, February 5, 1958.

CHAPTER 7

Note: Page numbers which appear at end of quotations throughout this chapter refer to the McClellan Committee Reports.

1. Marten S. Estey (Philip Taft and Martin Wagner, Editors), *Regulating Union Government* (Industrial Relations Research Association Series. Harper & Row, New York (1964), p. 34.
2. John J. McClellan, *Crime Without Punishment*, Duell, Sloan and Pearce, New York (1962), p. 69.
3. Robert F. Kennedy, *The Enemy Within*, Harper & Row, New York. (1960), p. 254.
4. *Ibid.*, p. 256.

5. *Ibid.*, p. 258.
6. *Ibid.*, p. 258.
7. *Ibid.*, p. 259.
8. *Ibid.*, p. 260.
9. *Ibid.*, p. 263.

10. *Ibid.*, p. 272.
11. Taped interview with Harvey Kitzman and Ray Majerus, Milwaukee, September 21, 1964.

CHAPTER 8

1. From records of Federal Mediation and Conciliation Service on Kohler case. FMCS Archives, Washington, D.C.
2. From minutes taken at the meetings with the clergy, by E. H. Kohlhagen.
3. *Reporter and Kohlerian*, May 3, 1957.
4. Kohler Strike and Boycott *Bulletin*, UAW Local 833. Vol. II, No. 341, January 7, 1959.
5. *Sheboygan Press*, August 26, 1960.
6. *Ibid.*, August 27, 1960.
7. *Ibid.*
8. *Ibid.*, October 8, 1960.
9. NLRB Supplemental Decision and Supplemental Order, Case No. 30-CA-A, August 29, 1964.

10. From *Brief for the National Labor Relations Board*, U.S. Court of Appeals for the District of Columbia. U.S. Government Printing Office, 1961.
11. *Colorado Union Advocate*, December 27, 1963.
12. *Sheboygan Press*, June 28, 1962.
13. *Ibid.*, October 8, 1962.
14. *Ibid.*
15. From letter from E. H. Kohlhagen, September 23, 1965.
16. *Sheboygan Press*, December 6, 1964.
17. *Ibid.*
18. *Ibid.*

CHAPTER 9

1. *Rubin Bros. Footwear, Inc. et al v. National Labor Relations Board* No. 14155 United States Court of Appeals, Fifth Circuit, April 13, 1953 — cited in *Federal Reporter, 2nd series*, 203, p. 486.
2. *N.L.R.B. v. Burnup and Sims, Inc.*, 322 f. 2d 57 (1963).
3. *Joint Appendix*, Volume 1 — United States Court of Appeals for the District of Columbia. Intermediate Report and Recommended Order, October 9, 1957, p. 236.
4. *Ibid.*, p. 238.
5. *The United States Law Week* — Supreme Court Opinions, Vol. 33, No. 17. The Bureau of National Affairs, Washington, D.C., November 10, 1964.
6. *N.L.R.B. Petition v. Thayer Co. et al Respondents*, (CA-1.1954) 213 F. 2d 748. *Certiorari* denied. U.S. CCH 26 Labor Cases. 68, 457. Reproduced from *CCH Labor Cases*, published and copyright, June 10, 1954. Commerce Clearing House, Inc., Chicago, Illinois.
7. *45 American Law Reports (Annotated)*, 2d Series, p. 896.

8. *Labor Cases* CCH 26, 1954, *op. cit.*
9. *Sheboygan Press*, September 30, 1964.
10. *Joint Appendix*, Volume 1, U.S. Court of Appeals, *op. cit.*, p. 245.
11. *45 American Law Reports (Annotated)*, 2d Series, p. 890.
12. Supplemental Decision and Supplemental Order, N.L.R.B. Case No. 30-CA-3 (formerly 13-CA-1780) 148 NLRB No. 147 September 29, 1964.
13. *Sheboygan Press*, September 30, 1964.
14. Board Supplemental Order at 148 N.L.R.B., No. 147 Court Opinion at 58 LRRM 2847.
15. Special Master's Report by Edward M. DuQuaine for U.S. District Court of Appeals for the District of Columbia Circuit *N.L.R.B. v. Kohler Co.* No. 16,031, February 1, 1965.
16. *Sheboygan Press*, October 11, 1965.
17. *Ibid.*, October 12, 1965.

CHAPTER 10

1. U.S. Department of Commerce, Bureau of the Census, 1950.
2. *The Milwaukee Journal*, August 21, 1956.
3. Jack Barbash (editor). *Unions and Union Leadership*. Harper & Brothers, New York (1959), pp. 27–76. Parts of article reproduced by permission of *Wisconsin State Journal*.
4. Taped interview with Rudolph J. Ploetz, Sheboygan; December 30, 1964. Copy of taped statement in possession of writer.
5. Robert Wallace, "The Long Strike's Human Damage," *Life* magazine, May 20, 1957.
6. *Sheboygan Press*, September, 1955.
7. Rev. Charles Owen Rice, "Verdict at Kohler," *The Commonweal*, November 11, 1960.
8. Rev. Edward A. Keller, "Can Reuther's Boycott Bring Kohler to Its Knees?" *Human Events*, Vol. XIV, No. 8, February 23, 1957.

9. McClellan Committee, *op. cit.*, pp. 8989–8990.
10. *Ibid.*, p. 9880.
11. *Ibid.*, p. 9449.
12. Taped interview with Leo Breirather, September 20, 1964.
13. Paul McMahon, *Milwaukee Journal*, August 15, 1955.
14. *Sheboygan Press*, September 10, 1964.
15. McClellan Committee, *op. cit.*, p. 8485.
16. *Ibid.*, p. 9419.
17. *Milwaukee Journal*, August 15, 1955.
18. *Ibid.*, August 15, 1955.
19. President Kennedy had appointed Attorney Rabinovitz as Federal Judge in September, 1963, and President Johnson reappointed him. He served from January 7, 1964, to October 7, 1964.

CHAPTER 11

1. McClellan Committee, *op. cit.*, p. 8519.
2. Abraham L. Gitlow, *Labor and Industrial Society*. Richard D. Irwin, Inc., Homewood, Illinois (1963), pp. 461–62.
3. L. Reed Tripp, *Labor Problems and Processes*, Harper & Row, New York (1961), p. 257.
4. *America* (magazine), September 10, 1960. p. 606.
5. Taped interview with Albert Gore, Chicago, December 29, 1964.
6. Fred J. Cook, *Barry Goldwater, Extremist of the Right*. Grove Press, Inc., New York (1964), p. 126.
7. UAW *Strike Bulletin*, November 13, 1957.
8. Group Research, Inc., 1404 New York Ave., Washington 5, D.C., September 8, 1965. Letter to Sam Fishman, United Auto Workers.

9. From UAW-AFL-CIO files.
10. Sylvester Petro, *The Kohler Strike — Union Violence and Administrative Law*. Henry Regnery Company, Chicago (1961).
11. James P. Finucan, from letter to H. V. Kohler, June 13, 1961.
12. Herbert V. Kohler, from letter to James P. Finucan, July 11, 1961.
13. James P. Finucan, from letter to H. V. Kohler, July 12, 1961.
14. Sylvester Petro, *The Kohler Strike — Union Violence and Administrative Law, op. cit.*, pp. 92–93.
15. From interview with Waldemar G. Capelle, October 7, 1965.
16. *Milwaukee Journal*, August 15, 1955. Paul McMahon.

EPILOGUE — 1966

1. *Sheboygan Press*, December 17, 1965.

2. *Ibid.*, December 18, 1965.
3. *Ibid.*, December 17, 1965.

INDEX